The
X Window System
in a Nutshell

Desktop Quick Reference

The
X Window System
in a Nutshell

*for Version 11 Release 4
and Release 5 of the
X Window System*

Edited by
Ellie Cutler, Daniel Gilly, and Tim O'Reilly

O'Reilly & Associates, Inc.

The X Window System in a Nutshell
Edited by Ellie Cutler, Daniel Gilly, and Tim O'Reilly

X Series Editor: Adrian Nye

Printing History:

May 1990:	First Edition.
May 1992:	Second Edition. Updated for X11 R5 by Ellie Cutler.

This book is printed on acid-free paper with 50% recycled content, 10-15% post-consumer waste. O'Reilly & Associates is committed to using paper with the highest recycled content available consistent with high quality.

ISBN 0-56592-017-1   [3/94]

Table of Contents

Preface

Finally, here is a quick reference that presents the major features of the X Window System in one, easy-to-use handbook.

Once you've mastered the concepts behind X and learned how to program in Xlib and Xt, there is still a mass of details to remember. *The X Window System in a Nutshell* contains essential information from the other volumes of our X Window System Series, in a quick-reference format. Not only is the information easy to find, but as a handbook, it is compact and can lie flat on your desk.

People who are less familiar with the X Window System might also benefit from this book, since it reveals the breadth of the X Window System; that is, it allows you to see "what X is all about."

In the current edition of this book, we've expanded descriptions of each of the Xlib and Xt functions, added comments to the Xt function arguments, and added all information relevant to Release 5 of the X Window System.

Scope of This Handbook

This handbook covers material in X Version 11, for both Release 4 and Release 5. *The X Window System in a Nutshell* is organized as follows:

Section 1, *Xlib Functions and Macros*, presents the Xlib functions and macros. They are grouped by categories and then described alphabetically along with their calling sequence. New R5 functions are marked as such.

Section 2, *Xlib Data Types*, presents all public Xlib structures (excluding events) and other typedefs, along with various defined symbols and function prototypes.

Section 3, *Events*, lists the XEvent union and event masks. It also summarizes the event structures and any associated defined symbols.

Section 4, *Xt Functions and Macros*, summarizes the Xt functions and macros. As in Section 1, these routines are grouped by categories and then described alphabetically along with their calling sequence. New R5 functions are marked as such.

Section 5, *Xt Data Types*, presents all public Xt Intrinsics structures and data types, along with various defined symbols and function prototypes.

Section 6, *Inside a Widget*, describes widgets—the fundamental data type of the X Toolkit.

Section 7, *Clients*, describes the clients available in R4 and R5, along with available options and resource variables.

Section 8, *Fonts, Colors, Cursors, and Bitmaps*, lists and illustrates various features that allow you to customize your X environment.

Section 9, *Translations*, describes translation table syntax and how to use modifier names and event types in building translation tables.

Section 10, *Xlib Functions and Macros*, summarizes the errors and warnings generated by routines in Xlib and Xt.

Conventions in This Handbook

The following typographic conventions are used in this book.

Italics
> are used for file and directory names, UNIX command names, and X client names when they appear in the body of a paragraph.

Helvetica Narrow
> is used for displaying the contents of X11 source files, such as structures, functions, and symbols.

Helvetica Narrow Bold
> is used within examples to show command lines and options that should be typed verbatim on the screen.

Helvetica Narrow Oblique
> is used within code displays to show a parameter that requires context-dependent substitution (such as a variable). For example, *filename* means to specify some appropriate filename; *options* means to use some appropriate options to the command.

Related Documents

This handbook is compiled primarily from five books published by O'Reilly & Associates, Inc. These books are part of our X Window Series:

Volume One	*Xlib Programming Manual*
Volume Two	*Xlib Reference Manual*
Volume Three	*X Window System User's Guide*
Volume Four	*X Toolkit Intrinsics Programming Manual*
Volume Five	*X Toolkit Intrinsics Reference Manual*

Acknowledgements

We'd like to thank the staff at O'Reilly & Associates, Inc. who helped significantly with this book.

Jean Diaz compiled portions of and provided technical support for Section 7, *Clients*. Technical consultants were Ted Stefanik and O'Reilly authors David Flanagan, Adrian Nye, and Valerie Quercia.

Chris Reilley created the illustrations and Edie Freedman designed the cover. The production department, especially Colleen Urban, prepared the camera ready copy.

Kismet McDonough capably handled production for the R5 edition.

Despite the efforts of these people, we issue the standard disclaimer: any errors that remain are our own.

Xlib Functions and Macros

This section presents the Xlib functions and macros available in R4 and R5. (We'll refer to functions and macros collectively as routines.) The information is in two main parts:

- **Category listing.** Routines that perform related tasks are listed alphabetically under various categories.

- **Calling sequences.** Each function or macro is presented in alphabetical order, along with a brief description and its calling sequence.

Summary by Category

Sometimes you know the general task you need to do, but not the exact routine that does it. If this is the case, browse the categories here to find the routine you need. For more information about the function or macro, you can turn ahead to the alphabetical summary. The categories are presented on the next page.

Category Headings

Xlib routines have been grouped under the following categories. (*Xrm* refers to routines that involve the Resource Manager; *Housekeeping* refers to miscellaneous maintenance activity.)

Association Table	Device-independent color	Font
Bitmap	Display Macro	GC
Color	Drawing	Host Access
Colormap	Error	Housekeeping
ConnectionHost	Event	Image
Cut Buffer	Extension	Image Macro

Category Headings (Continued)

Internationalization	Property	Visual
Keyboard	Region	Window Location
Keysym Macro	Screen Saver	Window Manager
Pixmap	Standard Geometry	Xrm
Pointer	Selection	Xrm Macro
Preference	Text	

Category Listings

In the following lists, the routines new to R5 are preceded by a bullet (•).

Association Table
XCreateAssocTable
XDeleteAssoc
XDestroyAssocTable
XLookUpAssoc
XMakeAssoc

Bitmap
XCreateBitmapFromData
XReadBitmapFile
XWriteBitmapFile

Color
XAllocColor
XAllocColorCells
XAllocColorPlanes
XAllocNamedColor
XFreeColors
XLookupColor
XParseColor
XQueryColor
XQueryColors
XStoreColor
XStoreColors
XStoreNamedColor

Colormap
XAllocStandardColormap
XCopyColormapAndFree
XCreateColormap
XFreeColormap

XGetRGBColormaps
XGetStandardColormap
XInstallColormap
XListInstalledColormaps
XSetRGBColormaps
XSetStandardColormap
XUninstallColormap

Connection
XKillClient
XSetCloseDownMode

Context
XDeleteContext
XFindContext
XSaveContext
XUniqueContext

Cursor
XCreateFontCursor
XCreateGlyphCursor
XDefineCursor
XFreeCursor
XQueryBestCursor
XRecolorCursor
XUndefineCursor

Cut Buffer
XFetchBuffer
XFetchBytes
XRotateBuffers

XStoreBuffer
XStoreBytes

Device-Independent Color
- XcmsAddColorSpace
- XcmsAddFunctionSet
- XcmsAllocColor
- XcmsAllocNamedColor
- XcmsCCCOfColormap
- XcmsCIELabQueryMaxC
- XcmsCIELabQueryMaxL
- XcmsCIELabQueryMaxLC
- XcmsCIELabQueryMinL
- XcmsCIELuvQueryMaxC
- XcmsCIELuvQueryMaxL
- XcmsCIELuvQueryMaxLC
- XcmsCIELuvQueryMinL
- XcmsClientWhitePointOfCCC
- XcmsCompressionProc
- XcmsConvertColors
- XcmsCreateCCC
- XcmsDefaultCCC
- XcmsDisplayOfCCC
- XcmsFormatOfPrefix
- XcmsFreeCCC
- XcmsLookupColor
- XcmsPrefixOfFormat
- XcmsQueryBlack
- XcmsQueryBlue
- XcmsQueryColor
- XcmsQueryColors
- XcmsQueryGreen
- XcmsQueryRed
- XcmsQueryWhite
- XcmsScreenFreeProc
- XcmsScreenInitProc
- XcmsScreenNumberOfCCC
- XcmsScreenWhitePointOfCCC
- XcmsSetCCCOfColormap
- XcmsSetCompressionProc
- XcmsSetWhitePoint
- XcmsStoreColor
- XcmsStoreColors
- XcmsTekHVCQueryMaxC

- XcmsTekHVCQueryMaxV
- XcmsTekHVCQueryMaxVC
- XcmsTekHVCQueryMaxVSamples
- XcmsTekHVCQueryMinV
- XcmsVisualOfCCC
- XcmsWhiteAdjustProc

Display Macro
AllPlanes
BlackPixel
BlackPixelOfScreen
CellsOfScreen
ConnectionNumber
DefaultColormap
DefaultColormapOfScreen
DefaultDepth
DefaultDepthOfScreen
DefaultGC
DefaultGCOfScreen
DefaultRootWindow
DefaultScreen
DefaultScreenOfDisplay
DefaultVisual
DefaultVisualOfScreen
DisplayCells
DisplayHeight
DisplayHeightMM
DisplayOfScreen
DisplayPlanes
DisplayString
DisplayWidth
DisplayWidthMM
DoesBackingStore
DoesSaveUnders
dpyno
EventMaskOfScreen
HeightMMOfScreen
HeightOfScreen
Keyboard
LastKnownRequestProcessed
MaxCmapsOfScreen
MinCmapsOfScreen
NextRequest
PlanesOfScreen

ProtocolRevision
ProtocolVersion
QLength
RootWindow
RootWindowOfScreen
ScreenCount
ScreenOfDisplay
ServerVendor
VendorRelease
WhitePixel
WhitePixelOfScreen
WidthMMOfScreen
WidthOfScreen
XDisplayMotionBufferSize
XMaxRequestSize
XScreenNumberOfScreen
XVisualIDFromVisual

Plus these functions:
XListDepths
XListPixmapFormats

Drawing
XClearArea
XClearWindow
XCopyArea
XCopyPlane
XDraw (X10)
XDrawArc
XDrawArcs
XDrawFilled (X10)
XDrawLine
XDrawLines
XDrawPoint
XDrawPoints
XDrawRectangle
XDrawRectangles
XDrawSegments
XFillArc
XFillArcs
XFillPolygon
XFillRectangle
XFillRectangles

Error
XDisplayName
XGetErrorDatabaseText
XGetErrorText
XSetAfterFunction
XSetErrorHandler
XSetIOErrorHandler
XSynchronize

Event
XAllowEvents
XCheckIfEvent
XCheckMaskEvent
XCheckTypedEvent
XCheckTypedWindowEvent
XCheckWindowEvent
XEventsQueued
XFlush
XGetInputFocus
XGetMotionEvents
XGrabServer
XIfEvent
XMaskEvent
XNextEvent
XPeekEvent
XPeekIfEvent
XPending
XPutBackEvent
XSelectInput
XSendEvent
XSetInputFocus
XSync
XUngrabServer
XWindowEvent

Extension
XFreeExtensionList
XListExtensions
XQueryExtension

Fonts
• XBaseFontNameListOfFontSet
• XCreateFontSet
• XExtentsOfFontSet

- XFontsOfFontSet
XFreeFont
XFreeFontInfo
XFreeFontNames
XFreeFontPath
- XFreeFontSet
XGetFontPath
XListFonts
XListFontsWithInfo
XLoadFont
XLoadQueryFont
- XLocaleOfFontSet
XQueryFont
XSetFont
XSetFontPath
XUnloadFont

GC

XChangeGC
XCopyGC
XCreateGC
- XFlushGC
XFreeGC
XGContextFromGC
XGetGCValues
XQueryBestSize
XQueryBestStipple
XQueryBestTile
XSetArcMode
XSetBackground
XSetClipMask
XSetClipOrigin
XSetClipRectangles
XSetDashes
XSetFillRule
XSetFillStyle
XSetForeground
XSetFunction
XSetGraphicsExposures
XSetLineAttributes
XSetPlaneMask
XSetState
XSetStipple
XSetSubwindowMode

XSetTile
XSetTSOrigin

Host Access

XAddHost
XAddHosts
XDisableAccessControl
XEnableAccessControl
XListHosts
XRemoveHost
XRemoveHosts
XSetAccessControl

Housekeeping

XCloseDisplay
XFree
XFreeStringList
XNoOp
XOpenDisplay

Image

XAddPixel
XCreateImage
XDestroyImage
XGetImage
XGetPixel
XGetSubImage
XPutImage
XPutPixel
XSubImage

Image Macro

BitmapBitOrder
BitmapPad
BitmapUnit
ImageByteOrder

Internationalization

- ClientWhitePointOfCCC
- DisplayOfCCC
- ScreenNumberOfCCC
- ScreenWhitePointOfCCC
- XCloseIM
- XContextDependentDrawing
- XCreateIC

- XDefaultString
- XDestroyIC
- XDisplayOfIM
- XDrawString
- XFilterEvent
- XGetICValues
- XGetIMValues
- XIMOfIC
- XLocaleOfIM
- XmbDrawImageString
- XmbDrawString
- XmbDrawText
- XmbLookupString
- XmbResetIC
- XmbTextEscapement
- XmbTextExtents
- XmbTextListToTextProperty
- XmbTextPerCharExtents
- XmbTextPropertyToTextList
- XOpenIM
- XSetICFocus
- XSetICValues
- XSetLocaleModifiers
- XSupportsLocale
- XUnsetICFocus
- XVaCreateNestedList
- XwcDrawImageString
- XwcDrawString
- XwcDrawText
- XwcFreeStringList
- XwcLookupString
- XwcResetIC
- XwcTextEscapement
- XwcTextExtents
- XwcTextListToTextProperty
- XwcTextPerCharExtents
- XwcTextPropertyToTextListXlib

Keyboard
XChangeKeyboardControl
XChangeKeyboardMapping
XDeleteModifiermapEntry
XDisplayKeycodes
XFreeModifiermap

XGetKeyboardControl
XGetKeyboardMapping
XGetModifierMapping
XGrabKey
XGrabKeyboard
XInsertModifiermapEntry
XKeycodeToKeysym
XKeysymToKeycode
XKeysymToString
XLookupKeysym
XLookupString
XNewModifiermap
XQueryKeymap
XRebindKeysym
XRefreshKeyboardMapping
XSetModifierMapping
XStringToKeysym
XUngrabKey
XUngrabKeyboard

Keysym Macro
IsCursorKey
IsFunctionKey
IsKeypadKey
IsMiscFunctionKey
IsModifierKey
IsPFKey

Pixmap
XCreatePixmap
XCreatePixmapCursor
XCreatePixmapFromBitmapData
XFreePixmap

Pointer
XChangeActivePointerGrab
XChangePointerControl
XGetPointerControl
XGetPointerMapping
XGrabButton
XGrabPointer
XQueryPointer
XSetPointerMapping
XUngrabButton

XUngrabPointer
XWarpPointer

Preference
XAutoRepeatOff
XAutoRepeatOn
XBell
XGetDefault

Property
XChangeProperty
XDeleteProperty
XGetAtomName
XGetFontProperty
XGetTextProperty
XGetWindowProperty
XInternAtom
XListProperties
XRotateWindowProperties
XSetStandardProperties
XSetTextProperty
XStringListToTextProperty
XTextPropertyToStringList

Region
XClipBox
XCreateRegion
XDestroyRegion
XEmptyRegion
XEqualRegion
XIntersectRegion
XOffsetRegion
XPointInRegion
XPolygonRegion
XRectInRegion
XSetRegion
XShrinkRegion
XSubtractRegion
XUnionRectWithRegion
XUnionRegion
XXorRegion

Screen Saver
XActivateScreenSaver
XForceScreenSaver
XGetScreenSaver
XResetScreenSaver
XSetScreenSaver

Selection
XConvertSelection
XGetSelectionOwner
XSetSelectionOwner

Standard Geometry
XGeometry
XParseGeometry
XTranslateCoordinates

Text
XDrawImageString
XDrawImageString16
XDrawString16
XDrawText
XDrawText16
XQueryTextExtents
XQueryTextExtents16
XTextExtents
XTextExtents16
XTextWidth
XTextWidth16

Visual
XGetVisualInfo
XMatchVisualInfo

Window Location
XAddToSaveSet
XChangeSaveSet
XChangeWindowAttributes
XCirculateSubwindows
XCirculateSubwindowsDown
XCirculateSubwindowsUp
XConfigureWindow
XCreateSimpleWindow
XCreateWindow
XDestroySubwindows

Xlib Routines

XDestroyWindow
XGetGeometry
XGetWindowAttributes
XLowerWindow
XMapRaised
XMapSubwindows
XMapWindow
XMoveResizeWindow
XMoveWindow
XQueryTree
XRaiseWindow
XRemoveFromSaveSet
XReparentWindow
XResizeWindow
XRestackWindows
XSetWindowBackground
XSetWindowBackgroundPixmap
XSetWindowBorder
XSetWindowBorderPixmap
XSetWindowBorderWidth
XSetWindowColormap
XUnmapSubwindows
XUnmapWindow

Window Manager

XAllocClassHint
XAllocIconSize
XAllocSizeHints
XAllocWMHints
XFetchName
XGetClassHint
XGetIconName
XGetIconSizes
XGetNormalHints
XGetSizeHints
XGetTransientForHint
XGetWMHints
XGetWMIconName
XGetWMName
XGetWMNormalHints
XGetWMSizeHints
XGetZoomHints
XIconifyWindow
XReconfigureWMWindow

XSetClassHint
XSetCommand
XSetIconName
XSetIconSizes
XSetNormalHints
XSetSizeHints
XSetTransientForHint
XSetWMClientMachine
XSetWMColormapWindows
XSetWMHints
XSetWMIconName
XSetWMName
XSetWMNormalHints
XSetWMProperties
XSetWMProtocols
XSetWMSizeHints
XSetZoomHints
XStoreName
XWithdrawWindow
XWMGeometry

Xrm

Xpermalloc
• XResourceManagerString
• XrmCombineDatabase
• XrmCombineFileDatabase
XrmDestroyDatabase
• XrmEnumerateDatabase
• XrmGetDatabase
XrmGetFileDatabase
XrmGetResource
XrmGetStringDatabase
XrmInitialize
• XrmLocaleOfDatabase
XrmMergeDatabases
XrmParseCommand
XrmPutFileDatabase
XrmPutLineResource
XrmPutResource
XrmPutStringResource
XrmQGetResource
XrmQGetSearchList
XrmQGetSearchResource
XrmQPutResource

XrmQPutStringResource
XrmQuarkToString
• XrmSetDatabase
XrmStringToBindingQuarkList
XrmStringToQuark
XrmStringToQuarkList
XrmUniqueQuark
• XScreenResourceString
XVisualIDFromVisual

Xrm Macro

XResourceManagerString
XrmClassToString
XrmNameToString
XrmRepresentationToString
XrmStringToClass
XrmStringToName
XrmStringToRepresentation

Alphabetical Summary

For each function and macro, a brief description is followed by the calling sequence of the routine. (Most of the macros appear first, since their names don't start with *X*.)

In the descriptions of the calling sequence for each function, comments indicate the use of any non-standard arguments. For a description of any structures or other special Xlib data types used as arguments or return values, see Section 2, *Xlib Data Types*.

Section 2 also lists any defined symbols used for filling in structure members or for specifying the value of other special data types. The reason for this separation is to avoid the necessity for repeating the explanation of commonly used arguments.

However, Xlib also makes use of numerous mask arguments, which are simply declared as unsigned long (rather than via some typedef which could be listed in Section 2). The symbols used to specify these masks are listed along with the function in which they are used.

In the descriptions of macros, the argument *screen* refers to a pointer to a Screen structure (see Section 2, *Xlib Data Types*), while the argument *screen_number* refers to an integer screen number starting at 0, for a given screen associated with the current display.

AllPlanes

Return a value with all bits set suitable for use as a plane mask argument.

```
unsigned long AllPlanes()
```

BitmapBitOrder

Within each BitmapUnit, the leftmost bit in the bitmap as displayed on the screen is either the least or the most significant bit in the unit. Returns LSBFirst or MSBFirst.

```
int BitmapBitOrder(display)
    Display *display;                    /* pointer to a Display structure */
```

BitmapPad

Each scan line must be padded to a multiple of bits specified by the value returned by this macro.

```
int BitmapPad(display)
    Display *display;                    /* pointer to a Display structure */
```

BitmapUnit

Return the size of a bitmap's unit. The scan line is quantized (calculated) in multiples of this value.

```
int BitmapUnit(display)
    Display *display;                    /* pointer to a Display structure */
```

BlackPixel

Return the black pixel value in the default colormap that is created by XOpenDisplay.

```
BlackPixel(display, screen_number)
    Display *display;                    /* pointer to a Display structure */
    int screen_number;                   /* number of display screen to be queried */
```

BlackPixelOfScreen

Return the black pixel value in the default colormap of the specified screen.

```
unsigned long BlackPixelOfScreen(screen)
    Screen *screen;                      /* pointer to screen structure to be queried */
```

CellsOfScreen

Return the number of colormap cells in the default colormap of the specified screen.

```
int CellsOfScreen(screen)
    Screen *screen;                      /* pointer to screen structure to be queried */
```

ClientWhitePointOfCCC

Return the white point of the screen associated with the specified color conversion context. (New in R5.)

```
ClientWhitePointOfCCC(ccc)
    XcmsCCC ccc;                         /* color conversion context */
```

ConnectionNumber

Return a connection number for the specified display. On a UNIX system, this is the file descriptor of the connection.

```
int ConnectionNumber(display)
    Display *display;                    /* pointer to a Display structure */
```

DefaultColormap

Return the default colormap for the specified screen. Most routine allocations of color should be made out of this colormap.

```
Colormap DefaultColormap(display, screen_number)
    Display *display;                    /* pointer to a Display structure */
    int *screen_number;                  /* number of display screen to be queried */
```

DefaultColormapOfScreen

Return the default colormap of the specified screen.

```
Colormap DefaultColormapOfScreen(screen)
    Screen *screen;                      /* pointer to screen structure to be queried */
```

DefaultDepth

Return the depth (number of planes) of the root window for the specified screen. Other depths may also be supported on this screen.

```
int DefaultDepth(display, screen_number)
    Display *display;                    /* pointer to a Display structure */
    int *screen_number;                  /* number of display screen to be queried */
```

DefaultDepthOfScreen

Return the default depth of the specified screen.

```
int DefaultDepthOfScreen(screen)
    Screen *screen;                         /* pointer to screen structure to be queried */
```

DefaultGC

Return the default graphics context for the specified screen.

```
GC DefaultGC(display, screen_number)
    Display *display;                       /* pointer to a Display structure */
    int *screen_number;                     /* number of display screen to be queried */
```

DefaultGCOfScreen

Return the default graphics context of the specified screen.

```
GC DefaultGCOfScreen(screen)
    Screen *screen;                         /* pointer to screen structure to be queried */
```

DefaultRootWindow

Return the ID of the root window on the default screen. Most applications should use RootWindow instead so that screen selection is supported.

```
DefaultRootWindow(display)
```

DefaultScreen

Return the integer that was specified in the last segment of the string passed to XOpenDisplay or from the DISPLAY environment variable if NULL was used. For example, if the DISPLAY environment were Ogre:0.1, then DefaultScreen would return 1.

```
int DefaultScreen(display)
    Display *display;                       /* pointer to a Display structure */
```

DefaultScreenOfDisplay

Return the default screen of the specified display.

```
Screen *DefaultScreenOfDisplay(display)
    Display *display;                       /* pointer to a Display structure */
```

DefaultVisual

Return a pointer to the default visual structure for the specified screen.

```
Visual *DefaultVisual(display, screen_number)
    Display *display;                    /* pointer to a Display structure */
    int screen_number;                   /* number of display screen to be queried */
```

DefaultVisualOfScreen

Return the default visual of the specified screen.

```
Visual *DefaultVisualOfScreen(screen)
    Screen *screen;                      /* pointer to screen structure to be queried */
```

DisplayCells

Return the maximum possible number of colormap cells on the specified screen. This macro is misnamed: it should have been ScreenCells.

```
int DisplayCells(display, screen_number)
    Display *display;                    /* pointer to a Display structure */
    int screen_number;                   /* number of display screen to be queried */
```

DisplayHeight

Return the height in pixels of the screen. This macro is misnamed: it should have been ScreenHeight.

```
int DisplayHeight(display, screen_number)
    Display *display;                    /* pointer to a Display structure */
    int screen_number;                   /* number of display screen to be queried */
```

DisplayHeightMM

Return the height in millimeters of the specified screen. This macro is misnamed: it should have been ScreenHeightMM.

```
int DisplayHeightMM(display, screen_number)
    Display *display;                    /* pointer to a Display structure */
    int screen_number;                   /* number of display screen to be queried */
```

DisplayOfCCC

Return the display associated with a Color Conversion Context. (New in R5.)

```
DisplayOfCCC(ccc)
    XcmsCCC ccc;  /* color conversion context */
```

DisplayOfScreen

Return the display associated with the specified screen.

```
Display *DisplayOfScreen(screen)
    Screen *screen;                    /* pointer to screen structure to be queried */
```

DisplayPlanes

Return the number of planes on the specified screen. This macro is misnamed: it should have been ScreenPlanes.

```
int DisplayPlanes(display, screen_number)
    Display *display;                  /* pointer to a Display structure */
    int screen_number;                 /* number of display screen to be queried */
```

DisplayString

Return the string that was passed to XOpenDisplay when the current display was opened (or, if that was NULL, the value of the DISPLAY environment variable). This macro is useful in applications which invoke the fork system call and want to open a new connection to the same display from the child process.

```
char *DisplayString(display)
    Display *display;                  /* pointer to a Display structure */
```

DisplayWidth

Return the width in pixels of the screen. This macro is misnamed: it should have been ScreenWidth.

```
int DisplayWidth(display, screen_number)
    Display *display;                  /* pointer to a Display structure */
    int screen_number;                 /* number of display screen to be queried */
```

DisplayWidthMM

Return the width in millimeters of the specified screen. This macro is misnamed: it should have been ScreenWidthMM.

```
int DisplayWidthMM(display, screen_number)
    Display *display;                  /* pointer to a Display structure */
    int screen_number;                 /* number of display screen to be queried */
```

DoesBackingStore

Return a value indicating whether the screen supports backing stores. Values are WhenMapped, NotUseful, or Always.

```
int DoesBackingStore(screen)
    Screen *screen;                    /* pointer to screen structure to be queried */
```

DoesSaveUnders

Return a Boolean value indicating whether the screen supports save unders. If True, the screen supports save unders. If False, the screen does not support save unders.

```
Bool DoesSaveUnders(screen)
    Screen *screen;                    /* pointer to screen structure to be queried */
```

dpyno

Return the file descriptor of the connected display. On a UNIX system, you can then pass this returned file descriptor to the *select*(3) system call when your application program is driving more than one display at a time.

```
dpyno(display)
```

EventMaskOfScreen

Return the initial event mask for the root window of the specified screen.

```
long EventMaskOfScreen(screen)
    Screen *screen;                    /* pointer to screen structure to be queried */
```

HeightMMOfScreen

Return the height in millimeters of the specified screen.

```
int HeightMMOfScreen(screen)
    Screen *screen;                    /* pointer to screen structure to be queried */
```

HeightOfScreen

Return the height in pixels of the specified screen.

```
int HeightOfScreen(screen)
    Screen *screen;                    /* pointer to screen structure to be queried */
```

ImageByteOrder

Returns the byte order for images required by the server for each scan line unit in XY format (bitmap) or for each pixel value in Z format. Values are LSBFirst or MSBFirst.

```
int ImageByteOrder(display)
    Display *display;                  /* pointer to a Display structure */
```

IsCursorKey

Return True if the keysym represents a cursor key.

```
int IsCursorKey(keysym)
    unsigned int keysym;                    /* keysym value to be checked */
```

IsFunctionKey

Return True if the keysym represents a function key.

```
int IsFunctionKey(keysym)
    unsigned int keysym;                    /* keysym value to be checked */
```

IsKeypadKey

Return True if the keysym represents a key pad.

```
int IsKeypadKey(keysym)
    unsigned int keysym;                    /* keysym value to be checked */
```

IsMiscFunctionKey

Return True if the keysym represents a miscellaneous function key.

```
int IsMiscFunctionKey(keysym)
    unsigned int keysym;                    /* keysym value to be checked */
```

IsModifierKey

Return True if the keysym represents a modifier key.

```
int IsModifierKey(keysym)
    unsigned int keysym;                    /* keysym value to be checked */
```

IsPFKey

Return True if the keysym represents a Programmable Function key.

```
int IsPFKey(keysym)
    unsigned int keysym;                    /* keysym value to be checked */
```

Keyboard

Return the device ID for the main keyboard connected to the display.

```
Keyboard(display)
```

LastKnownRequestProcessed

Return the serial ID of the last known protocol request to have been issued. This can be useful in processing errors, since the serial number of failing requests are provided in the XErrorEvent structure.

```
unsigned long LastKnownRequestProcessed(display)
    Display *display;                      /* pointer to a Display structure */
```

MaxCmapsOfScreen

Return the maximum number of installed (hardware) colormaps supported by the specified screen.

```
int MaxCmapsOfScreen(screen)
    Screen *screen;                        /* pointer to screen structure to be queried */
```

MinCmapsOfScreen

Return the minimum number of installed (hardware) colormaps supported by the specified screen.

```
int MinCmapsOfScreen(screen)
    Screen *screen;                        /* pointer to screen structure to be queried */
```

NextRequest

Return the serial ID of the next protocol request to be issued. This can be useful in processing errors, since the serial number of failing requests are provided in the XErrorEvent structure.

```
unsigned long NextRequest(display)
    Display *display;                      /* pointer to a Display structure */
```

PlanesOfScreen

Return the number of planes in the specified screen.

```
int PlanesOfScreen(screen)
    Screen *screen;                        /* pointer to screen structure to be queried */
```

ProtocolRevision

Return the minor protocol revision number of the X server.

```
int ProtocolRevision(display)
    Display *display;                      /* pointer to a Display structure */
```

ProtocolVersion

Return the version number of the X protocol associated with the connected display. This is currently 11.

```
int ProtocolVersion(display)
    Display *display;                    /* pointer to a Display structure */
```

QLength

Return the number of events that can be queued by the specified display.

```
QLength(display)
    Display *display;                    /* pointer to a Display structure */
```

RootWindow

Return the ID of the root window. This macro is necessary for routines that reference the root window or create a top-level window for an application.

```
Window RootWindow(display, screen_number)
    Display *display;                    /* pointer to a Display structure */
    int screen_number;                   /* number of display screen to be queried */
```

RootWindowOfScreen

Return the ID of the root window of the specified screen.

```
Window RootWindowOfScreen(screen)
    Screen *screen;                      /* pointer to screen structure to be queried */
```

ScreenCount

Return the number of available screens on a specified display.

```
int ScreenCount(display)
    Display *display;                    /* pointer to a Display structure */
    int screen_number;                   /* number of display screen to be queried */
```

ScreenNumberOfCCC

Count screens associated with the specified color conversion context. There is also a macro version of this function, ScreenNumberOfCCC. (New in R5.)

```
ScreenNumberOfCCC(ccc)
    XcmsCCC ccc;                         /* color conversion context */
```

ScreenOfDisplay

Return the specified screen of the specified display.

```
Screen *ScreenOfDisplay(display, screen_number)
    Display *display;                    /* pointer to a Display structure */
    int screen_number;                   /* number of display screen to be queried */
```

ScreenWhitePointOfCCC

Return the white point of the screen associated with a specified color conversion context. (New in R5.)

```
ScreenWhitePointOfCCC(ccc)
    XcmsCCC ccc;                         /* color conversion context */
```

ServerVendor

Return a pointer to a NULL-terminated string giving some identification of the owner of the X server implementation.

```
char *ServerVendor(display)
    Display *display;                    /* pointer to a Display structure */
```

VendorRelease

Return a number related to the release of the X server by the vendor.

```
int VendorRelease(display)
    Display *display;                    /* pointer to a Display structure */
```

WhitePixel

Return the white pixel value in the default colormap that is created by XOpen-Display.

```
unsigned long WhitePixel(display, screen_number)
    Display *display;                    /* pointer to a Display structure */
    int screen_number;                   /* number of display screen to be queried */
```

WhitePixelOfScreen

Return the white pixel value in the default colormap of the specified screen.

```
unsigned long WhitePixelOfScreen(screen)
    Screen *screen;                      /* pointer to screen structure to be queried */
```

WidthMMOfScreen

Return the width of the specified screen in millimeters.

```
int WidthMMOfScreen(screen)
    Screen *screen;                     /* pointer to screen structure to be queried */
```

WidthOfScreen

Return the width of the specified screen in pixels.

```
int WidthOfScreen(screen)
    Screen *screen;                     /* pointer to screen structure to be queried */
```

XActivateScreenSaver

Turn on the screen saver using the parameters set with XSetScreenSaver.

```
XActivateScreenSaver(display)
    Display *display;
```

XAddHost

Add a host to the access control list.

```
XAddHost(display, host)
    Display *display;
    XHostAddress *host;
```

XAddHosts

Add multiple hosts to the access control list.

```
XAddHosts(display, hosts, num_hosts)
    Display *display;
    XHostAddress *hosts;
    int num_hosts;
```

XAddPixel

Add a constant value to every pixel value in an image.

```
XAddPixel(ximage, value)
    XImage *ximage;
    unsigned long value;
```

XAddToSaveSet

Add a window to the client's save-set. To remove a window from the client's save-set, use XRemoveFromSaveSet.

```
XAddToSaveSet(display, w)
    Display *display;
    Window w;
```

XAllocClassHint

Allocate an XClassHint structure, for use in calling XSetWMProperties, XGetClassHint, or XSetClassHint. By avoiding compiled-in structure sizes, XAlloc-ClassHint keeps object files compatible with later releases that may have new structure members.

```
XClassHint *XAllocClassHint( )
```

XAllocColor

Allocate a read-only colormap cell with closest hardware-supported color.

```
Status XAllocColor(display, cmap, colorcell_def)
    Display *display;
    Colormap cmap;
    XColor *colorcell_def;              /* desired color; returns closest match */
```

XAllocColorCells

Allocate read/write (nonshared) colorcells in a read/write colormap.

```
Status XAllocColorCells(display, cmap, contig, plane_masks, nplanes, pixels, ncolors)
    Display *display;
    Colormap cmap;
    Bool contig;                              /* which planes should be contiguous */
    unsigned long plane_masks[nplanes];  /* returns array of plane masks */
    unsigned int nplanes;                    /* number of values in plane masks */
    unsigned long pixels[ncolors];         /* returns pixel values */
    unsigned int ncolors;                    /* number of values in pixels */
```

XAllocColorPlanes

Allocate read/write (nonshareable) color planes.

```
Status XAllocColorPlanes(display, cmap, contig, pixels, ncolors, nreds, ngreens, nblues, rmask,
            gmask, bmask)
    Display *display;
    Colormap cmap;
    Bool contig;                              /* whether planes should be contiguous */
    unsigned long pixels[ncolors];         /* returns array of pixel values */
```

```
int ncolors;                    /* number of color cells to be added */
int nreds, ngreens, nblues;     /* # of shades needed */
unsigned long *rmask;           /* returns bit masks for red, ... */
unsigned long *gmask;           /* green, and ... */
unsigned long *bmask;           /* blue planes */
```

XAllocIconSize

Allocate an XIconSize structure for use in calling XGetIconSizes or XSetIconSizes.

```
XIconSize *XAllocIconSize()
```

XAllocNamedColor

Allocate a read-only colorcell given a color name from the color database.

```
Status XAllocNamedColor(display, cmap, colorname, colorcell_def, rgb_db_def)
    Display *display;
    Colormap cmap;
    char *colorname;            /* see Colors in Section 8 */
    XColor *colorcell_def;      /* closest RGB match in colormap */
    XColor *rgb_db_def;         /* returns exact RGB equivalent to name */
```

XAllocSizeHints

Allocate an XSizeHints structure for use in calling XSetWMProperties, XSetWMNormalHints, or XGetWMNormalHints.

```
XSizeHints *XAllocSizeHints()
```

XAllocStandardColormap

Allocate an XStandardColormap structure for use in calling XGetRGBColormaps or XSetRGBColormaps.

```
XStandardColormap *XAllocStandardColormap()
```

XAllocWMHints

Allocate an XWMHints structure for use in calling XSetWMProperties, XSetWMHints, or XGetWMHints.

```
XWMHints *XAllocWMHints()
```

XAllowEvents

Control the behavior of keyboard and pointer events when the keyboard or pointer is grabbed.

```
XAllowEvents(display, event_mode, time)
    Display *display;
    int event_mode;                        /* one of symbols below */
    Time time;                             /* when grab should take place */
```

The values for *event_mode* are defined in <X11/X.h>:

```
#define AsyncPointer      0    /* resume pointer events */
#define SyncPointer       1    /* resume pointer events, until next one */
#define ReplayPointer     2    /* release queued events, if pointer frozen */
#define AsyncKeyboard     3    /* resume keyboard events */
#define SyncKeyboard      4    /* resume keyboard events, until next one */
#define ReplayKeyboard    5    /* release queued events, if keyboard frozen */
#define AsyncBoth         6    /* resume pointer and keyboard events */
#define SyncBoth          7    /* same, but only until next one */
```

XAutoRepeatOff

Turn off auto-repeat for the keyboard.

```
XAutoRepeatOff(display)
    Display *display;
```

XAutoRepeatOn

Turn on auto-repeat for the keyboard.

```
XAutoRepeatOn(display)
    Display *display;
```

XBaseFontNameListOfFontSet

Get the base font list of a font set. A NULL-terminated string containing a list of comma-separated font names is returned as the value of the function. (New in R5.)

```
char *XBaseFontNameListOfFontSet(font_set)
    XFontSet font_set;
```

XBell

Ring the bell (Control G) at a percent relative to its default volume, which is set up with XChangeKeyboardControl.

```
XBell(display, percent)
    Display *display;
    int percent;                           /* -100 (off) to 100 (loudest) */
```

XChangeActivePointerGrab

Change the parameters of an active pointer grab, if the specified time is no earlier than the last pointer grab time and no later than the current X server time.

```
XChangeActivePointerGrab(display, event_mask, cursor, time)
    Display *display;
    unsigned int event_mask;              /* see Section 3 */
    Cursor cursor;
    Time time;                            /* when grab should take place */
```

XChangeGC

Change the components of a given graphics context.

```
XChangeGC(display, gc, valuemask, values)
    Display *display;
    GC gc;
    unsigned long valuemask;              /* see Section 2: XGCValues */
    XGCValues *values;
```

XChangeKeyboardControl

Change the keyboard preferences such as key click, bell volume and duration, LED state, and keyboard auto-repeat.

```
XChangeKeyboardControl(display, value_mask, values)
    Display *display;
    unsigned long value_mask;             /* see Section 2: XKeyboardControl */
    XKeyboardControl *values;
```

XChangeKeyboardMapping

Change the keyboard mapping. This function defines the keysysms for the specified number of keycodes, starting with *first_keycode*.

```
XChangeKeyboardMapping(display, first_code, keysyms_per_code, keysyms, num_codes)
    Display *display;
    int first_keycode;
    int keysyms_per_keycode;
    KeySym *keysyms;
    int num_keycodes;
```

XChangePointerControl

Change the pointer preferences regarding acceleration (how fast the pointer moves in proportion to the pointing device) and threshold (how far it has to move before acceleration starts).

```
XChangePointerControl(display, do_accel, do_threshold, accel_numerator, accel_denominator,
            threshold)
Display *display;
Bool do_accel, do_threshold;       /* whether other args are used */
int accel_numerator;               /* acceleration multiplier */
int accel_denominator;             /* acceleration multiplier */
int threshold;                     /* number of pixels to move before acceleration */
                                   /* starts */
```

XChangeProperty

Change a property associated with a window and generate PropertyNotify events if it has been selected.

```
XChangeProperty(display, w, property, type, format, mode, data, nelements)
Display *display;
Window w;
Atom property, type;               /* see Section 2 for list */
int format;                        /* 8, 16, or 32 bit data ? */
int mode;                          /* one of symbols below */
unsigned char *data;
int nelements;                     /* number of elements in property */
```

The values for *mode* are defined in <*X11/X.h*>:

```
#define PropModeReplace    0   /* replace property with new data */
#define PropModePrepend    1   /* insert data at start of property */
#define PropModeAppend     2   /* add data to end of property */
```

XChangeSaveSet

Add or remove a subwindow from the client's save-set.

```
XChangeSaveSet(display, w, change_mode)
Display *display;
Window w;
int change_mode;                   /* SetModeInsert or SetModeDelete */
```

The values for *change_mode* are defined in <*X11/X.h*>:

```
#define SetModeInsert    0   /* add window to save set */
#define SetModeDelete    1   /* delete window from save set */
```

XChangeWindowAttributes

Set window attributes.

```
XChangeWindowAttributes(display, w, valuemask, attributes)
    Display *display;
    Window w;
    unsigned long valuemask;          /* Section 2, XSetWindowAttributes */
    XSetWindowAttributes *attributes;
```

XCheckIfEvent

Return the next event in the queue that is matched by the specified predicate procedure. The predicate procedure is passed *display*, *event*, and any *arg*s.

```
Bool XCheckIfEvent(display, event, predicate, arg)
    Display *display;
    XEvent *event;
    Bool (*predicate)();
    char *arg;
```

XCheckMaskEvent

Return the next event that matches the passed mask; don't wait.

```
Bool XCheckMaskEvent(display, event_mask, event)
    Display *display;
    long event_mask;                  /* OR of event mask symbols */
    XEvent *event;                    /* returns matching event */
```

XCheckTypedEvent

Return the next event in queue that matches event type; don't wait.

```
Bool XCheckTypedEvent(display, event_type, report)
    Display *display;
    int event_type;                   /* see Section 2: XEvent */
    XEvent *report;                   /* returns matching event */
```

XCheckTypedWindowEvent

Return the next event in queue that matches type and window.

```
Bool XCheckTypedWindowEvent(display, w, event_type, report)
    Display *display;
    Window w;
    int event_type;                   /* event type, not mask */
    XEvent *report;                   /* returned event */
```

XCheckWindowEvent

Return the next event that matches both passed window and passed mask; don't wait.

```
Bool XCheckWindowEvent(display, w, event_mask, event)
    Display *display;
    Window w;
    long event_mask;              /* OR of event mask symbols */
    XEvent *event;                /* returned event */
```

XCirculateSubwindows

Circulate the stacking order of children up or down.

```
XCirculateSubwindows(display, w, direction)
    Display *display;
    Window w;                     /* parent of windows to be circulated */
    int direction;                /* RaiseLowest or LowerHighest */
```

The values for *direction* are defined in *<X11/X.h>*:

```
#define RaiseLowest        0    /* from bottom of stack to top */
#define LowerHighest       1    /* from top of stack to bottom */
```

XCirculateSubwindowsDown

Circulate the bottom child to the top of the stacking order. Equivalent to XCirculateSubwindows (*display, w, LowerHighest*).

```
XCirculateSubwindowsDown(display, w)
    Display *display;
    Window w;                     /* parent of windows to be circulated */
```

XCirculateSubwindowsUp

Circulate the top child to the bottom of the stacking order. Equivalent to XCirculateSubWindows (*display, w, RaiseLowest*).

```
XCirculateSubwindowsUp(display, w)
    Display *display;
    Window w;                     /* parent of windows to be circulated */
```

XClearArea

Clear a rectangular area in a window.

```
XClearArea(display, w, x, y, width, height, exposures)
    Display *display;
    Window w;
```

```
    int x, y;
    unsigned int width, height;
    Bool exposures;                         /* whether to generate Expose events */
```

XClearWindow

Clear an entire window. Equivalent to XClearArea (display, w, 0, 0, 0, 0, False).

```
XClearWindow(display, w)
    Display *display;
    Window w;
```

XClipBox

Generate the smallest rectangle enclosing a region.

```
XClipBox(r, rect)
    Region r;
    XRectangle *rect;                       /* returns rectangle enclosing region*/
```

XCloseDisplay

Disconnect a client program from an X server and display.

```
XCloseDisplay(display)
    Display *display;
```

XCloseIM

Close an input method. (New in R5.)

```
Status XCloseIM(im)
    XIM im;
```

XcmsAddColorSpace

Add a device-independent color space. (New in R5.)

```
Status XcmsAddColorSpace(color_space)
    XcmsColorSpace *color_space;            /* device-independent color space to add */
```

XcmsAddFunctionSet

Add a Color Characterization function set. (New in R5.)

```
Status XcmsAddFunctionSet(function_set)
    XcmsFunctionSet *function_set;          /* Color Characterization Function Set to add */
```

XcmsAllocColor

Allocate device-independent color. This function is similar to XAllocColor except the color can be specified in any format. (New in R5.)

```
Status XcmsAllocColor(display, colormap, color_in_out, result_format)
    Display *display;
    Colormap colormap;
    XcmsColor *color_in_out;          /* returns pixel and color actually used in colormap */
    XcmsColorFormat result_format;    /* color format for returned color specification */
```

XcmsAllocNamedColor

Allocate a named device-independent color. This function is similar to XcmsAlloc-Color except the color returned can be in any format specified. (New in R5.)

```
Status XcmsAllocNamedColor(display, colormap, color_string, color_screen_return,
            color_exact_return, result_format)
    Display *display;
    Colormap colormap;
    char *color_string;                /* the color name or specification */
    XcmsColor *color_screen_return;    /* returns pixel value of color cell and color */
                                       /* specification */
    XcmsColor *color_exact_return;     /* returns color specification parsed from color string */
    XcmsColorFormat result_format;     /* color format for returned color specification */
```

XcmsCCCOfColormap

Get the color conversion context of a colormap. (New in R5.)

```
XcmsCCC XcmsCCCOfColormap(display, colormap)
    Display *display;
    Colormap colormap;
```

XcmsCIELabQueryMaxC

Find the point in CIE L*a*b* color space of maximum chroma displayable by the screen, given a hue angle and lightness. (New in R5.)

```
Status XcmsCIELabQueryMaxC(ccc, hue_angle, L_star, color_return)
    XcmsCCC ccc;                      /* Color conversion context */
    XcmsFloat hue_angle;              /* Hue angle in degrees at which to find maximum */
                                      /* Chroma */
    XcmsFloat L_star;                 /* lightness (L*) at which to find maximum */
                                      /* Chroma */
    XcmsColor *color_return;          /* returns maximum Chroma given Hue angle and */
                                      /* lightness */
```

XcmsCIELabQueryMaxL

Find the point in CIE L*a*b* color space of maximum lightness (L*) displayable by the screen, given a hue angle and chroma. (New in R5.)

```
Status XcmsCIELabQueryMaxL(ccc, hue_angle, chroma, color_return)
    XcmsCCC ccc;                    /* color conversion context */
    XcmsFloat hue_angle;            /* Hue angle in degrees at which to find maximum */
                                    /* Chroma */
    XcmsFloat chroma;               /* Chroma at which to find maximum lightness */
    XcmsColor *color_return;        /* returns maximum lightness given Hue angle and */
                                    /* Chroma */
```

XcmsCIELabQueryMaxLC

Find the point in CIE L*a*b* color space of maximum chroma displayable by the screen, given a hue angle. (New in R5.)

```
Status XcmsCIELabQueryMaxLC(ccc, hue_angle, color_return)
    XcmsCCC ccc;                    /* color conversion context */
    XcmsFloat hue_angle;            /* Hue angle at which to find maximum Chroma*/
    XcmsColor *color_return;        /* returns maximum chroma for given Hue angle */
```

XcmsCIELabQueryMinL

Find the point in CIE L*a*b* color space of minimum lightness (L*) displayable by the screen, given a Hue angle and Chroma. (New in R5.)

```
Status XcmsCIELabQueryMinL(ccc, hue_angle, chroma, color_return)
    XcmsCCC ccc;                    /* color conversion context */
    XcmsFloat hue_angle;            /* Hue angle at which to find maximum Chroma*/
    XcmsFloat chroma;               /* Chroma at which to find minimum lightness */
    XcmsColor *color_return;        /* returns minimum lightness given Hue angle and */
                                    /* Chroma */
```

XcmsCIELuvQueryMaxC

Find the point in CIE L*u*v* color space of maximum Chroma displayable by the screen, given a Hue angle and lightness. (New in R5.)

```
Status XcmsCIELuvQueryMaxC(ccc, hue_angle, L_star, color_return)
    XcmsCCC ccc;                    /* color conversion context */
    XcmsFloat hue_angle;            /* Hue angle at which to find maximum Chroma*/
    XcmsFloat L_star;               /* lightness (L*) at which to find maximum Chroma */
    XcmsColor *color_return;        /* returns maximum chroma given Hue angle and */
                                    /* lightness */
```

XcmsCIELuvQueryMaxL

Find the point in CIE L*u*v* color space of maximum lightness (L*) displayable by the screen, given a Hue angle and Chroma. (New in R5.)

```
Status XcmsCIELuvQueryMaxL(ccc, hue_angle, chroma, color_return)
    XcmsCCC ccc;                     /* color conversion context */
    XcmsFloat hue_angle;             /* hue angle at which to find maximum lightness */
    XcmsFloat chroma;                /* Chroma at which to find maximum lightness */
    XcmsColor *color_return;         /* returns maximum lightness given Hue angle and */
                                     /* Chroma */
```

XcmsCIELuvQueryMaxLC

Find the point in CIE L*u*v* color space of maximum Chroma displayable by the screen, given a Hue angle. (New in R5.)

```
Status XcmsCIELuvQueryMaxLC(ccc, hue_angle, color_return)
    XcmsCCC ccc;                     /* color conversion context */
    XcmsFloat hue_angle;             /* Hue angle in degrees at which to find maximum */
                                     /* Chroma */
    XcmsColor *color_return;         /* returns maximum chroma given Hue angle */
```

XcmsCIELuvQueryMinL

Find the point in CIE L*u*v* color space of minimum lightness (L*) displayable by the screen, given a Hue angle and Chroma. (New in R5.)

```
Status XcmsCIELuvQueryMinL(ccc, hue_angle, chroma, color_return)
    XcmsCCC ccc;                     /* color conversion context */
    XcmsFloat hue_angle;             /* Hue angle in degrees at which to find minimum */
                                     /* lightness */
    XcmsFloat chroma;                /* Chroma at which to find minimum lightness */
    XcmsColor *color_return;         /* returns minimum lightness given Hue angle and */
                                     /* Chroma */
```

XcmsClientWhitePointOfCCC

Return the white point of the screen associated with the specified color conversion context. There is a macro version of this function, ClientWhitePointOfCCC. (New in R5.)

```
XcmsColor *XcmsClientWhitePointOfCCC(ccc)
    XcmsCCC ccc;                     /* color conversion context */
```

XcmsConvertColors

Convert a color specification from one format to another. (New in R5.)

```
Status XcmsConvertColors(ccc, colors_in_out, ncolors, target_format,
                compression_flags_return)
    XcmsCCC ccc;                          /* color conversion context */
    XcmsColor colors_in_out[];            /* array of color specifications */
    unsigned int ncolors;                 /* number of XcmsColor structures in color */
                                          /* specification array */
    XcmsColorFormat target_format;        /* target color specification format */
    Bool compression_flags_return[];      /* returns color conversion compression status */
```

XcmsCreateCCC

Create a color conversion context. (New in R5.)

```
XcmsCCC XcmsCreateCCC(display, screen_number, visual, client_white_point,
                compression_proc, compression_client_data, white_adjust_proc,
                white_adjust_client_data)
    Display *display;
    int screen_number;                    /* appropriate screen number on host server */
    Visual *visual;                       /* visual type */
    XcmsColor *client_white_point;        /* Client White Point */
    XcmsCompressionProc compression_proc; /* gamut compression procedure to be applied */
    XPointer compression_client_data;     /* client data for use by gamut compression */
                                          /* procedure */
    XcmsWhiteAdjustProc white_adjust_proc; /* white adjustment procedure to be applied */
    XPointer white_adjust_client_data;    /* client data for use with white point */
                                          /* adjustment procedure */
```

XcmsDefaultCCC

Get the default color conversion context for a screen. (New in R5.)

```
XcmsCCC XcmsDefaultCCC(display, screen_number)
    Display *display;
    int screen_number;
```

XcmsDisplayOfCCC

Return the display associated with a color conversion context. There is also a macro version of this function, DisplayOfCCC. (New in R5.)

```
Display *XcmsDisplayOfCCC(ccc)
    XcmsCCC ccc;                          /* color conversion context */
```

Xlib Routines

XcmsFormatOfPrefix

Obtain the format associated with the color space associated with a specified color string prefix. (New in R5.)

```
XcmsColorFormat XcmsFormatOfPrefix(prefix)
    char *prefix;                    /* string containing color space prefix */
```

XcmsFreeCCC

Free a color conversion context. (New in R5.)

```
void XcmsFreeCCC(ccc)
    XcmsCCC ccc;                     /* color conversion context */
```

XcmsLookupColor

Return device-independent color structures corresponding exactly to the named color and to the nearest color reproducible on the screen of the colormap. (New in R5.)

```
Status XcmsLookupColor(display, colormap, color_string, color_exact_return,
            color_screen_return, result_format)
    Display *display;
    Colormap colormap;
    char *color_string;              /* color string */
    XcmsColor *color_exact_return;   /* returns color specification parsed from color */
                                     /* string */
    XcmsColor *color_screen_return;  /* returns color reproducible on Screen */
    XcmsColorFormat result_format;   /* color format for returned color specifications */
```

XcmsPrefixOfFormat

Obtain the color string prefix associated with the color space specified by a color format. (New in R5.)

```
char *XcmsPrefixOfFormat(format)
    XcmsColorFormat format;          /* color specification format */
```

XcmsQueryBlack

Obtain a device-independent specification for RGBi:0.0/0.0/0.0. (New in R5.)

```
Status XcmsQueryBlack(ccc, target_format, color_return)
    XcmsCCC ccc;                     /* color conversion context */
    XcmsColorFormat target_format;   /* target color specification format */
    XcmsColor *color_return;         /* returns color specification in specified target */
                                     /* format */
```

XcmsQueryBlue

Obtain a device-independent specification for RGBi:0.0/0.0/1.0. (New in R5.)

```
Status XcmsQueryBlue(ccc, target_format, color_return)
    XcmsCCC ccc;                      /* color conversion context */
    XcmsColorFormat target_format;    /* target color specification format */
    XcmsColor *color_return;          /* returns color specification in specified target format */
```

XcmsQueryColors

Return, in the format specified by *result_format*, the color values specified by the *pixel* field of the specified XcmsColor structures. (New in R5.)

```
Status XcmsQueryColors(display, colormap, colors_in_out, ncolors, result_format)
    Display *display;
    Colormap colormap;
    XcmsColor *colors_in_out[];        /* array of XcmsColor structures; allocated by */
                                       /* caller */
    unsigned int ncolors;              /* number of XcmsColor structures in */
                                       /* colors_in_out array */
    XcmsColorFormat result_format;     /* color format for returned color specifications */
```

XcmsQueryGreen

Obtain a device-independent specification for RGBi:0.0/1.0/0.0. (New in R5.)

```
Status XcmsQueryGreen(ccc, target_format, color_return)
    XcmsCCC ccc;                      /* color conversion context */
    XcmsColorFormat target_format;    /* target color specification format */
    XcmsColor *color_return;          /* returns color specification in specified target */
                                      /* format */
```

XcmsQueryRed

Obtain a device-independent specification for RGBi:1.0/0.0/0.0. (New in R5.)

```
Status XcmsQueryRed(ccc, target_format, color_return)
    XcmsCCC ccc;                      /* color conversion context */
    XcmsColorFormat target_format;    /* target color specification format */
    XcmsColor *color_return;          /* returns color specification in specified target */
                                      /* format */
```

XcmsQueryWhite

Obtain a device-independent specification for RGBi:1.0/1.0/1.0. (New in R5.)

```
Status XcmsQueryWhite(ccc, target_format, color_return)
    XcmsCCC ccc;                      /* color conversion context */
    XcmsColorFormat target_format;    /* target color specification format */
    XcmsColor *color_return;          /* returns color specification in specified target */
                                      /* format */
```

XcmsScreenNumberOfCCC

Return the number of the screen associated with the specified color conversion context. (New in R5.)

```
int XcmsScreenNumberOfCCC(ccc)
    XcmsCCC ccc;                    /* color conversion context */
```

XcmsScreenWhitePointOfCCC

Return the white point of the screen associated with a specified color conversion context. There is also a macro version of this function, ScreenWhitePointOfCCC. (New in R5.)

```
XcmsColor *XcmsScreenWhitePointOfCCC(ccc)
    XcmsCCC ccc;                    /* color conversion context */
```

XcmsSetCCCOfColormap

Change the color conversion context associated with a colormap. (New in R5.)

```
XcmsCCC XcmsSetCCCOfColormap(display, colormap, ccc)
    Display *display;
    Colormap colormap;
    XcmsCCC ccc;                    /* color conversion context */
```

XcmsSetWhitePoint

Set white point of color conversion context. (New in R5.)

```
Status XcmsSetWhitePoint(ccc, color)
    XcmsCCC ccc;                    /* color conversion context */
    XcmsColor *color;               /* new Client White Point */
```

XcmsStoreColor

Set a device-independent color in a read/write colormap cell.

```
Status XcmsStoreColor(display, colormap, color)
    Display *display;
    Colormap colormap;
    XcmsColor *color;
```

XcmsStoreColors

Set device-independent colors in read/write colormap cells. (New in R5.)

```
Status XcmsStoreColors(display, colormap, colors, ncolors, compression_flags_return)
    Display *display;
    Colormap colormap;
    XcmsColor colors[];             /* array of XcmsColor structures */
```

```
       int ncolors;                               /* number of XcmsColor structures in color */
                                                   /* specification array */
       Boolcompression_flags_return[];            /* returns compression status; caller must allocate */
```

XcmsTekHVCQueryMaxC

Find maximum Chroma for a given TekHVC Hue and Value.

```
    Status XcmsTekHVCQueryMaxC(ccc, hue, value, color_return)
       XcmsCCC ccc;                               /* color conversion context */
       XcmsFloat hue;                             /* Hue at which to find maximum Chroma */
       XcmsFloat value;                           /* Value at which to find maximum Chroma */
       XcmsColor *color_return;                   /* returns maximum Chroma along with Hue and */
                                                   /* Value */
```

XcmsTekHVCQueryMaxV

Find the maximum Value for a given TekHVC Hue and Chroma.

```
    Status XcmsTekHVCQueryMaxV(ccc, hue, chroma, color_return)
       XcmsCCC ccc;                               /* color conversion context */
       XcmsFloat hue;                             /* Hue at which to find maximum Value */
       XcmsFloat chroma;                          /* Chroma at which to find maximum Value */
       XcmsColor *color_return;                   /* returns maximum Value along with Hue and */
                                                   /* Chroma */
```

XcmsTekHVCQueryMaxVSamples

Return the boundaries of the TekHVC gamut for a given Hue.

```
    Status XcmsTekHVCQueryMaxVSamples(ccc, hue, colors_return, nsamples)
       XcmsCCC ccc;                               /* color conversion context */
       XcmsFloat hue;                             /* Hue at which to find maximum Chroma/Value */
                                                   /* samples */
       XcmsColor colors_return[];                 /* array of nsamples XcmsColor structures; caller must */
                                                   /* allocate */
       unsigned int nsamples;                     /* number of samples */
```

XcmsTekHVCQueryMinV

Find the minimum Value for a given TekHVC Hue and Chroma. (New in R5.)

```
    Status XcmsTekHVCQueryMinV(ccc, hue, chroma, color_return)
       XcmsCCC ccc;                               /* color conversion context */
       XcmsFloat hue;                             /* Hue at which to find minimum Value */
       XcmsFloat chroma;                          /* Chroma at which to find minimum Value */
       XcmsColor *color_return;                   /* returns minimum Value and actual Hue and */
                                                   /* Chroma */
```

XcmsVisualOfCCC

Return the visual associated with a specified color conversion context. (New in R5.)

```
Visual *XcmsVisualOfCCC(ccc)
    XcmsCCC ccc;                        /* color conversion context */
    VisualOfCCC(ccc)
    XcmsCCC ccc;
```

XConfigureWindow

Change the window position, size, border width, or stacking order.

```
XConfigureWindow(display, w, value_mask, values)
    Display *display;
    Window w;
    unsigned int value_mask;            /* see Section 2: XWindowChanges */
    XWindowChanges *values;
```

XContextDependentDrawing

Get a hint about context dependencies in the text of the locale. If this function returns True, text in locale of specified font set may contain context dependencies. If False, text drawn with font set does not contain context dependencies. (New in R5.)

```
Bool XContextDependentDrawing(font_set)
    XFontSet font_set;
```

XConvertSelection

Use the value of a selection. Cause a SelectionRequest event to be sent to the current selection owner specifying property to store the data in, format to convert data into, property to place information in, window that wants the information, and the time to make the conversion.

```
XConvertSelection(display, selection, target, property, requestor, time)
    Display *display;
    Atom selection, target;             /* see Section 2 for list */
    Atom property;                      /* where to store result */
    Window requestor;
    Time time;                          /* when conversion should happen */
```

XCopyArea

Copy an area of a drawable.

```
XCopyArea(display, src, dest, gc, src_x, src_y, width, height, dest_x, dest_y)
    Display *display;
    Drawable src, dest;
    GC gc;
    int src_x, src_y;
    unsigned int width, height;
    int dest_x, dest_y;
```

XCopyColormapAndFree

Copy a colormap and return a new colormap ID. This function is used to obtain a new virtual colormap when allocating colorcells out of a previous colormap has failed because too many cells or planes were in use in the original colormap.

```
Colormap XCopyColormapAndFree(display, cmap)
    Display *display;
    Colormap cmap;                       /* to be copied */
```

XCopyGC

Copy selected elements of one graphics context to another.

```
XCopyGC(display, src, valuemask, dest)
    Display *display;
    GC src, dest;
    unsigned long valuemask;             /* see Section 2: XGCValues */
```

XCopyPlane

Copy a single plane of a drawable into a drawable with depth, applying pixel values.

```
XCopyPlane(display, src, dest, gc, src_x, src_y, width, height, dest_x, dest_y, plane)
    Display *display;
    Drawable src, dest;
    GC gc;
    int src_x, src_y;                    /* position of source rectangle */
    unsigned int width, height;          /* width and height in pixels */
    int dest_x, dest_y;                  /* position of destination rectangle */
    unsigned long plane;                 /* source bit plane */
```

XCreateAssocTable

Create a new association table (provided for compatibility with X Version 10).

```
XAssocTable *XCreateAssocTable(size)
    int size;
```

XCreateBitmapFromData

Create a bitmap from X11 bitmap format data.

```
Pixmap XCreateBitmapFromData(display, drawable, data, width, height)
    Display *display;
    Drawable drawable;
    char *data;                        /* location of bitmap data * /
    unsigned int width, height;        /* size of bitmap, in pixels */
```

Data uses the following default format:

```
format=XYPixmap
bit_order=LSBFirst
byte_order=LSBFirst
bitmap_unit=8
bitmap_pad=8
xoffset=0
no extra bytes per line
```

XCreateColormap

Create a colormap and return colormap ID.

```
Colormap XCreateColormap(display, w, visual, alloc)
    Display *display;
    Window w;
    Visual *visual;
    int alloc;                         /* AllocNone or AllocAll */
```

alloc must be AllocNone for StaticColor, StaticGray, or TrueColor visuals. The values for alloc are defined in <X11/X.h>:

```
#define AllocNone    0                 /* create map with no entries */
#define AllocAll     1                 /* allocate entire map writeable */
```

XCreateFontCursor

Create a cursor from the standard cursor font. (See Section 8.)

```
#include <X11/cursorfont.h>
Cursor XCreateFontCursor(display, shape)
    Display *display;
    unsigned int shape;                /* which character in font to use */
```

XCreateFontSet

Create a font set for a specified display. (New in R5.)

```
XFontSet XCreateFontSet(display, base_font_name_list, missing_charset_list_return,
          missing_charset_count_return, def_string_return)
    Display *display;
    char *base_font_name_list;              /* base font names */
    char ***missing_charset_list_return;    /* returns missing charsets */
    int *missing_charset_count_return;      /* returns number of missing charsets */
    char **def_string_return;               /* returns string drawn for missing charsets */
```

XCreateGC

Create a new graphics context for a given display with the depth of the specified drawable.

```
GC XCreateGC(display, drawable, valuemask, values)
    Display *display;
    Drawable drawable;
    unsigned long valuemask;                /* see Section 2: XGCValues */
    XGCValues *values;
```

XCreateGlyphCursor

Create a cursor from font glyphs. If mask_char is 0, all bits of source_char are displayed. XCreateGlyphCursor is similar to XCreatePixmapCursor, but the source and mask bitmaps are obtained from separate font characters.

```
Cursor XCreateGlyphCursor(display, source_font, mask_font, source_char, mask_char,
          foreground_color, background_color)
    Display *display;
    Font source_font, mask_font;            /* mask_font 0 if not needed */
    unsigned int source_char, mask_char;    /* index into font */
    XColor *foreground_color;
    XColor *background_color;
```

XCreateIC

Create an input context associated with a specified input method. The first argument to this function is the input context, and it is followed by NULL-terminated variable-length argument list of attribute name/value pairs. (New in R5.)

```
XIC XCreateIC(im, ...)
    XIM im;
    ...;                                    /* variable length argument list to set XIC values */
```

XCreateImage

Allocate memory for an XImage structure. (See Section 2.)

```
#include <X11/Xutil.h>
XImage *XCreateImage(display, visual, depth, format, offset, data, width, height, bitmap_pad,
              bytes_per_line)
    Display *display;
    Visual *visual;
    unsigned int depth;
    int format;                          /* XYPixmap or ZPixmap */
    int offset;                          /* if data not aligned */
    char *data;
    unsigned int width, height;
    int bitmap_pad, bytes_per_line;
```

XCreatePixmap

Create a pixmap and return its ID.

```
Pixmap XCreatePixmap(display, drawable, width, height, depth)
    Display *display;
    Drawable drawable;
    unsigned int width, height;          /* in pixels */
    unsigned int depth;                  /* see Section 2: XImage */
```

XCreatePixmapCursor

Create a cursor from two bitmaps and return its ID.

```
Cursor XCreatePixmapCursor(display, source, mask, foreground_color, background_color,
           x_hot, y_hot)
    Display *display;
    Pixmap source;                       /* depth 1:  shape of cursor */
    Pixmap mask;                         /* depth 1:  bits to be displayed */
    XColor *foreground_color;
    XColor *background_color;
    unsigned int x_hot, y_hot;
```

XCreatePixmapFromBitmapData

Create a pixmap with depth from bitmap data. For the format of data, see
XCreateBitmapFromData.

```
Pixmap XCreatePixmapFromBitmapData(display, drawable, data, width, height, fg, bg, depth)
    Display *display;
    Drawable drawable;
    char *data;                          /* location of data */
    unsigned int width, height;
```

```
unsigned long fg, bg;                /* pixel values */
unsigned int depth;
```

XCreateRegion

Create a new, empty region of undefined size. XPolygonRegion can be used to create a region with a defined shape and size.

```
Region XCreateRegion()
```

XCreateSimpleWindow

Create an unmapped InputOutput window. Window attributes are either inherited from the parent (depth, class, and visual) or have their default values. If you want to set window attributes while creating a window, use XCreateWindow.

```
Window XCreateSimpleWindow(display, parent, x, y, width, height, border_width, border,
              background)
   Display *display;
   Window parent;
   int x, y;
   unsigned int width, height, border_width;
   unsigned long border;                /* pixel value */
   unsigned long background;            /* pixel value */
```

XCreateWindow

Create a window and set attributes. To create a window without setting specific attributes, use XCreateSimpleWindow.

```
Window XCreateWindow(display, parent, x, y, width, height, border_width, depth, class, visual,
              valuemask, attributes)
   Display *display;
   Window parent;
   int x, y;
   unsigned int width, height;
   unsigned int border_width;
   int depth;
   unsigned int class;                  /* one of symbols below */
   Visual *visual
   unsigned long valuemask;             /* Section 2: XSetWindowAttributes */
   XSetWindowAttributes *attributes;
```

The values for *class* are defined in *<X11/X.h>*:

```
#define CopyFromParent        0L
#define InputOutput           1
#define InputOnly             2
```

XDefaultString

Return the default string used for text conversion. The default string is the string in the current locale that is output when an unconvertible character is found during text conversion. Caller must not free or modify this string. (New in R5.)

```
char *XDefaultString()
```

XDefineCursor

Assign a cursor to a window.

```
XDefineCursor(display, w, cursor)
    Display *display;
    Window w;
    Cursor cursor;                    /* None = parent's cursor */
```

XDeleteAssoc

Delete an entry from an association table (provided for compatibility with X Version 10).

```
XDeleteAssoc(display, table, x_id)
    Display *display;
    XAssocTable *table;
    XID x_id;
```

XDeleteContext

Delete a context entry for a given window and type.

```
int XDeleteContext(display, w, context)
    Display *display;
    Window w;
    XContext context;
```

XDeleteModifiermapEntry

Delete an entry from an XModifierKeymap structure. This function is normally used by calling XGetModifierMapping to get a pointer to the current XModifierKeymap structure for use as modmap.

```
XModifierKeymap *XDeleteModifiermapEntry(modmap, keysym_entry, modifier)
    XModifierKeymap *modmap;
    KeyCode keysym_entry;
    int modifier;                     /* modifier to be deleted */
```

XDeleteProperty

Delete a window property.

```
XDeleteProperty(display, w, property)
    Display *display;
    Window w;
    Atom property;                      /* see Section 2 for list */
```

XDestroyAssocTable

Free the memory allocated for an association table (provided for compatibility with X Version 10).

```
XDestroyAssocTable(table)
    XAssocTable *table;
```

XDestroyIC

Destroy an input context. (New in R5.)

```
void XDestroyIC(ic)
    XIC ic;
```

XDestroyImage

Deallocate storage associated with an XImage structure.

```
int XDestroyImage(ximage)
    XImage *ximage;
```

XDestroyRegion

Deallocate storage associated with a region.

```
XDestroyRegion(r)
    Region r;
```

XDestroySubwindows

Destroy all subwindows of a window. Do not use this function with the window argument set to the root window as it will destroy all applications on the screen. XCloseDisplay destroys all windows created by that client on the specified display.

```
XDestroySubwindows(display, w)
    Display *display;
    Window w;
```

XDestroyWindow

Unmap and destroy a specified window and all subwindows.

```
XDestroyWindow(display, w)
    Display *display;
    Window w;
```

XDisableAccessControl

Allow access from any host.

```
XDisableAccessControl(display)
    Display *display;
```

XDisplayKeycodes

Obtain the legal keycodes for a server. Not all keycodes in the *min_keycodes/max_keycodes* range are required to have corresponding keys.

```
XDisplayKeycodes(display, min_keycodes, max_keycodes)
    Display *display;
    int *min_keycodes, *max_keycodes;
```

XDisplayMotionBufferSize

Return the size of the motion buffer (an *unsigned long* value) on the server. If this function returns zero, the server has no motion history buffer.

```
unsigned long XDisplayMotionBufferSize(display)
    Display *display;                    /* pointer to a Display structure */
```

XDisplayName

Report the display name (when attempt to open with XOpenDisplay fails).

```
char *XDisplayName(string)
    char *string;                        /* display name */
```

XDisplayOfIM

Get the display of an input method. (New in R5.)

```
Display *XDisplayOfIM(im)
    XIM im;
```

XDraw

Draw a polyline or curve from a list of vertices (provided for compatibility with X Version 10).

```
Status XDraw(display, drawable, gc, vlist, vcount)
    Display *display;
    Drawable drawable;
    GC gc;
    Vertex *vlist;
    int vcount;                         /* number of vertices */
```

XDrawArc

Draw an arc fitting inside a rectangle.

```
XDrawArc(display, drawable, gc, x, y, width, height, angle1, angle2)
    Display *display;
    Drawable drawable;
    GC gc;
    int x, y;
    unsigned int width, height;
    int angle1, angle2;                 /* 64ths of a degree; 3 o'clock as 0 */
```

XDrawArcs

Draw multiple arcs. To determine how many arcs can be drawn in a single cell, use XMaxRequestSize.

```
XDrawArcs(display, drawable, gc, arcs, narcs)
    Display *display;
    Drawable drawable;
    GC gc;
    XArc *arcs;
    int narcs;
```

XDrawFilled

Draw a polygon or curve from list of vertices (according to XDraw rules), then fill them (from X10).

```
Status XDrawFilled(display, drawable, gc, vlist, vcount)
    Display *display;
    Drawable drawable;
    GC gc;
    Vertex *vlist;
    int vcount;
```

XDrawImageString

Draw 8-bit image text characters. Unlike XDrawString, this functions draws both the foreground and background of the characters,

```
XDrawImageString(display, drawable, gc, x, y, string, length)
    Display *display;
    Drawable drawable;
    GC gc;
    int x, y;                        /* baseline starting position */
    char *string;
    int length;                      /* length of string */
```

XDrawImageString16

Draw 16-bit image text characters. This function draws both the foreground and background of the characters, unlike XDrawString16.

```
XDrawImageString16(display, drawable, gc, x, y, string, length)
    Display *display;
    Drawable drawable;
    GC gc;
    int x, y;                        /* baseline starting position */
    XChar2b *string;
    int length;                      /* length of string */
```

XDrawLine

Draw a line between two points (x1,y1 to x2,y2) using the specified graphics context.

```
XDrawLine(display, drawable, gc, x1, y1, x2, y2)
    Display *display;
    Drawable drawable;
    GC gc;
    int x1, y1, x2, y2;
```

XDrawLines

Draw multiple connected lines. To determine the limit of lines that can be drawn in a single cell, use XMaxRequestSize.

```
XDrawLines(display, drawable, gc, points, npoints, mode)
    Display *display;
    Drawable drawable;
    GC gc;
    XPoint *points;
    int npoints;
    int mode;                        /* one of symbols below */
```

The values for *mode* are defined in *<X11/X.h>*:

```
#define CoordModeOrigin        0    /* relative to the origin */
#define CoordModePrevious      1    /* relative to previous point */
```

XDrawPoint

Draw a point (at *x,y*) using the specified graphics context.

```
XDrawPoint(display, drawable, gc, x, y)
    Display *display;
    Drawable drawable;
    GC gc;
    int x, y;
```

XDrawPoints

Draw multiple points. To determine maximum number of points that can be drawn in a single cell, use XMaxRequestSize

```
XDrawPoints(display, drawable, gc, points, npoints, mode)
    Display *display;
    Drawable drawable;
    GC gc;
    XPoint *points;
    int npoints;
    int mode;                    /* CoordModeOrigin or CoordModePrevious */
```

XDrawRectangle

Draw an outline of a rectangle using *x* and *y* coordinates, *width* and *height*, and specified graphics context.

```
XDrawRectangle(display, drawable, gc, x, y, width, height)
    Display *display;
    Drawable drawable;
    GC gc;
    int x, y;
    unsigned int width, height;
```

XDrawRectangles

Draw the outlines of multiple rectangles. To determine maximum number of rectangles that can be drawn in a single cell, use XMaxRequestSize.

```
XDrawRectangles(display, drawable, gc, rectangles, nrectangles)
    Display *display;
    Drawable drawable;
```

```
GC gc;
XRectangle rectangles[];
int nrectangles;
```

XDrawSegments

Draw multiple disconnected line segments into the specified drawable. To determine maximum number of segments that can be drawn in a single cell, use XMax-RequestSize.

```
XDrawSegments(display, drawable, gc, segments, nsegments)
    Display *display;
    Drawable drawable;
    GC gc;
    XSegment *segments;
    int nsegments;
```

XDrawString

Draw an 8-bit text string, foreground only.

```
XDrawString(display, drawable, gc, x, y, string, length)
    Display *display;
    Drawable drawable;
    GC gc;
    int x, y;
    char *string;
    int length;
```

XDrawString16

Like XDrawString, but draw two-byte (16-bit) text strings.

```
XDrawString16(display, drawable, gc, x, y, string, length)
    Display *display;
    Drawable drawable;
    GC gc;
    int x, y;
    XChar2b *string;
    int length;
```

XDrawText

Draw 8-bit polytext strings. Each XTextItem structure contains a string, number of characters in the string, the number of pixels to be moved horizontally prior to drawing the string, and the font.

```
XDrawText(display, drawable, gc, x, y, items, nitems)
    Display *display;
    Drawable drawable;
```

```
GC gc;
int x, y;
XTextItem *items;
int nitems;
```

XDrawText16

Like XDrawText, but draw 16-bit polytext strings.

```
XDrawText16(display, drawable, gc, x, y, items, nitems)
    Display *display;
    Drawable drawable;
    GC gc;
    int x, y;
    XTextItem16 *items;
    int nitems;
```

XEmptyRegion

Determine if a region is empty.

```
Bool XEmptyRegion(r)
    Region r;
```

XEnableAccessControl

Use access control list to allow or deny connection requests. If access has not been disabled with XDisableAccessControl or XSetAccessControl, this routine does nothing.

```
XEnableAccessControl(display)
    Display *display;
```

XEqualRegion

Determine if two regions have the same size, offset, and shape.

```
Bool XEqualRegion(r1, r2)
    Region r1, r2;
```

XEventsQueued

Return the number of events in the event queue. Using QueuedAfterFlush mode is identical in behavior to XPending.

```
int XEventsQueued(display, mode)
    Display *display;
    int mode;                          /* how to count the events read */
```

The values for *mode* are defined in *<X11/X.h>*:

```
#define QueuedAlready        0       /* flush nothing; read nothing more */
#define QueuedAfterReading   1       /* don't flush output, but read more */
#define QueuedAfterFlush     2       /* flush output, and read more */
```

XExtentsOfFontSet

Obtain the maximum extents structure for a font set. (New in R5.)

```
XFontSetExtents *XExtentsOfFontSet(font_set)
    XFontSet font_set;
```

XFetchBuffer

Return data (*nbytes* or NULL) from a cut buffer.

```
char *XFetchBuffer(display, nbytes, buffer)
    Display *display;
    int *nbytes;                     /* returns number of bytes in buffer */
    int buffer;                      /* 0 to 7 */
```

XFetchBytes

Like XFetchBuffer, but returns data from cut buffer 0.

```
char *XFetchBytes(display, nbytes)
    Display *display;
    int *nbytes;                     /* returns number of bytes in buffer */
```

XFetchName

Get a window's name (XA_WM_NAME property). This function has been superseded by XGetWMName in R4 and later releases.

```
Status XFetchName(display, w, window_name)
    Display *display;
    Window w;
    char **window_name;              /* NULL-terminated string */
```

XFillArc

Fill an arc. Unfilled arcs are drawn with XDrawArc.

```
XFillArc(display, drawable, gc, x, y, width, height, angle1, angle2)
    Display *display;
    Drawable drawable;
    GC gc;
```

```
int x, y;
unsigned int width, height;
int angle1, angle2;                          /* 64ths of a degree */
```

XFillArcs

Fill multiple arcs. To determine maximum number of arcs allowed in a single call, use XMaxRequestSize. (Multiple unfilled arcs are drawn with XDrawArcs.)

```
XFillArcs(display, drawable, gc, arcs, narcs)
    Display *display;
    Drawable drawable;
    GC gc;
    XArc *arcs;
    int narcs;
```

XFillPolygon

Fill a polygon region closed by specified path. Path is closed automatically if last point in point list does not coincide with first point. *shape* allows the fill routine to optimize its performance, given tips on the configuration of the area.

```
XFillPolygon(display, drawable, gc, points, npoints, shape, mode)
    Display *display;
    Drawable drawable;
    GC gc;
    XPoint *points;
    int npoints;
    int shape;               /* Complex, Convex, or NonConvex */
    int mode;                /* CoordModeOrigin or CoordModePrevious */
```

XFillRectangle

Fill a rectangular area. Unfilled rectangles are drawn by XDrawRectangle.

```
XFillRectangle(display, drawable, gc, x, y, width, height)
    Display *display;
    Drawable drawable;
    GC gc;
    int x, y;
    unsigned int width, height;
```

XFillRectangles

Fill multiple rectangular areas. Multiple unfilled rectangles are drawn by XDrawRectangles.

```
XFillRectangles(display, drawable, gc, rectangles, nrectangles)
    Display *display;
    Drawable drawable;
    GC gc;
    XRectangle *rectangles;
    int nrectangles;
```

XFilterEvent

Filter X events for an input method—pass the specified event to any event filters registered for the specified window. Internationalized clients should call this function from their event loops, generally directly after calling XNextEvent. (New in R5.)

```
Bool XFilterEvent(event, w)
    XEvent *event;              /* event to filter */
    Window w;                   /* window filter applied to */
```

XFindContext

Get data from the context manager (not graphics context).

```
int XFindContext(display, w, context, data)
    Display *display;
    Window w;
    XContext context;
    XPointer *data;
```

XFlush

Flush the request buffer (display all queued requests). Flushing may be done automatically by calls to XPending, XNextEvent, or XWindowEvent.

```
XFlush(display)
    Display *display;
```

XFlushGC

Force cached GC changes to the server.

```
void XFlushGC(display, gc)
    Display *display;
    GC gc;
```

XFontsOfFontSet

Get the list of fonts used by a font set. A list of pointers to the XFontStruct structures is returned to font_struct_list_return, a list of pointers to font name strings in the font set locale is returned to *font_name_list_return*, and the number of elements in each array is returned as the value of the function. (New in R5.)

```
int XFontsOfFontSet(font_set, font_struct_list_return, font_name_list_return)
    XFontSet font_set;
    XFontStruct ***font_struct_list_return;    /* returns list of font structs; caller must free */
    char ***font_name_list_return;             /* returns list of font names; caller must free */
```

XForceScreenSaver

Turn the screen saver on or off.

```
XForceScreenSaver(display, mode)
    Display *display;
    int mode                                   /* one of symbols below */
```

The values for *mode* are defined in *<X11/X.h>*:

```
#define ScreenSaverReset     0    /* deactivate and rest timer */
#define ScreenSaverActive    1    /* active screen saver now */
```

XFree

Free specified memory allocated by an Xlib function.

```
XFree(data)
    Xpointer data;                             /* pointer to data to be freed */
```

XFreeColormap

Delete a colormap and install the default colormap.

```
XFreeColormap(display, cmap)
    Display *display;
    Colormap cmap;
```

XFreeColors

Free colormap cells or planes. If cells are read/write, they become available for reuse (unless allocated with **XAllocColorPlanes**, in which case all related pixels may need to be freed before any are available). If cells are read-only, they become available only if this is the last client to have allocated these shared cells.

```
XFreeColors(display, cmap, pixels, npixels, planes)
    Display *display;
    Colormap cmap;
    unsigned long pixels[];                    /* values map to cells in colormap */
    int npixels;
    unsigned long planes;                      /* planes you want to free */
```

XFreeCursor

Release a cursor.

```
XFreeCursor(display, cursor)
    Display *display;
    Cursor cursor;
```

XFreeExtensionList

Free memory allocated by XListExtensions for a list of installed extensions.

```
XFreeExtensionList(list)
    char **list;                        /* returned from XListExtensions */
```

XFreeFont

Free storage for a font structure, and unload font if no other client has loaded it.

```
XFreeFont(display, font_struct)
    Display *display;
    XFontStruct *font_struct;
```

XFreeFontInfo

Free the memory allocated by XListFontsWithInfo. This function does not unload specific fonts themselves.

```
XFreeFontInfo(names, info, actual_count)
    char **names;
    XFontStruct *info;                  /* returned from XListFontsWithInfo */
    int actual_count;                   /* returned from XListFontsWithInfo */
```

XFreeFontNames

Free the memory allocated by XListFonts.

```
XFreeFontNames(list)
    char *list[];
```

XFreeFontPath

Free the memory allocated by XGetFontPath.

```
XFreeFontPath(list)
    char **list;
```

XFreeFontSet

Free a font set. The associated base font name list, font name list, XFontStruct list, and XFontSetExtents, if any, are freed. (New in R5.)

```
void XFreeFontSet(display, font_set)
    Display *display
    XFontSet font_set;
```

XFreeGC

Free a graphics context and remove it from the server and display hardware.

```
XFreeGC(display, gc)
    Display *display;
    GC gc;
```

XFreeModifiermap

Destroy and free a keyboard modifier mapping structure originally allocated by XNewModifierMap or XGetModifierMapping.

```
XFreeModifiermap(modmap)
    XModifierKeymap *modmap;
```

XFreePixmap

Free a pixmap ID.

```
XFreePixmap(display, pixmap)
    Display *display;
    Pixmap pixmap;
```

XFreeStringList

Free the in-memory data associated with the specified string list allocated by XTextPropertyToStringList.

```
void XFreeStringList(list)
    char **list;
```

XGContextFromGC

Obtain the GContext (resource ID) associated with the specified graphics context.

```
GContext XGContextFromGC(gc)
    GC gc;
```

XGeometry

Calculate a window's geometry, given the user-supplied geometry string and the default geometry. Geometry strings have the following form: *width* x *height* ± *xoffset* ± *yoffset*. This function has been superseded by XWMGeometry in R4 and later releases.

```
int XGeometry(display, screen, user_geom, default_geom, bwidth, fwidth, fheight, xadder,
              yadder, x, y, width, height)
    Display *display;
    int screen;
    char *user_geom, *default_geom;   /* geometry strings */
    unsigned int bwidth;              /* border width */
    unsigned int fwidth, fheight;     /* font width and height, for size increments */
    int xadder, yadder;               /* interior padding */
    int *x, *y, *width, *height;
```

XGetAtomName

Get a string name for a property given its atom.

```
char *XGetAtomName(display, atom)
    Display *display;
    Atom atom;                        /* Atom you want string name for */
```

XGetClassHint

Get the XA_WM_CLASS property of a window.

```
Status XGetClassHint(display, w, class_hints)
    Display *display;
    Window w;
    XClassHint *class_hints;
```

XGetDefault

Extract an option value from the resource database.

```
char *XGetDefault(display, program, option)
    Display *display;
    char *program;                    /* usually argv[0] */
    char *option;                     /* resource name */
```

XGetErrorDatabaseText

Obtain error messages from the error database.

```
XGetErrorDatabaseText(display, name, message, default_string, buffer, length)
    Display display;
    char *name;                       /* name of application */
    char *message;                    /* XProtoError, XlibMessage, or XRequestMajor */
```

```
      char *default_string;              /* default error message */
      char *buffer;                      /* returns error description*/
      int length;
```

XGetErrorText

Obtain a description of error code.

```
   XGetErrorText(display, code, buffer, length)
      Display *display;
      int code;                          /* # of error code wanted */
      char *buffer;                      /* returns message */
      int length;
```

XGetFontPath

Get the current font search path.

```
   char **XGetFontPath(display, npaths)
      Display *display;
      int *npaths;                       /* number of strings in font path array */
```

XGetFontProperty

Get a font property given its atom. Predefined atoms for font properties can be found in <X11/XAtom.h>.

```
   Bool XGetFontProperty(font_struct, atom, value)
      XFontStruct *font_struct;          /* which font to look at */
      Atom atom;                         /* which font property */
      unsigned long *value;              /* value of font property */
```

XGetGCValues

Obtain components of a given GC from Xlib's GC cache.

```
   Status XGetGCValues(display, gc, valuemask, values)
      Display *display;
      GC gc;
      unsigned long valuemask;           /* see Section 2: XGCValues */
      XGCValues *values;                 /* returns values in XGCValues structure*/
```

XGetGeometry

Obtain the current geometry of specified drawable.

```
   Status XGetGeometry(display, drawable, root, x, y, width, height, border_width, depth)
      Display *display;
      Drawable drawable;
      Window *root;                      /* returns root window ID */
```

```
int *x, *y;                          /* returns window border coordinates */
unsigned int *width, *height;        /* returns dimensions of drawable */
unsigned int *border_width;          /* returns border width */
unsigned int *depth;                 /* returns depth of pixmap or window */
```

XGetIconName

Get the name to be displayed in an icon. This function has been superseded by XGetWMIconName in R4.

```
Status XGetIconName(display, w, icon_name)
    Display *display;
    Window w;
    char **icon_name;                /* returns pointer to name*/
```

XGetIconSizes

Get preferred icon sizes. This function should be called by all programs to determine icon sizes preferred by the window manager. The application should then use XSetWMHints to supply window manager with an icon pixmap or window in a supported size.

```
Status XGetIconSizes(display, w, size_list, count)
    Display *display;
    Window w;
    XIconSize **size_list;           /* returns preferred sizes */
    int *count;                      /* returns number of sizes */
```

XGetICValues

Get input context attributes. The first argument to this function is the input context, and it is followed by a NULL-terminated variable-length argument list of attribute name/value pairs. (New in R5.)

```
char * XGetICValues(ic, ... )
    XIC ic;
    ... ;                            /* variable argument list to get XIC values */
```

XGetIMValues

Obtain input method information. The first argument to this function is the input method, and it is followed by a NULL-terminated variable-length argument list of attribute name/value pairs. (New in R5.)

```
char *XGetIMValues(im, ... )
    XIM im;
    ... ;                            /* variable argument list to get XIM values */
```

XGetImage

Place contents of a rectangle from drawable into a client-side XImage structure, in a specified format. XYPixmap gets only the bit planes passed to *plane_mask*; ZPixmap sets bits not specified in *plane_mask* to 0, no range checking is performed, and extraneous bits are ignored.

```
XImage *XGetImage(display, drawable, x, y, width, height, plane_mask, format)
    Display *display;
    Drawable drawable;
    int x, y;
    unsigned int width, height;
    unsigned long plane_mask;          /* which planes in image? */
    int format;                        /* XYPixmap or ZPixmap */
```

XGetInputFocus

Return the current keyboard focus window.

```
XGetInputFocus(display, focus, revert_to)
    Display *display;
    Window *focus;                     /* returns window ID, PointerRoot, or None */
    int *revert_to;                    /* returns RevertToNone, RevertToPointerRoot, or */
                                       /* RevertToParent */
```

The symbols above are defined in *<X11/X.h>*:

```
#define None                 0L
#define PointerRoot          1L
#define RevertToNone         (int)None
#define RevertToPointerRoot  (int)PointerRoot
#define RevertToParent       2
```

XGetKeyboardControl

Obtain a list of the current keyboard preferences, including key click volume; bell volume; pitch and duration; LEDs; and auto-repeat controls.

```
XGetKeyboardControl(display, values)
    Display *display;
    XKeyboardState *values;            /* returns filled XKeyboardState structure */
```

XGetKeyboardMapping

Return symbols for keycodes.

```
KeySym *XGetKeyboardMapping(display, first_keycode, keycode_count, keysyms_per_keycode)
    Display *display;
    KeyCode first_keycode;
```

```
int keycode_count;                    /* number of keycodes to be returned */
int keysyms_per_keycode;              /* returns number of keysyms per keycode */
```

XGetModifierMapping

Obtain a mapping of modifier keys (Shift, Control, etc.)

```
XModifierKeymap *XGetModifierMapping(display)
    Display *display;
```

XGetMotionEvents

Get events from the pointer motion history buffer during a given time interval, and that have coordinates that lie within the specified window at its present placement.

```
XTimeCoord *XGetMotionEvents(display, w, start, stop, nevents)
    Display *display;
    Window w;
    Time start, stop;
    int *nevents;                     /* returns number of events in buffer */
```

XGetNormalHints

Get the size hints property of a window in normal state (not zoomed or iconified). This function has been superseded by WMXGetNormalHints in R4 and later releases.

```
Status XGetNormalHints(display, w, hints)
    Display *display;
    Window w;
    XSizeHints *hints;                /* returns sizing hints */
```

XGetPixel

Obtain a single pixel value from an image.

```
unsigned long XGetPixel(ximage, x, y)
    XImage *ximage;
    int x, y;                         /* coordinates of pixel in image */
```

XGetPointerControl

Get the current pointer preferences. *accel_numerator* divided by *accel_denominator* is the number of pixels the cursor moves per unit of pointer motion, applied only to the amount of movement over *threshold*.

```
XGetPointerControl(display, accel_numerator, accel_denominator, threshold)
    Display *display;
    int accel_numerator;              /* acceleration multiplier */
```

```
int accel_denominator;          /* acceleration multiplier */
int threshold;                  /* number of pixels to move before*/
                                /* acceleration starts */
```

XGetPointerMapping

Get the mapping between logical and physical pointer buttons. Return value is the actual number of elements in the pointer list.

```
int XGetPointerMapping(display, map, nmap)
Display *display;
unsigned char map[];            /* returns mapping list */
int nmap;                       /* size of map */
```

XGetRGBColormaps

Obtain the XStandardColormap structure associated with the specified property. This function supersedes XGetStandardColormap in R4 and later releases.

```
Status XGetRGBColormaps(display, w, std_colormap, count, property)
Display *display;
Window w;
XStandardColormap **std_colormap;   /* returns XStandardColormap structure */
int *count;                         /* returns the number of colormaps*/
Atom property;                      /* XA_RGB_COLOR_MAP */
```

XGetScreenSaver

Get the current screen saver parameters, which may be set with XSetScreenSaver.

```
XGetScreenSaver(display, timeout, interval, prefer_blanking, allow_exposures)
Display *display;
int *timeout, *interval;            /* in seconds */
int *prefer_blanking;               /* one of symbols below */
int *allow_exposures;               /* one of symbols below */
```

The values for prefer_blanking are defined in <X11/X.h>:

```
#define DontPreferBlanking      0
#define PreferBlanking          1
#define DefaultBlanking         2
```

The values for allow_exposures are defined in <X11/X.h>:

```
#define DontAllowExposures      0
#define AllowExposures          1
#define DefaultExposures        2
```

XGetSelectionOwner

Return the owner of a selection.

```
Window XGetSelectionOwner(display, selection)
    Display *display;
    Atom selection;
```

XGetSizeHints

Returns the XSizeHints structure for the named property and specified window. This is used by XGetNormalHints and XGetZoomHints, and can be used to retrieve the value of any property of type XA_WM_SIZE_HINTS.

```
Status XGetSizeHints(display, w, hints, property)
    Display *display;
    Window w;
    XSizeHints *hints;              /* returns size hints structure */
    Atom property;                  /* usually normal hints or zoom hints */
```

XGetStandardColormap

Get the standard colormap property. This function is superseded by XGetWMColormap in R4.

```
Status XGetStandardColormap(display, w, cmap_info, property)
    Display *display;
    Window w;
    XStandardColormap *cmap_info;   /* returns filled colormap information structure*/
    Atom property;                  /* see Section 2 for list */
```

XGetSubImage

Copy a rectangle in a drawable to a location within the pre-existing image. If format is XYPixmap, only bit planes specified in plane_mask are transmitted. If format is ZPixmap, bit planes not specified in plane_mask are returned as zero.

```
XImage *XGetSubImage(display, drawable, x, y, width, height, plane_mask, format,
            dest_image, dest_x, dest_y)
    Display *display;
    Drawable drawable;
    int x, y;
    unsigned int width, height;
    unsigned long plane_mask;       /* which planes to take */
    int format;                     /* XYPixmap or ZPixmap */
    XImage *dest_image;             /* destination image */
    int dest_x, dest_y;             /* upper-left corner in dest_image */
```

XGetTextProperty

Read one of a window's text properties and store data in *value* field of *text_prop*, datatype in *encoding* field, format of data in data field, and number of items in *nitems* field.

```
Status XGetTextProperty(display, w, text_prop, property)
    Display *display;
    Window w;
    XTextProperty *text_prop;
    Atom property;                    /* see Section 2 for list */
```

XGetTransientForHint

Get the XA_WM_TRANSIENT_FOR property of a window.

```
Status XGetTransientForHint(display, w, prop_window)
    Display *display;
    Window w;
    Window *prop_window;              /* returns window */
```

XGetVisualInfo

Find the visual information structures that match the specified template.

```
XVisualInfo *XGetVisualInfo(display, vinfo_mask, vinfo_template, nitems)
    Display *display;
    long vinfo_mask;                  /* see Section 2: XVisualInfo */
    XVisualInfo *vinfo_template;      /* returns visual attributes */
    int *nitems;                      /* returns number of matching visual structures*/
```

XGetWindowAttributes

Obtain the current attributes of a window.

```
Status XGetWindowAttributes(display, w, window_attributes)
    Display *display;
    Window w;
    XWindowAttributes *window_attributes;
```

XGetWindowProperty

Obtain the atom type and property format for a window.

```
int XGetWindowProperty(display, w, property, long_offset, long_length, delete, req_type,
            actual_type, actual_format, nitems, bytes_after, prop)
    Display *display;
    Window w;
    Atom property;
    long long_offset, long_length;
```

Bool *delete*;	/* delete property after read? */
Atom *req_type*;	/* actual property, or AnyPropertyType (0L) */
Atom *actual_type*;	/* returns actual type of property */
int *actual_format*;	/* returns actual data type of returned data */
unsigned long *nitems*;	/* returns actual number of items returned in *prop* */
unsigned long *bytes_after*;	/* returns bytes left over from partial read */
unsigned char **prop*;	/* returns actual data, plus one NULL byte */

XGetWMHints

Read the window manager hints property for a window.

```
XWMHints *XGetWMHints(display, w)
    Display *display;
    Window w;
```

XGetWMIconName

Read a window's XA_WM_ICON_NAME property.

```
Status XGetWMIconName(display, w, text_prop)
    Display *display;
    Window w;
    XTextProperty *text_prop;
```

XGetWMName

Read a window's XA_WM_NAME property.

```
Status XGetWMName(display, w, text_prop)
    Display *display;
    Window w;
    XTextProperty *text_prop;
```

XGetWMNormalHints

Read a window's XA_WM_NORMAL_HINTS property.

```
Status XGetWMNormalHints(display, w, hints, supplied)
    Display *display;
    Window w;
    XSizeHints *hints;
    long *supplied;                    /* returns user-supplied hints */
```

XGetWMSizeHints

Read a window's XA_WM_SIZE_HINTS property.

```
Status XGetWMSizeHints(display, w, hints, supplied, property)
    Display *display;
    Window w;
    XSizeHints *hints;
    long *supplied;                    /* returns user-supplied hints */
    Atom property;
```

XGetZoomHints

Read the size hints property of a zoomed window. This function is obsolete beginning in R4.

```
Status XGetZoomHints(display, w, zhints)
    Display *display;
    Window w;
    XSizeHints *zhints;                /* returns pointer to zoom hints */
```

XGrabButton

Grab a pointer button—establish a passive grab such that an active grab may take place when the specified key/button combination is pressed in the specified window.

```
XGrabButton(display, button, modifiers, grab_window, owner_events, event_mask,
            pointer_mode, keyboard_mode, confine_to, cursor)
    Display *display;
    unsigned int button;                    /* button to grab */
    unsigned int modifiers;                 /* modifiers that must be pressed */
    Window grab_window;                     /* ID of window in which grab to occur */
    Bool owner_events;                      /* should grab window get all events? */
    unsigned int event_mask;                /* events to grab on */
    int pointer_mode, keyboard_mode;        /* GrabModeSync or GrabModeAsync */
    Window confine_to;                      /* ID of window in which to confine pointer, or None*/
    Cursor cursor;                          /* cursor to display during grab */
```

The values for *button* are defined in *<X11/X.h>*:

```
#define AnyButton    0        /* cannot be ORed */
#define Button1      1
#define Button2      2
#define Button3      3
#define Button4      4
#define Button5      5
```

The values for *modifiers* are defined in *<X11/X.h>*:

```
#define ShiftMask             (1<<0)
```

```
#define LockMask           (1<<1)
#define ControlMask        (1<<2)
#define Mod1Mask           (1<<3)
#define Mod2Mask           (1<<4)
#define Mod3Mask           (1<<5)
#define Mod4Mask           (1<<6)
#define Mod5Mask           (1<<7)
#define AnyModifier        (1<<15)
```

Values for *pointer_mode* and *keyboard_mode* are defined in *<X11/X.h>*:

```
#define GrabModeSync      0      /* wait for XallowEvents to release events */
#define GrabModeAsync     1      /* keep sending events normally */
```

XGrabKey

Grab a key—establish a passive grab on the specified keys such that when the specified key/modifier combination is pressed, the keyboard may be grabbed and all keyboard events sent to the application. See XGrabButton for relevant symbols.

```
XGrabKey(display, keycode, modifiers, grab_window, owner_events, pointer_mode,
         keyboard_mode)
    Display *display;
    int keycode;                              /* key to grab */
    unsigned int modifiers;                   /* modifiers that must be pressed */
    Window grab_window;                       /* window in which grab to occur */
    Bool owner_events;                        /* should grab window get all events? */
    int pointer_mode, keyboard_mode;          /* GrabModeSync or GrabModeAsync */
```

XGrabKeyboard

Actively grab the keyboard. Further key events are reported only to the grabbing client. See XGrabButton for relevant symbols.

```
int XGrabKeyboard(display, grab_window, owner_events, pointer_mode, keyboard_mode, time)
    Display *display;
    Window grab_window;
    Bool owner_events;                        /* should grab window get all events? */
    int pointer_mode, keyboard_mode;
    /* GrabModeSync or GrabModeAsync */
    Time time;                                /* timestamp or CurrentTime */
```

XGrabPointer

Actively grab the pointer. Further pointer events are only reported to the grabbing client until XUngrabPointer is called. See XGrabButton for relevant symbols.

```
int XGrabPointer(display, grab_window, owner_events, event_mask, pointer_mode,
         keyboard_mode, confine_to, cursor, time)
```

```
Display *display;
Window grab_window;                      /* ID of window in which grab to occur */
Bool owner_events;                       /* should grab window get all events? */
unsigned int event_mask;                 /* event(s) to grab on */
int pointer_mode, keyboard_mode;         /* GrabModeSync or GrabModeAsync */
Window confine_to;                       /* ID of window in which to confine pointer, or None */
Cursor cursor;                           /* cursor to display during grab */
Time time;                               /* timestamp or CurrentTime */
```

XGrabServer

Grab the server.

```
XGrabServer(display)
    Display *display;
```

XIconifyWindow

Request that a top-level window be iconified. A WM_CHANGE_STATE ClientMessage event with a format of 32 and a first data element of IconicState is sent to the root window of the specified screen.

```
Status XIconifyWindow(display, w, screen_number)
    Display *display;
    Window w;
    int screen_number;
```

XIfEvent

Check the event queue for matching events, and, if found, remove from queue. This routine returns only when the specified predicate procedure returns true for an event.

```
XIfEvent(display, event, predicate, args)
    Display *display;
    XEvent *event;                       /* returns matched event */
    Bool (*predicate)();                 /* procedure to determine if event satisfies criteria */
    char *args;
```

XIMOfIC

Obtain the input method of an input context. (New in R5.)

```
XIM XIMOfIC(ic)
    XIC ic;
```

XInsertModifiermapEntry

This function returns an XModifierKeymap structure suitable for calling XSetModifier-Mapping, in which the specified keycode is deleted from the set of keycodes mapped to the specified modifier. XInsertModifiermapEntry is normally used by calling XGetModifierMapping to get a pointer to the current XModifierKeymap structure for use as *modmap*.

```
XModifierKeymap *XInsertModifiermapEntry(modmap, keysym_entry, modifier)
    XModifierKeymap *modmap;
    KeyCode keysym_entry;
    int modifier;                           /* one of symbols below */
```

The values for *modifier* are defined in *<X11/X.h>*:

```
#define ShiftMapIndex        0
#define LockMapIndex         1
#define ControlMapIndex      2
#define Mod1MapIndex         3
#define Mod2MapIndex         4
#define Mod3MapIndex         5
#define Mod4MapIndex         6
#define Mod5MapIndex         7
```

XInstallColormap

Install a virtual colormap into a hardware colormap. If there is only one hardware colormap, XInstallColormap loads a virtual colormap into the hardware colormap.

```
XInstallColormap(display, cmap)
    Display *display;
    Colormap cmap;
```

XInternAtom

Return an atom ID for a given property name string. This function is the opposite of XGetAtomName, which returns the atom name when given an atom ID.

```
Atom XInternAtom(display, property_name, only_if_exists)
    Display *display;
    char *property_name;                 /* string you want atom for */
    Bool only_if_exists;                 /* if True, return None if atom doesn't exist */
```

XIntersectRegion

Compute the intersection of two regions.

```
XIntersectRegion(sra, srb, dr)
    Region sra, srb;
    Region dr;                           /* returns intersection */
```

XKeycodeToKeysym

Convert a keycode to a keysym.

```
KeySym XKeycodeToKeysym(display, keycode, index)
    Display *display;
    KeyCode keycode;
    int index;                    /* if more than one keysym for that keycode */
```

XKeysymToKeycode

Convert a keysym to the appropriate keycode.

```
KeyCode XKeysymToKeycode(display, keysym)
    Display *display;
    Keysym keysym;
```

XKeysymToString

Convert a keysym symbol to a string. The returned string is in a static area and must not be modified.

```
char *XKeysymToString(keysym)
    KeySym keysym;
```

XKillClient

Destroy a client or its remaining resources. If the client has already terminated in either RetainPermanent or RetainTemporary mode, all the client's resources are destroyed. If AllTemporary is specified in the *resource* argument, then the resources of all clients that have terminated in RetainTemporary are destroyed.

```
XKillClient(display, resource)
    Display *display;
    XID resource;                 /* any resource of client or AllTemporary */
```

XListDepths

Determine the depths available on a given screen.

```
int *XListDepths(display, screen_number, count)
    Display *display;
    int screen_number;
    int *count;                   /* number of possible depths */
```

XListExtensions

Return a list of all extensions to X supported by Xlib and the server.

```
char **XListExtensions(display, nextensions)
    Display *display;
    int *nextensions;
```

XListFonts

Return a list of the available font names.

```
char **XListFonts(display, pattern, maxnames, actual_count)
    Display *display;
    char *pattern;
    int maxnames;                       /* maximum number of names to be returned */
    int *actual_count;                  /* actual number of names returned */
```

XListFontsWithInfo

Obtain the names and information about loaded fonts. The information returned for each font is identical to what XQueryFont would return, except that the per-character metrics (lbearing, rbearing, width, ascent, descent for single characters) are not returned.

```
char **XListFontsWithInfo(display, pattern, maxnames, count, info)
    Display *display;
    char *pattern;                      /* NULL-terminated */
    int maxnames;                       /* maximum number of names to be returned */
    int *count;                         /* returns number of fonts in list */
    XFontStruct **info;                 /* returns pointer to font information structures*/
```

XListHosts

Obtain a list of hosts having access to this display.

```
XHostAddress *XListHosts(display, nhosts, state)
    Display *display;
    int *nhosts;                        /* returns number of hosts */
    Bool *state;                        /* returns True if access list enabled */
```

XListInstalledColormaps

Return a list of currently installed colormaps for the screen containing the specified window.

```
Colormap *XListInstalledColormaps(display, w, num)
    display *display;
    Window w;
    int *num;                           /* returns number of installed colormaps */
```

XListPixmapFormats

Obtain the supported pixmap formats (an array of XPixmapFormatValues structures) for a given server.

```
XPixmapFormatValues *XListPixmapFormats(display, count)
    Display *display;
    int *count;
```

XListProperties

Get the property list for a window.

```
Atom *XListProperties(display, w, num_prop)
    Display *display;
    Window w;
    int *num_prop;                      /* returns length of properties array */
```

XLoadFont

Load a font if not already loaded and get font ID. Font information is usually necessary for locating the text. Call XLoadFontWithInfo to get the info at the time you load the font, or call XQueryFont if you used XLoadFont to load the font.

```
Font XLoadFont(display, name)
    Display *display;
    char *name;                         /* NULL-terminated font name string */
```

XLoadQueryFont

Load a font and fill information structure. This function performs an XLoadFont and XQueryFont in a single operation. That is, it both opens (loads) the specified font and returns a pointer to the appropriate XFontStruct structure.

```
XFontStruct *XLoadQueryFont(display, name)
    Display *display;
    char *name;                         /* NULL-terminated font name string */
```

XLocaleOfFontSet

Return the name of the locale bound to the specified XFontSet, as a NULL-terminated string. (New in R5.)

```
char *XLocaleOfFontSet(font_set)
    XFontSet font_set;
```

XLocaleOfIM

Get the locale of an input method. (New in R5.)

```
char * XLocaleOfIM(im)
    XIM im;
```

XLookUpAssoc

Obtain data from an association table (provided for compatibility with X Version 10.)

```
Xpointer XLookUpAssoc(display, table, x_id)
    Display *display;
    XAssocTable *table;
    XID x_id;
```

XLookupColor

Get database RGB values and closest hardware-supported RGB values from color name.

```
Status XLookupColor(display, cmap, colorname, rgb_db_def, hardware_def)
    Display *display;
    Colormap cmap;
    char *colorname;              /* see Section 8 */
    XColor *rgb_db_def,;          /* returns exact RGB values */
    XColor *hardware_def;         /* returns closest RGB on hardware */
```

XLookupKeysym

Get the keysym corresponding to a keycode in structure. This function simply calls XKeycodeToKeysym, using arguments taken from the specified event structure. To generate *index*, interpret the state member of the XKeyEvent structure. For additional values of *index*, see the *modifiers* argument in XInsertModifiermapEntry.

```
KeySym XLookupKeysym(event, index)
    XKeyEvent *event;
    int index;                    /* which keysym to return */
```

XLookupString

Map a key event to ASCII string, keysym, and ComposeStatus.

```
int XLookupString(event, buffer, num_bytes, keysym, status)
    XKeyEvent *event;
    char *buffer;                 /* returns the string */
    int num_bytes;                /* how many bytes we want */
    KeySym *keysym;               /* returns the keysym */
    XComposeStatus *status;       /* can be NULL */
```

XLowerWindow

Lower a window in the stacking order of its siblings so that it does not obscure any sibling windows.

```
XLowerWindow(display, w)
    Display *display;
    Window w;
```

XMakeAssoc

Create an entry in an association table. (Provided for compatibility with X Version 10.)

```
XMakeAssoc(display, table, x_id, data)
    Display *display;
    XAssocTable *table;
    XID x_id;
    Xpointer data;
```

Xlib Routines

XMapRaised

Map a window on top of its siblings. This function is similar to XMapWindow, except it additionally raises the specified window to the top of the stack among its siblings.

```
XMapRaised(display, w)
    Display *display;
    Window w;
```

XMapSubwindows

Map all subwindows of a window.

```
XMapSubwindows(display, w)
    Display *display;
    Window w;                    /* parent whose subwindows are mapped */
```

XMapWindow

Map a window. If all ancestors are mapped, and the window is not obscured by siblings higher in the stacking order, the window and all of its mapped subwindows are displayed.

```
XMapWindow(display, w)
    Display *display;
    Window w;
```

XMaskEvent

Remove the next event that matches the passed mask. If no such event has been queued, the request buffer is flushed and the routine waits until one is received. Use XCheckMaskEvent if you do not wish to wait.

```
XMaskEvent(display, event_mask, rep)
    Display *display;
    long event_mask;              /* see Section 3 */
    XEvent *rep;                  /* returns event removed from queue */
```

XMatchVisuallnfo

Obtain the visual information that matches the desired depth and class.

```
Status XMatchVisualInfo(display, screen, depth, class, vinfo)
    Display *display;
    int screen;
    int depth;
    int class;                    /* PseudoColor, etc.; see Section 2: VisualID */
    XVisualInfo *vinfo;
```

XMaxRequestSize

Return a long value containing the maximum size of a protocol request for the specified server, in units of four bytes.

```
long XMaxRequestSize(display)
    Display *display;             /* pointer to a Display structure */
```

XmbDrawImageString

Draw internationalized multi-byte image text. The destination rectangle is filled with the background pixel defined in the GC, then the specified multi-byte text is painted with the foreground pixel. (New in R5.)

```
void XmbDrawImageString(display, drawable, font_set, gc, x, y, string, num_bytes)
    Display *display;
    Drawable drawable;
    XFontSet font_set;
    GC gc;
    int x, y;                     /* starting position and baseline of text */
    char *string;                 /* character string */
    int num_bytes;                /* number of bytes in string argument */
```

XmbDrawString

Draw internationalized multi-byte text. This function allows complex spacing and font set shifts between internationalized multi-byte text strings. Only the foreground color is drawn; the background is not modified. (New in R5.)

```
void XmbDrawString(display, drawable, font_set, gc, x, y, string, num_bytes)
    Display *display;
    Drawable drawable;
    XFontSet font_set;
    GC gc;
    int x, y;              /* starting position and baseline of text */
    char *string;          /* character string */
    int num_bytes;         /* number of bytes in string argument */
```

XmbDrawText

Draw internationalized multi-byte text using multiple font sets. This function allows complex spacing and font set shifts between internationalized multi-byte text strings. Only the foreground color is drawn; the background is not modified. (New in R5.)

```
void XmbDrawText(display, drawable, gc, x, y, items, nitems)
    Display *display;
    Drawable drawable;
    GC gc;
    int x, y;              /* starting position and baseline of text */
    XmbTextItem *items;    /* array of text items */
    int nitems;            /* number of text items in array */
```

XmbLookupString

Obtain composed multi-byte input from an input method. This function passes a KeyPress event to an input context, returns composed text in the encoding of the input context locale (if ready), and may also return a keysym corresponding to the KeyPress event. (New in R5.)

```
int XmbLookupString(ic, event, buffer_return, bytes_buffer, keysym_return, status_return)
    XIC ic;
    XKeyPressedEvent *event;   /* keypress event to be used */
    char *buffer_return;       /* returns multibyte string from input */
                               /* method */
    int bytes_buffer;          /* number of bytes in return buffer */
    KeySym *keysym_return;     /* returns KeySym computed from event */
    Status *status_return;     /* returns value indicating kind of data returned */
```

The values returned in *status_return* are:

XBufferOverflow	/* input string too large for *buffer_return* */
XLookupNone	/* no consistent input composed yet */
XLookupChars	/* some input characters composed */
XLookupKeySym	/* KeySym returned instead of string */
XLookupBoth	/* both KeySym and string returned */

XmbResetIC

Reset the state of an input context. Any input pending on that context is deleted, and the input method is required to clear the Preedit area, if any, and update the Status area accordingly. May return any partially composed text. (New in R5.)

```
char * XmbResetIC(ic)
    XIC ic;
```

XmbTextEscapement

Return the width, in pixels, of the specified multi-byte string using the fonts loaded for the specified font set. (New in R5.)

```
int XmbTextEscapement(font_set, string, num_bytes)
    XFontSet font_set;
    char *string;                /* character string */
    int num_bytes;               /* number of bytes in string argument */
```

XmbTextExtents

Compute the size of internationalized multi-byte string. This function sets the components of the *overall_ink_return* and *overall_logical_return* to the overall bounding box of the string image plus inter-line and inter-character spacing. (New in R5.)

```
int XmbTextExtents(font_set, string, num_bytes, overall_ink_return, overall_logical_return)
    XFontSet font_set;
    char *string;                        /* character string */
    int num_bytes;                       /* number of bytes in string argument */
    XRectangle *overall_ink_return;      /* returns overall ink dimensions */
    XRectangle *overall_logical_return;  /* returns overall logical dimensions */
```

XmbTextListToTextProperty

Convert an internationalized multi-byte text list to a text property structure—set the specified XTextProperty value to a set of NULL-separated elements representing the concatenation of the specified list of NULL-terminated text strings. (New in R5.)

The X Window System in a Nutshell

```
int XmbTextListToTextProperty(display, list, count, style, text_prop_return)
    Display *display;
    char **list;                         /* array of NULL-terminated multi-byte strings */
    int count;                           /* number of strings specified */
    XICCEncodingStyle style;             /* manner in which property is encoded */
    XTextProperty *text_prop_return;     /* returns XTextProperty structure; */
                                         /* caller must free value field */
```

XmbTextPerCharExtents

Obtain per-character measurements of an internationalized multi-byte text string—return the text dimensions of each character of the specified text, using the fonts loaded for the specified font set. (New in R5.)

```
Status XmbTextPerCharExtents(font_set, string, num_bytes, ink_array_return,
            logical_array_return, array_size, num_chars_return, overall_ink_return,
            overall_logical_return)
    XFontSet font_set;
    char *string;                        /* character string */
    int num_bytes;                       /* number of bytes in string argument */
    XRectangle *ink_array_return;        /* returns ink dimensions for each character; */
                                         /* allocated by caller */
    XRectangle *logical_array_return;    /* returns logical dimensions for each character; */
                                         /* allocated by caller */
    int array_size;                      /* size of ink_array_return and logical_array_return */
    int *num_chars_return;               /* returns number characters in string argument */
    XRectangle *overall_ink_return;      /* returns overall ink extents of entire string */
    XRectangle *overall_logical_return;  /* returns overall logical extents of entire string */
```

The possible return values of this function are:

```
#define      XNoMemory              -1
#define      XLocaleNotSupported    -2
#define      XConverterNotFound     -3
```

XmbTextPropertyToTextList

Return a list of multi-byte text strings encoded in the current locale representing the NULL-separated elements of the specified XTextProperty structure. (New in R5.)

```
int XmbTextPropertyToTextList(display, text_prop, list_return, count_return)
    Display *display
    XTextProperty *text_prop;            /* XTextProperty structure to be used */
    char ***list_return;                 /* returns list of NULL-terminated character strings; */
                                         /* caller must free with XwcFreeStringList */
    int *count_return;                   /* returns number of strings */
```

The possible return values of this function are:
```
#define  XNoMemory                -1
#define  XLocaleNotSupported      -2
#define  XConverterNotFound       -3
```

XMoveResizeWindow

Change the size and position of a window.

```
XMoveResizeWindow(display, w, x, y, width, height)
    Display *display;
    Window w;
    int x, y;
    unsigned int width, height;
```

XMoveWindow

Move a window. This function neither raises the window nor changes its mapping state, size, or stacking order.

```
XMoveWindow(display, w, x, y)
    Display *display;
    Window w;
    int x, y;
```

XNewModifiermap

Create a keyboard modifier mapping structure. This function is used when more than one XModifierKeymap structure is needed. *max_keys_per_mod* depends on the server and should be gotten from the XModifierKeymap returned by XGetModifier-Mapping.

```
XModifierKeymap *XNewModifiermap(max_keys_per_mod)
    int max_keys_per_mod;              /* get from XGetModifierMapping */
```

XNextEvent

Get the next event of any type or window. If the event queue is empty, the request buffer is flushed and the routine waits until an event is received. Use XCheckMaskEvent or XCheckIfEvent if you do not want to wait.

```
XNextEvent(display, report)
    Display *display;
    XEvent *report;                    /* returns event removed from queue */
```

XNoOp

Send a NoOperation request to the X server, thereby exercising the connection.

```
XNoOp(display)
    Display *display;
```

XOffsetRegion

Change offset of a region.

```
XOffsetRegion(r, dx, dy)
    Region r;
    int dx, dy;                          /* relative to origin of all regions */
```

XOpenDisplay

Connect a client program to an X server. If *display_name* is NULL, the value defaults to the contents of the DISPLAY environment variable on UNIX-based systems. On non-UNIX-based systems, see that operating system's Xlib manual for the default *display_name*.

```
Display *XOpenDisplay(display_name)
    char *display_name;                  /* hostname:server[.screen] */
```

XOpenIM

Open an input method. (New in R5.)

```
XIM XOpenIM(display, db, res_name, res_class)
    Display *display;
    XrmDatabase db;                      /* resource database */
    char *res_name;                      /* full resource name of application */
    char *res_class;                     /* full class name of application */
```

XParseColor

Look up RGB values from ASCII color name or translate hexadecimal value. This function takes a string specification of a color, typically from a command line or XGetDefault option, and returns the corresponding red, green, and blue values, suitable for a subsequent call to XAllocColor or XStoreColor.

```
Status XParseColor(display, colormap, spec, rgb_db_def)
    Display *display;
    Colormap colormap;
    char *spec;                          /* color name or hex string */
    XColor *rgb_db_def;                  /* returns RGB values */
```

XParseGeometry

Generate position and size from standard window geometry string (*width* x *height* ±*xoffset* ±*yoffset*).

```
int XParseGeometry(parsestring, x, y, width, height)
    char *parsestring;                    /* returns string to parse */
    int *x, *y;                           /* returns coordinates from string */
    unsigned int *width, *height;         /* returns width and height from string */
```

XParseGeometry returns a bitmask that indicates which of the four values in the parsed geometry string were found. These values are defined in *<X11/Xutil.h>*.

```
#define NoValue       0x0000    /* none found */
#define XValue        0x0001    /* xoffset found */
#define YValue        0x0002    /* yoffset found */
#define WidthValue    0x0004    /* width found */
#define HeightValue   0x0008    /* height found */
#define AllValues     0x000F    /* all four values found */
#define XNegative     0x0010    /* x value is negative */
#define YNegative     0x0020    /* y value is negative */
```

XPeekEvent

Get an event without removing it from the queue. If the queue is empty, the request buffer is flushed and the routine waits until an event is received. If you do not want to wait, use the QLength macro to determine if there are any events to peek at, or use XCheckIfEvent.

```
XPeekEvent(display, report)
    Display *display;
    XEvent *report;                       /* returns event peeked from input queue */
```

XPeekIfEvent

Get an event matched by predicate procedure without removing it from the queue. Predicate procedure is passed *display, event*, and *args*.

```
XPeekIfEvent(display, event, predicate, args)
    Display *display;
    XEvent *event;
    Bool (*predicate)();
    char *args;
```

XPending

Flush the request buffer and return the number of pending input events.

```
int XPending(display)
    Display *display;
```

Xpermalloc

Allocate memory never to be freed. This function is used by some toolkits for permanently allocated storage and allows some performance and space savings over the completely general memory allocator.

```
char *Xpermalloc(size)
    unsigned int size;                    /* rounded to nearest 4-byte boundary */
```

XPointInRegion

Determine if a point is inside a region.

```
Bool XPointInRegion(r, x, y)
    Region r;
    int x, y;
```

XPolygonRegion

Generate a region from points.

```
Region XPolygonRegion(points, n, fill_rule)
    XPoint points[];
    int n;
    int fill_rule;                        /* see XGCValues in Section 2 */
```

XPutBackEvent

Push an event back on the input queue. There is no limit to how many times you can call XPutBackEvent in succession.

```
XPutBackEvent(display, event)
    Display *display;
    XEvent *event;
```

XPutImage

Draw a section of an image on a window or pixmap. The section of the image is defined by src_x, src_y, width, and height. The following graphics context components are used: function, plane_mask, subwindow_mode, clip_x_origin, clip_y_origin, and clip_mask. There is no limit to the size of image that can be sent to the server.

```
XPutImage(display, drawable, gc, image, src_x, src_y, dst_x, dst_y, width, height)
    Display *display;
    Drawable drawable;
    GC gc;
    XImage *image;
    int src_x, src_y;
    int dst_x, dst_y;
    unsigned int width, height;
```

XPutPixel

Set a pixel value in an image.

```
int XPutPixel(ximage, x, y, pixel)
    XImage *ximage;
    int x, y;                       /* pixel to be set */
    unsigned long pixel;            /* new pixel value */
```

XQueryBestCursor

Get the closest supported cursor sizes for a given drawable.

```
Status XQueryBestCursor(display, drawable, width, height, rwidth, rheight)
    Display *display;
    Drawable drawable;
    unsigned int width, height;             /* preferred size */
    unsigned int *rwidth, *rheight;         /* returns closest supported size */
```

XQueryBestSize

Obtain the best supported cursor, tile, or stipple size for a given drawable. For cursors, this is the closest size that can be fully displayed on the screen. For tiles and stipples, this is the closest size that can be tiled or stippled fastest.

```
Status XQueryBestSize(display, class, drawable, width, height, rwidth, rheight)
    Display *display;
    int class;
    Drawable drawable;
    unsigned int width, height;             /* preferred size */
    unsigned int *rwidth, *rheight;         /* returns closest supported size */
```

XQueryBestStipple

Obtain the fastest supported stipple shape for a given drawable.

```
Status XQueryBestStipple(display, drawable, width, height, rwidth, rheight)
    Display *display;
    Drawable drawable;
```

```
unsigned int width, height;              /* preferred size */
unsigned int *rwidth, *rheight;          /* returns closest supported size */
```

XQueryBestTile

Obtain the fastest supported fill tile shape for a given drawable.

```
Status XQueryBestTile(display, drawable, width, height, rwidth, rheight)
    Display *display;
    Drawable drawable;
    unsigned int width, height;          /* preferred size */
    unsigned int *rwidth, *rheight;      /* returns closest supported size */
```

XQueryColor

Obtain the RGB values and flags for a specified colorcell.

```
XQueryColor(display, cmap, colorcell_def)
    Display *display;
    Colormap cmap;
    XColor *colorcell_def;               /* specifies pixel value; returns RGB */
```

XQueryColors

Obtain RGB values for an array of colorcells.

```
XQueryColors(display, cmap, colorcell_defs, ncolors)
    Display *display;
    Colormap cmap;
    XColor colorcell_defs[ncolors];      /* specifies pixel; returns RGB */
    int ncolors;                         /* number of XColors in array */
```

XQueryExtension

Get extension information. Returns True if extension exists. The available extensions can be listed with XListExtensions.

```
Bool XQueryExtension(display, name, major_opcode, first_event, first_error)
    Display *display;
    char *name;
    int *major_opcode;
    int *first_event;                    /* custom event defined by extension */
    int *first_error;                    /* custom error defined by extension */
```

XQueryFont

Return information about a loaded font. This function should be used if you loaded the with XLoadFont, but also need the font information for multiple calls to determine the extent of text.

```
XFontStruct *XQueryFont(display, font_ID)
    Display *display;
    XID font_ID;                          /* font ID or graphics ID */
```

XQueryKeymap

Obtain a bit vector for the current state of the keyboard, where each bit set to 1 indicates that the corresponding key is currently pressed down.

```
XQueryKeymap(display, keys)
    Display *display;
    char keys[32];                        /* return; see Section 2: XKeyBoardState */
```

XQueryPointer

Get the current pointer location relative to a window and to the root window. Also get the *root* window ID and the window ID (if any) of the child window the pointer is currently in, and the current state of modifier keys and buttons.

```
Bool XQueryPointer(display, w, root, child, root_x, root_y, win_x, win_y, keys_buttons)
    Display *display;
    Window w;
    Window *root, *child;                 /* returns root window ID of pointer, ID of child */
    int *root_x, *root_y;                 /* returns */
    int *win_x, *win_y;                   /* returns */
    unsigned int *keys_buttons;           /* return.  OR of symbols below */
```

The mask symbols for *keys_buttons* are defined in *<X11/X.h>*:

```
#define ShiftMask           (1<<0)
#define LockMask            (1<<1)
#define ControlMask         (1<<2)
#define Mod1Mask            (1<<3)
#define Mod2Mask            (1<<4)
#define Mod3Mask            (1<<5)
#define Mod4Mask            (1<<6)
#define Mod5Mask            (1<<7)
#define Button1Mask         (1<<8)
#define Button2Mask         (1<<9)
#define Button3Mask         (1<<10)
#define Button4Mask         (1<<11)
#define Button5Mask         (1<<12)
```

XQueryTextExtents

Query the server for string and font metrics. Although this function queries the server and suffers the round trip overhead that is avoided by XTextExtents, it does not require a filled XFontInfo structure stored on the client side. Therefore, it is useful when memory is precious or when just a small number of text width calculations are to be done.

```
XQueryTextExtents(display, font_ID, string, nchars, direction, ascent, descent, overall)
    Display *display;
    XID font_ID;
    char *string;
    int nchars;
    int *direction;              /* returns direction for font */
    int *ascent, *descent;       /* returns ascent/descent for font */
    XCharStruct *overall;        /* returns overall characteristics of string */
```

XQueryTextExtents16

Query the server for string and font metrics of a 16-bit character string. Although this function queries the server and, therefore suffers the round trip overhead that is avoided by XTextExtents16, it does not require a filled XFontInfo structure.

```
XQueryTextExtents16(display, font_ID, string, nchars, direction, ascent, descent, overall)
    Display *display;
    XID font_ID;
    XChar2b *string;
    int nchars;
    int *direction;              /* returns direction for font */
    int *ascent, *descent;       /* returns ascent/descent for font */
    XCharStruct *overall;        /* returns overall characteristics of string */
```

XQueryTree

Return a list of children, parent, and root.

```
Status XQueryTree(display, w, root, parent, children, nchildren)
    Display *display;
    Window w;
    Window *root;                /* returns window's root ID */
    Window *parent;              /* returns window's parent window */
    Window **children;           /* returns window's list of children */
    unsigned int *nchildren;     /* returns number of children */
```

XRaiseWindow

Raise a window to the top of the stacking order.

```
XRaiseWindow(display, w)
    Display *display;
    Window w;
```

XReadBitmapFile

Read a bitmap file and use it to create a pixmap. This function reads files created with the X Version 10 or X Version 11 bitmap format.

```
int XReadBitmapFile(display, drawable, filename, width, height, bitmap, x_hot, y_hot)
    Display *display;
    Drawable drawable;
    char *filename;
    unsigned int *width, *height;         /* returns dimensions of bitmap */
    Pixmap *bitmap;                        /* returns pixmap resource ID created */
    int *x_hot, *y_hot;                    /* returns hotspot, or -1, -1 if none */
```

For XReadBitmapFile, the following return codes are defined in *<X11/Xutil.h>*.

```
    #define BitmapSuccess       0     /* file is readable and valid */
    #define BitmapOpenFailed    1     /* file cannot be opened */ ·
    #define BitmapFileInvalid   2     /* file contains invalid data */
    #define BitmapNoMemory      3     /* insufficient working storage */
```

XRebindKeysym

Rebind a keysym to a string for client. This function binds the ASCII *string* to the specified *keysym*, so that *string* and *keysym* are returned by XLookukpString when that key is pressed and the modifier(s) specified in *mod_list* are also being held down.

```
XRebindKeysym(display, keysym, mod_list, mod_count, string, num_bytes)
    Display *display;
    KeySym keysym;                    /* keysym to rebind */
    KeySym *mod_list;                 /* keysyms used as modifiers */
    int mod_count;                    /* number of modifiers */
    unsigned char *string;            /* for XLookupString */
    int num_bytes;                    /* length of string */
```

XRecolorCursor

Change the color of a cursor.

```
XRecolorCursor(display, cursor, foreground_color, background_color)
    Display *display;
    Cursor cursor;
    XColor *foreground_color, *background_color;
```

XReconfigureWMWindow

Request that a top-level window be reconfigured. This function issues a ConfigureWindow request on the specified top-level window. If the stacking mode is changed and the request fails with a BadMatch error, the error event is trapped and a synthetic ConfigureRequest event containing the same configuration parameters is sent to the root of the specified window. This function differs from XConfigureWindow in that it detects errors that might arise from trying to change the stacking order.

```
Status XReconfigureWMWindow(display, w, screen_number, value_mask, values)
    Display *display;
    Window w;
    int screen_number;
    unsigned int value_mask;          /* see Section 2: XWindowChanges */
    XWindowChanges *values;
```

XRectInRegion

Determine if a rectangle resides in a region.

```
int XRectInRegion(r, x, y, width, height)
    Region r;
    int x, y;
    unsigned int width, height;
```

For XRectInRegion, the following return codes are defined in *<X11/Xutil.h>*.

```
#define RectangleOut    0    /* completely outside region */
#define RectangleIn     1    /* completely inside */
#define RectanglePart   2    /* part of rect is inside */
```

XRefreshKeyboardMapping

Read keycode-keysym mapping from server into Xlib. This function should be called when a MappingNotify event occurs, which happens when XChangeKeyboardMapping has been called by a client.

```
XRefreshKeyboardMapping(event)
    XMappingEvent *event;
```

XRemoveFromSaveSet

Remove a window from the client's save-set. This call is not necessary when a window is destroyed since destroyed windows are automatically removed from the save-set.

```
XRemoveFromSaveSet(display, w)
    Display *display;
    Window w;
```

XRemoveHost

Remove a host from the server's access control list. The server must be on the same host as the process issuing the command.

```
XRemoveHost(display, host)
    Display *display;
    XHostAddress *host;
```

XRemoveHosts

Remove multiple hosts from the server's access control list. The server must be on the same host as the process issuing the command.

```
XRemoveHosts(display, hosts, num_hosts)
    Display *display;
    XHostAddress *hosts;
    int num_hosts;
```

XReparentWindow

Insert a window between another window and its parent. This function is usually used by a window manager to put a decoration window behind each application window.

```
XReparentWindow(display, win, parent, x, y)
    Display *display;
    Window win;
    Window parent;                    /* new parent */
    int x, y;
```

XResetScreenSaver

Reset the screen saver. This may result in exposure events to all visible windows if the server cannot save the screen contents. If the screen is already active, nothing happens.

```
XResetScreenSaver(display)
    Display *display;
```

XResizeWindow

Change the inside dimensions of the window (width, height). This function does not raise the window or change its origin.

```
XResizeWindow(display, w, width, height)
    Display *display;
    Window w;
    unsigned int width, height;
```

XResourceManagerString

Return the RESOURCE_MANAGER property from the root window of screen zero, which was returned when the connection was opened with XOpenDisplay. The property is converted from type STRING to the current locale. The conversion is identical to that produced by XmbTextPropertyToTextList for a singleton STRING property. (New in R5.)

```
char *XResourceManagerString(display)
    Display *display;
```

XRestackWindows

Change the stacking order of siblings.

```
XRestackWindows(display, windows, nwindows);
    Display *display;
    Window windows[];                   /* must all have a common parent */
    int nwindows;
```

XrmClassToString

Convert XrmClass to string. Same as XrmQuarkToString.

```
XrmClassToString(class)
```

XrmCombineDatabase

Combine the contents of two resource databases. (New in R5.)

```
void XrmCombineDatabase(source_db, target_db, override)
    XrmDatabase source_db;              /* source database to be merged */
    XrmDatabase *target_db;             /* address of target database */
    Bool override;                      /* whether source should override target */
```

XrmCombineFileDatabase

Combine the contents of a resource file and a resource database. (New in R5.)

```
Status XrmCombineFileDatabase(filename, target_db, override)
    char *filename;                     /* name of resource file */
    XrmDatabase *target_db;             /* address of resource database */
    Bool override;                      /* whether file should override database */
```

XrmDestroyDatabase

Destroy a resource database and free its allocated memory.

```
void XrmDestroyDatabase(database)
    XrmDatabase database;
```

XrmEnumerateDatabase

Enumerate resource database entries—call the specified procedure for each resource in the database that would match some completion of the given name/class resource prefix. (New in R5.)

```
Bool XrmEnumerateDatabase(database, name_prefix, class_prefix, mode, proc, arg)
    XrmDatabase database;
    XrmNameList name_prefix;        /* resource name prefix */
    XrmClassList class_prefix;      /* resource class prefix */
    int mode;                       /* XrmEnumOneLevel or XrmEnumAllLevels */
    Bool (*proc)();                 /* procedure to be called for each matching entry */
    XPointer arg;                   /* user-supplied argument passed to procedure */
```

Values for mode are:

XrmEnumOneLevel   Resource must match given name/class prefix with just single name and class appended.

XrmEnumAllLevels   Resource must match given name/class prefix with one or more names and classes appended.

XrmGetDatabase

Retrieve the resource database associated with a display. (New in R5.)

```
XrmDatabase XrmGetDatabase(display)
    Display *display;
```

XrmGetFileDatabase

Open the specified file, create a new resource database, and load the database with the data read in from the file.

```
XrmDatabase XrmGetFileDatabase(filename)
    char *filename;
```

XrmGetResource

Get a resource from specified database of lines containing resource name/class strings followed by a colon and the value of the resource. This function is very similar to XrmQGetResource, except that in XrmQGetResource, the equivalent arguments to *str_name*, *str_class*, and *str_type* are quarks instead of strings.

```
Bool XrmGetResource(database, str_name, str_class, str_type, value)
    XrmDatabase database;
    char *str_name;      /* resource name string */
    char *str_class;     /* resource class string */
    char **str_type;     /* returns representation type as string */
    XrmValue *value;     /* actual resource value; do not modify or free */
```

XrmGetStringDatabase

Create a new database and store in it the resources specified by the *data* string. This function is similar to XrmGetFileDatabase, except that it reads the information out of a string instead of a file.

```
XrmDatabase XrmGetStringDatabase(data)
    char *data;                          /* resources as a string */
```

XrmInitialize

Initialize the resource manager. This function creates a representation type of "String" for values defined as strings. This representation type is used by XrmPutStringResource and XrmQPutStringResource, which require a value as a string.

```
void XrmInitialize();
```

XrmLocaleOfDatabase

Return, as a NULL-terminated string, the name of the locale bound to the specified database. (New in R5.)

```
char *XrmLocaleOfDatabase(database)
    XrmDatabase database;
```

XrmMergeDatabases

Merge the contents of one database into another. The source database is destroyed, and the target database is modified.

```
void XrmMergeDatabases(source_db, target_db)
    XrmDatabase source_db, *target_db;
```

XrmNameToString

Convert XrmName to string. Same as XrmQuarkToString.

```
XrmNameToString(name)
```

XrmParseCommand

Load a resource database from command-line arguments. After the call, *argc* returns the number of arguments not parsed, and *argv* contains a pointer to a string containing the arguments that couldn't be parsed.

```
void XrmParseCommand(db, table, table_count, name, argc, argv)
    XrmDatabase *db;
    XrmOptionDescList table;
    int table_count;
    char *name;
```

```
    int *argc;                          /* sends and returns */
    char **argv;                        /* sends and returns */
```

XrmPutFileDatabase

Store a resource database in a file.

```
    void XrmPutFileDatabase(database, stored_db)
    XrmDatabase database;
    char *stored_db;                    /* filename for stored db */
```

XrmPutLineResource

Add a resource specification to a resource database. This function is similar to
XrmPutStringResource, except that instead of having separate string arguments for
the resource and its value, XrmPutLineResource takes a single string argument (*line*)
which consists of the resource name, a colon, then the value.

```
    void XrmPutLineResource(database, line)
    XrmDatabase *database;              /* send, and if NULL, return */
    char *line;                         /* resource name: value pair */
```

XrmPutResource

Store a resource specification into a resource database. This routine first converts
specifier into a binding list and a quark list by calling XrmStringToBindingQuarkList,
and converts *type* into an XrmRepresentation by calling XrmStringToRepresentation.
Finally, it puts the data into the database.

```
    void XrmPutResource(database, specifier, type, value)
    XrmDatabase *database;
    char *specifier;                    /* resource class or name string */
    char *type;                         /* resource type */
    XrmValue *value;                    /* resource value */
```

XrmPutStringResource

Add a resource specification with separate resource name and value. The *resource*
string may contain both names and classes, bound with either loose (*) or tight (.)
bindings.

```
    void XrmPutStringResource(database, resource, value)
    XrmDatabase *database;
    char *resource;                     /* resource string */
    char *value;                        /* resource value */
```

XrmQGetResource

Get a resource value using name and class as quarks. This function is very similar to XrmGetResource, except that in XrmGetResource, the equivalent arguments to *quark_name*, *quark_class*, and *quark_type* arguments are strings instead of quarks.

```
Bool XrmQGetResource(database, quark_name, quark_class, quark_type, value)
    XrmDatabase database;
    XrmNameList quark_name;
    XrmClassList quark_class;
    XrmRepresentation *quark_type;      /* returns pointer to quark type */
    XrmValue *value;                    /* returns pointer to value in database */
```

XrmQGetSearchList

Return a search list of database levels where a resource might be found. This function is used in combination with XrmQGetSearchResource, which searches the returned list.

```
Bool XrmQGetSearchList(database, names, classes, search_list, list_length)
    XrmDatabase database;
    XrmNameList names;                  /* quarks for desired names */
    XrmClassList classes;               /* quarks for desired classes */
    XrmSearchList search_list;          /* most likely levels to match */
    int list_length;                    /* size allocated for list */
```

XrmQGetSearchResource

Search a prepared search list of database levels for a given resource. This function is used in combination with XrmQGetSearchList, which returns the list to be searched.

```
Bool XrmQGetSearchResource(search_list, name, class, type, value)
    XrmSearchList search_list;          /* from XrmQGetSearchList */
    XrmName name;                       /* resource name */
    XrmClass class;                     /* resource class */
    XrmRepresentation *type;            /* returns data representation type */
    XrmValue *value;                    /* returns value from database */
```

XrmQPutResource

Store a resource specification into a database using quarks. *database* can be a previously defined database, as returned by XrmGetStringDatabase, XrmGetFileDatabase, or from XrmMergeDatabases.

```
void XrmQPutResource(database, bindings, quarks, type, value)
    XrmDatabase *database;
    XrmBindingList bindings;            /* bindings between corresponding quarks */
    XrmQuarkList quarks;                /* name or class components */
```

```
XrmRepresentation type;              /* representation type */
XrmValue *value;                     /* value */
```

XrmQPutStringResource

Add a resource specification to a database using a quark resource name and string value. This function is a cross between XrmQPutResource and XrmPutStringResource. Like XrmQPutResource, it specifies the resource by *quarks* and *bindings*—two lists that together make a name/class list with loose and tight bindings. Like XrmPutStringResource, it specifies the value to be stored as a string—that value is converted into an XrmValue, and the default representation type String is used.

```
void XrmQPutStringResource(database, bindings, quarks, value)
    XrmDatabase *database;
    XrmBindingList bindings;         /* bindings between corresponding quarks */
    XrmQuarkList quarks;             /* name or class components */
    char *value;                     /* value */
```

XrmQuarkToString

Convert a quark to a string.

```
char *XrmQuarkToString(quark)
    XrmQuark quark;
```

XrmRepresentationToString

Convert XrmRepresentation to string. Same as XrmQuarkToString.

```
XrmRepresentationToString(type)
```

XrmSetDatabase

Associate a resource database with a display. (New in R5.)

```
void XrmSetDatabase(display, database)
    Display *display;
    XrmDatabase database;
```

XrmStringToBindingQuarkList

Convert a resource specification string to a binding list and a quark list. Component names in the list are separated by a dot (.) indicating a tight binding or an asterisk (*) indicating a loose binding. XrmStringToQuark performs the inverse function.

```
XrmStringToBindingQuarkList(string, bindings, quarks)
    char *string;                        /* resource name or class string */
    XrmBindingList bindings;             /* bindings between components */
    XrmQuarkList quarks;                 /* quarks for each component */
```

XrmStringToClass

Convert string to XrmClass. Same as XrmStringToQuark.

```
XrmStringToClass(string)
```

XrmStringToName

Convert string to XrmName. Same as XrmStringToQuark.

```
XrmStringToName(string)
```

XrmStringToQuark

Convert a string to a quark. XrmQuarkToString performs the inverse function.

```
XrmQuark XrmStringToQuark(string)
    char *string;
```

XrmStringToQuarkList

Convert a resource specification string to a quark list. Components of the string may be separated by a tight binding (.) or a loose binding (*). Use XrmStringTo-BindingQuarkList for lists which contain both tight and loose bindings.

```
void XrmStringToQuarkList(string, quarks)
    char *string;
    XrmQuarkList quarks;
```

XrmStringToRepresentation

Convert string to XrmRepresentation. Same as XrmStringToQuark.

```
XrmStringToRepresentation(string)
```

XrmUniqueQuark

Allocate a new quark. For most applications, XrmStringToQuark is more useful, as it binds a quark to a string. This function allocates a quark that is guaranteed not to represent any existing string.

```
XrmQuark XrmUniqueQuark()
```

XRotateBuffers

Rotate the cut buffers. All 8 buffers must be loaded with XStoreBuffer. This routine will not work if any of the buffers have not been stored into with XStoreBuffer or XStoreBytes.

```
XRotateBuffers(display, rotate)
    Display *display;
    int rotate;                          /* number of positions to rotate */
```

XRotateWindowProperties

Rotate properties in the properties array.

```
XRotateWindowProperties(display, w, properties, num_prop, npositions)
    Display *display;
    Window w;
    Atom properties[];                   /* numbered from 0 */
    int num_prop;                        /* number of properties in array */
    int npositions;                      /* number of positions to rotate; */
                                         /* sign controls direction of rotation */
```

XSaveContext

Save a data value corresponding to a window and context type (not graphics context). The client must have called XUniqueContext to get the *context* ID before calling this function. If an entry with the specified window and *context* ID already exists, it is written over with the specified data.

```
int XSaveContext(display, w, context, data)
    Display *display;
    Window w;
    XContext context;
    Xpointer data;
```

XScreenNumberOfScreen

Return the integer screen number corresponding to the specified pointer to a Screen structure.

```
int XScreenNumberOfScreen(screen)
    Screen *screen;                      /* screen whose screen number to be returned */
```

XScreenResourceString

Return the SCREEN_RESOURCES property from the root window of the specified screen. The property is converted from type STRING to the current locale in a conversion identical to that produced by XmbTextPropertyToTextList for a singleton STRING property. (New in R5.)

```
char *XScreenResourceString(screen)
    Screen *screen;
```

XSelectInput

Select the event types to be sent to a window.

```
XSelectInput(display, w, event_mask)
    Display *display;
    Window w;
    long event_mask;                    /* see Section 3 */
```

XSendEvent

Send an event from one client to another.

```
Status XSendEvent(display, w, propagate, event_mask, event)
    Display *display;
    Window w;
    Bool propagate;
    long event_mask;                    /* see Section 3 */
    XEvent *event;
```

XSetAccessControl

Disable or enable access control. This function can only be called from a client running on the same host as the server.

```
XSetAccessControl(display, mode)
    Display *display;
    int mode;                           /* EnableAccess or DisableAccess */
```

The values for mode are defined in <X11/X.h>:

```
#define EnableAccess        1
#define DisableAccess       0
```

XSetAfterFunction

Set a function to be called after all Xlib functions. To make sure that the input and request buffers are flushed after every Xlib routine, use XSynchronize.

```
int (*XSetAfterFunction(display, func))( )
    Display *display;
    int (*func)( );
```

XSetArcMode

Set the arc mode in a graphics context, which controls filling in the XFillArcs function.

```
XSetArcMode(display, gc, arc_mode)
    Display *display;
    GC gc;
    int arc_mode;                          /* ArcChord or ArcPieSlice */
```

XSetBackground

Set the background pixel value in a graphics context. Note that this is different from the background of a window, which can be set with either XSetWindowBackground or XSetWindowBackgroundPixmap.

```
XSetBackground(display, gc, background)
    Display *display;
    GC gc;
    unsigned long background;
```

XSetClassHint

Set the XA_WM_CLASS property of a window.

```
XSetClassHint(display, w, class_hints)
    Display *display;
    Window w;
    XClassHint *class_hints;
```

XSetClipMask

Set clip_mask to a pixmap in a graphics context. Use XSetClipRectangles to set clip_mask to a set of rectangles, or XSetRegion to set clip_mask to a region.

```
XSetClipMask(display, gc, clip_mask)
    Display *display;
    GC gc;
    Pixmap clip_mask;
```

XSetClipOrigin

Set the clip origin in a graphics context.

```
XSetClipOrigin(display, gc, clip_x_origin, clip_y_origin)
    Display *display;
    GC gc;
    int clip_x_origin, clip_y_origin;
```

XSetClipRectangles

Change clip_mask in a graphics context to a list of rectangles.

```
XSetClipRectangles(display, gc, clip_x_origin, clip_y_origin, rectangles, nrects, ordering)
    Display *display;
    GC gc;
    int clip_x_origin, clip_y_origin;
    XRectangle rectangles[];        /* rectangles for clip mask */
    int nrects;                     /* number of rectangles */
    int ordering;                   /* one of symbols below */
```

The values for *ordering* are defined in *<X11/X.h>*:

```
#define Unsorted    0    /* arbitrary order */
#define YSorted     1    /* non-decreasing in y origin */
#define YXSorted    2    /* non-decreasing in x as well */
#define YXBanded    3    /* for each y scan line, each rectangle has */
                         /* identical y origin and y extent */
```

XSetCloseDownMode

Change the close down mode of a client. A connection between a client and the server starts in DestroyAll mode, and all resources associated with that connection will be freed when the client process dies. If the close down mode is RetainTemporary or RetainPermanent when the client dies, its resources live on until a call to XKillClient.

```
XSetCloseDownMode(display, close_mode)
    Display *display;
    int close_mode;                 /* one of symbols below */
```

The values for *close_mode* are defined in *<X11/X.h>*:

```
#define DestroyAll        0
#define RetainPermanent   1    /* keep resources till XKillClient */
#define RetainTemporary   2    /* keep resources till XKillClient with AllTemporary */
```

XSetCommand

Set the XA_WM_COMMAND atom (command-line arguments). Use this command only if XSetStandardProperties or XSetWMProperties are not called. This function has been superseded by XSetWMCommand in R4.

```
XSetCommand(display, w, argv, argc)
    Display *display;
    Window w;
    char **argv;
    int argc;
```

XSetDashes

Set a pattern of line dashes in a graphics context.

```
XSetDashes(display, gc, dash_offset, dash_list, n)
    Display *display;
    GC gc;
    int dash_offset;                    /* start of pattern on line */
    char dash_list[];                   /* on-off pattern */
    int n;                              /* length of list */
```

XSetErrorHandler

Set a nonfatal error event handler.

```
XSetErrorHandler(handler)              /* In Release 3 */
    int (*handler)(Display *, XErrorEvent *)

int (*XSetErrorHandler(handler))()     /* In Release 4 */
    int (*handler)(Display *, XErrorEvent *)
```

XSetFillRule

Set the fill rule in a graphics context. *fill_rule* determines what pixels are drawn in XFillPolygon requests.

```
XSetFillRule(display, gc, fill_rule)
    Display *display;
    GC gc;
    int fill_rule;                     /* see XGCValues in Section 2 */
```

XSetFillStyle

Set the fill style in a graphics context. *fill_style* defines the contents of the source for line, text, and fill requests.

```
XSetFillStyle(display, gc, fill_style)
    Display *display;
    GC gc;
    int fill_style;                    /* see XGCValues in Section 2 */
```

XSetFont

Set the current font in a graphics context. Text-drawing requests using this graphics context will use this font only if it is loaded; otherwise, text will not be drawn.

```
XSetFont(display, gc, font)
    Display *display;
    GC gc;
    Font font;
```

XSetFontPath

Set the font search path.

```
XSetFontPath(display, directories, ndirs)
    Display *display;
    char **directories;                /* empty string restores default */
    int ndirs;                         /* number of directories in path */
```

XSetForeground

Set the foreground pixel value in a graphics context.

```
XSetForeground(display, gc, foreground)
    Display *display;
    GC gc;
    unsigned long foreground;
```

XSetFunction

Set the bitwise logical operation in a graphics context.

```
XSetFunction(display, gc, function)
    Display *display;
    GC gc;
    int function;                      /* see XGCValues in Section 2 */
```

XSetGraphicsExposures

Set the graphics_exposures component in a graphics context. If *graphics_exposures* is True, the following events will be generated: GraphicsExpose, when XCopyArea and XCopyPlane requests cannot be completely satisfied because a source region is obscured; NoExpose, when they *can* be completely satisfied. If *graphics_exposures* is False, these events are not generated.

```
XSetGraphicsExposures(display, gc, graphics_exposures)
    Display *display;
    GC gc;
    Bool graphics_exposures;           /* see XGCValues in Section 2 */
```

XSetICFocus

Set input context focus. Notify an input method that the window associated with the specified input context has received keyboard focus. (New in R5.)

```
void XSetICFocus(ic)
    XIC ic;
```

XSetIconName

Set the name to be displayed in a window's icon (XA_WM_ICON_NAME property). This function has been superseded by XSetWMIconName in R4. XSetStandardProperties or XSetWMProperties also set this property.

```
XSetIconName(display, w, icon_name)
    Display *display;
    Window w;
    char *icon_name;
```

XSetICValues

Set input context attributes. The first argument is the input context, and it is followed by a NULL-terminated variable-length argument list of name/value pairs. (New in R5.)

```
char * XSetICValues(ic, ...)
    XIC ic;                             /* input context */
    ...;                                /* argument list to set XIC values */
```

XSetIconSizes

Set the value of the XA_WM_ICON_SIZE property. The property can then be read with XGetIconSizes.

```
XSetIconSizes(display, w, size_list, count)
    Display *display;
    Window w;
    XIconSize *size_list;               /* preferred icon sizes */
    int count;                          /* number of atoms in size list */
```

XSetInputFocus

Set the keyboard focus window. This function has no effect if *time* is earlier than the current last-focus-change time or later than the current X server time. Otherwise, the last-focus-change time is set to the specified time, with CurrentTime replaced by the current X server time.

```
XSetInputFocus(display, focus, revert_to, time)
    Display *display;
    Window focus;                       /* window ID, PointerRoot, or None */
    int revert_to;                      /* RevertToNone, RevertToPointerRoot, or */
                                        /* RevertToParent */
    Time time;                          /* when change should take place */
```

The symbols above are defined in *<X11/X.h>*:

```
#define None            0L
#define PointerRoot     1L
```

```
#define RevertToNone            (int)None
#define RevertToPointerRoot     (int)PointerRoot
#define RevertToParent          2
```

XSetIOErrorHandler

Set a nonfatal error event handler.

```
int (*XSetIOErrorHandler(handler))()
    int (*handler)(Display *, XErrorEvent *)
```

XSetLineAttributes

Set the line drawing components in a graphics context.

```
XSetLineAttributes(display, gc, line_width, line_style, cap_style, join_style)
    Display *display;
    GC gc;
    unsigned int line_width;
    int line_style;              /* see XGCValues in Section 2 */
    int cap_style;
    int join_style;
```

XSetLocaleModifiers

Configure locale modifiers. This function sets or queries the X modifiers for the current locale setting. If *modifier_list* is NULL, the current settings are returned. Otherwise, *modifier_list* is the empty string or a string having zero or more concatenated entries of the form "@*category* = *value*}", where *category* is a category name and *value* is the setting for that category. (New in R5.)

```
char *XSetLocaleModifiers(modifier_list)
    char *modifier_list;         /* modifiers */
```

XSetModifierMapping

Set keycodes to be used as modifiers (Shift, Control, etc.), specifying all the keycodes for all the modifiers at once. The other, easier, way to specify keycodes is to use XInsertModifiermapEntry and XDeleteModifiermapEntry, which add or delete a single keycode for a single modifier key. XSetModifierMapping does the work in a single call, but the price of this call is that you need to manually set up the XModifierKeymap structure pointed to by *mod_map*.

```
int XSetModifierMapping(display, mod_map)
    Display *display;
    XModifierKeymap *mod_map;
```

XSetNormalHints

Set the size hints property (XA_WM_NORMAL_HINTS property) of a window in normal state (not zoomed or iconified). This function has been superseded by XSetWMNormalHints in R4 and later releases.

```
void XSetNormalHints(display, w, hints)
    Display *display;
    Window w;
    XSizeHints *hints;
```

XSetPlaneMask

Set the plane mask in a graphics context.

```
XSetPlaneMask(display, gc, plane_mask)
    Display *display;
    GC gc;
    unsigned long plane_mask;
```

XSetPointerMapping

Set the pointer button mapping. Elements of the *map* list are indexed starting from 1. The length of the list *nmap* must be the same as is returned by XGetPointer-Mapping.

```
int XSetPointerMapping(display, map, nmap)
    Display *display;
    unsigned char map[];
    int nmap;
```

Symbols used by this function are defined in *<X11/X.h>*:

```
#define MappingSuccess        0
#define MappingBusy           1
#define MappingFailed         2
```

XSetRGBColormaps

Set an XStandardColormap structure. This function replaces the RGB colormap definition in the specified property on the named window. The property is stored with a type of RGB_COLOR_MAP and a format of 32.

```
void XSetRGBColormaps(display, w, std_colormap, count, property)
    Display *display;
    Window w;
    XStandardColormap *std_colormap;
    int count;
    Atom property;                         /* standard colormap to set */
```

XSetRegion

Set clip_mask of the graphics context to the specified region.

```
XSetRegion(display, gc, r)
    Display *display;
    GC gc;
    Region r;
```

XSetScreenSaver

Set the parameters of the screen saver. (See also XGetScreenSaver.)

```
XSetScreenSaver(display, timeout, interval, prefer_blanking, allow_exposures)
    Display *display;
    int timeout, interval;          /* in seconds */
    int prefer_blanking;            /* one of symbols below */
    int allow_exposures;            /* one of symbols below */
```

Values for prefer_blanking: Values for allow_exposures:

```
#define DontPreferBlanking    0      #define DontAllowExposures    0
#define PreferBlanking        1      #define AllowExposures        1
#define DefaultBlanking       2      #define DefaultExposures      2
```

XSetSelectionOwner

Set the owner and last-change time of a selection. This makes the information available so that other applications can request the data from the new selection owner using XConvertSelection, which generates a SelectionRequest event specifying the desired type and format of the data.

```
XSetSelectionOwner(display, selection, owner, time)
    Display *display;
    Atom selection;                 /* XA_PRIMARY or XA_SECONDARY */
    Window owner;                   /* ID of current owner, or None */
    Time time;                      /* when selection should take place */
```

XSetSizeHints

Set the value of any property of type XA_WM_SIZE_HINTS. This has been superseded by XSetWMSizeHints in R4 and later releases.

```
XSetSizeHints(display, w, hints, property)
    Display *display;
    Window w;
    XSizeHints *hints;              /* pointer to the size hints */
    Atom property;                  /* usually normal hints or zoom hints */
```

XSetStandardColormap

Change the standard colormap property. This function has been superseded by XSetRGBColormap as of R4.

```
void XSetStandardColormap(display, w, cmap_info, property)
    Display *display;
    Window w;
    XStandardColormap *cmap_info;      /* values for colormap */
    Atom property;                     /* standard colormap property to set */
```

XSetStandardProperties

Set the minimum set of properties for the window manager. This function has been superseded by XSetWMProperties in R4 and later releases.

```
XSetStandardProperties(display, w, window_name, icon_name, icon_pixmap, argv, argc, hints)
    Display *display;
    Window w;
    char *window_name;
    char *icon_name;
    Pixmap icon_pixmap;
    char **argv;
    int argc;
    XSizeHints *hints;                 /* window in normal state */
```

XSetState

Set the foreground, background, logical function, and plane mask in a graphics context.

```
XSetState(display, gc, foreground, background, function, plane_mask)
    Display *display;
    GC gc;
    unsigned long foreground, background;
    int function;                      /* see XGCValues in Section 2 */
    unsigned long plane_mask;
```

XSetStipple

Set the stipple in a graphics context. The *stipple* is a pixmap of depth one.

```
XSetStipple(display, gc, stipple)
    Display *display;
    GC gc;
    Pixmap stipple;
```

XSetSubwindowMode

Set the subwindow mode in a graphics context. ClipByChildren mode means that graphics requests will be clipped by all viewable children. IncludeInferiors mode means draw through all subwindows.

```
XSetSubwindowMode(display, gc, subwindow_mode)
    Display *display;
    GC gc;
    int subwindow_mode;                 /* ClipByChildren or IncludeInferiors */
```

The values for *subwindow_mode* are defined in *<X11/X.h>*:

```
#define ClipByChildren    0    /* default - graphics will not show through
                                /* any other window that has a background */
#define IncludeInferiors  1    /* graphics appear through all mapped
                                /* subwindows, but not through siblings */
```

XSetTextProperty

Set one of a window's text properties. This function sets the specified property for the named window with the data, type, format, and number of items determined by the *value* field, the *encoding* field, the *format* field, and the *nitems* field, respectively, of the specified XTextProperty structure.

```
void XSetTextProperty(display, w, text_prop, property)
    Display *display;
    Window w;
    XTextProperty *text_prop;           /* which text property to use */
    Atom property;
```

XSetTile

Set the fill tile in a graphics context. The tile must have the same depth as the destination drawable.

```
XSetTile(display, gc, tile)
    Display *display;
    GC gc;
    Pixmap tile;
```

XSetTransientForHint

Set the XA_WM_TRANSIENT_FOR property for a window. This should be done when the window *w* is a temporary child (for example, a dialog box) and the main top-level window of its application is *prop_window*.

```
XSetTransientForHint(display, w, prop_window)
    Display *display;
    Window w;
    Window prop_window;
```

XSetTSOrigin

Set the tile/stipple origin in a graphics context. The origin is measured relative to the origin of the drawable specified in the drawing request that uses the graphics context.

```
XSetTSOrigin(display, gc, ts_x_origin, ts_y_origin)
    Display *display;
    GC gc;
    int ts_x_origin, ts_y_origin;
```

XSetWindowBackground

Set the background pixel value attribute of a window. This overrides any previous call to XSetWindowBackground or XSetWindowBackgroundPixmap on the same window.

```
XSetWindowBackground(display, w, background_pixel)
    Display *display;
    Window w;
    unsigned long background_pixel;
```

XSetWindowBackgroundPixmap

Change the background tile attribute of a window. This function overrides any previous background_pixel or background_pixmap attribute set with XSetWindowBackgroundPixmap, XSetWindowBackground, or XChangeWindowAttributes.

```
XSetWindowBackgroundPixmap(display, w, background_tile)
    Display *display;
    Window w;
    Pixmap background_tile;
```

XSetWindowBorder

Change a window border pixel attribute and repaint the border. The border is also automatically repainted after Expose events. To create a tiled border, use XSetWindowBorderPixmap.

```
XSetWindowBorder(display, w, border_pixel)
    Display *display;
    Window w;
    unsigned long border_pixel;
```

XSetWindowBorderPixmap

Change a window border tile attribute and repaint the border. The border_tile can be freed immediately after the call if no further explicit references to it are to be made. This function can only be performed on an InputOutput window.

```
XSetWindowBorderPixmap(display, w, border_tile)
    Display *display;
    Window w;
    Pixmap border_tile;
```

XSetWindowBorderWidth

Change the border width of a window.

```
XSetWindowBorderWidth(display, w, width)
    Display *display;
    Window w;
    unsigned int width;
```

XSetWindowColormap

Set the colormap attribute for a window. The colormap must have the same visual as the window.

```
XSetWindowColormap(display, w, cmap)
    Display *display;
    Window w;
    Colormap cmap;
```

XSetWMClientMachine

Set a window's XA_WM_CLIENT_MACHINE property to the list of window resource IDs provided in windows.

```
void XSetWMClientMachine(display, w, text_prop)
    Display *display;
    Window w;
    XTextProperty *text_prop;          /* which text property to use */
```

XSetWMColormapWindows

Set a window's XA_WM_COLORMAP_WINDOWS property to the list of window resource IDs provided in colormap_windows.

```
Status XSetWMColormapWindows(display, w, colormap_windows, count)
    Display *display;
    Window w;
    Window *colormap_windows;          /* list of windows */
    int count;                         /* number of windows in list */
```

XSetWMHints

Set window manager hints, including icon information and location, initial state of the window, and whether the application relies on the window manager to get keyboard input.

```
XSetWMHints(display, w, wmhints)
    Display *display;
    Window w;
    XWMHints *wmhints;
```

XSetWMIconName

Set a window's XA_WM_ICON_NAME property. If the property already exists, it is replaced by the values provided in *text_prop*.

```
void XSetWMIconName(display, w, text_prop)
    Display *display;
    Window w;
    XTextProperty *text_prop;              /* XA_WM_ICON_NAME */
```

XSetWMName

Set a window's XA_WM_NAME property. If the property already exists, it is replaced by the values provided in *text_prop*.

```
void XSetWMName(display, w, text_prop)
    Display *display;
    Window w;
    XTextProperty *text_prop;              /* XA_WM_NAME */
```

XSetWMNormalHints

Set a window's XA_WM_NORMAL_HINTS property to the values provided in *hints*. If the property already exists, it is replaced by the values in *hints*.

```
void XSetWMNormalHints(display, w, hints)
    Display *display;
    Window w;
    XSizeHints *hints;
```

XSetWMProperties

Set a window's standard window manager properties. If *window_name* is non-NULL, the WM_NAME property is set by calling XSetWMName. If *icon_name* is non-NULL, the WM_ICON_NAME property is set by calling XSetWMIconName. If *argv* is non-NULL, the WM_COMMAND property is set by calling XSetCommand. XSetWM-ClientMachine is called to store the host name of the client machine. If *normal_hints* is non-NULL, XSetWMNormalHints is called to set the WM_NORMAL_HINTS property.

If *class_hints* is non-NULL, the WM_CLASS property is set by calling XSetClassHint. This function supersedes XSetStandardProperties for R4.

```
void XSetWMProperties(display, w, window_name, icon_name, argv, argc, normal_hints,
            wm_hints, class_hints)
    Display *display;
    Window w;
    XTextProperty *window_name;        /* NULL-terminated */
    XTextProperty *icon_name;          /* NULL-terminated */
    char **argv;
    int argc;
    XSizeHints *normal_hints;          /* hints for window in its normal state */
    XWMHints *wm_hints;                /* hints for window manager */
    XClassHint *class_hints;           /* hints for application class */
```

XSetWMProtocols

Set a window's XA_WM_PROTOCOLS property to list of atoms provided in *protocols*. The property is stored with a type of ATOM and a format of 32.

```
Status XSetWMProtocols(display, w, protocols, count)
    Display *display;
    Window w;
    Atom *protocols;
    int count;
```

XSetWMSizeHints

Set a window's XA_WM_SIZE_HINTS property to values provided in *hints*. The property is stored with a type of WM_SIZE_HINTS and a format of 32. To set a window's normal size hints, you can use XSetWMNormalHints instead. XSetWMSizeHints supersedes XSetSizeHints.

```
void XSetWMSizeHints(display, w, hints, property)
    Display *display;
    Window w;
    XSizeHints *hints;
    Atom property;
```

XSetZoomHints

Set the size hints property of a zoomed window. This function is obsolete for R4.

```
XSetZoomHints(display, w, zhints)
    Display *display;
    Window w;
    XSizeHints *zhints;
```

XShrinkRegion

Reduce or expand the size of a region. Positive values shrink the region; negative values expand the region.

```
XShrinkRegion(r, dx, dy)
    Region r;
    int dx, dy;                              /* positive to expand, negative to shrink */
```

XStoreBuffer

Store data in a cut buffer. Data is stored in any of the eight cut buffers (numbered 0 through 7). All eight buffers must be stored before they can be circulated with XRotateBuffers. Use XFetchBuffer to recover data from any cut buffer.

```
XStoreBuffer(display, bytes, nbytes, buffer)
    Display *display;
    char bytes[];
    int nbytes;
    int buffer;                              /* 1 to 7 */
```

XStoreBytes

Store data in cut buffer 0. Data to be stored need not be text, so NULL bytes are not special. To store data in buffers 1-7, use XStoreBuffer.

```
XStoreBytes(display, bytes, nbytes)
    Display *display;
    char bytes[];
    int nbytes;
```

XStoreColor

Set or change the RGB values of a read/write colormap entry to the closest possible hardware color.

```
XStoreColor(display, cmap, colorcell_def)
    Display *display;
    Colormap cmap;
    XColor *colorcell_def;
```

XStoreColors

Set or change the RGB values of read/write colorcells to the closest possible hardware colors.

```
XStoreColors(display, cmap, colorcell_defs, ncolors)
    Display *display;
    Colormap cmap;
```

```
XColor colorcell_defs[ncolors];
int ncolors;
```

XStoreName

Set the WM_NAME property for the specified window. This function was superseded in R4 and later releases by XSetWMName.

```
XStoreName(display, w, window_name)
    Display *display;
    Window w;
    char *window_name;          /* NULL-terminated */
```

XStoreNamedColor

Set RGB values of a read/write colorcell by color name. Look up the named *color*
in the database with respect to the screen associated with *cmap*, then store the
result in the read/write colorcell of *cmap* specified by *pixel*.

```
XStoreNamedColor(display, cmap, colorname, pixel, flags)
    Display *display;
    Colormap cmap;
    char *colorname;
    unsigned long pixel;
    int flags;                  /* see XColor in Section 2 */
```

XStringListToTextProperty

Set the specified list of strings to an XTextProperty structure.

```
Status XStringListToTextProperty(list, count, text_prop)
    char **list;
    int count;
    XTextProperty *text_prop;
```

XStringToKeysym

Convert a keysym name string to a keysym by translating the character string version of the name to the matching keysym, which is a constant. Valid keysym
names are listed in <X11/keysymdef.h>. This string is *not* the string returned in the
buffer argument of XLookUpString.

```
KeySym XStringToKeysym(string)
    char *string;
```

XSubImage

Create a subimage from part of an image by allocating memory necessary for the new XImage structure, and return a pointer to it. Data is copied from the source image, and the rectangle defined by x, y, subimage_width, and subimage_height must be contained in the image.

```
XImage *XSubImage(ximage, x, y, subimage_width, subimage_height)
    XImage *ximage;
    int x, y;
    unsigned int subimage_width, subimage_height;
```

XSubtractRegion

Subtract one region from another.

```
XSubtractRegion(sra, srb, dr)
    Region sra, srb;                    /* subtract srb from sra */
    Region dr;                          /* returns result in dr */
```

XSupportsLocale

Determine locale support. If True is returned, Xlib functions are capable of operating under current locale; if False, client should usually switch to a supported locale or exit. (New in R5.)

```
Bool XSupportsLocale()
```

XSync

Flush the request buffer and wait for all events and errors to be processed by the server.

```
XSync(display, discard)
    Display *display;
    Bool discard;                       /* if True, discard all events in queue */
```

XSynchronize

Enable or disable synchronization for debugging.

```
int (*XSynchronize(display, onoff))()
    Display *display;
    Bool onoff;                         /* 0 disable; nonzero, enable */
```

XTextExtents

Get string and font metrics of an 8-bit character string. This function performs the size computation locally, thereby avoiding the roundtrip overhead of XQueryTextExtents.

XTextExtents(*font_struct*, *string*, *nchars*, *direction*, *ascent*, *descent*, *overall*)
    XFontStruct *font_struct;   /* see Section 2 */
    char *string;
    int *nchars*;
    int *direction;   /* returns direction element of XFontStruct */
    int *ascent, *descent;   /* returns font ascent/descent element of XFontStruct */
    XCharStruct *overall;   /* returns overall characteristics of string */

XTextExtents16

Get string and font metrics of a 16-bit character string.

XTextExtents16(*font_struct*, *string*, *nchars*, *direction*, *ascent*, *descent*, *overall*)
    XFontStruct *font_struct;   / see Section 2 */
    XChar2b *string;
    int *nchars*;
    int *direction;   /* returns direction element of the XFontStruct */
    int *ascent, *descent;   /* returns ascent/descent element of the XFontStruct */
    XCharStruct *overall;   /* returns overall characteristics of the string */

XTextPropertyToStringList

Obtain a list of strings from a specified XTextProperty structure. The data in *text_prop* must be of type STRING and format 8. To free the storage for the list and its contents, use XFreeStringList.

Status XTextPropertyToStringList(*text_prop*, *list*, *count*)
    XTextProperty *text_prop;   /* data of type STRING; format 8 */
    char ***list;   /* list of NULL-terminated char strings */
    int *count;   /* number of strings */

XTextWidth

Get the width in pixels of an 8-bit character string.

int XTextWidth(*font_struct*, *string*, *count*)
    XFontStruct *font_struct;
    char *string;
    int *count*;   /* number of chars in string */

XTextWidth16

Get the width in pixels of a 16-bit character string.

int XTextWidth16(*font_struct*, *string*, *count*)
    XFontStruct *font_struct;
    XChar2b *string;
    int *count*;   /* number of chars in string */

XTranslateCoordinates

Change the coordinate system from one window to another.

```
Bool XTranslateCoordinates(display, src_w, frame_w, src_x, src_y, new_x, new_y, child)
    Display *display;
    Window src_w, frame_w;
    int src_x, src_y;
    int *new_x, *new_y;              /* returns translated x and y coordinates */
    Window *child;                    /* returns child ID, if coords in child of frame_w */
```

XUndefineCursor

Disassociate a cursor from a window. This function undoes a previous call to XDefineCursor.

```
XUndefineCursor(display, w)
    Display *display;
    Window w;
```

XUngrabButton

Release a button from a passive grab. A *modifiers* of AnyModifier is equivalent to issuing the ungrab request for all possible modifier combinations. A *button* of AnyButton is equivalent to issuing the request for all possible buttons.

```
XUngrabButton(display, button, modifiers, w)
    Display *display;
    unsigned int button;             /* see symbols below */
    unsigned int modifiers;          /* bitwise OR of symbols below */
    Window w;
```

The values for *button* are defined in <*X11/X.h*>:

```
#define AnyButton       0
#define Button1         1        /* cannot be ORed */
#define Button2         2
#define Button3         3
#define Button4         4
#define Button5         5
```

Key masks for *modifiers* are defined in <*X11/X.h*>:

```
#define ShiftMask       (1<<0)
#define LockMask        (1<<1)
#define ControlMask     (1<<2)
#define Mod1Mask        (1<<3)
#define Mod2Mask        (1<<4)
#define Mod3Mask        (1<<5)
#define Mod4Mask        (1<<6)
#define Mod5Mask        (1<<7)
```

XUngrabKey

Release a key from a passive grab. A *modifiers* of AnyModifier is equivalent to issuing the ungrab request for all possible modifier combinations. A *keycode* of Any-Key is equivalent to issuing the request for all possible nonmodifier keycodes. See XUngrabButton for #defines.

```
XUngrabKey(display, keycode, modifiers, w)
    Display *display;
    int keycode;                        /* a keycode or AnyKey (0L) */
    unsigned int modifiers;
    Window w;
```

XUngrabKeyboard

Release the keyboard from an active grab performed by XGrabKeyboard or XGrab-Key.

```
XUngrabKeyboard(display, time)
    Display *display;
    Time time;
```

XUngrabPointer

Release the pointer from an active grab performed by XGrabPointer, XGrabButton, or a normal button press.

```
XUngrabPointer(display, time)
    Display *display;
    Time time;
```

XUngrabServer

Release the server from a grab and begin execution of all requests queued during the grab. This funtion is called automatically when a client closes its connection.

```
XUngrabServer(display)
    Display *display;
```

XUninstallColormap

Uninstall a colormap; install default if not already installed.

```
XUninstallColormap(display, cmap)
    Display *display;
    Colormap cmap;
```

XUnionRectWithRegion

Add a rectangle to a region by computing the union of the specified rectangle and region, and returning the resulting region in *dest_region*.

```
XUnionRectWithRegion(rectangle, src_region, dest_region)
    XRectangle *rectangle;
    Region src_region;
    Region dest_region;                    /* may be same as src */
```

XUnionRegion

Compute the union of two regions, returning resulting region in *dr*.

```
XUnionRegion(sra, srb, dr)
    Region sra, srb;
    Region dr;                             /* returns result */
```

XUniqueContext

Create a new context ID that can be used in subsequent calls to XFindContext, XDeleteContext, and XSaveContext.

```
XContext XUniqueContext()
```

XUnloadFont

Unload a font.

```
XUnloadFont(display, font)
    Display *display;
    Font font;
```

XUnmapSubwindows

Unmap all subwindows of a given window, in bottom-to-top stacking order.

```
XUnmapSubwindows(display, w)
    Display *display;
    Window w;
```

XUnsetICFocus

Unset input context focus—allow a client to notify an input method that the specified input context has lost the keyboard focus and no more input is expected on the focus window attached to that input context. (New in R5.)

```
void XUnsetICFocus(ic)
    XIC ic;
```

XUnmapWindow

Unmap a window. Descendants of the window are removed from the screen but not unmapped, and remain invisible until the window is remapped.

```
XUnmapWindow(display, w)
    Display *display;
    Window w;
```

XVaCreateNestedList

Allocate a nested variable argument list. The arguments consist of an unused (but required) integer value, followed by a NULL-terminated variable length argument list. Generally, the arguments will be input method or input context attribute name/value pairs. (New in R5.)

```
XVaNestedList XVaCreateNestedList(dummy, ...)
    int dummy;                      /* unused argument (required by ANSI C) */
    ...;                            /* variable length argument list */
```

XVisualIDFromVisual

Returns the ID of the server resource associated with a visual structure. This is useful when storing standard colormap properties. This macro is a shortcut for the identically named function, XVisualIDFromVisual.

```
VisualID XVisualIDFromVisual(visual)
    Visual *visual;                 /* visual type whose visual ID to be returned */
```

XWarpPointer

Move the pointer to another point on the screen.

```
XWarpPointer(display, src_w, dest_w, src_x, src_y, src_width, src_height, dest_x, dest_y)
    Display *display;
    Window src_w, dest_w;           /* window ID or None */
    int src_x, src_y;
    unsigned int src_width, src_height;    /* size of src window */
    int dest_x, dest_y;
```

XwcDrawImageString

Draw internationalized wide-character image text. This function fills the destination rectangle with the background pixel defined in the GC, then paints the specified wide-character text with the foreground pixel.

```
void XwcDrawImageString(display, drawable, font_set, gc, x, y, string, num_wchars)
    Display *display;
    Drawable drawable;
    XFontSet font_set;
```

```
GC gc;
int x, y;                              /* starting position and baseline of text */
wchar_t *string;                       /* character string */
int num_wchars;                        /* number of characters in string argument */
```

XwcDrawString

Draw internationalized wide-character text, painting foreground pixels and leaving the background unmodified. (New in R5.)

```
void XwcDrawString(display, drawable, font_set, gc, x, y, string, num_wchars)
    Display *display;
    Drawable drawable;
    XFontSet font_set;
    GC gc;
    int x, y;                          /* starting position and baseline of text */
    wchar_t *string;                   /* character string */
    int num_wchars;                    /* number of characters in string argument */
```

XwcDrawText

Draw internationalized wide-character text using multiple font sets. This function allows complex spacing and font set shifts between wide-character text strings. (New in R5.)

```
void XwcDrawText(display, drawable, gc, x, y, items, nitems)
    Display *display;
    Drawable drawable;
    GC gc;
    int x, y;                          /* starting position and baseline of text */
    XwcTextItem *items;                /* number of text items in array */
    int nitems;                        /* array of text items */
```

XwcFreeStringList

Free memory allocated by XwcTextPropertyToTextList. (New in R5.)

```
void XwcFreeStringList(list)
    wchar_t **list;                    /* list of strings to be freed */
```

XwcLookupString

Obtain composed wide-character input from an input method. This function passes a KeyPress event to an input context, returns composed text, if any, in the encoding of the input context locale, and may also return a keysym corresponding to the KeyPress event. (New in R5.)

```
int XwcLookupString(ic, event, buffer_return, bytes_buffer, keysym_return, status_return)
  XIC ic;
  XKeyPressedEvent *event;        /* keypress event to be used */
  wchar_t *buffer_return;         /* returns wide-character string from input method */
  int wchars_buffer;             /* number of wide-characters in return buffer */
  KeySym *keysym_return;         /* returns KeySym if argument not NULL */
  Status *status_return;         /* returns value indicating kind of data returned */
```

The values returned in *status_return* are:

```
  XBufferOverflow                /* input string too large for buffer_return */
  XLookupNone                    /* No consistent input composed yet */
  XLookupChars                   /* Some input characters composed */
  XLookupKeySym                  /* KeySym returned instead of string */
  XLookupBoth                    /* Both KeySym and string returned */
```

XwcResetIC

Reset the state of an input context. (New in R5.)

```
wchar_t * XwcResetIC(ic)
  XIC ic;
```

XwcTextEscapement

Return the width in pixels of the specified wide-character string using the fonts
loaded for the specified font set. (New in R5.)

```
int XwcTextEscapement(font_set, string, num_wchars)
  XFontSet font_set;
  wchar_t *string;               /* character string */
  int num_wchars;                /* number of characters in string argument */
```

XwcTextExtents

Compute the size of a wide-character string. This function sets the components
of *overall_ink_return* and *overall_logical_return* to the bounding box of the string's
image and the overall logical bounding box of the string's image plus inter-line
and inter-character spacing. (New in R5.)

```
int XwcTextExtents(font_set, string, num_wchars, overall_ink_return,
           overall_logical_return)
  XFontSet font_set;
  wchar_t *string;               /* character string */
  int num_wchars;                /* number of characters in string argument */
  XRectangle *overall_ink_return;    /* returns overall ink dimensions */
  XRectangle *overall_logical_return; /* returns overall logical dimensions */
```

XwcTextListToTextProperty

Convert an internationalized wide-character text list to a text property structure. This function sets the specified XTextProperty value to a set of NULL-separated elements representing the concatenation of the specified list of NULL-terminated wide-character strings. (New in R5.)

```
int XwcTextListToTextProperty(display, list, count, style, text_prop_return)
    Display *display;
    wchar_t **list;                  /* array of NULL-terminated wide-character strings */
    int count;                       /* number of strings specified */
    XICCEncodingStyle style;         /* how property encoded */
    XTextProperty *text_prop_return; /* returns XTextProperty structure */
```

The possible return values of this function are:

```
#define    OXNoMemory            -1
#define    XLocaleNotSupported   -2
#define    XConverterNotFound    -3
```

XwcTextPerCharExtents

Obtain per-character measurements of an internationalized wide-character text string using the fonts loaded for the specific font set. *ink_array_return* and *logical_array_return* are arrays allocated by the caller. (New in R5.)

```
Status XwcTextPerCharExtents(font_set, string, num_wchars, ink_array_return,
               logical_array_return, array_size, num_chars_return, overall_ink_return,
               overall_logical_return)
    XFontSet font_set;
    wchar_t *string;                      /* character string */
    int num_wchars;                       /* number of characters in string argument */
    XRectangle *ink_array_return;         /* returns ink dimensions for each character; */
                                          /* allocated by caller */
    XRectangle *logical_array_return;     /* returns logical dimensions for each character */
    int array_size;                       /* size of ink_array_return and logical_array_return */
    int *num_chars_return;                /* returns number characters in string argument */
    XRectangle *overall_ink_return;       /* returns overall ink extents of entire string */
    XRectangle *overall_logical_return;   /* returns overall logical extents of entire string */
```

XwcTextPropertyToTextList

Convert an internationalized text property to a list of wide-character strings. This function returns a list of wide-character text strings encoded in the current locale representing the NULL-separated elements of the specified XTextProperty structure. The data in *text_prop* must be format 8. (New in R5.)

```
int XwcTextPropertyToTextList(display, text_prop, list_return, count_return)
    Display *display;
    XTextProperty *text_prop;        /* XTextProperty structure to be used */
```

```
wchar_t ***list_return;          /* returns list of NULL-terminated character strings */
int *count_return;               /* returns number of strings */
```

The possible return values of this function are:

```
#define     XNoMemory              -1
#define     XLocaleNotSupported    -2
#define     XConverterNotFound     -3
```

XWindowEvent

Remove the next event that matches the specified mask and window.

```
XWindowEvent(display, w, event_mask, rep)
    Display *display;
    Window w;
    long event_mask;             /* see Section 3 */
    XEvent *rep;                 /* returns event removed from queue */
```

XWithdrawWindow

Request that a top-level window be withdrawn. This function unmaps the specified window and sends a synthetic UnMapNotify event to the root window of the specified screen.

```
Status XWithdrawWindow(display, w, screen_number)
    Display *display;
    Window w;
    int screen_number;
```

XWMGeometry

Obtain a window's geometry information.

```
int XWMGeometry(display, screen, user_geom, def_geom, bwidth, hints, x, y, width, height,
                gravity)
    Display *display;
    int screen;
    char *user_geom;             /* NULL, or user-specified geometry */
    char *def_geom;              /* NULL, or application's default geometry */
    unsigned int bwidth;         /* border width */
    XSizeHints *hints;           /* size hints for window in its normal state */


    int *x, *y;                  /* returns computed window position */
    int *width, *height;         /* returns computed window size, in pixels */
    int *gravity;                /* returns window gravity */
```

XWriteBitmapFile

Write a bitmap to a file. See XReadBitmapFile for return codes.

```
int XWriteBitmapFile(display, filename, bitmap, width, height, x_hot, y_hot)
    Display *display;
    char *filename;
    Pixmap bitmap;
    unsigned int width, height;
    int x_hot, y_hot;                      /* hotspot; or –1; –1 for none */
```

XXorRegion

Calculate the difference between the union and intersection of two regions. Xor is short for "ExclusiveOr", meaning that a pixel is included in *dr* if it is set in either *sra* or *srb* but not both.

```
XXorRegion(sra, srb, dr)
    Region sra, srb;
    Region dr;                             /* returns result */
```

2
Xlib Data Types

This section lists all public Xlib structure definitions in *<X11/Xlib.h>*, *<X11/Xutil.h>*, *<X11/Xresource.h>*, and *<X11/Xcms.h>* as well as various other typedefs and defined symbols from *<X11/X.h>*.

Our objective was to list every special X data type that is used as an argument or return value to an Xlib function, or as a member of another structure. The only exception is the event structures, which are listed in Section 3, *Events*.

The Xlib data types are listed in alphabetical order. The section also lists any defined symbols or other special values used in conjunction with particular members in each structure. Wherever possible, these values are described together with the structure in which they are used. If a value is used in more than one structure, a cross-reference may be provided rather than a complete listing. The actual values for defined constants are given, as well as their symbolic names, to aid in debugging.

Unlike Xt, which uses typedefs for every possible argument type to maximize portability, various Xlib calls use masks as arguments, which are simply defined as an unsigned long. In cases where these masks identify which elements in a particular structure are to be read, the symbols that are ORed into the mask are described in this section along with the structure they affect. Masks that aren't associated with a structure or any other data type in this section are described in Section 1, *Xlib Functions and Macros*, along with the Xlib function in which they appear. Also included in this section are the Xcms function prototypes.

The names of opaque internal structures begin with an underscore (_). They are not described here.

Unless otherwise noted, the data types described in this section are defined in *<X11/Xlib.h>*.

Atom

A unique numeric ID corresponding to a string, such as the name of a property, type, or selection. Atoms are used in order to avoid the overhead of passing arbitrary-length strings between clients and the server. An Atom is defined in <XI1/X.h> as an unsigned long; individual standard atoms are defined in <XI1/Xatom.h> using defined symbols beginning with XA_. For example:

```
#define XA_PRIMARY          ((Atom) 1)
#define XA_SECONDARY        ((Atom) 2)
```

These atoms are listed below, in abbreviated form:

PRIMARY	1	RGB_COLOR_MAP	24
SECONDARY	2	RGB_BEST_MAP	25
ARC	3	RGB_BLUE_MAP	26
ATOM	4	RGB_DEFAULT_MAP	27
BITMAP	5	RGB_GRAY_MAP	28
CARDINAL	6	RGB_GREEN_MAP	29
COLORMAP	7	RGB_RED_MAP	30
CURSOR	8	STRING	31
CUT_BUFFER0	9	VISUALID	32
CUT_BUFFER1	10	WINDOW	33
CUT_BUFFER2	11	WM_COMMAND	34
CUT_BUFFER3	12	WM_HINTS	35
CUT_BUFFER4	13	WM_CLIENT_MACHINE	36
CUT_BUFFER5	14	WM_ICON_NAME	37
CUT_BUFFER6	15	WM_ICON_SIZE	38
CUT_BUFFER7	16	WM_NAME	39
DRAWABLE	17	WM_NORMAL_HINTS	40
FONT	18	WM_SIZE_HINTS	41
INTEGER	19	WM_ZOOM_HINTS	42
PIXMAP	20	MIN_SPACE	43
POINT	21	NORM_SPACE	44
RECTANGLE	22	MAX_SPACE	45
RESOURCE_MANAGER	23	END_SPACE	46
SUPERSCRIPT_X	47	POINT_SIZE	59
SUPERSCRIPT_Y	48	RESOLUTION	60
SUBSCRIPT_X	49	COPYRIGHT	61
SUBSCRIPT_Y	50	NOTICE	62
UNDERLINE_POSITION	51	FONT_NAME	63
UNDERLINE_THICKNESS	52	FAMILY_NAME	64
STRIKEOUT_ASCENT	53	FULL_NAME	65
STRIKEOUT_DESCENT	54	CAP_HEIGHT	66
ITALIC_ANGLE	55	WM_CLASS	67
X_HEIGHT	56	WM_TRANSIENT_FOR	68

Non-standard atoms can be obtained from the server by calling the Xlib function XInternAtom. The Xmu library supports an atom-caching mechanism to reduce the number of XInternAtom calls that may be required.

Bool

A Boolean value (defined as an int in *<X11/Xlib.h>*). Use the values False (0) and True (1).

Colormap

A server-maintained structure that maps pixel values to RGB values. There is at least one hardware colormap, and additional virtual colormaps. A Colormap is identified in Xlib functions by an XID value returned by the server in response to a call to XCreateColormap. (A Colormap is a typedef in *X.h* for an XID, which, in the standard MIT X distribution at least, is in turn a typedef for an unsigned long.)

Cursor

An XID (server resource ID) that identifies a cursor resource (hardware or software) maintained by the server. A Cursor can be returned from any of the calls XCreateFontCursor (which creates a cursor from the set of standard cursors contained in the cursor font), XCreateGlyphCursor (which creates a cursor from any other font glyph), or XCreatePixmapCursor (which creates a cursor from a bitmap image). The returned cursor is assigned to a window with XDefineCursor.

Depth

Defines a valid depth (number of planes) and list of associated visuals. A list of these structures is contained in the Screen structure, which is itself a member of the Display structure. Not used directly in any Xlib function. This structure should not be accessed directly, but instead through XGetVisualInfo and XMatchVisualInfo.

```
typedef struct {
    int depth;              /* number of planes */
    int nvisuals;           /* number of Visual classes at this depth */
    Visual *visuals;        /* list of Visuals possible at this depth */
} Depth;
```

Display

Describes the connection to the X server. A pointer to a structure of this type is returned by XOpenDisplay and is subsequently the first argument to nearly every Xlib routine. Macros are provided to access most members of this structure.

```
typedef struct _XDisplay {
    XExtData *ext_data;                    /* hook for extension to hang data */
    struct _XDisplay *next;                /* next open Display on list */
    int fd;                                /* network socket */
    int lock;                              /* is someone in critical section? */
    int proto_major_version;               /* major version of server's X protocol */
    int proto_minor_version;               /* minor version of server's X protocol */
    char *vendor;                          /* vendor of the server hardware */
    long resource_base;                    /* resource ID base */
    long resource_mask;                    /* resource ID mask bits */
    long resource_id;                      /* allocator current ID */
    int resource_shift;                    /* allocator shift to correct bits */
    XID (*resource_alloc)();               /* allocator function */
    int byte_order;                        /* screen byte order, LSBFirst, MSBFirst */
    int bitmap_unit;                       /* padding and data requirements */
    int bitmap_pad;                        /* padding requirements on bitmaps */
    int bitmap_bit_order;                  /* LeastSignificant or MostSignificant */
    int nformats;                          /* number of pixmap formats in list */
    ScreenFormat *pixmap_format;           /* pixmap format list */
    int vnumber;                           /* Xlib's X protocol version number */
    int release;                           /* release of the server */
    struct _XSQEvent *head, *tail;         /* input event queue */
    int qlen;                              /* length of input event queue */
    int last_request_read;                 /* sequence number of last event read */
    int request;                           /* sequence number of last request */
    char *last_req;                        /* beginning of last request, or dummy */
    char *buffer;                          /* request buffer starting address */
    char *bufptr;                          /* request buffer index pointer */
    char *bufmax;                          /* request buffer maximum+1 address */
    unsigned max_request_size;             /* maximum number 32 bit words in request */
    struct _XrmHashBucketRec *db;
    int (*synchandler)();                  /* synchronization handler */
    char *display_name;                    /* "host:display" string used on this connect */
    int default_screen;                    /* default screen for operations */
    int nscreens;                          /* number of screens on this server */
    Screen *screens;                       /* pointer to list of screens */
    int motion_buffer;                     /* size of motion buffer */
    Window current;                        /* for use internally for Keymap notify */
    int min_keycode;                       /* minimum defined keycode */
    int max_keycode;                       /* maximum defined keycode */
    KeySym *keysyms;                       /* this server's keysyms */
    XModifierKeymap *modifiermap;          /* this server's modifier keymap */
    int keysyms_per_keycode;               /* number of rows */
    char *xdefaults;                       /* contents of defaults from server */
    char *scratch_buffer;                  /* place to hang scratch buffer */
    unsigned long scratch_length;          /* length of scratch buffer */
    int ext_number;                        /* extension number on this display */
    _XExtension *ext_procs;                /* extensions initialized on this display */
```

```
        Bool (*event_vec[128])();       /* vector for wire to event */
        Status (*wire_vec[128])();      /* vector for event to wire */
} Display;
```

Drawable

An XID (server resource ID) returned by the server to identify a window or pix-map that has been allocated for drawing via a call to XCreateWindow or XCreatePix-map.

Font

An XID (server resource ID) returned by the server in response to a call to XLoad-Font. Once a font has been loaded, it is referred to by its Font ID.

GC

Describes a graphics context. A pointer to a structure of this type is returned by XCreateGC and subsequently used in all routines that draw or modify the GC. The members of this structure must not be accessed directly.

```
typedef struct _XGC {
        XExtData *ext_data;       /* hook for extension to hang data */
        GContext gid;             /* protocol ID for graphics context */
        Bool rects;               /* Boolean; TRUE if clipmask is list of rectangles */
        Bool dashes;              /* Boolean; TRUE if dash-list is really a list */
        unsigned long dirty;      /* cache dirty bits */
        XGCValues values;         /* shadow structure of values */
} *GC;
```

GContext

An XID that identifies a unique graphics context. Used as part of the GC structure.

KeyCode

A value in the range 8-255, inclusive, that represents a physical or logical key on the keyboard. The mapping between keys and keycodes is defined for each server, and cannot be changed. KeyCode is a typedef from <X11/X.h> for an unsigned char. The KeyCodes returned in KeyPress and KeyRelease events should be translated into KeySyms with XLookupString or XLookupKeySym.

KeySym

A portable representation of the symbol on the cap of a key. Individual KeySyms are symbols defined in <X11/keysymdef.h>. The keycode-to-keysym lookup tables are maintained by the server, and hence a KeySym is actually an XID, which is returned for a given KeyCode via a call to XLookupString or XLookupKeyCode. The special keysym NoSymbol is sometimes used as a placeholder for any keysym.

Xlib Data Types

Pixmap

An XID (server resource ID) returned by a call to XCreatePixmap and representing a two-dimensional array of pixels—a drawable with a specified width, height, and depth (number of planes), but no screen coordinates. The contents of a Pixmap are initially undefined, but can be drawn into with subsequent Xlib calls. A Pixmap can be displayed by copying it into a Window.

Region

An arbitrary area of the screen, independent of any drawable.

```
/*
 * opaque reference to Region data type
 */
typedef struct _XRegion *Region;
```

Screen

Describes the characteristics of a screen. Each Display structure has a member that points to a list of Screen structures. A pointer to a structure of this type is returned by XGetWindowAttributes. Macros are provided to access most members of this structure.

```
typedef struct {
    XExtData *ext_data;         /* hook for extension to hang data */
    struct _XDisplay *display;  /* back pointer to display structure */
    Window root;                /* root window ID */
    int width, height;          /* width and height of screen */
    int mwidth, mheight;        /* width and height of in millimeters */
    int ndepths;                /* number of depths possible */
    Depth *depths;              /* list of allowable depths on the screen */
    int root_depth;             /* bits per pixel */
    Visual *root_visual;        /* root visual */
    GC default_gc;              /* GC for the root root visual */
    Colormap cmap;              /* default colormap */
    unsigned long white_pixel;
    unsigned long black_pixel;  /* white and black pixel values */
    int max_maps, min_maps;     /* max and min colormaps */
    int backing_store;          /* NotUseful, WhenMapped, Always */
    Bool save_unders;           /* should bits under popups be saved */
    long root_input_mask;       /* initial root input mask */
} Screen;
```

ScreenFormat

A member of the Display structure. This structure is used internally for image operations. It is not used as an argument to or returned by any Xlib function. Macros are provided to access the members of this structure.

```
typedef struct {
    XExtData *ext_data;          /* hook for extension to hang data */
    int depth;                   /* depth of this image format */
    int bits_per_pixel;          /* bits/pixel at this depth */
    int scanline_pad;            /* scan line must be padded to this multiple */
} ScreenFormat;
```

Status

A value (defined as an int in <X11/Xlib.h>) that is used as the return value of a function. Status is 0 on failure, 1 (or in some cases, any non-zero value) on success.

Time

An unsigned long value representing the time in milliseconds since the last server reset, or the constant CurrentTime, which is used by clients to represent the current server time, and which is defined as follows in <X11/X.h>:

```
#define CurrentTime          0L      /* special Time */
```

Vertex

Used in XDraw and XDrawFilled.

```
typedef struct {
    short x, y;                  /* position */
    unsigned short flags;        /* constants defined below */
} Vertex;
```

This typedef, along with the following values for the flags member, is defined in <X11/X10.h>. If the bit is 1, then the predicate is true.

```
#define VertexRelative          0x0001     /* else absolute */
#define VertexDontDraw          0x0002     /* else draw */
#define VertexCurved            0x0004     /* else straight */
#define VertexStartClosed       0x0008     /* else not */
#define VertexEndClosed         0x0010     /* else not */
/* #define VertexDrawLastPoint  0x0020 */  /* else don't */
```

The VertexDrawLastPoint symbol has not been implemented in XDraw and XDrawFilled, so it shouldn't be defined.

Visual

Describes a way of using color on a particular screen. A pointer to a visual structure is an argument to XCreateColormap, XCreateImage, and XCreateWindow. The valid visual structures for a screen can be determined with XGetVisualInfo or XMatchVisualInfo or with the DefaultVisual(screen) macro. The visual used to create a window is returned by XGetWindowAttributes.

```
typedef struct {
    XExtData *ext_data;          /* hook for extension to hang data */
```

```
VisualID visualid;              /* visual ID of this visual */
int class;                      /* class of screen (PseudoColor, etc.) */
unsigned long red_mask;         /* TrueColor, DirectColor only */
unsigned long green_mask;       /* TrueColor, DirectColor only */
unsigned long blue_mask;        /* TrueColor, DirectColor only */
int bits_per_rgb;               /* log base 2 of distinct color values */
int map_entries;                /* number of colormap entries */
} Visual;
```

VisualID

An unsigned long that is used to uniquely identify a given visual class. Possible values are given by the following constants defined in <X11/X.h>:

```
#define StaticGray      0
#define GrayScale       1
#define StaticColor     2
#define PseudoColor     3
#define TrueColor       4
#define DirectColor     5
```

Note that the statically allocated visual classes are even-numbered and the dynamically changeable ones are odd-numbered.

wchar_t

The "wide character" type used in internationalization. It is not an X datatype; it is required by ANSI-C, and is generally defined in <stdlib.h>. (New in R5.)

Window

An XID (server resource ID) returned by XCreateWindow or XCreateSimpleWindow to identify a newly-created window, and used thereafter in any Xlib calls that perform operations on that window.

XArc

Specifies the bounding box for an arc and two angles in 64ths of a degree, with the 3 o'clock position at 0, indicating the extent of the arc within the box. A list of these structures is used in XDrawArcs and XFillArcs.

```
typedef struct {
    short x, y;
    unsigned short width, height;
    short angle1, angle2;       /* 64ths of a degree */
} XArc;
```

XAssoc

Associations used in the XAssocTable structure. The associations are used as circular queue entries in the association table, which contains an array of circular queues (buckets). XAssoc is defined as follows in <X11/X10.h>:

```
typedef struct _XAssoc {
    struct _XAssoc *next;          /* next object in this bucket */
    struct _XAssoc *prev;          /* previous object in this bucket */
    Display *display;              /* display which owns the ID */
    XID x_id;                      /* X Window System ID */
    char *data;                    /* pointer to untyped memory */
} XAssoc;
```

XAssocTable

A structure defined in <*X11/X10.h*> and used only in the compatibility routines XCreateAssocTable, XMakeAssoc, XLookupAssoc, XDeleteAssoc, and XDestroyAssocTable. Association tables make it possible to associate pointers to your own data structures with X resource IDs (XIDs), for fast lookup.

An XAssocTable is a hash table whose buckets are circular queues of XAssocs. It is constructed from an array of XAssocs, which are the circular queue headers (bucket headers).

```
typedef struct {
    XAssoc *buckets;               /* pointer to first bucket in bucket array */
    int size;                      /* table size (number of buckets) */
} XAssocTable;
```

XChar2b

Specifies a character in a two-byte font. A list of structures of this type is an argument to XDrawImageString16, XDrawString16, XDrawText16, XQueryTextExtents16, XTextExtents16, and XTextWidth16. The only two-byte font currently available is Kanji (Japanese).

```
typedef struct {                   /* normal 16 bit characters are two bytes */
    unsigned char byte1;
    unsigned char byte2;
} XChar2b;
```

XCharStruct

Describes the metrics (in pixels) of a single character in a font or the overall characteristics of a font. This structure is used to return the overall characteristics of a string in XQueryTextExtents, XQueryTextExtents16, XTextExtents, and XTextExtents16.

```
typedef struct {
    short lbearing;                /* origin to left edge of raster */
    short rbearing;                /* origin to right edge of raster */
    short width;                   /* advance to next char's origin */
    short ascent;                  /* baseline to top edge of raster */
    short descent;                 /* baseline to bottom edge of raster */
    unsigned short attributes;     /* per char flags (not predefined) */
} XCharStruct;
```

The meaning of the various members in an XCharStruct and XFontStruct are illustrated below:

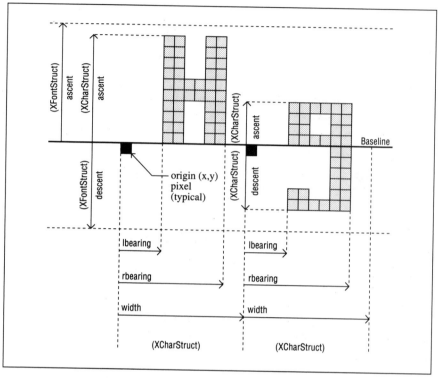

XClassHint

A structure defined in *<X11/Xutil.h>* used to set or get the XA_WM_CLASS property for an application's top-level window, as arguments to XSetClassHint or XGetClassHint. The structure holds the application's name and class, to be used when retrieving the application's resources from the resource database.

```
typedef struct {
    char *res_name;              /* application name */
    char *res_class;             /* application class */
} XClassHint;
```

XcmsCCC

A color conversion context used to control the details of device-independent color conversions. It is an opaque type created by XcmsCreateCCC. There are Xcms functions to get and set the values of each field of an XcmsCCC. (New in R5.)

XcmsCIELab

Describes a color in the CIE L*a*b* color space. (New in R5.)

```
typedef double XcmsFloat;
typedef struct {
    XcmsFloat L_star;              */0.0 to 100.0 */
    XcmsFloat a_star;
    XcmsFloat b_star;
} XcmsCIELab;                      /* CIE L*a*b* */
```

XcmsCIELuv

Describes a color in the CIE L*u*v* color space.

```
typedef double XcmsFloat;
typedef struct {
    XcmsFloat L_star;              /* 0.0 to 100.0 */
    XcmsFloat u_star;
    XcmsFloat v_star;
} XcmsCIELuv;                      /* CIE L*u*v* */
```

XcmsCIEuvY

Describes a color in the CIE u'v'Y color space. (New in R5.)

```
typedef double XcmsFloat;
typedef struct {
    XcmsFloat u_prime;            /* 0.0 to ~0.6 */
    XcmsFloat v_prime;            /* 0.0 to ~0.6 */
    XcmsFloat Y;                  /* 0.0 to 1.0 */
} XcmsCIEuvY;                     /* CIE u'v'Y */
```

XcmsCIExyY

Describes a color in the CIE xyY space. (New in R5.)

```
typedef double XcmsFloat;
typedef struct {
    XcmsFloat x;                  /* 0.0 to ~.75 */
    XcmsFloat y;                  /* 0.0 to ~.85 */
    XcmsFloat Y;                  /* 0.0 to 1.0 */
} XcmsCIExyY;                     /* CIE xyY */
```

XcmsCIEXYZ

Describes a color in the CIE XYZ color space. (New in R5.)

```
typedef double XcmsFloat;
typedef struct {
    XcmsFloat X;
    XcmsFloat Y;                  /* 0.0 to 1.0 */
```

```
        XcmsFloat Z;
} XcmsCIEXYZ;                        /* CIE XYZ */
```

XcmsColor

A union of substructures, each of which describes a color in a particular color space. The XcmsColor structure contains:

```
typedef unsigned long XcmsColorFormat;      /* Color Specification Format */

#define XcmsUndefinedFormat            (XcmsColorFormat)0x00000000
#define XcmsCIEXYZFormat               (XcmsColorFormat)0x00000001
#define XcmsCIEuvYFormat               (XcmsColorFormat)0x00000002
#define XcmsCIExyYFormat               (XcmsColorFormat)0x00000003
#define XcmsCIELabFormat               (XcmsColorFormat)0x00000004
#define XcmsCIELuvFormat               (XcmsColorFormat)0x00000005
#define XcmsTekHVCFormat               (XcmsColorFormat)0x00000006
#define XcmsRGBFormat                  (XcmsColorFormat)0x80000000
#define XcmsRGBiFormat                 (XcmsColorFormat)0x80000001

typedef struct {
        union {
                XcmsRGB RGB;
                XcmsRGBi RGBi;
                XcmsCIEXYZ CIEXYZ;
                XcmsCIEuvY CIEuvY;
                XcmsCIExyY CIExyY;
                XcmsCIELab CIELab;
                XcmsCIELuv CIELuv;
                XcmsTekHVC TekHVC;
                XcmsPad Pad;
        } spec;
        XcmsColorFormat format;
        unsigned long pixel;
} XcmsColor;         /* Xcms Color Structure */
```

XcmsCompressionProc

Interface definition for gamut compression procedure. (New in R5.)

```
typedef Status (*XcmsCompressionProc)(ccc, colors_in_out, ncolors, index, compression_flags_return)
        XcmsCCC ccc;                     /* conversion color context */
        XcmsColor colors_in_out[ ];      /* array of color specifications */
        unsigned int ncolors;            /* number of XcmsColor structures in color specification array */
        unsigned int index;              /* index for color specification lying outside color gamut */
        Bool compression_flags_return[ ]; /* array of Boolean values for returned color compression info */
```

XcmsPad

Supports color specification for future or user-defined color spaces. (New in R5.)

```
typedef double XcmsFloat;
typedef struct {
    XcmsFloat pad0;
    XcmsFloat pad1;
    XcmsFloat pad2;
    XcmsFloat pad3;
} XcmsPad;                        /* space reserved for future or user-defined color spaces */
```

XcmsRGB

Describes a color in the RGB device-dependent color space. (New in R5.)

```
typedef double XcmsFloat;
typedef struct {
    unsigned short red;           /* 0x0000 to 0xffff */
    unsigned short green;         /* 0x0000 to 0xffff */
    unsigned short blue;          /* 0x0000 to 0xffff */
} XcmsRGB;                        /* RGB Device */
```

XcmsRGBi

Describes a color in the RGBi device-dependent color space. (New in R5.)

```
typedef double XcmsFloat;
typedef struct {
    XcmsFloat red;                /* 0.0 to 1.0 */
    XcmsFloat green;              /* 0.0 to 1.0 */
    XcmsFloat blue;              /* 0.0 to 1.0 */
} XcmsRGBi;                       /* RGB Intensity */
```

XcmsScreenFreeProc

Software interface specification for the screen free callback. (New in R5.)

```
typedef void (*XcmsScreenFreeProc)(screenData)
    XPointer screenData;          /* data to be freed */
```

XcmsScreenInitProc

Interface specification for the screen initialization callback. (New in R5.)

```
typedef Status (*XcmsScreenInitProc)(display, screen_number, screen_info)
    Display *display;
    int screen_number;            /* appropriate screen number on host server */
    XcmsPerScrnInfo *screen_info; /* XcmsPerScrnInfo structure */
```

XcmsSetCompressionProc

Set the gamut compression procedure and corresponding client data in a specified conversion color context. (New in R5.)

```
XcmsCompressionProc XcmsSetCompressionProc(ccc, compression_proc, client_data)
    XcmsCCC ccc;                              /* conversion color context */
    XcmsCompressionProc compression_proc;  /* compression procedure to be applied */
    XPointer client_data;                    /* client data for compression procedure */
```

XcmsSetWhiteAdjustProc

Interface definition for white point adjustment procedure of a conversion color context. (New in R5.)

```
XcmsWhiteAdjustProc XcmsSetWhiteAdjustProc(ccc, white_adjust_proc, client_data)
    XcmsCCC ccc;                            /* conversion color context */
    XcmsWhiteAdjustProc white_adjust_proc;  /* white point adjustment procedure */
    XPointer client_data;                   /* client data for white point adjustment procedure */
```

XColor

Describes a single colorcell. This structure is used to specify and return the pixel value and RGB values for a colorcell. The flags indicate which of the RGB values should be changed when used in XStoreColors, XAllocNamedColor, or XAlloc-Color. Also used in XCreateGlyphCursor, XCreatePixmapCursor, XLookupColor, XParseColor, XQueryColor, XQueryColors, and XRecolorCursor.

```
typedef struct {
    unsigned long pixel;
    unsigned short red, green, blue;
    char flags;                  /* which members contain valid values */
    char pad;                    /* pad to even word boundary; unused */
} XColor;
```

The flags member is constructed as a bitwise OR of the following symbols, which are defined in <X11/X.h>:

```
#define DoRed              (1<<0)
#define DoGreen            (1<<1)
#define DoBlue             (1<<2)
```

XComposeStatus

A structure defined in <X11/Xutil.h> that describes the current state of a multikey character sequence. Used in calling XLookupString.

```
typedef struct _XComposeStatus {
    char *compose_ptr;           /* state table pointer */
    int chars_matched;           /* match state */
} XComposeStatus;
```

XContext

An integer value (a quark, actually) returned by a call to XUniqueContext and used to identify a unique context type. Xlib context manager routines allow a client to maintain a set of data relative to a window and a locally-defined context type.

XEvent

A union of the 30 event structures. See Section 3, *Events*, for details on the individual event structures. However, note that the first member of each event structure is the type, which you can switch on to find the actual event type. The valid event types are identified by the following symbols defined in *<X11/X.h>*:

```
#define KeyPress           2
#define KeyRelease         3
#define ButtonPress        4
#define ButtonRelease      5
#define MotionNotify       6
#define EnterNotify        7
#define LeaveNotify        8
#define FocusIn            9
#define FocusOut           10
#define KeymapNotify       11
#define Expose             12
#define GraphicsExpose     13
#define NoExpose           14
#define VisibilityNotify   15
#define CreateNotify       16
#define DestroyNotify      17
#define UnmapNotify        18
#define MapNotify          19
#define MapRequest         20
#define ReparentNotify     21
#define ConfigureNotify    22
#define ConfigureRequest   23
#define GravityNotify      24
#define ResizeRequest      25
#define CirculateNotify    26
#define CirculateRequest   27
#define PropertyNotify     28
#define SelectionClear     29
#define SelectionRequest   30
#define SelectionNotify    31
#define ColormapNotify     32
#define ClientMessage      33
#define MappingNotify      34
#define LASTEvent          35    /* must be bigger than any event # */
```

Note that numbering of event types starts at 2, since 0 and 1 are reserved in the X Protocol for errors and replies. Also, be sure not to confuse these event type symbols with the event mask symbols used to select events in the XSetWindowAttributes structure.

XExtCodes

Is a structure used by the extension mechanism. This structure is returned by XInitExtension, which is not a standard Xlib routine but should be called within the extension code. Its contents are not normally accessible to the application.

```
typedef struct {                       /* public to extension, cannot be changed */
    int extension;                     /* extension number */
    int major_opcode;                  /* major opcode assigned by server */
    int first_event;                   /* first event number for the extension */
    int first_error;                   /* first error number for the extension */
} XExtCodes;
```

XExtData

Provides a way for extensions to attach private data to the existing structure types GC, Visual, Screen, Display, and XFontStruct. This structure is not used in normal Xlib programming.

```
typedef struct _XExtData {
    int number;                        /* number returned by XRegisterExtension */
    struct _XExtData *next;            /* next item on list of data for structure */
    int (*free_private)();             /* called to free private storage */
    char *private_data;                /* data private to this extension */
} XExtData;
```

XFontProp

Is used in XFontStruct. This structure allows the application to find out the names of additional font properties beyond the predefined set, so that they too can be accessed with XGetFontProperty. This structure is not used as an argument or return value for any core Xlib function.

```
typedef struct {
    Atom name;
    unsigned long card32;
} XFontProp;
```

XFontSet

An abstraction that is used in internationalized applications. (New in R5.) R5 bases its new text output routines on XFontSet rather than XFontStruct. An XFontSet is bound to the locale in which it is created, and contains all the fonts needed to display text in that locale. Font sets are created with a call to XCreateFontSet. The following routines also use or operate on font sets:

XFreeFontSet	/* frees an XFontSet */
XFontsOfFontSet	/* returns the list of XFontStructs and font names */
	/* associated with an XFontSet */
XBaseFontNameListOfFontSet	/* returns string containing base font name list for FontSet */
XLocaleOfFontSet	/* returns name of XFontSet locale */

XFontSetExtents

Describes the bounding box of the largest glyph in an XFontSet. Returned by XExtentsOfFontSet. (New in R5.)

```
typedef struct {
    XRectangle max_ink_extent;      /*over all drawable characters*/
    XRectangle max_logical_extent;  /*over all drawable characters*/
} XFontSetExtents;
```

XFontStruct

Specifies metric information (in pixels) for an entire font. This structure is filled with the XLoadQueryFont and XQueryFont routines. XListFontsWithInfo also fills it, but with metric information for the entire font only, not for each character. A pointer to this structure is used in the routines XFreeFont, XFreeFontInfo, XGetFontProp, XTextExtents, XTextExtents16, XTextWidth, and XTextWidth16. See XCharStruct for more information on individual members.

```
typedef struct {
    XExtData *ext_data;              /* hook for extension to hang data */
    Font fid;                        /* font ID for this font */
    unsigned direction;              /* direction the font is painted */
    unsigned min_char_or_byte2;      /* first character */
    unsigned max_char_or_byte2;      /* last character */
    unsigned min_byte1;              /* first row that exists */
    unsigned max_byte1;              /* last row that exists */
    Bool all_chars_exist;            /* flag if all characters have nonzero size*/
    unsigned default_char;           /* char to print for undefined character */
    int n_properties;                /* how many properties there are */
    XFontProp *properties;           /* pointer to array of additional properties*/
    XCharStruct min_bounds;          /* minimum bounds over all existing char*/
    XCharStruct max_bounds;          /* maximum bounds over all existing char*/
    XCharStruct *per_char;           /* first_char to last_char information */
    int ascent;                      /* logical extent of largest character above baseline */
    int descent;                     /* logical descent of largest character below baseline */
} XFontStruct;
```

The direction member is specified with one of the following constants defined in <X11/X.h>:

```
#define FontLeftToRight          0
#define FontRightToLeft          1

#define FontChange             255
```

XGCValues

Is used to set or change members of the GC by the routines XCreateGC and XChangeGC. In cases where alternate values are shown in the comments, the symbol in boldface type is the default. The various values are explained further and illustrated on the following pages.

```
typedef struct {
    int function;               /* logical operation, default GXcopy */
    unsigned long plane_mask;   /* plane mask */
    unsigned long foreground;   /* foreground pixel, default 1 */
    unsigned long background;   /* background pixel, default 0 */
    int line_width;             /* line width, default 0 */
    int line_style;             /* LineSolid, LineOnOffDash, LineDoubleDash */
    int cap_style;              /* CapNotLast, CapButt, CapRound, CapProjecting */
    int join_style;             /* JoinMiter, JoinRound, JoinBevel */
    int fill_style;             /* FillSolid, FillTiled, FillStippled */
    int fill_rule;              /* EvenOddRule, WindingRule */
    int arc_mode;               /* ArcPieSlice, ArcChord */
    Pixmap tile;                /* tile pixmap for tiling operations */
    Pixmap stipple;             /* stipple 1 plane pixmap for stippling */
    int ts_x_origin;            /* offset for tile or stipple operations */
    int ts_y_origin;            /* default for both is 0 */
    Font font;                  /* default text font for text operations */
    int subwindow_mode;         /* ClipByChildren, IncludeInferiors */
    Bool graphics_exposures;    /* should exposures be generated, default True */
    int clip_x_origin;          /* origin for clipping */
    int clip_y_origin;          /* default for both is 0 */
    Pixmap clip_mask;           /* bitmap clipping; other calls for rects */
    int dash_offset;            /* starting point for patterned/dashed lines */
    char dashes;                /* dash length; see explanation below */
} XGCValues;
```

In calls to XCreateGC and XChangeGC, there is also a *valuemask* argument, which specifies which members in the XGCValues structure are to be used. The *valuemask* is a bitwise OR of the following symbols, which are defined in <X11/X.h>:

```
#define GCFunction              (1L<<0)
#define GCPlaneMask             (1L<<1)
#define GCForeground            (1L<<2)
```

```
#define GCBackground            (1L<<3)
#define GCLineWidth             (1L<<4)
#define GCLineStyle             (1L<<5)
#define GCCapStyle              (1L<<6)
#define GCJoinStyle             (1L<<7)
#define GCFillStyle             (1L<<8)
#define GCFillRule              (1L<<9)
#define GCTile                  (1L<<10)
#define GCStipple               (1L<<11)
#define GCTileStipXOrigin       (1L<<12)
#define GCTileStipYOrigin       (1L<<13)
#define GCFont                  (1L<<14)
#define GCSubwindowMode         (1L<<15)
#define GCGraphicsExposures     (1L<<16)
#define GCClipXOrigin           (1L<<17)
#define GCClipYOrigin           (1L<<18)
#define GCClipMask              (1L<<19)
#define GCDashOffset            (1L<<20)
#define GCDashList              (1L<<21)
```

Many of the GC members take values specified by symbols from *<X11/X.h>*. The definitions for these symbols are shown below. In some cases, their effects are illustrated immediately following the symbol definitions.

The function member specifies the logical function to be used for drawing:

```
#define GXclear         0x0     /* 0 */
#define GXand           0x1     /* src AND dst */
#define GXandReverse    0x2     /* src AND NOT dst */
#define GXcopy          0x3     /* src - this is the default */
#define GXandInverted   0x4     /* NOT src AND dst */
#define GXnoop          0x5     /* dst */
#define GXxor           0x6     /* src XOR dst */
#define GXor            0x7     /* src OR dst */
#define GXnor           0x8     /* NOT src AND NOT dst */
#define GXequiv         0x9     /* NOT src XOR dst */
#define GXinvert        0xa     /* NOT dst */
#define GXorReverse     0xb     /* src OR NOT dst */
#define GXcopyInverted  0xc     /* NOT src */
#define GXorInverted    0xd     /* NOT src OR dst */
#define GXnand          0xe     /* NOT src OR NOT dst */
#define GXset           0xf     /* 1 */
```

The line_style member specifies whether lines should be solid or dashed:

```
#define LineSolid       0       /* default */
#define LineOnOffDash   1       /* draw foreground dashes only */
#define LineDoubleDash  2       /* alternate dash and space in fg and bg colors */
```

The cap_style member specifies how endpoints of lines should be drawn:

```
#define CapNotLast          0
#define CapButt             1        /* default */
#define CapRound            2
#define CapProjecting       3
```

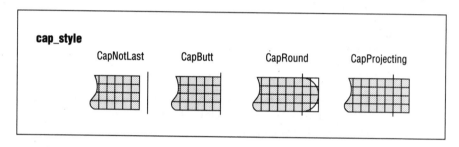

cap_style

CapNotLast   CapButt   CapRound   CapProjecting

The join_style member specifies how corners (endpoints of connected lines) should be drawn:

```
#define JoinMiter           0        /* default */
#define JoinRound           1
#define JoinBevel           2
```

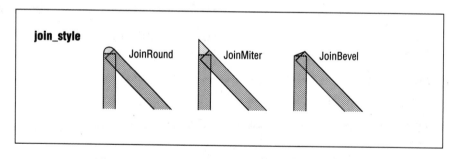

join_style

JoinRound   JoinMiter   JoinBevel

The fill_style member specifies how filled figures should be drawn:

```
#define FillSolid           0        /* default */
#define FillTiled           1
#define FillStippled        2
#define FillOpaqueStippled  3
```

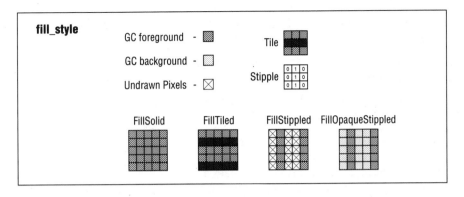

The fill_rule member controls the filling of complex, closed polygons with intersecting lines:

```
#define EvenOddRule          0        /* default */
#define WindingRule          1
```

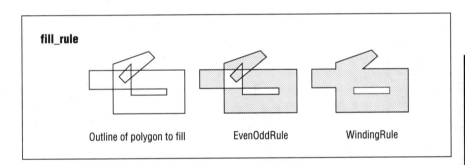

The arc_mode member controls how the endpoints of arcs should be drawn:

```
#define ArcChord             0        /* join endpoints of arc */
#define ArcPieSlice          1        /* default - join endpoints to center of arc */
```

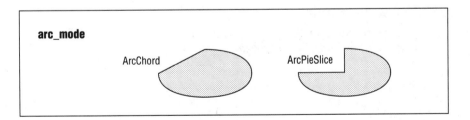

The subwindow_mode member controls how graphics are displayed when windows overlap:

```
#define ClipByChildren    0    /* default-graphics won't show through windows with backgrounds */
#define IncludeInferiors  1    /* graphics appear through mapped subwindows */
```

The graphics_exposures member is a Boolean specifying whether or not to generate GraphicsExpose or NoExpose events. If True (the default), these events will be generated when XCopyArea or XCopyPlane is called with this GC. If False, they will not be generated.

The dashes member in XGCValues is actually a single value (by default, 4), which is repeated as an on-off pattern (e.g., 4,4). If the client has specified a true dashlist by calling XSetDashes, the Boolean dashes member in the actual GC is set to True, and the actual dash list is stored in the bowels of the server.

XHostAddress

Specifies the address of a host machine that is to be added or removed from the host access list for a server. Used in XAddHost, XAddHosts, XListHosts, XRemoveHost, and XRemoveHosts.

```
typedef struct {
    int family;             /* for example Family_Internet */
    int length;             /* length of address, in bytes */
    char *address;          /* pointer to where to find the bytes */
} XHostAddress;
```

The family member is specified using one of the following symbols defined in <X11/X.h>:

```
#define FamilyInternet    0
#define FamilyDECnet      1
#define FamilyChaos       2
```

XIC

An opaque structure that serves as a handle to an input context. (New in R5.)

XICCEncodingStyle

Specifies the encoding of the XTextProperty returned by calls to XmbTextListToTextProperty and XwcTextListToTextProperty. (New in R5.)

```
typedef enum  {
    XStringStyle,           /* STRING */
    XCompoundTextStyle,     /* COMPOUND_TEXT */
    XTextStyle,             /* text in owner's encoding (current locale) */
    XStdICCTextStyle        /* STRING, else COMPOUND_TEXT */
} XICCEncodingStyle;
```

XIconSize

A structure defined in *<X11/Xutil.h>* that is used to set or read the XA_WM_ICON_SIZE property. This is normally set by the window manager with XSetIconSizes and read by each application with XGetIconSizes.

```
typedef struct {
    int min_width, min_height;      /* minimum size */
    int max_width, max_height;      /* maximum size */
    int width_inc, height_inc;      /* preferred size increments when resizing */
} XIconSize;
```

XID

An unsigned long value representing a unique ID for a server-maintained resource such as a Colormap, a Font, or a Cursor. Routines that load a colormap or font, create a cursor, and so on, return an XID of the appropriate type, which is passed to them by the server. If the resource has already been allocated, the XID may point to a resource that is also used by other clients.

XIM

An opaque structure that serves as a handle to an input method. (New in R5.)

XImage

Describes an area of the screen; used in XCreateImage, XDestroyImage, XGetPixel, XPutPixel, XSubImage, XAddPixel, XGetImage, XGetSubImage, and XPutImage.

```
typedef struct _XImage {
    int width, height;              /* size of image in pixels */
    int xoffset;                    /* number of pixels offset in X direction */
    int format;                     /* XYBitmap, XYPixmap, ZPixmap */
    char *data;                     /* pointer to image data */
    int byte_order;                 /* data byte order, LSBFirst, MSBFirst */
    int bitmap_unit;                /* quant. of scan line 8, 16, 32 */
    int bitmap_bit_order;           /* LSBFirst, MSBFirst */
    int bitmap_pad;                 /* 8, 16, 32 */
    int depth;                      /* depth of image */
    int bytes_per_line;             /* accelerator to next line */
    int bits_per_pixel;             /* bits per pixel (ZPixmap only) */
    unsigned long red_mask;         /* bits in z arrangement */
    unsigned long green_mask;
    unsigned long blue_mask;
    char *obdata;                   /* hook for the object routines to hang on */
    struct funcs {                  /* image manipulation routines */
    struct _XImage *(*create_image)();
        int (*destroy_image)();
        unsigned long (*get_pixel)();
        int (*put_pixel)();
        struct _XImage *(*sub_image)();
```

```
        int (*add_pixel)();
      } f;
  } XImage;
```

The format member is specified using one of the following symbols defined in
<X11/X.h>:

```
#define XYBitmap        0       /* depth 1, XYFormat */
#define XYPixmap        1       /* pixmap viewed as stack of planes; */
                                /* depth == drawable depth */
#define ZPixmap         2       /* pixels in scan-line order; */
                                /* depth == drawable depth */
```

The byte_order and bitmap_bit_order members are specified using one of the following symbols defined in *<X11/X.h>*:

```
#define LSBFirst        0
#define MSBFirst        1
```

XIMStyles

Describes input styles. Returned by a call to XGetIMValues. (New in R5.)

```
typedef unsigned long XIMStyle;

typedef struct {
    unsigned short count_styles;
    XIMStyle *supported_styles;
} XIMStyles;
```

Each XIMStyle in the list of supported styles is an unsigned long in which various bit flags describing the style are set. The valid flags and their meanings are
described below:

```
#define XIMPreeditArea          0x0001L
#define XIMPreeditCallbacks     0x0002L
#define XIMPreeditPosition      0x0004L
#define XIMPreeditNothing       0x0008L
#define XIMPreeditNone          0x0010L
#define XIMStatusArea           0x0100L
#define XIMStatusCallbacks      0x0200L
#define XIMStatusNothing        0x0400L
#define XIMStatusNone           0x0800L
```

```
XIMPreeditArea              /* client must provide geometry management of area */
                            /* in which IM can do pre-editing */
XIMPreeditCallbacks          /* client must provide pre-edit callback procedures */
XIMPreeditPosition           /* client must provide location of insertion cursor */
XIMPreeditNothing            /* IM can pre-edit root window with no geometry */
                            /* management provided by client */
```

XIMPreeditNone	/* IM does no pre-editing or display of pre-edit data */
XIMStatusCallbacks	/* client must provide status callback procedures */
XIMStatusArea	/* client must provide geometry management of area */
	/* in which IM can display status values */
XIMStatusNothing	/* IM can display status information in root window */
	/* with no geometry management provided by client */
XIMStatusNone	/* IM does not display any status information */

XKeyboardControl

Is used to set user preferences with XChangeKeyboardControl.

```
typedef struct {
    int key_click_percent;        /* range: 0 (off) to 100 (loudest) */
    int bell_percent;             /* range: 0 (off) to 100 (loudest) */
    int bell_pitch;               /* in Hertz */
    int bell_duration;            /* in milliseconds */
    int led;                      /* which LED? Range: 1-32 */
    int led_mode;                 /* LedModeOn or LedModeOff */
    int key;                      /* between 7 and 255, inclusive */
    int auto_repeat_mode;         /* AutoRepeatModeOn, AutoRepeatModeOff,
                                     AutoRepeatModeDefault */

} XKeyboardControl;
```

A value of −1 in either the key_click_percent, bell_percent, bell_pitch, or bell_duration members restores the default value. If no value is specified for led or key, the default is all leds or all keys, respectively. Otherwise, the value of led_mode or auto_repeat_mode is applied only to the specified led or key.

The led_mode member is specified using one of the following symbols defined in <X11/X.h>:

```
#define LedModeOff        0
#define LedModeOn         1        /* default - Led's flash */
```

The auto_repeat_mode member is specified using one of the following symbols defined in <X11/X.h>:

```
#define AutoRepeatModeOff      0    /* key doesn't repeat if held down */
#define AutoRepeatModeOn       1    /* key does auto_repeat */
#define AutoRepeatModeDefault  2    /* all non-modal keys repeat */
```

In calls to XChangeKeyboardControl, a *valuemask* argument specifies which members in the XKeyboardControl structure are to be used. The mask is made up of a bitwise OR of the following symbols, which are defined in <X11/X.h>:

```
#define KBKeyClickPercent    (1L<<0)
#define KBBellPercent        (1L<<1)
#define KBBellPitch          (1L<<2)
#define KBBellDuration       (1L<<3)
#define KBLed                (1L<<4)
```

```
#define KBLedMode               (1L<<5)
#define KBKey                   (1L<<6)
#define KBAutoRepeatMode        (1L<<7)
```

XKeyboardState

Is used to return the current settings of user preferences with XGetKeyboardControl.

```
typedef struct {
    int key_click_percent;
    int bell_percent;
    unsigned int bell_pitch, bell_duration;
    unsigned long led_mask;
    int global_auto_repeat;
    char auto_repeats[32];
} XKeyboardState;
```

See XKeyboardControl for a description of the members, with the following exceptions: global_auto_repeat is either AutoRepeatModeOn or AutoRepeatModeOff; and auto_repeats[32] is a bit vector in which each bit set to 1 indicates a key for which auto-repeat is enabled. Byte N (from 0) contains the bits for keys $8N$ to $8N+7$, with the LSB representing key $8N$.

XmbTextItem

Describes a component of a complex multi-byte string to be drawn by XmbDrawText. (New in R5.)

```
typedef struct {
    char *chars;            /* pointer to string */
    int nchars;             /* number of characters */
    int delta;              /* pixel delta between strings */
    XFontSet font_set;      /* fonts, None means don't change */
} XmbTextItem;
```

XModifierKeymap

Specifies which physical keys are mapped to modifier functions. This structure is returned by XGetModifierMapping and is an argument to XDeleteModifiermapEntry, XFreeModifiermap, XInsertModifiermapEntry, XNewModifiermap, and XSetModifierMapping.

```
typedef struct {
    int max_keypermod;      /* server's max # of keys per modifier */
    KeyCode *modifiermap;   /* an 8 by max_keypermod array of modifiers */
} XModifierKeymap;
```

This structure is often accompanied in Xlib calls by a *modifier* argument, which identifies the modifier to be affected; one of the following symbols from *<X11/X.h>*:

```
#define ShiftMapIndex              0
#define LockMapIndex               1
#define ControlMapIndex            2
#define Mod1MapIndex               3
#define Mod2MapIndex               4
#define Mod3MapIndex               5
#define Mod4MapIndex               6
#define Mod5MapIndex               7
```

XPixmapFormatValues

Describes a ZPixmap format that is supported on the server. A list of these structures is returned by XListPixmapFormats.

```
typedef struct {
    int depth;                    /* depth of this image format */
    int bits_per_pixel;           /* bits/pixel at this depth */
    int scanline_pad;             /* scan line must be padded to this multiple */
} XPixmapFormatValues;
```

XPoint

Specifies the coordinates of a point. Used in XDrawPoints, XDrawLines, XFillPolygon, and XPolygonRegion.

```
typedef struct {
    short x, y;
} XPoint;
```

XRectangle

Specifies a rectangle.

```
typedef struct {
    short x, y;
    unsigned short width, height;
} XRectangle;
```

XrmBindingList

An enum that specifies the type of binding between adjoining elements in a resource specification that has been converted to an XrmQuarkList (or XrmClassList or XrmNameList). The enum is used in XrmQPutResource, XrmQPutStringResource and XrmStringToBindingQuarkList, and is defined as follows in *<X11/Xresource.h>*:

```
typedef enum {XrmBindTightly, XrmBindLoosely} XrmBinding, *XrmBindingList;
```

Xlib Data Types

XrmClass

A typedef for an XrmQuark, used to uniquely specify a resource class.

XrmClassList

A typedef for a pointer to a list of XrmClass quarks.

XrmDatabase

A pointer to an internal resource manager data type. Members of this structure should not be accessed directly. An XrmDatabase is created or loaded by a call to XrmQPutResource or XrmQPutStringResource, among others.

XrmName

A typedef for an XrmQuark, used to uniquely specify a resource name.

XrmNameList

A typedef for a pointer to a list of XrmName quarks.

XrmOptionDescList

See XrmOptionDescRec.

XrmOptionDescRec

A structure used to parse command-line options and load them into a resource database. It is used by the XrmParseCommand routine, and is defined as follows in *<X11/Xresource.h>*:

```
typedef struct {
    char *option;                    /* option abbreviation in argv */
    char *specifier;                 /* resource specifier */
    XrmOptionKind argKind;           /* which style of option it is */
    XPointer value;                  /* value to provide if XrmoptionNoArg */
} XrmOptionDescRec, *XrmOptionDescList;
```

The value for the argKind element is specified by one of the following enum values, defined in the same file:

```
typedef enum {
    XrmoptionNoArg,          /* value specified in OptionDescRec.value */
    XrmoptionIsArg,          /* value is the option string itself */
    XrmoptionStickyArg,      /* value immediately follows option */
    XrmoptionSepArg,         /* value is next argument in argv */
    XrmoptionResArg,         /* resource and value in next arg in argv */
    XrmoptionSkipArg,        /* ignore this opt and next arg in argv */
    XrmoptionSkipLine        /* ignore this opt and rest of argv */
} XrmOptionKind;
```

XrmQuark

A unique integer value returned by a call to XrmStringToQuark. Quarks are assigned to strings, and used both to speed string comparisons, and to ensure that only a single value is assigned for each unique string. The string corresponding to a quark can be returned by a call to XrmQuarkToString.

XrmQuarkList

A typedef for a pointer to a list of quarks. The XrmStringToBindingQuarkList function converts a resource string into an XrmQuarkList and an accompanying XrmBindingList that describes the bindings — tight (.) or loose (*) — between adjoining components in the string.

XrmRepresentation

A typedef for an XrmQuark, used to uniquely specify a resource representation type (e.g., XtRstring). Various standard representation types are defined in the file *<X11/StringDefs.h>*.

XrmSearchList

A typedef for an array of resource manager hash tables, the structure of which is private.

XrmValue

A structure defined in *<X11/Xresource.h>* that is used to identify the size and position of a resource value within a resource database.

```
typedef struct {
    unsigned int size;
    XPointer addr;
} XrmValue, *XrmValuePtr;
```

XrmValuePtr

See XrmValue.

XSegment

Specifies the x and y coordinates of the endpoints of a line segment. Used in XDrawSegments.

```
typedef struct {
    short x1, y1, x2, y2;
} XSegment;
```

XSetWindowAttributes

Contains all the attributes that can be set without window manager intervention. Used in XChangeWindowAttributes and XCreateWindow.

```
typedef struct {
    Pixmap background_pixmap;          /* pixmap, None, or ParentRelative */
    unsigned long background_pixel;    /* background pixel */
    Pixmap border_pixmap;              /* pixmap, None, or CopyFromParent */
    unsigned long border_pixel;        /* pixel value - default, undefined */
    int bit_gravity;                   /* where to put contents on resize */
    int win_gravity;                   /* where to put window on parent's resize */
    int backing_store;                 /* NotUseful, WhenMapped, Always */
    unsigned long backing_planes;      /* planes to be preserved if possible */
    unsigned long backing_pixel;       /* value to use in restoring planes */
    Bool save_under;                   /* should bits under be saved? False */
    long event_mask;                   /* set of events that should be saved */
    long do_not_propagate_mask;        /* set of events that should not */
    Bool override_redirect;            /* default False */
    Colormap colormap;                 /* colormap to be associated with window */
    Cursor cursor;                     /* cursor to be displayed (None - copy from parent) */
} XSetWindowAttributes;
```

In calls to XChangeWindowAttributes and XCreateWindow, this structure is always accompanied by a *valuemask* argument that identifies which members in the structure are to be used. The values for this argument are defined as follows in *<X11/X.h>*:

```
#define CWBackPixmap        (1L<<0)
#define CWBackPixel         (1L<<1)
#define CWBorderPixmap      (1L<<2)
#define CWBorderPixel       (1L<<3)
#define CWBitGravity        (1L<<4)
#define CWWinGravity        (1L<<5)
#define CWBackingStore      (1L<<6)
#define CWBackingPlanes     (1L<<7)
#define CWBackingPixel      (1L<<8)
#define CWOverrideRedirect  (1L<<9)
#define CWSaveUnder         (1L<<10)
#define CWEventMask         (1L<<11)
#define CWDontPropagate     (1L<<12)
#define CWColormap          (1L<<13)
#define CWCursor            (1L<<14)
```

The event_mask and do_not_propagate_mask members take event mask values, which are specified as a bitwise OR of the following symbols defined in *<X11/X.h>*:

```
#define NoEventMask         0L        /* no events */
#define KeyPressMask        (1L<<0)   /* keyboard up events */
#define KeyReleaseMask      (1L<<1)   /* keyboard down events */
#define ButtonPressMask     (1L<<2)   /* pointer button down events */
#define ButtonReleaseMask   (1L<<3)   /* pointer button up events */
#define EnterWindowMask     (1L<<4)   /* pointer window entry events */
```

The X Window System in a Nutshell

```
#define LeaveWindowMask          (1L<<5)   /* pointer window leave events */
#define PointerMotionMask        (1L<<6)   /* all pointer motion events */
#define PointerMotionHintMask    (1L<<7)   /* fewer pointer motion events */
#define Button1MotionMask        (1L<<8)   /* pointer motion while button 1 down */
#define Button2MotionMask        (1L<<9)   /* pointer motion while button 2 down */
#define Button3MotionMask        (1L<<10)  /* pointer motion while button 3 down */
#define Button4MotionMask        (1L<<11)  /* pointer motion while button 4 down */
#define Button5MotionMask        (1L<<12)  /* pointer motion while button 5 down */
#define ButtonMotionMask         (1L<<13)  /* pointer motion while any button down */
#define KeymapStateMask          (1L<<14)  /* keyboard state change on Notify/Focus events */
#define ExposureMask             (1L<<15)  /* any exposure but GraphicsExpose/NoExpose */
#define VisibilityChangeMask     (1L<<16)  /* any change in visibility */
#define StructureNotifyMask      (1L<<17)  /* any change in window configuration */
#define ResizeRedirectMask       (1L<<18)  /* redirect resize of this window */
#define SubstructureNotifyMask   (1L<<19)  /* notify about reconfiguration of children */
#define SubstructureRedirectMask (1L<<20)  /* redirect reconfiguration of children */
#define FocusChangeMask          (1L<<21)  /* any change in keyboard focus */
#define PropertyChangeMask       (1L<<22)  /* any change in property */
#define ColormapChangeMask       (1L<<23)  /* any change in colormap */
#define OwnerGrabButtonMask      (1L<<24)  /* modifies handling of pointer events */
```

The bit_gravity member is specified using one of the following symbols from <X11/X.h>:

```
#define ForgetGravity      0    /* default - discard window contents */
#define NorthWestGravity   1    /* move contents to upper left corner */
#define NorthGravity       2    /* move contents to upper middle */
#define NorthEastGravity   3    /* move contents to upper right */
#define WestGravity        4    /* and so on */
#define CenterGravity      5
#define EastGravity        6
#define SouthWestGravity   7
#define SouthGravity       8
#define SouthEastGravity   9
#define StaticGravity      10   /* don't move relative to root origin /*
```

The win_gravity member uses the same symbols, with the exception of the following, which is used instead of ForgetGravity:

```
#define UnmapGravity       0    /* unmap the window instead */
```

The default for win_gravity is NorthWestGravity.

The backing_store member is specified using one of the following symbols:

```
#define NotUseful          0
#define WhenMapped         1
#define Always             2
```

XSizeHints

A structure defined in *<X11/Xutil.h>* that describes a range of preferred sizes and aspect ratios. It is used to set the XA_WM_NORMAL_HINTS and XA_WM_ZOOM_HINTS properties for the window manager with XSetStandardProperties, XSetNormalHints, XSetSizeHints, or XSetZoomHints in R3, and XSetWMProperties, XSetWMNormalHints, and XSetWMSizeHints in R4. Also used in reading these properties with XGetNormalHints, XGetSizeHints, or XGetZoomHints in R3, and XGetWMNormalHints and XGetWMSizeHints in R4.

```
typedef struct {
    long flags;                        /* marks defined members in structure */
    int x, y;                          /* obsolete in R4 */
    int width, height;                 /* obsolete in R4 */
    int min_width, min_height;
    int max_width, max_height;
    int width_inc, height_inc;
    struct {
        int x;                         /* numerator */
        int y;                         /* denominator */
    } min_aspect, max_aspect;
    int base_width, base_height;
    int win_gravity;
} XSizeHints;
```

The flags member is for window manager properties that clients and applications use for communication. It is made up of a bitwise OR of the following symbols defined in *<X11/Xutil.h>*.

```
#define USPosition   (1L << 0)   /* user specified x, y */
#define USSize       (1L << 1)   /* user specified width, height */
#define PPosition    (1L << 2)   /* program specified position */
#define PSize        (1L << 3)   /* program specified size */
#define PMinSize     (1L << 4)   /* program specified minimum size */
#define PMaxSize     (1L << 5)   /* program specified maximum size */
#define PResizeInc   (1L << 6)   /* program specified resize increments */
#define PAspect      (1L << 7)   /* program specified min and max aspect ratios */
#define PBaseSize    (1L << 8)   /* program specified base for incrementing */
#define PWinGravity  (1L << 9)   /* program specified window gravity */
```

In addition, the following value is obsolete:

```
#define PAllHints (PPosition|PSize|PMinSize|PMaxSize|PResizeInc|PAspect)
```

In R4, the new base_width and base_height members are used instead of min_width and min_height, which are retained for backward compatibility. The win_gravity member is used to allow some corner of the window other than the top left to be used as the placement point for interactive window placement. For example, if a window were displaying text in a language that reads from right to left, the user might want to place the top right corner instead of the top left.

XStandardColormap

A structure defined in *<X11/Xutil.h>* that describes a standard colormap, giving its ID and its color characteristics. This is the format of the standard colormap properties set on the root window, which can be changed with XSetRGBColormaps and read with XGetRGBColormaps.

```
typedef struct {
    Colormap colormap;
    unsigned long red_max;
    unsigned long red_mult;
    unsigned long green_max;
    unsigned long green_mult;
    unsigned long blue_max;
    unsigned long blue_mult;
    unsigned long base_pixel;
    VisualID visualid;
    XID killid;
} XStandardColormap;
```

The killid member uses the following symbol:

```
#define ReleaseByFreeingColormap ((XID) 1L)
```

XTextItem

Describes a string, the font to print it in, and the horizontal offset from the previous string drawn or from the location specified by the drawing command. Used in XDrawText.

```
typedef struct {
    char *chars;          /* pointer to string */
    int nchars;           /* number of characters */
    int delta;            /* delta between strings */
    Font font;            /* font to print it in, None don't change */
} XTextItem;
```

XTextItem16

Describes a string in a two-byte font, the font to print it in, and the horizontal offset from the previous string drawn or from the location specified by the drawing command. Used in XDrawText16.

```
typedef struct {
    XChar2b *chars;       /* two-byte characters */
    int nchars;           /* number of characters */
    int delta;            /* delta between strings */
    Font font;            /* font to print it in, None don't change */
} XTextItem16;
```

XTextProperty

Stores a concatenated array of strings in a standard format and encoding suitable for the value of a window property. Conversions between arrays of strings and XTextProperties are performed by:

StringListToTextProperty, XTextPropertyToStringList
XmbTextListToTextProperty, XmbTextPropertyToTextList,
XwcTextListToTextProperty, and XwcTextPropertyToTextList.

```
typedef struct {
      unsigned char *value;         /* same as Property routines */
      Atom encoding;                /* property type */
      int format;                   /* property data format: 8, 16, or 32 */
      unsigned long nitems;         /* number of data items in value */
} XTextProperty;
```

XTimeCoord

Specifies a time and position pair, for use in tracking the pointer with XGetMotionEvents. This routine is not supported on all systems.

```
typedef struct {
      Time time;
      short x, y;
} XTimeCoord;
```

XVisualInfo

A structure defined in *<X11/Xutil.h>* that contains all the information about a particular visual. It is used in XGetVisualInfo and XMatchVisualInfo to specify the desired visual type. The visual member of XVisualInfo is used for the *visual* argument of XCreateColormap or XCreateWindow.

```
typedef struct {
      Visual *visual;
      VisualID visualid;
      int screen;
      unsigned int depth;
#if defined(__cplusplus) || defined(c_plusplus)
      int c_class;                  /* C++ */
#else
      int class;
#endif
      unsigned long red_mask;
      unsigned long green_mask;
      unsigned long blue_mask;
      int colormap_size;
      int bits_per_rgb;
} XVisualInfo;
```

In the XGetVisualInfo call, there is a *vinfo_mask* argument that specifies which elements of the XVisualInfo structure are to be returned. It is made up of a bitwise OR of the following symbols:

```
#define VisualNoMask            0x0
#define VisualIDMask            0x1
#define VisualScreenMask        0x2
#define VisualDepthMask         0x4
#define VisualClassMask         0x8
#define VisualRedMaskMask       0x10
#define VisualGreenMaskMask     0x20
#define VisualBlueMaskMask      0x40
#define VisualColormapSizeMask  0x80
#define VisualBitsPerRGBMask    0x100
#define VisualAllMask           0x1FF
```

XwcTextItem

Describes a component of a complex wide-character string to be drawn by XwcDrawText. (New in R5.)

```
typedef struct {
    wchar_t *chars;         /* pointer to wide char string */
    int nchars;             /* number of wide characters */
    int delta;              /* pixel delta between strings */
    XFontSet font_set;      /* fonts; None means don't change */
} XwcTextItem;
```

XWindowAttributes

Describes the complete set of window attributes, including those that cannot be set without window manager interaction. This structure is returned by XGetWindowAttributes. It is *not* used by XChangeWindowAttributes or XCreateWindow.

```
typedef struct {
    int x, y;                           /* location of window */
    int width, height;                  /* width and height of window */
    int border_width;                   /* border width of window */
    int depth;                          /* depth of window */
    Visual *visual;                     /* the associated visual structure */
    Window root;                        /* root of screen containing window */
#if defined(__cplusplus) || defined(c_plusplus)
    int c_class;                        /* C++ InputOutput, InputOnly*/
#else
    int class;                          /* InputOutput, InputOnly*/
#endif
    int bit_gravity;                    /* one of bit gravity values */
    int win_gravity;                    /* one of the window gravity values */
    int backing_store;                  /* NotUseful, WhenMapped, Always */
    unsigned long backing_planes;       /* planes to be preserved if possible */
```

```
        unsigned long backing_pixel;        /* value to be used when restoring planes */
        Bool save_under;                     /* Boolean; should bits under be saved */
        Colormap colormap;                   /* colormap to be associated with window */
        Bool map_installed;                  /* Boolean; is colormap currently installed*/
        int map_state;                       /* IsUnmapped, IsUnviewable, IsViewable */
        long all_event_masks;                /* events all people have interest in*/
        long your_event_mask;                /* my event mask */
        long do_not_propagate_mask;          /* set of events that should not propagate */
        Bool override_redirect;              /* Boolean value for override-redirect */
        Screen *screen;
    } XWindowAttributes;
```

XWindowChanges

Describes a configuration for a window. Used in XConfigureWindow, which can change the screen layout and therefore can be intercepted by the window manager. This sets some of the remaining members of XWindowAttributes that cannot be set with XChangeWindowAttributes or XCreateWindow.

```
typedef struct {
    int x, y;
    int width, height;
    int border_width;
    Window sibling;          /* comparison window for stack mode */
    int stack_mode;          /* how window should appear relative to sibling */
} XWindowChanges;
```

The stack_mode member specifies the relationship between the current window and a sibling window specified in the same XConfigureWindow call. It is specified using one of the following symbols defined in <X11/X.h>:

```
#define Below            1
#define TopIf            2
#define BottomIf         3
#define Opposite         4
```

In the XConfigureWindow call, the *value_mask* argument specifies which members in the XWindowChanges structure are to be read. The *value_mask* is a bitwise OR of the following symbols defined in <X11/X.h>:

```
#define CWX              (1<<0)
#define CWY              (1<<1)
#define CWWidth          (1<<2)
#define CWHeight         (1<<3)
#define CWBorderWidth    (1<<4)
#define CWSibling        (1<<5)
#define CWStackMode      (1<<6)
```

XWMHints

A structure defined in *<X11/Xutil.h>* that describes various application preferences for communication to the window manager via the XA_WM_HINTS property.
Used in XSetWMHints and XGetWMHints.

```
typedef struct {
    long flags;                /* marks defined members in structure */
    Bool input;                /* whether window manager needed for keyboard input */
    int initial_state;         /* see below */
    Pixmap icon_pixmap;        /* pixmap to be used as icon */
    Window icon_window;        /* window to be used as icon */
    int icon_x, icon_y;        /* initial position of icon */
    Pixmap icon_mask;          /* icon mask bitmap */
    XID window_group;          /* ID of related window group */
                               /* this structure may be extended in the future */
} XWMHints;
```

The flags member is for window manager properties that clients and applications
use for communication. It is made up of a bitwise OR of the following symbols
defined in *<X11/Xutil.h>*.

```
#define InputHint         (1L << 0)
#define StateHint         (1L << 1)
#define IconPixmapHint    (1L << 2)
#define IconWindowHint    (1L << 3)
#define IconPositionHint  (1L << 4)
#define IconMaskHint      (1L << 5)
#define WindowGroupHint   (1L << 6)
#define AllHints          (InputHint|StateHint|IconPixmapHint|IconWindowHint\
                           |IconPositionHint|IconMaskHint|WindowGroupHint)
```

The initial_state member specifies how application windows are first displayed. It
can take one of the following values defined in *<X11/Xutil.h>*:

```
#define WithdrawnState 0    /* for windows that are not mapped */
#define NormalState 1       /* most applications want to start this way */
#define IconicState 3       /* application wants to start as an icon */
```

The following values for initial_state are obsolete as of R4.

```
#define DontCareState 0     /* don't know or care */
#define ZoomState 2         /* application wants to start zoomed */
#define InactiveState 4     /* application believes it is seldom used */
```

3
Events

This section presents the following information about events:

- The XEvent union.
- Event mask symbols and values.
- Table of event masks, event types, and event structures.
- The 33 event types, in alphabetical order.

The XEvent Union

```
typedef union _XEvent {
    int                          type;    /* must not be changed; first element */
    XAnyEvent                    xany;
    XButtonEvent                 xbutton;
    XCirculateEvent              xcirculate;
    XCirculateRequestEvent       xcirculaterequest;
    XClientMessageEvent          xclient;
    XColormapEvent               xcolormap;
    XConfigureEvent              xconfigure;
    XConfigureRequestEvent       xconfigurerequest;
    XCreateWindowEvent           xcreatewindow;
    XCrossingEvent               xcrossing;
    XDestroyWindowEvent          xdestroywindow;
    XErrorEvent                  xerror;
    XExposeEvent                 xexpose;
    XFocusChangeEvent            xfocus;
    XGraphicsExposeEvent         xgraphicsexpose;
    XGravityEvent                xgravity;
    XKeyEvent                    xkey;
    XKeymapEvent                 xkeymap;
    XMapEvent                    xmap;
    XMappingEvent                xmapping;
    XMapRequestEvent             xmaprequest;
    XMotionEvent                 xmotion;
    XNoExposeEvent               xnoexpose;
    XPropertyEvent               xproperty;
    XReparentEvent               xreparent;
    XResizeRequestEvent          xresizerequest;
    XSelectionClearEvent         xselectionclear;
    XSelectionEvent              xselection;
    XSelectionRequestEvent       xselectionrequest;
    XUnmapEvent                  xunmap;
    XVisibilityEvent             xvisibility;
    long                         pad[24];
} XEvent;
```

One member of this union is the simple event structure called XAnyEvent, which
contains members that are used by many or all of the event structures:

```
typedef struct {
    int type;
    unsigned long serial;      /* # of last request processed by server */
    Bool send_event;           /* true if this came from SendEvent request */
    Display *display;          /* display the event was read from */
    Window window;             /* window on which event was requested in event mask */
} XAnyEvent;
```

All event structures contain the members type, serial, and send_event. Most event structures also contain the members display and window.

Event Masks and Defined Values

In many Xlib calls, events are selected with an event mask. Event mask values are specified as a bitwise OR of the following symbols defined in *<X11/X.h>*:

```
#define NoEventMask            0L        /* no events */
#define KeyPressMask           (1L<<0)   /* keyboard up events */
#define KeyReleaseMask         (1L<<1)   /* keyboard down events */
#define ButtonPressMask        (1L<<2)   /* pointer button down events */
#define ButtonReleaseMask      (1L<<3)   /* pointer button up events */
#define EnterWindowMask        (1L<<4)   /* pointer window entry events */
#define LeaveWindowMask        (1L<<5)   /* pointer window leave events */
#define PointerMotionMask      (1L<<6)   /* all pointer motion events */
#define PointerMotionHintMask  (1L<<7)   /* fewer pointer motion events */
#define Button1MotionMask      (1L<<8)   /* pointer motion while button 1 down */
#define Button2MotionMask      (1L<<9)   /* pointer motion while button 2 down */
#define Button3MotionMask      (1L<<10)  /* pointer motion while button 3 down */
#define Button4MotionMask      (1L<<11)  /* pointer motion while button 4 down */
#define Button5MotionMask      (1L<<12)  /* pointer motion while button 5 down */
#define ButtonMotionMask       (1L<<13)  /* pointer motion: any button down */
#define KeymapStateMask        (1L<<14)  /* any keyboard state change on */
                                         /* Notify or Focus events */
#define ExposureMask           (1L<<15)  /* any exposure (except GraphicsExpose */
                                         /* and NoExpose) */
#define VisibilityChangeMask   (1L<<16)  /* any change in visibility */
#define StructureNotifyMask    (1L<<17)  /* any change in window configuration */
#define ResizeRedirectMask     (1L<<18)  /* redirect resize of this window */
#define SubstructureNotifyMask (1L<<19)  /* notify about reconfiguration of children */
#define SubstructureRedirectMask (1L<<20) /* redirect reconfiguration of children */
#define FocusChangeMask        (1L<<21)  /* any change in keyboard focus */
#define PropertyChangeMask     (1L<<22)  /* any change in property */
#define ColormapChangeMask     (1L<<23)  /* any change in colormap */
#define OwnerGrabButtonMask    (1L<<24)  /* modifies handling of pointer events */
```

Event Masks, Event Types, and Event Structures

Event Mask	Event Type	Event Structure
(always selected)	MappingNotify ClientMessage SelectionClear SelectionNotify SelectionRequest	XMappingEvent XClientMessageEvent XSetSelectClearEvent XSelectionEvent XSelectionRequestEvent
ButtonPressMask ButtonReleaseMask	ButtonPress ButtonRelease	XButtonPressedEvent XButtonReleasedEvent
PointerMotionMask PointerMotionHintMask ButtonMotionMask Button1MotionMask Button2MotionMask Button3MotionMask Button4MotionMask Button5MotionMask	MotionNotify	XPointerMovedEvent
ColormapChangeMask	ColormapNotify	XColormapEvent
EnterWindowMask LeaveWindowMask	EnterNotify LeaveNotify	XEnterWindowEvent XLeaveWindowEvent
FocusChangeMask	FocusIn FocusOut	XFocusInEvent XFocusOutEvent
ExposureMask graphics_expose member (in GC) VisibilityChangeMask	Expose GraphicsExpose NoExpose VisibilityNotify	XExposeEvent XGraphicsExposeEvent XNoExposeEvent XVisibilityEvent
KeyPressMask KeyReleaseMask KeymapStateMask	KeyPress KeyRelease KeymapNotify	XKeyPressedEvent XKeyReleasedEvent XKeymapEvent
OwnerGrabButtonMask	n/a	n/a
PropertyChangeMask	PropertyNotify	XPropertyEvent

Event Mask	Event Type	Event Structure
ResizeRedirectMask	ResizeRequest	XResizeRequestEvent
StructureNotifyMask or SubstructureNotifyMask	CirculateNotify ConfigureNotify DestroyNotify GravityNotify MapNotify ReparentNotify UnmapNotify	XCirculateEvent XConfigureEvent XDestroyWindowEvent XGravityEvent XMapEvent XReparentEvent XUnmapEvent
SubstructureRedirectMask	CirculateRequest ConfigureRequest MapRequest	XCirculateRequestEvent XConfigureRequestEvent XMapRequestEvent

Event Types

Each event listing begins with a brief description, which includes the conditions that generate and select the event. Following the description is the event structure, and each member is described with a comment.

Presented with the event structures are any defined symbols or other special values used in conjunction with particular members. If a value is used in more than one structure, a cross-reference may be provided rather than a complete listing. The actual values for defined constants are given, as well as their symbolic names, to aid in debugging.

Events

ButtonPress, ButtonRelease

Generated when a pointer button has been pressed or released. May be selected separately, using ButtonPressMask and ButtonReleaseMask.

```
typedef struct {
        int type;                       /* type of event */
        unsigned long serial;           /* # of last request processed by server */
        Bool send_event;                /* true if this came from SendEvent request */
        Display *display;               /* display the event was read from */
        Window window;                  /* window being restacked */
        Window root;                    /* root window that the event occurred under */
        Window subwindow;               /* child window */
        Time time;                      /* when event occurred, in milliseconds */
        int x, y;                       /* pointer coords relative to receiving window */
        int x_root, y_root;             /* coordinates relative to root */
        unsigned int state;             /* mask of all buttons and modifier keys */
        unsigned int button;            /* button that triggered event */
        Bool same_screen;               /* same screen flag */
} XButtonEvent;
typedef XButtonEvent XButtonPressedEvent;
typedef XButtonEvent XButtonReleasedEvent;
```

The button member is specified with one of the following constants defined in <X11/X.h>:

```
#define Button1          1
#define Button2          2
#define Button3          3
#define Button4          4
#define Button5          5
```

The state member is made up of a bitwise OR of the following symbols defined in <X11/X.h>:

```
#define ShiftMask        (1<<0)
#define LockMask         (1<<1)
#define ControlMask      (1<<2)
#define Mod1Mask         (1<<3)
#define Mod2Mask         (1<<4)
#define Mod3Mask         (1<<5)
#define Mod4Mask         (1<<6)
#define Mod5Mask         (1<<7)
#define Button1Mask      (1<<8)
#define Button2Mask      (1<<9)
#define Button3Mask      (1<<10)
#define Button4Mask      (1<<11)
#define Button5Mask      (1<<12)
```

CirculateNotify

Generated when a window is actually restacked from a call to XCirculateSubwindows, XCirculateSubwindowsDown, or XCirculateSubwindowsUp. This event is selected with StructureNotifyMask in the XSelectInput call for the window to be moved or with SubstructureNotifyMask for the parent of the window to be moved.

```
typedef struct {
        int type;                  /* type of event */
        unsigned long serial;      /* # of last request processed by server */
        Bool send_event;           /* true if this came from SendEvent request */
        Display *display;          /* display the event was read from */
        Window event;              /* ID of window receiving the event */
        Window window;             /* window that was restacked */
        int place;                 /* where window was placed */
} XCirculateEvent;
```

The place member is specified with one of the following constants defined in <X11/X.h>:

```
#define PlaceOnTop       0
#define PlaceOnBottom    1
```

CirculateRequest

Generated when XCirculateSubwindows, XCirculateSubwindowsDown, XCirculateSubwindowsUp, or XRestackWindows is called to change the stacking order of a group of children. (CirculateNotify, a related event, indicates the *final* outcome of the request.) This event is selected for the parent window with SubstructureRedirectMask.

```
typedef struct {
        int type;                  /* type of event */
        unsigned long serial;      /* # of last request processed by server */
        Bool send_event;           /* true if this came from SendEvent request */
        Display *display;          /* display the event was read from */
        Window parent;             /* parent of the window that was restacked */
        Window window;             /* window being restacked */
        int place;                 /* PlaceOnTop, PlaceOnBottom */
} XCirculateRequestEvent;
```

The values for the place member are listed under CirculateNotify.

ClientMessage

Generated when there is a call to XSendEvent by a client to a particular window. There is no event mask for ClientMessage events, and they are not selected with XSelectInput. Instead XSendEvent directs them to a specific window, which is given as a window ID: the PointerWindow or the InputFocus.

```
typedef struct {
    int type;                      /* type of event */
    unsigned long serial;          /* # of last request processed by server */
    Bool send_event;               /* true if this came from SendEvent request */
    Display *display;              /* display the event was read from */
    Window window;                 /* window receiving the event */
    Atom message_type;             /* how data is interpreted by the receiving client */
    int format;                    /* format of property: 8, 16, 32 */
    union {
        char b[20];
        short s[10];
        long l[5];
    } data;                        /* data passed to the receiving client */
} XClientMessageEvent;
```

ColormapNotify

Generated when the colormap attribute of a window changes or when the color-map specified by the attribute is installed, uninstalled, or freed. Generated by XChangeWindowAttributes, XFreeColormap, XInstallColormap, and XUninstallColormap. This event is selected with ColormapChangeMask.

```
typedef struct {
    int type;                      /* type of event */
    unsigned long serial;          /* # of last request processed by server */
    Bool send_event;               /* true if this came from SendEvent request */
    Display *display;              /* display the event was read from */
    Window window;                 /* window whose colormap or attribute changes */
    Colormap colormap;             /* a colormap ID or None */
    Bool new;                      /* true (colormap attribute changed) or false */
                                   /* (colormap is installed or uninstalled) */
    int state;                     /* ColorMapInstalled, ColormapUninstalled */
} XColormapEvent;
```

The state member is specified with one of the following constants defined in <X11/X.h>:

```
#define ColormapUninstalled    0
#define ColormapInstalled      1
```

ConfigureNotify

Generated when a window's configuration (size, position, border, and stacking order) are actually changed. This event is selected for a single window by specifying the window ID of that window with StructureNotifyMask. To receive this event for all children of a window, specify the parent window ID with Substruc-tureNotifyMask.

```
typedef struct {
    int type;                      /* type of event */
    unsigned long serial;          /* # of last request processed by server */
```

```
        Bool send_event;            /* true if this came from SendEvent request */
        Display *display;           /* display the event was read from */
        Window event;               /* ID of window that selected the event */
        Window window;              /* ID of window whose configuration changed */
        int x, y;                   /* final coords of window relative to parent */
        int width, height;          /* of reconfigured window (in pixels) */
        int border_width;           /* of reconfigured window (in pixels) */
        Window above;               /* either None (on bottom) or above this sibling */
        Bool override_redirect;     /* true if window ignores this event */
} XConfigureEvent;
```

ConfigureRequest

Generated when another client attempts to change a window's size, position, border, and/or stacking order. (ConfigureNotify indicates the *final* outcome of the request.) This event is selected for any window in a group of children by specifying the parent window with SubstructureRedirectMask.

```
    typedef struct {
        int type;                   /* type of event */
        unsigned long serial;       /* # of last request processed by server */
        Bool send_event;            /* true if this came from SendEvent request */
        Display *display;           /* display the event was read from */
        Window parent;              /* ID of window that selected the event */
        Window window;              /* ID of window being configured */
        int x, y;                   /* border position relative to origin of parent */
        int width, height;          /* of window (in pixels) */
        int border_width;           /* of window's border width (in pixels) */
        Window above;               /* either None (on bottom) or above this sibling */
        int detail;                 /* Above, Below, TopIf, BottomIf, Opposite */
        unsigned long value_mask;
} XConfigureRequestEvent;
```

The detail member is specified with one of the following constants defined in *<X11/X.h>*:

```
    #define Above         0
    #define Below         1
    #define TopIf         2
    #define BottomIf      3
    #define Opposite      4
```

CreateNotify

Generated when a window is created. This event is selected on children of a window by specifying the parent window ID with SubstructureNotifyMask. (Note that this event type cannot be selected by StructureNotifyMask.)

```
    typedef struct {
        int type;                   /* type of event */
```

```
    unsigned long serial;        /* # of last request processed by server */
    Bool send_event;             /* true if this came from SendEvent request */
    Display *display;            /* display the event was read from */
    Window parent;               /* parent of the window that was restacked */
    Window window;               /* window being restacked */
    int x, y;                    /* window location */
    int width, height;           /* size of window */
    int border_width;            /* border width */
    Bool override_redirect;      /* true if window ignores this event */
} XCreateWindowEvent;
```

DestroyNotify

Generated when a window has been destroyed. To receive this event type on children of a window, specify the parent window ID and pass SubstructureNotifyMask as part of the *event_mask* argument to XSelectInput. This event type cannot be selected with StructureNotifyMask.

```
typedef struct {
    int type;                    /* type of event */
    unsigned long serial;        /* # of last request processed by server */
    Bool send_event;             /* true if this came from SendEvent request */
    Display *display;            /* display the event was read from */
    Window event;                /* ID of window that selected the event */
    Window window;               /* window that was destroyed */
} XDestroyWindowEvent;
```

EnterNotify, LeaveNotify

Generated when the pointer enters or leaves a window. Each of these events can be selected separately with XEnterWindowMask and XLeaveWindowMask.

```
typedef struct {
    int type;                    /* type of event */
    unsigned long serial;        /* # of last request processed by server */
    Bool send_event;             /* true if this came from SendEvent request */
    Display *display;            /* display the event was read from */
    Window window;               /* window being restacked */
    Window root;                 /* root window that the event occurred on */
    Window subwindow;            /* child window */
    Time time;                   /* milliseconds */
    int x, y;                    /* pointer x, y coordinates in receiving window */
    int x_root, y_root;          /* coordinates relative to root */
    int mode;                    /* NotifyNormal, NotifyGrab, NotifyUngrab */
    int detail;                  /* listed below */
    Bool same_screen;            /* same screen flag */
    Bool focus;                  /* is receiving window the focus? */
    unsigned int state;          /* mask of all buttons and modifier keys */
} XCrossingEvent;
```

```
typedef XCrossingEvent XEnterWindowEvent;
typedef XCrossingEvent XLeaveWindowEvent;
```

The mode member is specified with one of the following constants defined in
<X11/X.h>:

```
#define NotifyNormal      0
#define NotifyGrab        1
#define NotifyUngrab      2
```

The detail member is specified with one of the following constants defined in
<X11/X.h>:

```
#define NotifyAncestor          0
#define NotifyVirtual           1
#define NotifyInferior          2
#define NotifyNonlinear         3
#define NotifyNonlinearVirtual  4
```

The values for the state member are listed under ButtonPress.

The diagram below shows the events generated by a movement from window *A* to
a child (*B1*) of sibling *B*.

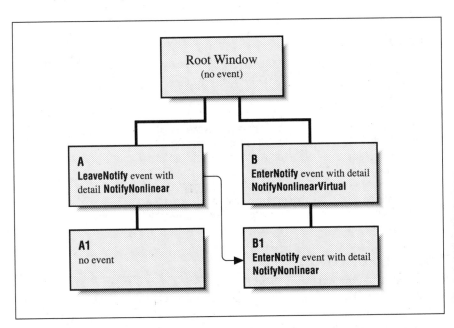

The diagram below shows the events and details caused by various pointer transitions. Pointer transitions, indicated by heavy arrows, are from a window *A* to a window *B*. Thin arrows ending with a bar indicate that the event type and detail described are delivered to all windows up to the bar.

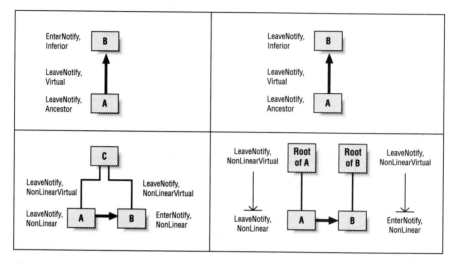

Expose

Generated when a window becomes visible or a previously invisible part of a window becomes visible. This event is selected with ExposureMask.

```
typedef struct {
    int type;                      /* type of event */
    unsigned long serial;          /* # of last request processed by server */
    Bool send_event;               /* true if this came from SendEvent request */
    Display *display;              /* display the event was read from */
    Window window;                 /* window that was destroyed */
    int x, y;                      /* coords of exposed region */
    int width, height;             /* of exposed region (in pixels) */
    int count;                     /* if nonzero, at least this many more */
} XExposeEvent;
```

Focusln, FocusOut

Generated when the keyboard focus window changes as a result of an XSetInput-Focus call. Similar to EnterNotify and LeaveNotify events, but tracking the focus rather than the pointer. Focusln and FocusOut events are selected with FocusChangeMask. They cannot be selected separately.

```
typedef struct {
    int type;                      /* Focusln or FocusOut */
    unsigned long serial;          /* # of last request processed by server */
```

```
    Bool send_event;         /* true if this came from SendEvent request */
    Display *display;        /* display the event was read from */
    Window window;           /* window being restacked */
    int mode;                /* NotifyNormal, NotifyGrab, NotifyUngrab */
    int detail;              /* one of the constants listed below * /
} XFocusChangeEvent;
typedef XFocusChangeEvent XFocusInEvent;
typedef XFocusChangeEvent XFocusOutEvent;
```

The values for the mode member are listed under EnterNotify.

The detail member is specified with one of the following constants defined in *<X11/X.h>*:

```
#define NotifyAncestor          0
#define NotifyVirtual           1
#define NotifyInferior          2
#define NotifyNonlinear         3
#define NotifyNonlinearVirtual  4
#define NotifyPointer           5
#define NotifyPointerRoot       6
#define NotifyDetailNone        7
```

The diagrams on the next two pages represent all possible combinations of focus transitions and of origin, destination, and pointer windows. The diagrams show the types of events generated and their associated detail member. Thin arrows ending with a bar indicate that the event type and detail described are delivered to all windows up to the bar.

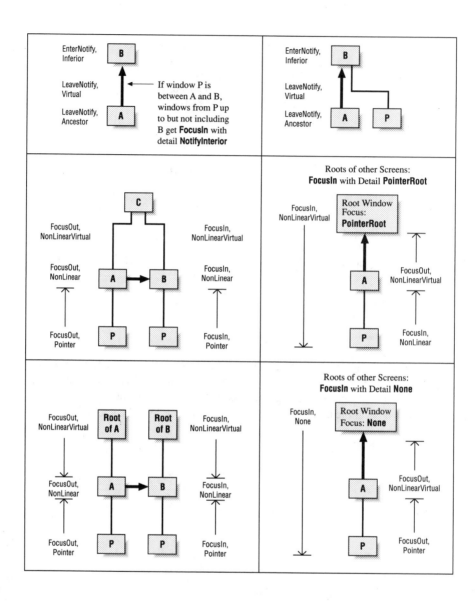

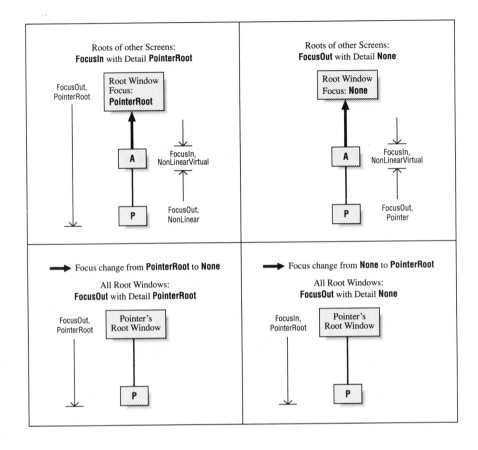

GraphicsExpose, NoExpose

Generated depending on the source area for an XCopyArea or XCopyPlane request. If the source area was not available because it was outside the source window or was obscured by a window, then a GraphicsExpose event occurs. If the source region was completely available, then a NoExpose event occurs.

These events are not selected with XSelectInput but are sent if the graphics context in the XCopyArea or XCopyPlane request had its graphics_exposures flag set to true. If graphics_exposures is true in the graphics context used for the copy, either one NoExpose event or one or more GraphicsExpose events will be generated for every XCopyArea or XCopyPlane call made.

```
typedef struct {
    int type;                   /* type of event */
    unsigned long serial;       /* # of last request processed by server */
    Bool send_event;            /* true if this came from SendEvent request */
    Display *display;           /* display the event was read from */
    Drawable drawable;          /* destination window or an off-screen pixmap */
    int x, y;                   /* coords of exposed region */
    int width, height;          /* of exposed region (in pixels) */
    int count;                  /* if nonzero, at least this many more */
    int major_code;             /* CopyArea, CopyPlane, or symbol defined by a loaded */
                                /* extension */
    int minor_code;             /* zero unless request is part of an extension */
} XGraphicsExposeEvent;

typedef struct {
    int type;                   /* type of event */
    unsigned long serial;       /* # of last request processed by server */
    Bool send_event;            /* true if this came from SendEvent request */
    Display *display;           /* display the event was read from */
    Drawable drawable;          /* destination window or an off-screen pixmap */
    int major_code;             /* CopyArea, CopyPlane, or symbol defined by a loaded */
                                /* extension */
    int minor_code;             /* zero unless request is part of an extension */
} XNoExposeEvent;
```

GravityNotify

Generated when a window is moved because of a change in the size of its parent. This happens when the win_gravity attribute of the child window is something other than StaticGravity or UnmapGravity.

This event is selected for a single window by specifying the window ID of that window with StructureNotifyMask. To receive notification of movement due to gravity for a group of siblings, specify the parent window ID with Substructure-NotifyMask.

```
typedef struct {
    int type;                   /* type of event */
    unsigned long serial;       /* # of last request processed by server */
    Bool send_event;            /* true if this came from SendEvent request */
    Display *display;           /* display the event was read from */
    Window event;               /* ID of window that selected the event */
    Window window;              /* ID of window that was moved */
    int x, y;                   /* new coords of window, relative to parent */
} XGravityEvent;
```

KeymapNotify

Generated when the pointer or keyboard focus enters a window. KeymapNotify events are reported immediately after EnterNotify or FocusIn events. This event is selected with KeymapStateMask.

```
typedef struct {
        int type;                    /* type of event */
        unsigned long serial;        /* # of last request processed by server */
        Bool send_event;             /* true if this came from SendEvent request */
        Display *display;            /* display the event was read from */
        Window window;               /* window member of preceding EnterNotify or FocusIn */
        char key_vector[32];         /* a 256-bit vector or mask, each bit representing key */
} XKeymapEvent;
```

KeyPress, KeyRelease

Generated for all keys, even those mapped to modifier keys such as Shift or Control. Each type of keyboard event may be selected separately with KeyPressMask and KeyReleaseMask.

```
typedef struct {
        int type;                    /* type of event */
        unsigned long serial;        /* # of last request processed by server */
        Bool send_event;             /* true if this came from SendEvent request */
        Display *display;            /* display the event was read from */
        Window window;               /* window being restacked */
        Window root;                 /* root window that the event occurred on */
        Window subwindow;            /* child window */
        Time time;                   /* milliseconds */
        int x, y;                    /* pointer coords relative to receiving window */
        int x_root, y_root;          /* coordinates relative to root */
        unsigned int state;          /* mask of all buttons and modifier keys */
        unsigned int keycode;        /* server-dependent code for key */
        Bool same_screen;            /* same screen flag */
} XKeyEvent;
typedef XKeyEvent XKeyPressedEvent;
typedef XKeyEvent XKeyReleasedEvent;
```

The values for the state member are listed under ButtonPress.

MapNotify, UnmapNotify

Generated when a window changes state from unmapped to mapped or vice versa. To receive these events on a single window, use StructureNotifyMask in the call to XSelectInput for the window. To receive these events for all children of a particular parent, specify the parent window ID and use SubstructureNotifyMask.

```
typedef struct {
        int type;                    /* type of event */
        unsigned long serial;        /* # of last request processed by server */
```

```
      Bool send_event;              /* true if this came from SendEvent request */
      Display *display;             /* display the event was read from */
      Window event;                 /* ID of window that selected this event */
      Window window;                /* ID of window that was just mapped or unmapped */
      Bool override_redirect;       /* true if window ignores this event */
} XMapEvent;

typedef struct {
      int type;                     /* type of event */
      unsigned long serial;         /* # of last request processed by server */
      Bool send_event;              /* true if this came from SendEvent request */
      Display *display;             /* display the event was read from */
      Window event;                 /* ID of window that selected this event */
      Window window;                /* ID of window that was just mapped or unmapped */
      Bool from_configure;          /* true if parent window was resized when window itself had */
                                    /* a win_gravity of UnmapGravity */
} XUnmapEvent;
```

MappingNotify

Generated when any of the following is changed by another client: the mapping between physical keyboard keys (keycodes) and keysyms, the mapping between modifier keys and logical modifiers, or the mapping between physical and logical pointer buttons. These events are triggered by a call to XSetModifierMapping or XSetPointerMapping, if the return status is MappingSuccess, or by any call to XChangeKeyboardMapping. The X server sends MappingNotify events to all clients. It is never selected and cannot be masked with the window attributes.

```
typedef struct {
      int type;                     /* type of event */
      unsigned long serial;         /* # of last request processed by server */
      Bool send_event;              /* true if this came from SendEvent request */
      Display *display;             /* display the event was read from */
      Window window;                /* window being restacked */
      int request;                  /* kind of mapping change that has occurred */
      int first_keycode;            /* first in a range of keycodes */
      int count;                    /* number of keycodes with altered mappings */
} XMappingEvent;
```

The members first_keycode and count are not set unless the request member is MappingKeyboard or MappingModifier.

The request member is specified with one of the following constants defined in *<X11/X.h>*:

```
#define MappingModifier          0
#define MappingKeyboard          1
#define MappingPointer           2
```

MapRequest

Generated when the functions XMapRaised and XMapWindow are called. (MapNotify indicates the *final* outcome of the request.) This event is selected by specifying the window ID of the parent of the receiving window with SubstructureRedirect-Mask. (In addition, the override_redirect member of the XSetWindowAttributes structure for the specified window must be False.)

```
typedef struct {
    int type;                 /* type of event */
    unsigned long serial;     /* # of last request processed by server */
    Bool send_event;          /* true if this came from SendEvent request */
    Display *display;         /* display the event was read from */
    Window parent;            /* ID of the parent of the window being mapped */
    Window window;            /* ID of the window being mapped */
} XMapRequestEvent;
```

MotionNotify

Generated when the user moves the pointer or when a program warps the pointer to a new position within a single window. This event is selected with Button-MotionMask, Button1MotionMask, Button2MotionMask, Button3MotionMask, Button4MotionMask, Button5MotionMask, PointerMotionHintMask, and PointerMotionMask. These masks determine the specific conditions under which the event is generated.

```
typedef struct {
    int type                  /* type of event */
    unsigned long serial;     /* # of last request processed by server */
    Bool send_event;          /* true if this came from SendEvent request */
    Display *display;         /* display the event was read from */
    Window window;            /* event window it is reported relative to */
    Window root;              /* root window that the event occurred on */
    Window subwindow;         /* child window */
    Time time;                /* milliseconds */
    int x, y;                 /* pointer coords relative to receiving window */
    int x_root, y_root;       /* coordinates relative to root */
    unsigned int state;       /* mask of all buttons and modifier keys */
    char is_hint;             /* NotifyNormal or NotifyHint */
    Bool same_screen;         /* same screen flag */
} XMotionEvent;
typedef XMotionEvent XPointerMovedEvent;
```

The is_hint member is specified with one of the following constants defined in <X11/X.h>:

```
#define NotifyNormal    0
#define NotifyHint      1
```

The values for the state member are listed under ButtonPress.

PropertyNotify

Generated when a property of a window has changed or been deleted. Generated by XChangeProperty, XDeleteProperty, XGetWindowProperty, or XRotateWindowProperties. This event is selected with PropertyChangeMask.

```
typedef struct {
    int type;                    /* type of event */
    unsigned long serial;        /* # of last request processed by server */
    Bool send_event;             /* true if this came from SendEvent request */
    Display *display;            /* display the event was read from */
    Window window;               /* ID of window whose property was changed */
    Atom atom;                   /* property that was changed */
    Time time;                   /* milliseconds */
    int state;                   /* new value or deleted */
} XPropertyEvent;
```

The state member is specified with one of the following constants defined in *<X11/X.h>*:

```
#define PropertyNewValue    0
#define PropertyDelete      1
```

ReparentNotify

A ReparentNotify event reports when a client successfully reparents a window. This event is selected with SubstructureNotifyMask by specifying the window ID of the old or the new parent window or with StructureNotifyMask by specifying the window ID.

```
typedef struct {
    int type;                    /* type of event */
    unsigned long serial;        /* # of last request processed by server */
    Bool send_event;             /* true if this came from SendEvent request */
    Display *display;            /* display the event was read from */
    Window event;                /* ID of event window */
    Window window;               /* ID of window whose parent window was changed */
    Window parent;               /* ID of new parent of the window */
    int x, y;                    /* pointer coords relative to receiving window */
    Bool override_redirect;      /* true if window ignores this event */
} XReparentEvent;
```

ResizeRequest

Generated when another client attempts to change the size of a window by calling XConfigureWindow, XMoveResizeWindow, or XResizeWindow. To receive this event type, specify a window ID and pass ResizeRedirectMask as part of the *event_mask* argument to XSelectInput. Only one client can select this event on a particular window. When selected, this event is triggered instead of resizing the window.

```
typedef struct {
    int type;                   /* type of event */
    unsigned long serial;       /* # of last request processed by server */
    Bool send_event;            /* true if this came from SendEvent request */
    Display *display;           /* display the event was read from */
    Window window;              /* window whose size another client wants to change */
    int width, height;          /* requested size of window, excluding its border */
} XResizeRequestEvent;
```

SelectionClear

Generated when a new owner is being defined. This event is not selected. It is
sent to the previous selection owner when another client calls XSetSelectionOwner
for the same selection.

```
typedef struct {
    int type;                   /* type of event */
    unsigned long serial;       /* # of last request processed by server */
    Bool send_event;            /* true if this came from SendEvent request */
    Display *display;           /* display the event was read from */
    Window window;              /* window that is receiving event and losing selection */
    Atom selection;             /* atom of selection that is changing ownership */
    Time time;                  /* last-change time recorded for the selection */
} XSelectionClearEvent;
```

SelectionNotify

Generated by clients, not by the server, when XSendEvent is called. There is no
event mask for SelectionNotify events, and they are not selected with XSelectInput.
Instead XSendEvent directs the event to a specific window, which is given as a
window ID: either PointerWindow, which identifies the window the pointer is in, or
InputFocus, which identifies the focus window.

The members of this structure have the values specified in the XConvertSelection
call that triggers the selection owner to send this event, except that the property
member will return either 1) the atom specifying a property on the requestor window with the data type specified in target or 2) None, which indicates that the data
could not be converted into the target type.

```
typedef struct {
    int type;                   /* type of event */
    unsigned long serial;       /* # of last request processed by server */
    Bool send_event;            /* true if this came from SendEvent request */
    Display *display;           /* display the event was read from */
    Window requestor;           /* the requesting window */
    Atom selection;             /* e.g., XA_PRIMARY or XA_SECONDARY */
    Atom target;                /* type property for desired format of data */
```

```
         Atom property;              /* Atom or None */
         Time time;                  /* milliseconds or CurrentTime */
    } XSelectionEvent;
```

SelectionRequest

Generated when another client requests the selection by calling XConvertSelection.
There is no event mask for SelectionRequest events, and they are not selected with
XSelectInput.

The members of this structure have the values specified in the XConvertSelection
call that triggers this event. The owner should convert the selection based on the
specified target type, if possible. If a property is specified, owner should store the
result as that property on the requestor window and then send a SelectionNotify
event to requestor by calling XSendEvent. If the selection cannot be converted as
requested, owner should send a SelectionNotify event with property set to the constant None.

```
    typedef struct {
         int type;                   /* type of event */
         unsigned long serial;       /* # of last request processed by server */
         Bool send_event;            /* true if this came from SendEvent request */
         Display *display;           /* display the event was read from */
         Window owner;               /* ID of current owner of selection */
         Window requestor;           /* ID of requesting client */
         Atom selection;             /* e.g., XA_PRIMARY or XA_SECONDARY */
         Atom target;                /* type property for desired format of data */
         Atom property;              /* Atom or None */
         Time time;                  /* milliseconds or CurrentTime */
    } XSelectionRequestEvent;
```

UnmapNotify

See MapNotify.

VisibilityNotify

Generated for any change in the visibility of the specified window. This event is
selected with VisibilityChangeMask.

```
    typedef struct {
         int type;                   /* type of event */
         unsigned long serial;       /* # of last request processed by server */
         Bool send_event;            /* true if this came from SendEvent request */
         Display *display;           /* display the event was read from */
         Window window;              /* ID of window affected by visibility event */
         int state;                  /* listed below */
    } XVisibilityEvent;
```

The state member is specified with one of the following constants defined in
<X11/X.h>:

```
#define VisibilityUnobscured            0
#define VisibilityPartiallyObscured     1
#define VisibilityFullyObscured         2
```

4

Xt Functions and Macros

Just as Section 1 summarizes Xlib, Section 4 provides an overview of the functions and macros in the Xt Intrinsics. The information is in two main parts:

- **Category listing.** Routines that perform related tasks are listed alphabetically under various categories.

- **Calling sequences.** Each function or macro is presented in alphabetical order, along with a brief description and its calling sequence.

Summary by Category

Sometimes you know the general task you need to do, but not the exact routine that does it. If this is the case, browse the categories here to find the routine you need. For more information about the function or macro, you can turn ahead to the alphabetical summary.

Category Headings

Action/Translation	Geometry	Object Information
Application Context	Graphics Context	Pop Up
Argument Lists	Initialization	Resource
Callback	Keyboard	Selection
Error	Locale Management	Widget Lifecycle
Event	Mouse Handling	Window Manipulation
File Searching	Memory	

Xt Routines

Category Listings

In the lists below, a bullet (•) precedes the name of any routine that is new in R5.

Action/Translation

XtAddActions
XtAppAddActionHook
XtAppAddActions
XtAugmentTranslations
XtCallActionProc
XtGetActionKeysym
• XtGetActionList
XtInstallAccelerators
XtInstallAllAccelerators
XtOverrideTranslations
XtParseAcceleratorTable
XtParseTranslationTable
XtRegisterGrabAction
XtRemoveActionHook
XtUninstallTranslations

Application Context

XtCreateApplicationContext
XtDestroyApplicationContext
XtDisplayInitialize
XtDisplayToApplicationContext
XtGetApplicationNameAndClass
XtOpenDisplay
XtToolkitInitialize
XtWidgetToApplicationContext

Argument Lists

XtMergeArgLists
XtNumber
XtOffset
XtOffsetOf
XtSetArg

Callback

XtAddCallback
XtAddCallbacks
XtCallbackReleaseCacheRef
XtCallbackReleaseCacheRefList
XtCallCallbackList
XtCallCallbacks
XtHasCallbacks
XtRemoveAllCallbacks
XtRemoveCallback
XtRemoveCallbacks

Error

XtAppError
XtAppErrorMsg
XtAppGetErrorDatabase
XtAppGetErrorDatabaseText
XtAppSetErrorHandler
XtAppSetErrorMsgHandler
XtAppSetWarningHandler
XtAppSetWarningMsgHandler
XtAppWarning
XtAppWarningMsg
XtDisplayStringConversionWarning
XtError
XtErrorMsg
XtGetErrorDatabase
XtGetErrorDatabaseText
XtSetErrorHandler
XtSetErrorMsgHandler
XtSetWarningHandler
XtSetWarningMsgHandler
XtStringConversionWarning
XtWarning
XtWarningMsg

Event

XtAddEventHandler
XtAddExposureToRegion
XtAddInput
XtAddRawEventHandler
XtAddTimeOut
XtAddWorkProc
XtAppAddInput
XtAppAddTimeOut
XtAppAddWorkProc
XtAppMainLoop
XtAppNextEvent
XtAppPeekEvent
XtAppPending
XtAppProcessEvent
XtBuildEventMask
XtDispatchEvent
XtInsertEventHandler
XtInsertRawEventHandler
XtLastTimestampProcessed

XtMainLoop
XtNextEvent
XtPeekEvent
XtPending
XtProcessEvent
XtRemoveEventHandler
XtRemoveInput
XtRemoveRawEventHandler
XtRemoveTimeOut
XtRemoveWorkProc

File Searching
XtFindFile
XtResolvePathname

Geometry
XtConfigureWidget
XtMakeGeometryRequest
XtMakeResizeRequest
XtMoveWidget
XtQueryGeometry
XtResizeWidget
XtUnmanageChild
XtUnmanageChildren

Graphics Context
• XtAllocateGC
XtDestroyGC
XtGetGC

Initialization
XtAppCreateShell
XtAppInitialize
XtCloseDisplay
XtCreateApplicationShell
XtInitialize
XtInitializeWidgetClass
XtVaAppCreateShell
XtVaAppInitialize

Keyboard
XtCallAcceptFocus
XtConvertCase
XtGetKeysymTable
XtGrabKey
XtGrabKeyboard
XtKeysymToKeycodeList
XtRegisterCaseConverter
XtSetKeyboardFocus

XtSetKeyTranslator
XtTranslateKeycode
XtUngrabKey
XtUngrabKeyboard

Locale Management
• XtSetLanguageProc

Memory
XtAppReleaseCacheRefs
XtCalloc
XtFree
XtMalloc
XtNew
XtNewString
XtRealloc
XtReleaseGC
XtVaCreateArgsList

Mouse Handling
XtGetMultiClickTime
XtGrabButton
XtGrabPointer
XtSetMultiClickTime
XtUngrabButton
XtUngrabPointer

Object Information
XtCheckSubclass
XtClass
XtDisplay
XtDisplayOfObject
XtIs*class*
XtIsManaged
XtIsRealized
XtIsSensitive
XtIsSubclass
XtName
XtNameToWidget
XtParent
XtScreen
XtScreenOfObject
XtSetWMColormapWindows
XtSuperclass
XtWindow
XtWindowOfObject
XtWindowToWidget

Pop Up

XtAddGrab
XtCallbackExclusive
XtCallbackNone
XtCallbackNonexclusive
XtCallbackPopdown
XtCreatePopupShell
XtMenuPopdown
XtMenuPopup
XtPopdown
XtPopup
XtPopupSpringLoaded
XtRemoveGrab
XtVaCreatePopupShell

Resource

XtAddConverter
XtAppAddConverter
XtAppSetFallbackResources
XtAppSetTypeConverter
XtCallConverter
XtConvert
XtConvertAndStore
XtDatabase
XtDirectConvert
XtGetApplicationResources
XtGetConstraintResourceList
XtGetResourceList
XtGetSubresources
XtGetSubvalues
XtGetValues
• XtScreenDatabase
XtSetMappedWhenManaged
XtSetSensitive
XtSetSubvalues
XtSetTypeConverter
XtSetValues
XtVaGetApplicationResources
XtVaGetSubresources
XtVaGetSubvalues
XtVaGetValues
XtVaSetSubvalues
XtVaSetValues

Selection

XtAppGetSelectionTimeout
XtAppSetSelectionTimeout
XtDisownSelection

XtGetSelectionRequest
XtGetSelectionTimeout
XtGetSelectionValue
XtGetSelectionValueIncremental
XtGetSelectionValues
XtGetSelectionValuesIncremental
XtOwnSelection
XtOwnSelectionIncremental
XtSetSelectionTimeout

Widget Lifecycle

XtCreateManagedWidget
XtCreateWidget
XtDestroyWidget
XtManageChild
XtManageChildren
XtMapWidget
XtRealizeWidget
XtUnmapWidget
XtUnrealizeWidget
XtVaCreateManagedWidget
XtVaCreateWidget

Window Manipulation

XtCreateWindow
XtResizeWindow
XtTranslateCoords

Some R3 functions are no longer used in R4. Although these R3 functions are retained for compatibility, their use is discouraged in later releases. The following table lists each of these functions, along with its R4 equivalent, if it has one.

Old R3 Functions	R4 Equivalent
XtAddActions	XtAppAddActions
XtAddConverter	XtSetTypeConverter
XtAddInput	XtAppAddInput
XtAddTimeOut	XtAppAddTimeOut
XtAddWorkProc	XtAppAddWorkProc
XtAppAddConverter	XtAppSetTypeConverter
XtConvert	XtConvertAndStore
XtCreateApplicationShell	XtAppCreateShell
XtDestroyGC	XtReleaseGC
XtDirectConvert	XtCallConverter
XtError	XtAppError
XtErrorMsg	XtAppErrorMsg
XtGetErrorDatabase	XtAppGetErrorDatabase
XtGetErrorDatabaseText	XtAppGetErrorDatabaseText
XtGetSelectionTimeout	XtAppGetSelectionTimeout
XtInitialize	XtAppInitialize
XtMainLoop	XtAppMainLoop
XtNextEvent	XtAppNextEvent
XtPeekEvent	XtAppPeekEvent
XtPending	XtAppPending
XtProcessEvent	XtAppProcessEvent
XtSetErrorHandler	XtAppSetErrorHandler
XtSetErrorMsgHandler	XtAppSetErrorMsgHandler
XtSetSelectionTimeout	XtAppSetSelectionTimeout

Old R3 Functions	R4 Equivalent
XtSetWarningHandler	XtAppSetWarningHandler
XtSetWarningMsgHandler	XtAppSetWarningMsgHandler
XtStringConversionWarning	XtDisplayStringConversionWarning
XtWarning	XtAppWarning
XtWarningMsg	XtAppWarningMsg

Alphabetical Listing

As in Section 1, *Xlib Functions and Macros*, the following alphabetical summary includes a brief description of each routine, followed by its calling sequence.

XtAddActions

Register an action table with the translation manager. This function has been superseded by XtAppAddActions.

```
void XtAddActions(actions, num_actions)
    XtActionList actions;
    Cardinal num_actions;
```

XtAddCallback

Add a callback procedure to a named callback list.

```
void XtAddCallback(w, callback_name, callback, client_data)
    Widget w;
    String callback_name;          /* callback list */
    XtCallbackProc callback;       /* callback procedure */
    XtPointer client_data;         /* argument passed to callback procedure */
```

XtAddCallbacks

Add an array of callback procedures to a named callback list.

```
void XtAddCallbacks(w, callback_name, callbacks)
    Widget w;
    String callback_name;          /* callback list */
    XtCallbackList callbacks;      /* callback procedures and client data */
```

XtAddConverter

Register an "old-style" resource converter. This function was superseded by XtSetTypeConverter in R4 and later releases.

```
void XtAddConverter(from_type, to_type, converter, convert_args, num_args)
    String from_type;
    String to_type;
    XtConverter converter;
    XtConvertArgList convert_args;
    Cardinal num_args;
```

XtAddEventHandler

Register a procedure to be called when specified events occur on a widget.

```
void XtAddEventHandler(w, event_mask, nonmaskable, proc, client_data)
    Widget w;                       /* widget for which event handler is to be registered */
    EventMask event_mask;           /* event mask to be used */
    Boolean nonmaskable;            /* event handler called on nonmaskable events? */
    XtEventHandler proc;            /* event handling procedure to be called */
    XtPointer client_data;          /* additional data to be passed to event handler */
```

XtAddExposureToRegion

Merge an Expose event or GraphicsExpose event into a region.

```
void XtAddExposureToRegion(event, region)
    XEvent *event;                  /* pointer to Expose or GraphicsExpose event */
    Region region;
```

XtAddGrab

Constrain or redirect user input to a modal widget. This function is automatically called by XtPopup.

```
void XtAddGrab(w, exclusive, spring_loaded)
    Widget w;                       /* widget to be added to modal cascade */
    Boolean exclusive;              /* events dispatched exclusively to this widget? */
    Boolean spring_loaded;          /* widget popped up by user pressing pointer button? */
```

XtAddInput

Register a procedure to be called when there is activity on a file descriptor. This function was superseded by XtAppAddInput in R4 and later releases.

```
XtInputId XtAddInput(source, condition, proc, client_data)
    int source;
    XtPointer condition;
    XtInputCallbackProc proc;
    XtPointer client_data;
```

XtAddRawEventHandler

Register an event handler without selecting for the event. This routine is similar to XtAddEventHandler, except that it never causes an XSelectInput call to be made for its events. Raw event handlers are removed with a call to XtRemoveRawEventHandler.

```
void XtAddRawEventHandler(w, event_mask, nonmaskable, proc, client_data)
    Widget w;                        /* widget for which event handler is being registered */
    EventMask event_mask;            /* call event handler on nonmaskable events? */
    Boolean nonmaskable;
    XtEventHandler proc;             /* procedure to be registered */
    XtPointer client_data;           /* additional data to be passed to event handler */
```

XtAddTimeOut

Register a procedure to be called when a specified time elapses. This function was superseded by XtAppAddTimeOut in R4 and later releases.

```
XtIntervalId XtAddTimeOut(interval, proc, client_data)
    unsigned long interval;
    XtTimerCallbackProc proc;
    XtPointer client_data;
```

XtAddWorkProc

Register a procedure to be called when the event loop is idle. This function was superseded by XtAppAddWorkProc in R4 and later releases.

```
XtWorkProcId XtAddWorkProc(proc, client_data)
    XtWorkProc proc;
    XtPointer client_data;
```

XtAllocateGC

Obtain a shareable graphics context with modifiable fields. This function returns a sharable graphics context with values as specified in *values* for each field set in *value_mask*. The GC is valid for the screen of the specified object and for drawable depth *depth*. The *dynamic_mask* and *dont_care_mask* arguments specify more information about the intended usage of the graphics context, which influences how it may be shared. (New in R5.)

```
GC XtAllocateGC (object, depth, value_mask, values, dynamic_mask, dont_care_mask)
    Widget object;
    Cardinal depth;                      /* depth graphics context  valid for */
    XtGCMask value_mask;                 /* fixed-value graphics context fields*/
    XtGCValues *values;                  /* values for fields in value_mask */
    XtGCMask dynamic_mask;               /* modifiable graphics context fields */
    XtGCMask dont_care_mask;             /* graphics context fields never used */
```

XtAppAddActionHook

Register a procedure to be called before any action is invoked. In the future, when any action routine is to be invoked for any widget in *app*, either through the translation manager or via XtCallActionProc, the action hook procedures will be called in reverse order of registration just prior to invoking the action routine.

```
XtActionHookId XtAppAddActionHook(app, proc, client_data)
    XtAppContext app;                    /* application context */
    XtActionHookProc proc;               /* action hook procedure */
    XtPointer client_data;               /* data passed to action hook */
```

XtAppAddActions

Register an action table with the Translation Manager.

```
void XtAppAddActions(app_context, actions, num_actions)
    XtAppContext app_context;
    XtActionList actions;                /* action table */
    Cardinal num_actions;                /* number of entries in action list */
```

XtAppAddConverter

Register an "old-style" resource converter. This function has been superseded by XtSetTypeConverter.

```
void XtAppAddConverter(app_context, from_type, to_type, converter, convert_args, num_args)
    XtAppContext app_context;
    String from_type;
    String to_type;
    XtConverter converter;
    XtConvertArgList convert_args;
    Cardinal num_args;
```

XtAppAddInput

Register a procedure to be called when there is activity on a file descriptor.

```
XtInputId XtAppAddInput(app_context, source, condition, proc, client_data)
    XtAppContext app_context;
```

```
int source;                          /* file descriptor or other device specification */
XtPointer condition;                 /* XtInputReadMask, XtInputWriteMask, */
                                     /* or XtInputExceptMask */
XtInputCallbackProc proc;            /* procedure called when condition is true */
XtPointer client_data;               /* data passed to input callback procedure when called */
```

XtAppAddTimeOut

Register a procedure to be called when a specified time elapses.

```
XtIntervalId XtAppAddTimeOut(app_context, interval, proc, client_data)
    XtAppContext app_context;
    unsigned long interval;          /* time interval in milliseconds */
    XtTimerCallbackProc proc;        /* procedure to be called when time expires */
    XtPointer client_data;           /* data passed to specified procedure */
```

XtAppAddWorkProc

Register a procedure to be called when the event loop is idle. Multiple work procedures can be registered, and the most recently added one is always the one called.

```
XtWorkProcId XtAppAddWorkProc(app_context, proc, client_data)
    XtAppContext app_context;
    XtWorkProc proc;
    XtPointer client_data;
```

XtAppCreateShell

Create a shell widget as the root of a widget tree.

```
Widget XtAppCreateShell(application_name, application_class, widget_class, display, args,
            num_args)
    String application_name;         /* name of application instance, or NULL */
    String application_class;        /* class name for application */
    WidgetClass widget_class;        /* class top level widget should be */
    Display *display;
    ArgList args;
    Cardinal num_args;
```

XtAppError

Call the low-level error handler. This function takes a simple string, which is printed out as the error message. In theory, most programs should use XtAppErrorMsg instead, so that messages can be easily customized.

```
void XtAppError(app_context, message)
    XtAppContext app_context;
    String message;                          /* message to be reported */
```

XtAppErrorMsg

Call the high-level fatal error handler. This function takes an error name and class and looks the message up in an error resource database.

```
void XtAppErrorMsg(app_context, name, type, class, default, params, num_params)
    XtAppContext app_context;
    String name;                    /* general error name */
    String type;                    /* detailed error type */
    String class;                   /* resource class */
    String default;                 /* default message to use if no message in database */
    String *params;                 /* pointer to list of values to be stored in error */
                                    /* message */
    Cardinal *num_params;
```

XtAppGetErrorDatabase

Obtain the default error database.

```
XrmDatabase *XtAppGetErrorDatabase(app_context)
    XtAppContext app_context;
```

XtAppGetErrorDatabaseText

Get the text of a named message from the error database.

```
void XtAppGetErrorDatabaseText(app_context, name, type, class, default, buffer_return, nbytes,
                database)
    XtAppContext app_context;
    String *name, *type, *class;    /* error name, error type, resource class */
    String *default;                /* default message to use if message not found */
    String *buffer_return;          /* buffer where message returned; allocated by caller */
    int nbytes;                     /* buffer size in bytes */
    XrmDatabase database;           /* database to use, NULL for default database */
```

XtAppGetSelectionTimeout

Get the current Intrinsics selection timeout value, in milliseconds, for the specified application context.

```
unsigned long XtAppGetSelectionTimeout(app_context)
    XtAppContext app_context;
```

XtAppInitialize

Initialize the X Toolkit internals, create an application context, open and initialize a display, and create the initial application shell instance.

```
Widget XtAppInitialize(app_context_return, application_class, options, num_options, argc_in_out,
            argv_in_out, fallback_resources, args, num_args)
```

```
XtAppContext *app_context_return;      /* returns application context, if non-NULL */
String application_class;              /* class name of application */
XrmOptionDescList options;             /* command-line options table */
Cardinal num_options;                  /* number of elements in options */
int *argc_in_out;                      /* address of number of command line arguments */
                                       /* (type Cardinal * in R4) */
String *argv_in_out;                   /* array of command-line arguments */
String *fallback_resources;            /* for use if application resource file cannot be */
                                       /* opened or read */
ArgList args;                          /* list to override other resource specifications */
Cardinal num_args;                     /* number of elements in args */
```

XtAppMainLoop

Continuously process events. This function is an infinite loop that reads the next incoming X Event by calling XtAppNextEvent, then dispatches it to the appropriate registered procedure by calling XtDispatchEvent.

```
void XtAppMainLoop(app_context)
    XtAppContext app_context;
```

XtAppNextEvent

Dispatch timer and alternate input event and return the next X event.

```
void XtAppNextEvent(app_context, event_return)
    XtAppContext app_context;
    XEvent *event_return;
```

XtAppPeekEvent

Return, but do not remove, the event at the head of an application's input queue; block if no events are available.

```
Boolean XtAppPeekEvent(app_context, event_return)
    XtAppContext app_context;
    XEvent *event_return;
```

XtAppPending

Determine if there are any events in an application's input queue. If there are pending events, a nonzero value is returned. The value indicates what types of event are pending and is a bitmask inclusive OR of any of the values XtIMXEvent, XtIMTimer, XtIMAlternateInput, or XtIMAll, which specifies all three event types.

```
XtInputMask XtAppPending(app_context)
    XtAppContext app_context;
```

XtAppProcessEvent

Process one X event, alternate input source event, or timer event in *app_context.*
mask specifies which types of events are to be processed; it is the bitwise inclusive OR of any of the values XtIMXEvent, XtIMTimer, XtIMAlternateInput, or the value XtIMAll, which specifies all three event types.

```
void XtAppProcessEvent(app_context, mask)
  XtAppContext app_context;
  XtInputMask mask;                    /* type of event to process */
```

XtAppReleaseCacheRefs

Decrement the reference counts for cached resources obtained from XtCallConverter. If any reference count reaches zero, the destructor registered with XtSetTypeConverter for that resource type, if any, will be called and the resource removed from the conversion cache.

```
void XtAppReleaseCacheRefs(app, refs)
  XtAppContext app;
  XtCacheRef *refs;                    /* NULL-terminated array of cache references */
```

XtAppSetErrorHandler

Set the low-level error handler procedure. The procedure *handler* is registered in *app_context* as the procedure to be invoked by XtAppError, and a pointer is returned to the previously installed low-level fatal error handler. The default low-level error handler is called _XtDefaultError and, on POSIX-based systems, prints the message to standard error and terminates the application.

```
XtErrorHandler XtAppSetErrorHandler(app_context, handler)
  XtAppContext app_context;
  XtErrorHandler handler;              /* fatal error procedure; should not return */
```

XtAppSetErrorMsgHandler

Set the high-level error handler. The procedure *msg_handler* is registered in *app_context* as the procedure to be invoked byXtAppErrorMsg, and a pointer is returned to the previously installed high-level error handler. The default high-level error handler is called _XtDefaultErrorMsg. It looks up a message in the error resource database, substitutes the supplied parameters into the message, and calls XtError.

```
void XtAppSetErrorMsgHandler(app_context, msg_handler)
  XtAppContext app_context;
  XtErrorMsgHandler msg_handler;       /* high-level fatal error message handling procedure */
```

XtAppSetFallbackResources

Specify a default set of resource values, *specification_list*, to be used in *app_context* to initialize the resource database if the application-class specific resource file cannot be found.

```
void XtAppSetFallbackResources(app_context, specification_list)
    XtAppContext app_context;
    String *specification_list;            /* NULL-terminated array of resource specs, */
                                           /* or NULL */
```

XtAppSetSelectionTimeout

Set the Intrinsics selection timeout value for *app_context*. This is the time within which two communicating applications must respond to one another. The initial timeout value is set by the selectionTimeout application resource, which has a default value of 5000 milliseconds (5 seconds).

```
void XtAppSetSelectionTimeout(app_context, timeout)
    XtAppContext app_context;
    unsigned long timeout;                 /* selection timeout in milliseconds */
```

XtAppSetTypeConverter

Register a "new-style" type converter in a single application context as a procedure to convert data of resource type *from_type* to resource type *to_type*.

```
void XtSetTypeConverter(from_type, to_type, converter, convert_args, num_args, cache_type,
        destructor)
    String from_type, to_type;            /* source and destination type */
    XtTypeConverter converter;            /* conversion procedure */
    XtConvertArgList convert_args;        /* additional conversion arguments, or NULL */
    Cardinal num_args;                    /* count of additional conversion arguments, or NULL */
    XtCacheType cache_type;               /* XtCacheNone, XtCacheAll, or XtCacheByDisplay */
    XtDestructor destructor;              /* free procedure for resources produced by this */
        /* converter, or NULL */
```

XtAppSetWarningHandler

Set the low-level warning handler. Register the procedure *handler* in *app_context* as the procedure to be invoked by XtAppWarning, and return a pointer to the previously installed low-level warning handler. The default low-level warning handler is called _XtDefaultWarning.

```
XtErrorHandler XtAppSetWarningHandler(app_context, handler)
    XtAppContext app_context;
    XtErrorHandler handler;               /* new nonfatal error handler */
```

XtAppSetWarningMsgHandler

Set the high-level warning handler. Register the procedure *msg_handler* in *app_context* as the procedure to be invoked by XtAppWarningMsg, and return a pointer to the previously installed high-level warning handler. The default high-level warning handler is called _XtDefaultWarningMsg.

```
void XtAppSetWarningMsgHandler(app_context, msg_handler)
    XtAppContext app_context;
    XtErrorMsgHandler msg_handler;
```

XtAppWarning

Call the low-level warning handler. On POSIX systems, the default handler is _XtDefaultWarning. It prints the message to the stderr stream and returns.

```
void XtAppWarning(app_context, message)
    XtAppContext app_context;
    String message;                     /* warning message to be reported */
```

XtAppWarningMsg

Call the high-level warning handler. The default high-level warning handler is called _XtDefaultWarningMsg. It calls XtAppGetErrorDatabaseText to lookup a message of the specified *name*, *type*, and *class* in the error database, and then calls XTWarning to display the message. If no such message is found, the specified *default* message is used.

```
void XtAppWarningMsg(app_context, name, type, class , default, params, num_params)
    XtAppContext app_context;
    String name;                        /* general error name */
    String type;                        /* detailed error type */
    String class;                       /* resource class */
    String default;                     /* default message */
    String *params;                     /* array of values to be inserted in message */
    Cardinal *num_params;               /* number of elements in params */
```

XtAugmentTranslations

Nondestructively merge new translations with widget's existing ones. The table *translations* is not altered by this process. Any #replace, #augment, or #override directives in *translations* are ignored by this function.

```
void XtAugmentTranslations(w, translations)
    Widget w;
    XtTranslations translations;        /* compiled translation table to merge in */
```

XtBuildEventMask

Retrieve a widget's event mask. This event mask is the logical OR of all event masks selected by adding event handlers and event translations (including accelerators).

```
EventMask XtBuildEventMask(w)
    Widget w;
```

XtCallAcceptFocus

Offer the input focus to a child widget—call the specified widget's Core class accept_focus method, passing it the specified widget and time and returns True if the widget took the input focus, or False otherwise. Generally, only widgets should call this function, and generally only on their descendants.

```
Boolean XtCallAcceptFocus(w, time)
    Widget w;
    Time *time;                          /* X time of event causing accept focus */
```

XtCallActionProc

Explicitly invoke a named action procedure—look up the action procedure and invoke it, passing *widget*, *event*, *params*, and *num_params* as arguments. Before calling the named action, invoke any action hook procedures that have been registered with XtAppAddActionHook.

```
void XtCallActionProc(widget, action, event, params, num_params)
    Widget widget;                       /* widget in which action to be invoked */
    String action;                       /* action name */
    XEvent *event;                       /* event passed to action routine */
    String *params;                      /* parameters passed to action routine */
    Cardinal num_params;                 /* number of parameters in params array */
```

XtCallCallbackList

Execute the procedures in a callback list, specifying the callback list by address. Invoke each procedure with *object* as the first argument, the data registered with the procedure as the second argument and *call_data* as the third argument. This function should only be called by widgets and objects; applications will never need to call it.

```
void XtCallCallbackList(object, callbacks, call_data)
    Widget object;
    XtCallbackList callbacks;            /* callback list to be invoked */
    XtPointer call_data;                 /* data value to be passed to each callback */
```

XtCallCallbacks

Execute the procedures on a widget's named callback list. Invoke each procedure with *object* as the first argument, the data registered with each procedure as the second argument, and *call_data* as the third argument. This function should only be called by widgets and objects; applications will never need to call it.

```
void XtCallCallbacks(object, callback_name, call_data)
    Widget object;
    String callback_name;          /* callback list to be executed */
    XtPointer call_data;           /* data value to be passed to each callback */
```

XtCallConverter

Explicitly invoke a "new-style" resource converter and cache result. Convert the value *from* as appropriate for the conversion procedure *converter* by looking a converted value up in the cache, or by invoking the converter with the *display, args, num_args, from,* and *to_in_out* arguments.

```
Boolean XtCallConverter( display, converter, args, num_args, from, to_in_out, cache_ref_return )
    Display* display;
    XtTypeConverter converter;     /* conversion procedure */
    XrmValuePtr args;              /* additional conversion arguments needed, or NULL */
    Cardinal num_args;             /* number of additional arguments */
    XrmValuePtr from;              /* source value to be converted */
    XrmValuePtr to_in_out;         /* returns actual size of converted value */
    XtCacheRef *cache_ref_return;  /* returns conversion cache ID, or NULL */
```

XtCallbackExclusive

Callback function to pop up a widget. This function calls **XtPopup** on the widget passed in the *client_data* argument, with *grab_mode* set to XtGrabExclusive, then calls XtSetSensitive on *w* to make that widget insensitive.

```
void XtCallbackExclusive(w, client_data, call_data)
    Widget w;
    XtPointer client_data;         /* pop-up shell */
    XtPointer call_data;           /* callback data; ignored /*
```

XtCallbackNone

Callback function to pop up a widget. This function calls **XtPopup** on the widget passed in the *client_data* argument, with *grab_mode* set to XtGrabNone, then calls XtSetSensitive on *w* to make that widget insensitive.

```
void XtCallbackNone(w, client_data, call_data)
    Widget w;
    XtPointer client_data;         /* pop-up shell */
    XtPointer call_data;           /* callback data; ignored */
```

XtCallbackNonexclusive

Callback function to pop up a widget. This function calls XtPopup on the widget passed in the *client_data* argument, with *grab_mode* set to XtGrabNonExclusive, then calls XtSetSensitive on *w* to make that widget insensitive.

```
void XtCallbackNonexclusive(w, client_data, call_data)
    Widget w;
    XtPointer client_data;          /* pop-up shell */
    XtPointer call_data;            /* callback data - ignored */
```

XtCallbackPopdown

Callback function to popdown a widget. Casts the *client_data* argument to an XtPopdownIDRec *, calls XtPopdown on the widget in the shell_widget field, then resensitizes the widget in the enable_widget field by calling XtSetSensitive. It is also possible to pop down a shell with XtMenuPopdown.

```
void XtCallbackPopdown(w, client_data, call_data)
    Widget w;
    XtPointer client_data;          /* pointer to an XtPopdownID structure */
    XtPointer call_data;            /* callback data - ignored */
```

XtCallbackReleaseCacheRef

Callback function to release a cached resource value. Casts the *client_data* argument to an XtCacheRef, places it in a NULL-terminated array of XtCacheRef, and passes this array to XtAppReleaseCacheRefs, which decrements the reference count on the specified object in the resource conversion cache and, if the count reaches zero, removes the object from the cache and calls the appropriate destructor procedures.

```
void XtCallbackReleaseCacheRef(object, client_data, call_data)
    Widget object;                  /* object with which resource associated */
    XtPointer client_data;          /* conversion cache entry to be released */
    XtPointer call_data;            /* ignored */
```

XtCallbackReleaseCacheRefList

Callback function to release a list of cached values. Casts the *client_data* argument to a NULL-terminated array of XtCacheRef and passes this array to XtAppReleaseCacheRefs, which decrements the reference count on the specified objects in the resource conversion cache and, if the count reaches zero on any of them, removes the object from the cache and calls the appropriate destructor procedures.

```
void XtCallbackReleaseCacheRefList(object, closure, call_data)
    Widget object;                          /* object with which resources associated */
    XtPointer client_data;                  /* conversion cache entries to be released */
    XtPointer call_data;                    /* ignored */
```

XtCalloc

Allocate memory for an array and initialize its bytes to zero. If there is insufficient memory, this function terminates by calling XtErrorMsg.

```
char *XtCalloc(num, size);
    Cardinal num;                           /* number of array elements to allocate */
    Cardinal size;                          /* size of an array element, in bytes */
```

XtCheckSubclass

Verify an object's class, if compiled with DEBUG defined. Check that *object* is of class *object_class* or a subclass. If it is not, call XtErrorMsg, passing *message* as the default message to be displayed.

```
void XtCheckSubclass(object, widget_class, message)
    Widget object;
    WidgetClass widget_class;               /* widget class to test against */
    String message;                         /* message to be displayed if object not a subclass */
```

XtClass

Obtain a widget's class.

```
WidgetClass XtClass(w)
    Widget w;
```

XtCloseDisplay

Close a display by calling XCloseDisplay, and removing it from an application context. Any converted resources associated with that display which are cached with an XtCacheType of XtCacheByDisplay are removed from the conversion cache and have their destructors, if any, called.

```
void XtCloseDisplay(display)
    Display *display;
```

XtConfigureWidget

Move and/or resize widget. If the new size and position are the same as the widget's current values, return immediately. Otherwise write the new *x, y, width, height,* and *border_width* values into instance fields of the object and, if the object is a widget and is realized, call XConfigureWindow on the widget's window.

```
void XtConfigureWidget(w, x, y, width, height, border_width)
    Widget w;
    Position x, y;                       /* new x and y coordinates of widget */
    Dimension width, height;             /* new size of widget */
    Dimension border_width;              /* new border width of widget */
```

XtConvert

Convert a value from one resource type to another. Look up the appropriate resource converter registered to convert from_type to to_type, compute any additional arguments required by that converter, then call XtDirectConvert or XtCallConverter, depending on whether the converter procedure is an "old-style" or a "new-style" converter.

```
void XtConvert(w, from_type, from, to_type, to_return)
    Widget w;
    String from_type;                    /* source type */
    XrmValuePtr from;                    /* value to be converted */
    String to_type;                      /* destination type */
    XrmValuePtr to_return;               /* returns address and size of converted value */
```

XtConvertAndStore

Look up and call a resource converter, copying the resulting value. Look up the type converter registered to convert from_type to to_type, compute any additional arguments needed, then call XtCallConverter (or XtDirectConvert for old-style converters) with the from and to_in_out arguments. Register XtCallbackReleaseCacheDef on the destroy callback list of object if the converted value is cached.

```
Boolean XtConvertAndStore(object, from_type, from, to_type, to_in_out)
    Widget object;
    String from_type;                    /* source data type */
    XrmValuePtr from;                    /* value to be converted */
    String to_type;                      /* destination type */
    XrmValuePtr to_in_out;               /* address and number of bytes for converted value */
```

XtConvertCase

Determine uppercase and lowercase versions of a keysym by calling the case converter procedure most recently registered for a range of keysyms that includes keysym.

```
void XtConvertCase(display, keysym, lower_return, upper_return)
    Display *display;
    KeySym keysym;                       /* keysym to convert */
    KeySym *lower_return;                /* returns lowercase equivalent of keysym */
    KeySym *upper_return;                /* returns uppercase equivalent of keysym */
```

XtCreateApplicationContext

Create and return an application context. The returned value is an opaque type. Every application must have at least one application context.

```
XtAppContext XtCreateApplicationContext()
```

XtCreateApplicationShell

Create an additional top-level widget. Call XtAppCreateShell, passing a NULL *application_name*, the *application_class* that was passed to XtInitialize, the display that was opened by XtInitialize, and the *widget_class*, *args*, and *num_args* arguments. This function was superseded by XtAppCreateShell in R4 and later releases.

```
Widget XtCreateApplicationShell(application_name, widget_class, args, num_args)
    String application_name;              /* ignored */
    WidgetClass widget_class;             /* widget class for created shell widget */
    ArgList args;                         /* argument list to override other resource */
        /* specifications */
    Cardinal num_args;
```

XtCreateManagedWidget

Create and manage a child widget by passing all of its arguments to XtCreateWidget, then calling XtManageChild on the resulting widget. Returns the created and managed widget.

```
Widget XtCreateManagedWidget(name, widget_class, parent, args, num_args)
    String name;
    WidgetClass widget_class;             /* widget class pointer for created widget */
    Widget parent;                        /* parent widget */
    ArgList args;                         /* argument list to override resource defaults */
    Cardinal num_args;
```

XtCreatePopupShell

Create a pop-up shell widget that is a subclass of Shell. The widget is not stored in the children array (maintained by Composite widgets), but rather in the popup_list array (which all widgets have).

```
Widget XtCreatePopupShell(name, widget_class, parent, args, num_args)
    String name;
    WidgetClass widget_class;
    Widget parent;                        /* parent widget */
    ArgList args;                         /* argument list to override the resource defaults */
    Cardinal num_args;
```

XtCreateWidget

Create an instance of a widget of the specified class. The resource name/resource value pairs in *args* are used to set resources in the widget and override resources from the resource database.

```
Widget XtCreateWidget( name, object_class, parent, args, num_args)
    String name;
    WidgetClass object_class;
    Widget parent;                     /* parent widget */
    ArgList args;                      /* argument list to override the resource defaults */
    Cardinal num_args;
```

XtCreateWindow

Create widget's window. Copy the depth, screen, x, y, width, height and border_width fields of the core part of the specified widget into the *attributes* structure. Then pass *attributes* and an appropriately modified *value_mask*, along with the widget's display, the widget's parent's window, *window_class*, and *visual* to the Xlib function XCreateWindow. Store the newly created Window in the widget's core part window field.

```
void XtCreateWindow( w, window_class, visual, value_mask, attributes)
    Widget w;
    unsigned int window_class;         /* InputOutput, InputOnly, or CopyFromParent */
    Visual *visual;
    XtValueMask value_mask;            /* attribute fields to use */
    XSetWindowAttributes *attributes;  /* window attributes for XCreateWindow call */
```

XtDatabase

Obtain the resource database for a particular display. In R4 and previous releases, this function returns the resource database built by XtDisplayInitialize for the display. In R5, which supports a resource database for each screen, it returns the resource database built by XtDisplayInitialize for the default screen of the display.

```
XrmDatabase XtDatabase( display)
    Display *display;
```

XtDestroyApplicationContext

Destroy an application context and close its displays. If called from within an event handler or a callback procedure, this function does not destroy the application context until the dispatch is complete.

```
void XtDestroyApplicationContext( app_context)
    XtAppContext app_context;
```

XtDestroyGC

This is a Release 2-compatible function to free up read-only graphics contexts; it has been superseded by XtReleaseGC.

```
void XtDestroyGC(w, gc)
    Widget w;
    GC gc;
```

XtDestroyWidget

Destroy a widget instance—destroys *object* and all of its normal and popup descendants, free all resources associated with that widget and its descendants, and call the Xlib function XDestroyWindow to destroy the windows (if any) of the affected objects.

```
void XtDestroyWidget(object)
    Widget object;
```

XtDirectConvert

Explicitly invoke an "old-style" resource converter and cache the result. Look in the converter cache to see if the named conversion procedure has previously been called with the specified arguments. If so, set the cached resource address and size in *to_return* and return. If no cached value is found, set *to_return*->addr to NULL and *to_return*->size to zero and call *converter* with the remaining arguments. The results of the conversion are stored in the cache and returned in *to_return*.

```
void XtDirectConvert(converter, args, num_args, from, to_return)
    XtConverter converter;
    XrmValuePtr args;              /* additional arguments needed for conversion */
    Cardinal num_args;             /* number of additional arguments */
    XrmValuePtr from;              /* value to be converted */
    XrmValuePtr to_return;         /* returns converted value */
```

XtDisownSelection

Indicate that selection data is no longer available—inform the Intrinsics selection mechanism that the specified widget is to lose ownership of the selection as of the specified time. If the widget does not currently own the selection, this function does nothing.

```
void XtDisownSelection(w, selection, time)
    Widget w;                      /* widget relinquishing ownership */
    Atom selection;                /* selection widget is giving up */
    Time time;                     /* timestamp indicating when relinquish request initiated */
```

XtDispatchEvent

Dispatch an event through registered event handlers, translations, and accelerators. In R5, this function also calls the new Xlib function XFilterEvent.

```
Boolean XtDispatchEvent( event)
    XEvent *event;                          /* pointer to event structure to be dispatched */
```

XtDisplay

Return the X Display pointer for the specified widget.

```
Display *XtDisplay( w)
    Widget w;
```

XtDisplayInitialize

Initialize a display and add it to an application context. This function parses the command line using the Xlib XrmParseCommand function, builds the resource database, and performs other per-display initialization.

```
void XtDisplayInitialize( app_context, display, application_name, application_class, options,
                num_options, argc, argv)
    XtAppContext app_context;
    Display *display;
    String application_name;
    String application_class;
    XrmOptionDescRec *options;              /* pointer to structure that defines how to parse */
                                            /* command line */
    Cardinal num_options;
    int *argc;                              /* pointer to number of command line arguments */
                                            /* (Cardinal * in R4) */
    String *argv;                           /* command line arguments */
```

XtDisplayOfObject

Return the display pointer for the nearest ancestor of an object that is of class Core. This function is identical to XtDisplay if the *object* is a widget.

```
Display *XtDisplayOfObject( object)
    Widget object;
```

XtDisplayStringConversionWarning

Issue a warning message during conversion of string resource values. The warning message is issued using XtAppWarningMsg, with *name* set to "conversionError", *type* set to "string", *class* set to "XtToolkitError" and the *default* message string set to: "Cannot convert *from_value* to type *to_type*".

```
void XtDisplayStringConversionWarning(display, from_value, to_type)
    Display *display;
    String from_value;                  /* string that could not be converted */
    String to_type;                     /* target representation type requested */
```

XtDisplayToApplicationContext

Retrieve the application context associated with a Display. If the display has not been initialized, an error message is issued.

```
XtAppContext XtDisplayToApplicationContext( display )
    Display *display;
```

XtError

Call the low-level fatal error handler. XtError has been superseded by XtAppError, which performs the same function on a per-application context basis.

```
void XtError( message)
    String message;
```

XtErrorMsg

Call the high-level fatal error handler. XtErrorMsg has been superseded by XtAppErrorMsg, which performs the same function on a per-application context basis.

```
void XtErrorMsg( name, type, class, default, params, num_params)
    String name;                        /* general error name */
    String type;                        /* detailed error type */
    String class;                       /* resource class of error */
    String default;                     /* default message */
    String *params;                     /* array of values to be stored in message */
    Cardinal *num_params;               /* number of elements in params */
```

XtFindFile

Search for a file by using substitutions in a path. Perform the substitutions specified by *substitutions* on each colon-separated element of *path* in turn, and pass the resulting string to *predicate*.

```
String XtFindFile(path, substitutions, num_substitutions, predicate)
    String path;                        /* path of file names */
    Substitution substitutions;         /* list of substitutions to make into path */
    Cardinal num_substitutions;         /* number of substitutions passed in */
    XtFilePredicate predicate;          /* procedure to judge each file name, or NULL */
```

XtFree

Free allocated memory.

```
void XtFree(ptr);
    char *ptr;                          /* pointer to memory to be freed */
```

XtGetActionKeysym

Retrieve the keysym and modifiers that matched the final event specification in the translation table entry.

```
KeySym XtGetActionKeysym(event, modifiers_return)
    XEvent* event;                      /* event pointer passed to action procedure */
    Modifiers* modifiers_return;        /* returns modifier state used to generate returned */
                                        /* keysym */
```

XtGetActionList

Get the action table of a widget class. (New in R5.)

```
void XtGetActionList (widget_class, actions_return, num_actions_return)
    WidgetClass widget_class;           /* widget class whose action table is return ed */
    XtActionList actions_return;        /* returns action table of widget class */
    Cardinal num_actions_return;        /* returns number of elements in action table */
```

XtGetApplicationNameAndClass

Return the application name and class passed to XtDisplayInitialize for a particular Display.

```
void XtGetApplicationNameAndClass(Display* display, String* name_return, String* class_return)
    Display *display;
    String *name_return;                /* returns application name; don't free or modify */
    String * class_return;              /* returns application class; don't free or modify */
```

XtGetApplicationResources

Set application variables from the resource database. This function retrieves resource settings that apply to an overall application rather than to a particular widget. For each resource in *resources*, a value is set in the structure pointed to by *base*. The value comes from the argument list *args* or, if no value for the resource is found there, from the resource database associated with *object* or, if no value is found in the database, from the *default_addr* field of the resource itself. Once determined, the value is copied into the structure at *base* using the resource_offset and resource_size fields of the resource.

```
void XtGetApplicationResources(object, base, resources, num_resources, args, num_args)
    Widget object;
    XtPointer base;                     /* base address of structure in which to write resources */
```

```
XtResourceList resources;           /* application's resource list */
Cardinal num_resources;             /* number of resources in resource list */
ArgList args;                       /* argument list to override other resource specs */
Cardinal num_args;                  /* number of arguments in argument list */
```

XtGetConstraintResourceList

Get the constraint resource list structure for a particular widget class. If it is
called before the widget class is initialized, the resource list as specified in the
widget class record will be returned. If it is called after the widget class has been
initialized, the merged resource list for the class and all constraint superclasses is
returned.

```
void XtGetConstraintResourceList(class, resources_return, num_resources_return)
  WidgetClass class;
  XtResourceList *resources_return;   /* returns constraint resource list; caller must free */
  Cardinal *num_resources_return;     /* returns number of entries in constraint resource list */
```

XtGetErrorDatabase

Obtain the error database. This function has been superseded by XtAppGetError-
Database, which performs the same function on a per-application context basis.

```
XrmDatabase *XtGetErrorDatabase
```

XtGetErrorDatabaseText

Get the text of a named message from the error database. This function has been
superseded by XtAppGetErrorDatabaseText.

```
void XtGetErrorDatabaseText(name, type, class, default, buffer_return, nbytes)
  char *name;                 /* name or general kind of message */
  char *type;                 /* type or detailed name of message */
  char *class;                /* resource clas of message */
  char *default;              /* default message */
  char *buffer_return;        /* buffer into which message to be returned */
  int nbytes;                 /* size of buffer_return in bytes */
```

XtGetGC

Obtain a read-only, sharable graphics context, with values as specified in *values*
for each bit set in *value_mask*. The graphics context is valid for the screen and
depth of *object*, or the nearest widget ancestor if *object* is not a subclass of Core.

```
GC XtGetGC(w, value_mask, values)
  Widget w;
  XtGCMask value_mask;        /* GC fields to be filled in with widget data */
  XGCValues *values;          /* actual values for graphics context */
```

XtGetKeysymTable

Return a pointer to the keysym-to-keycode mapping table for a particular display's table. This table is simply an array of KeySym. The number of keysyms
associated with each keycode is returned in *keysyms_per_keycode_return*. The first
keysyms in the table are for the keycode returned in *min_keycode_return*. The
returned table must not be modified or freed by the caller.

```
KeySym *XtGetKeysymTable(display, min_keycode_return, keysyms_per_keycode_return)
    Display *display;
    KeyCode *min_keycode_return;        /* minimum keycode valid for display */
    int *keysyms_per_keycode_return;    /* number of keysyms in each
    keycode */
```

XtGetMultiClickTime

Read the multi-click time—return the time in milliseconds that the translation
manager uses to determine if multiple events are to be interpreted as a repeated
event for purposes of matching a translation entry containing a repeat count.

```
int XtGetMultiClickTime(display)
    Display *display;
```

XtGetResourceList

Get the resource list of a widget class. If it is called before the widget class is initialized, it returns the resource list as specified in the widget class record. If it is
called after the widget class has been initialized, it returns a merged resource list
that includes the resources for all superclasses.

```
void XtGetResourceList(widget_class, resources_return, num_resources_return);
    WidgetClass widget_class;
    XtResourceList *resources_return;    /* returns resource list;
    caller must free */
    Cardinal *num_resources_return;      /* returns number of entries in resource list */
```

XtGetSelectionRequest

Retrieve the SelectionRequest event that triggered a XtConvertSelectionProc procedure.

```
XSelectionRequestEvent *XtGetSelectionRequest(w, selection, request_id)
    Widget w;
    Atom selection;              /* selection being processed */
    XtRequestId request_id;      /* request ID for incremental selections, or NULL */
```

XtGetSelectionTimeout

Get the current Intrinsics selection timeout value, in milliseconds. This function has been superseded by XtAppGetSelectionTimeout.

```
unsigned long XtGetSelectionTimeout()
```

XtGetSelectionValue

Request the value of a selection. This function initiates an ICCCM-compliant request to the owner of the *selection* to convert that selection to the type identified by *target*, and registers *callback* as the procedure to be called with *client_data* as one of its arguments when the converted value is ready.

```
void XtGetSelectionValue(w, selection, target, callback, client_data, time)
    Widget w;
    Atom selection;                         /* selection desired */
    Atom target;                            /* type of selection information needed */
    XtSelectionCallbackProc callback;       /* callback to be called when selection value obtained */
    XtPointer client_data;                  /* argument to be passed to callback */
    Time time;                              /* timestamp indicating when selection is desired */
```

XtGetSelectionValueIncremental

Obtain the selection value using incremental transfers. This function initiates an ICCCM-compliant request to the owner of the *selection* to convert the selected value to the type identified by *target*, and registers *callback* with the Intrinsics incremental selection interface as the procedure to call when segments of the requested value are delivered.

```
void XtGetSelectionValueIncremental(w, selection, target, selection_callback, client_data, time)
    Widget w;
    Atom selection;                         /* selection desired */
    Atom target;                            /* type of selection information needed */
    XtSelectionCallbackProc callback;       /* procedure called to receive data segments */
    XtPointer client_data;                  /* client data to be passed to callback */
    Time time;
```

XtGetSelectionValues

Obtain selection data in multiple formats. This function is similar to XtGetSelectionValue except it takes an array of target types and an array of client data and requests the current value of the selection converted to each of the targets. The callback is called once for each element of *targets*, and is passed the corresponding element of *client_data*.

```
void XtGetSelectionValues(w, selection, targets, count, callback, client_data, time)
    Widget w;
    Atom selection;
```

```
Atom *targets;                               /* type of selection information requested */
int count;                                   /* length of targets and client_data arrays */
XtSelectionCallbackProc callback;            /* callback for each selection value */
XtPointer client_data;                       /* array of client data */
Time time;                                   /* timestamp indicating when selection value is */
                                             /* desired */
```

XtGetSelectionValuesIncremental

Obtain multiple selection values using incremental transfers. This function is similar to XtGetSelectionValueIncremental except it takes an array of target types and an array of client data and requests the current value of the selection be converted to each of the targets.

```
void XtGetSelectionValuesIncremental(w, selection, targets, count, selection_callback,
            client_data, time)
    Widget w;
    Atom selection;
    Atom *targets;                               /* types of selection information requested */
    int count;                                   /* length of the targets and client_data arrays */
    XtSelectionIncrCallbackProc callback;        /* callback for each selection value */
    XtPointer *client_data;                      /* array of client data */
    Time time;                                   /* timestamp indicating when selection request was */
                                                 /* initiated */
```

XtGetSubresources

Copy resource values from a subpart data structure to an argument list. This function retrieves resource values for "subparts" of a widget or object that are not themselves widgets or objects. For each resource in *resources*, a value is set in the structure pointed to by *base*. This value comes from the argument list *args* or, if no value for the resource is found there, from the resource database associated with *object*, or if no value is found in the database, from the *default_addr* field of the resource itself. Once the value is determined, it is copied into the structure at *base* using the resource_offset and resource_size fields of the resource. This function is similar to XtGetApplicationResources.

```
void XtGetSubresources(w, base, name, class, resources, num_resources, args, num_args)
    Widget w;
    XtPointer base;                              /* base address of structure resources written into */
    String subpart_name;                         /* resource name of subpart */
    String class;                                /* resource class name of subpart */
    XtResourceList resources;                    /* resource list for subpart */
    Cardinal num_resources;                      /* number of resources in resource list */
    ArgList args;                                /* argument list to override other resource specs */
    Cardinal num_args;                           /* number of arguments in argument list */
```

XtGetSubvalues

Copy resource values from a subpart data structure to an argument list. This function uses each argument name field to look up the resource in *resources*, and uses the information in that resource structure to copy the resource value from the subpart structure pointed to by *base* to the location specified by the argument value field.

```
void XtGetSubvalues(base, resources, num_resources, args, num_args)
    XtPointer base;                    /* address of subpart data structure to retrieve */
        /* resources from */
    XtResourceList resources;          /* subpart resource list */
    Cardinal num_resources;            /* number of resources in resource list */
    ArgList args;                      /* list of name/address pairs */
    Cardinal num_args;
```

XtGetValues

Query widget resource values—retrieve the current values of one or more resources associated with a widget instance. Each element in *args* is an Arg structure which contains the resource name in the name field, and a pointer to the location at which the resource is to be stored in the *value* field.

```
void XtGetValues(object, args, num_args)
    Widget object;
    ArgList args;                      /* name/address pairs */
    Cardinal num_args;
```

XtGrabButton

Passively grab a single pointer button by calling XGrabButton. Passes the widget's window, and the remaining arguments directly to XGrabButton. If the widget is not realized, the call to XGrabButton will be performed when the widget is realized and its window becomes mapped. If the widget is unrealized and later realized again, the call to XGrabButton will be performed again.

```
void XtGrabButton(widget, button, modifiers, owner_events, event_mask, pointer_mode,
            keyboard_mode, confine_to, cursor)
    Widget widget;
    int button;                        /* mouse button to be grabbed */
    Modifiers modifiers;               /* modifiers that must be down */
    Boolean owner_events;              /* whether events are to be reported normally */
    unsigned int event_mask;           /* event mask to take effect during grab */
    int pointer_mode, keyboard_mode;   /* GrabModeSync or GrabModeAsync */
    Window confine_to;                 /* ID of window to confine pointer, or None */
    Cursor cursor;                     /* cursor to be displayed during grab */
```

XtGrabKey

Passively grab a key of the keyboard with XGrabKey. This function passes the widget's window and remaining arguments unmodified to XGrabKey.

```
void XtGrabKey(widget, keycode, modifiers, owner_events, pointer_mode, keyboard_mode)
  Widget widget;
  KeyCode keycode;                /* keycode of key to be grabbed */
  Modifiers modifiers;            /* mask specifying allowable modifier keys */
  Boolean owner_events;           /* whether events are to be reported normally */
  int pointer_mode;               /* GrabModeSync or GrabModeAsync */
  int keyboard_mode;              /* GrabModeSync or GrabModeAsync */
```

XtGrabKeyboard

Actively grab the keyboard. If the specified widget is realized, this function calls XGrabKeyboard, specifying the widget's window as the *grab_window*, passing its remaining argument unmodified, and returning whatever XGrabKeyboard returns. If the widget is not realized, GrabNotViewable is returned immediately.

```
int XtGrabKeyboard(widget, owner_events, pointer_mode, keyboard_mode, time)
  Widget widget;
  Boolean owner_events;           /* whether the pointer events to be reported normally */
  int pointer_mode, keyboard_mode;  /* GrabModeSync or GrabModeAsync */
  Time time;                      /* timestamp or CurrentTime */
```

XtGrabPointer

Actively grab the pointer. If the specified widget is realized, this function establishes an active pointer grab by calling XGrabPointer with the widget's window as the grab window, and passing the remaining arguments unmodified. It returns the value returned by XGrabPointer. If the widget is not realized, XGrabPointer immediately returns GrabNotViewable.

```
int XtGrabPointer(widget, owner_events, event_mask, pointer_mode, keyboard_mode,
                  confine_to, cursor, time)
  Widget widget;
  Boolean owner_events;           /whether events to be reported normally */
  unsigned int event_mask;        /* event mask to take effect during grab */
  int pointer_mode, keyboard_mode;  /* GrabModeSync or GrabModeAsync
  Window confine_to;              /* window in which to confine pointer, or None */
  Cursor cursor;                  /*  cursor to be displayed during grab, or None */
  Time time;                      / timestamp or CurrentTime */
```

XtHasCallbacks

Determine the status of a widget's callback list. This function checks the widget for a resource named *callback_name*. If the resource does not exist or is not of type

XtRCallback, XtCallbackNoList is returned. If the callback list exists but is empty, it returns XtCallbackHasNone. If the callback list contains at least one callback procedure, it returns XtCallbackHasSome.

```
XtCallbackStatus XtHasCallbacks(w, callback_name)
    Widget w;
    String callback_name;              /* callback list to be checked */
```

XtInitialize

Initialize toolkit and display. This is a convenience function for initializing an Xt application and has been superseded by XtAppInitialize. It calls XtToolkitInitialize to initialize the toolkit internals, creates a default application context for use by other superseded functions, calls XtOpenDisplay with *display_string* NULL and *application_name* NULL, and, finally calls XtAppCreateShell with *application_name* NULL and returns the created shell.

```
Widget XtInitialize(shell_name, application_class, options, num_options, argc, argv)
    String shell_name;                 /* ignored */
    String application_class;          /* class name of application */
    XrmOptionDescRec options[];        /* how to parse command line */
    Cardinal num_options;              /* number of entries in options list */
    int *argc;                         /* pointer to number of command line parameters */
    String argv[];                     /* command line parameters */
```

XtInitializeWidgetClass

Initialize a widget class without creating any widgets.

```
void XtInitializeWidgetClass(object_class)
    WidgetClass object_class;
```

XtInsertEventHandler

Register an event handler procedure that receives events before or after all previously registered event handlers.

```
void XtInsertEventHandler(w, event_mask, nonmaskable, proc, client_data, position)
    Widget w;
    EventMask event_mask;
    Boolean nonmaskable;               /* whether procedure should be called on */
                                       /* nonmaskable event */
    XtEventHandler proc;               /* procedure to be called */
    XtPointer client_data;             /* additional data passed to event handler */
    XtListPosition position;           /* XtListHead or XtListTail */
```

XtInsertRawEventHandler

Register an event handler procedure that receives events before or after all previously registered event handlers, without selecting for the events.

```
void XtInsertRawEventHandler(w, event_mask, nonmaskable, proc, client_data, position)
    Widget w;
    EventMask event_mask;
    Boolean nonmaskable;                /* whether procedure should be called on nonmaskable */
                                        /* events */
    XtEventHandler proc;                /* procedure to be registered */
    XtPointer client_data;              /* additional data passed to event handler when called */
    XtListPosition position;            /* XtListHead or XtListTail */
```

XtInstallAccelerators

Install a widget's accelerators on another widget—merge the accelerator table of *source* into the translation table of *destination*.

```
void XtInstallAccelerators(destination, source)
    Widget destination;
    Widget source;
```

XtInstallAllAccelerators

Install all accelerators from a widget and its descendants onto a destination widget. This function recursively traverses the widget tree rooted at *source* and installs the accelerator resource values of each widget onto *destination*.

```
void XtInstallAllAccelerators(destination, source)
    Widget destination;
    Widget source;
```

Xtls*class*

Test whether a widget is a subclass of the *class* widget class, where *class* is one of ApplicationShell, Composite, Constraint, Object, OverrideShell, RectObj, Shell, TopLevelShell, TransientShell, VendorShell, WMShell, or Widget.

```
Boolean Xtls class(object)
    Widget object;
```

XtIsManaged

Determine whether a widget is managed by its parent.

```
Boolean XtIsManaged(object)
    Widget object;                      /* object whose state is to be tested */
```

XtIsRealized

Determine whether a widget has been realized.

```
Boolean XtIsRealized(object)
    Widget object;
```

XtIsSensitive

Check the current sensitivity state of a widget.

```
Boolean XtIsSensitive(object)
    Widget object;
```

XtIsSubclass

Determine whether a widget is a subclass of a class.

```
Boolean XtIsSubclass(object, object_class)
    Widget object;
    WidgetClass object_class;          /* widget class to test against */
```

XtKeysymToKeycodeList

Return the list of keycodes that map to a particular keysym in the keyboard mapping table maintained by the Intrinsics.

```
void XtKeysymToKeycodeList(display, keysym, keycodes_return, keycount_return)
    Display *display;
    KeySym keysym;
    KeyCode **keycodes_return;         /* returns list of keycodes associated with  keysyms; */
                                       /* must be freed by caller */
    Cardinal *keycount_return;         /* returns number of keycodes in keycodes list */
```

XtLanguageProc

Prototype procedure to set locale. The procedure registered with XtSetLanguageProc and called by XtDisplayInitialize is of type XtLanguageProc. A language procedure is passed the language string, if any, from the application command line or per-display resources and should use that string to localize the application appropriately. (New in R5.)

```
typedef String (*XtLanguageProc)(Display*, String, XtPointer);
    Display                *display;
    String                 language;
    XtPointer              client_data;
```

XtLastTimestampProcessed

Retrieve the timestamp from the most recent event handled by XtDispatchEvent that contains a timestamp.

```
Time XtLastTimestampProcessed(display)
    Display *display;
```

XtMainLoop

Continuously process events. This function has been superseded by XtAppMain-Loop, which performs the same function on a per-application context basis.

```
void XtMainLoop()
```

XtMakeGeometryRequest

Request parent to change child's geometry. The request_mode field of *request* specifies which elements of its geometry the object is asking to have changed, and the remaining fields of this structure specify the values for each of those elements. XtGeometryYes is returned if the request was granted and performed, XtGeometryNo if the request was denied and XtGeometryAlmost if request could not be satisfied exactly, but the object's parent has proposed a compromise geometry in *geometry_return*.

```
XtGeometryResult XtMakeGeometryRequest(w, request, reply_return)
    Widget w;
    XtWidgetGeometry *request;          /* desired widget geometry */
    XtWidgetGeometry *reply_return;     /* returns compromise geometry for XtGeometryAlmost */
```

XtMakeResizeRequest

Request parent to change child's size. This is a simplified version of XtMak-eGeometryRequest that a child can use to ask its parent to change its size. It creates an XtWidgetGeometry structure, specifies *width*, and *height*, sets request_mode to Width | Height), and passes it to XtMakeGeometryRequest. The return values are as for XtMakeGeometryRequest.

```
XtGeometryResult XtMakeResizeRequest(w, width, height, width_return, height_return)
    Widget w;
    Dimension width, height;                    /* desired widget width and height */
    Dimension *width_return, *height_return;    /* returns compromise size for */
                                                /* XtGeometryAlmost */
```

XtMalloc

Allocate memory.

```
char *XtMalloc(size);
    Cardinal size;                      /* number of bytes of memory to allocate */
```

XtManageChild

Bring a widget under its parent's geometry management by constructing a Widget-List of length one and calling XtManageChildren.

```
void XtManageChild(w)
    Widget w;                         /* child widget to be managed */
```

XtManageChildren

Bring an array of widgets created with XtCreateWidget under their parent's geometry management.

```
void XtManageChildren(children, num_children)
    WidgetList children;              /* array of child widgets */
    Cardinal num_children;            /* number of children in array */
```

XtMapWidget

Map a widget's window. This is usually done automatically when a widget is managed.

```
XtMapWidget(w)
    Widget w;
```

XtMenuPopdown

Built-in action for popping down a widget. This is a predefined action procedure which does not have a corresponding public C routine, and can only be invoked from a translation table. In R3, this action is called MenuPopdown.

```
<Event sequence>: XtMenuPopdown([shell])
    shell;                            /* shell to be popped down */
```

XtMenuPopup

Built-in action for popping up a widget. This is a predefined action procedure which does not have a corresponding public C routine. It can only be invoked from a translation table. In R3, this function is called MenuPopup.

```
<Event sequence>: XtMenuPopup(shell_name)
    shell_name;                       /* name of shell to be popped up */
```

XtMergeArgLists

Merge two ArgList arrays—allocate a new ArgList large enough to hold *args1* and *args2*, and copy both into it.

```
ArgList XtMergeArgLists(args1, num_args1, args2, num_args2)
    ArgList args1;
```

```
Cardinal num_args1;
ArgList args2;
Cardinal num_args2;
```

XtMoveWidget

Move a widget within its parent. This function returns immediately if the specified geometry fields for the widget are the same as the current values. Otherwise
it writes the new *x* and *y* values into the widget and, if the widget is realized,
issues an Xlib XMoveWindow call on the widget's window.

```
void XtMoveWidget(w, x, y)
    Widget w;
    Position x, Position y;
```

XtName

Return to the name of the specified object.

```
String XtName(object)
    Widget object;
```

XtNameToWidget

Find a named widget—return a descendant of the *reference* widget whose name
matches the specified *names*. The *names* argument specifies a simple object name
or a series of simple object name components separated by periods or asterisks.

```
Widget XtNameToWidget(reference, names);
    Widget reference;          /* widget from which the search is to start */
    String names;              /* partially qualified name of desired widget */
```

XtNew

Allocate storage for a new instance of a data type. This macro is called with the
datatype (a type, not a variable) and returns a pointer to enough allocated memory to hold that type. The return value is correctly cast to *type* *.

```
type *XtNew(type)
    type;
```

XtNewString

Copy an instance of a string—allocate enough memory to hold a copy of the
specified string and copy the string into that memory. If there is insufficient
memory to allocate the new block, print an error message and terminate the application by calling XtErrorMsg.

```
String XtNewString(string)
    String string;            /* NULL-terminated string */
```

XtNextEvent

Return next event from input queue. If no events are pending, the output buffer and blocks are flushed. This function has been superseded by XtAppNextEvent.

```
void XtNextEvent(event_return)
    XEvent *event_return;              /* returns event information from dequeued event */
                                        /* structure */
```

XtNumber

Determine the number of elements in a fixed-size array (a static argument list or resource list, for example).

```
Cardinal XtNumber(array)
    ArrayVariable array;               /* fixed-size array of arbitrary type */
```

XtOffset

Determine byte offset of a field within a structure pointer type, given field name and a type which points to the structure. This macro has been superseded by XtOffsetOf, which takes the structure type itself rather than a pointer to the structure, and is defined in a more portable way.

```
Cardinal XtOffset(pointer_type, field_name)
    Type pointer_type;                 /* type declared as pointer to the structure */
    Field field_name;                  /* name of structure field pointed to by pointer_type */
```

XtOffsetOf

Determine byte offset of a field within a structure type. This macro expands to a constant expression that gives the offset in bytes of the specified structure member from the beginning of the structure.

```
Cardinal XtOffsetOf(structure_type, field_name)
    Type structure_type;               /* type declared as a structure */
    Field field_name;                  /* name of a field of the structure */
```

XtOpenDisplay

Open, initialize, and add a display to an application context. This function calls XOpenDisplay with the name of the display to open, then calls XtDisplayInitialize and passes it the rest of the arguments.

```
Display *XtOpenDisplay(app_context, display_name, application_name, application_class,
            options, num_options, argc, argv)
    XtAppContext app_context;
```

```
String display_name;                /* name of display to be opened */
String application_name;            /* name of application instance */
String application_class;           /* name of application class */
XrmOptionDescRec *options;          /* how to parse command line for application-specific */
                                    /* resources */
Cardinal num_options;               /* number of entries in options array */
int *argc;                          /* pointer to number of command line parameters /*
                                    /* (type Cardinal * in R4) */
String *argv;                       /* command line parameters */
```

XtOverrideTranslations

Merge new translations, overwriting widget's existing ones. The table *translations* is not altered by this process. Any #replace, #augment, or #override directives in *translations* are ignored by this function.

```
void XtOverrideTranslations(w, translations)
    Widget w;                       /* widget into which new translations to be merged */
    XtTranslations translations;    /* translation table to merge in */
```

XtOwnSelection

Make selection data available to other clients. This function tells the Intrinsics that as of time *time*, widget *w* has data it would like to make available to other clients through the selection named by *selection*. *convert_proc* will be called when a client requests the selection, *lose_proc*, if non-NULL, will be called when another widget or another client asserts ownership of the selection, and *done_proc*, if non-NULL, will be called after the requesting client has received the data converted by *convert_proc*.

```
Boolean XtOwnSelection(w, selection, time, convert_proc, lose_selection, done_proc)
    Widget w;
    Atom selection;
    Time time;
    XtConvertSelectionProc convert_proc;
    XtLoseSelectionProc lose_selection;
    XtSelectionDoneProc done_proc;
```

XtOwnSelectionIncremental

Make selection data available to other clients using the incremental transfer interface. This function tells the Intrinsics that as of time *time* widget *w* has data it would like to make available to other clients through the selection named by *selection*. *convert_callback* will be called when a client requests the value of the selection, *lose_callback* will be called, if non-NULL, when another widget or another client asserts ownership of the selection, *done_callback* will be called, if non-NULL, when all segments of a selection have been transferred, and *cancel_callback* will be called, if non-NULL, if a selection request is aborted because a timeout expires.

```
Boolean XtOwnSelectionIncremental(w, selection, time, convert_callback, lose_callback,
            done_callback, cancel_callback, client_data)
    Widget w;
    Atom selection;
    Time time;
    XtConvertSelectionIncrProc convert_callback;
    XtLoseSelectionIncrProc lose_callback;
    XtSelectionDoneIncrProc done_callback;
    XtCancelConvertSelectionProc cancel_callback;
    XtPointer client_data;
```

XtParent

Return the parent of the specified widget.

```
Widget XtParent(w)
    Widget w;
```

XtParseAcceleratorTable

Compile an accelerator table into its internal representation. This compiled table can be used to set the XtNaccelerators resource of a widget.

```
XtAccelerators XtParseAcceleratorTable(table)
    String table;                           /* accelerator table to compile */
```

XtParseTranslationTable

Compile a translation table into its internal representation. This compiled form can then be set as the value of a widget's XtNtranslations resource, or merged with a widget's existing translation table with XtAugmentTranslations or XtOverrideTranslations.

```
XtTranslations XtParseTranslationTable(table)
    String table;                           /* translation table to compile */
```

XtPeekEvent

Return, but do not remove, the event at the head of an application's input queue. This function has been superseded by XtAppPeekEvent.

```
Boolean XtPeekEvent(app_context, event_return)
    XEvent *event_return;
```

XtPending

Determine if there are any events in an application's input queue. This function has been superseded by XtAppPending, which performs the same function on a per-application context basis.

```
XtInputMask XtPending()
```

XtPopdown

Unmap a pop-up shell—pop down a pop-up shell and call the functions registered on the shell's XtNpopdownCallback list.

```
void XtPopdown(popup_shell)
    Widget popup_shell;                    /* widget shell to pop up */
```

XtPopup

Map a pop-up shell—call the functions registered on the shell's XtNpopupCallback list and pop up the shell widget (and its managed child).

```
void XtPopup(popup_shell, grab_kind)
    Widget popup_shell;                    /* widget shell to pop up */
    XtGrabKind grab_kind;                  /* XtGrabNone, XtGrabNonexclusive, or XtGrabExclusive */
```

XtPopupSpringLoaded

Map a spring-loaded pop-up—call the functions registered on the specified shell's XtNpopupCallback callback list and pop the shell up, making it spring-loaded.

```
void XtPopupSpringLoaded(popup_shell)
    Widget popup_shell;                    /* shell widget to be popped up */
```

XtProcessEvent

Get and process one input event of a specified type. This function has been superseded by XtAppProcessEvent, which performs the same function on a per-application context basis.

```
void XtProcessEvent(mask)
    XtInputMask mask;                      /* XtIMXEvent, XtIMTimer, or XtIMAlternateInput */
```

XtQueryGeometry

Query a child widget's preferred geometry by invoking its *query_geometry* method. The *intended* structure specifies the geometry values that the parent plans to set. The *geometry_return* structure returns the child's preferred geometry. The return value of the function may be one of the following values: XtGeometryYes (proposed change acceptable), XtGeometryAlmost (child does not agree entirely with proposed change), or XtGeometryNo (child would prefer that no changes were made).

```
XtGeometryResult XtQueryGeometry(w, intended, preferred_return)
    Widget w;
    XtWidgetGeometry *intended;            /* intended changes, or NULL */
    XtWidgetGeometry *preferred_return;    /* returns preferred geometry */
```

XtRealizeWidget

Realize a widget instance.

```
void XtRealizeWidget(w)
    Widget w;
```

XtRealloc

Change the size of an allocated block of storage pointed to by *ptr* to be at least *num* bytes large. If *ptr* is NULL, XtRealloc simply calls XtMalloc to allocate a block of memory of the requested size.

```
char *XtRealloc(ptr, num);
    char *ptr;          /* pointer to allocated memory */
    Cardinal num;       /* number of bytes of memory desired in block */
```

XtRegisterCaseConverter

Register a case converter *proc* with the Intrinsics as a procedure to be called in order to determine the correct uppercase and lowercase versions of any keysyms between *start* and *stop*, inclusive. The registered converter overrides any previous converters registered in that range.

```
void XtRegisterCaseConverter(display, proc, start, stop)
    Display *display;
    XtCaseProc proc;    /* procedure to perform case conversion */
    KeySym start;       /* first keysym for which converter valid */
    KeySym stop;        /* last keysym for which converter valid */
```

XtRegisterGrabAction

Register action procedure *action_proc* as one that needs a passive grab to function properly. The *owner_events*, *event_mask*, *pointer_mode*, and *keyboard_mode* arguments are passed to XtGrabKey or XtGrabButton when the action is triggered.

```
void XtRegisterGrabAction(action_proc, owner_events, event_mask, pointer_mode,
                keyboard_mode)
    XtActionProc action_proc;   /* action procedure requiring passive grab */
```

```
    Boolean owner_events;              /* whether events are to be reported normally */
    unsigned int event_mask;           /* event mask to take effect during grab */
    int pointer_mode, keyboard_mode;   /* GrabModeSync or GrabModeAsync */
```

XtReleaseGC

Deallocate a shared GC allocated with XtGetGC or XtAllocateGC when it is no longer needed.

```
    void XtReleaseGC(object, gc)
    Widget object;
    GC gc;
```

XtRemoveActionHook

Remove the specified action hook procedure from the list in which it was registered. The *id* argument is the value returned by XtAppAddActionHook when the action hook procedure was registered.

```
    void XtRemoveActionHook(id)
    XtActionHookId id;                 /* id for action hook to be removed */
```

XtRemoveAllCallbacks

Delete all procedures from a callback list named by *callback_name* in the object *object*.

```
    void XtRemoveAllCallbacks(object, callback_name)
    Widget object;
    String callback_name;              /* name of callback list */
    procedures to be removed */
```

XtRemoveCallback

Remove a callback from a callback list. This function removes the *callback/client_data* pair from the callback list named by *callback_name* of the object *object*. If no entry matches both *callback* and *client_data*, the function returns without generating a warning message.

```
    void XtRemoveCallback(object, callback_name, callback, client_data)
    Widget object;
    String callback_name;              /* name of callback list */
    XtCallbackProc callback;           /* callback procedure to be deleted */
    XtPointer client_data;             /* data registered with procedure */
```

XtRemoveCallbacks

Remove a list of callbacks from a callback list. This function removes the procedure/data pairs in *callbacks* from the callback list named by *callback_name* of object *object*.

```
void XtRemoveCallbacks( object, callback_name, callbacks)
    Widget object;
    String callback_name;          /* name of callback list */
    XtCallbackList callbacks;      /* callback procedure to be deleted */
```

XtRemoveEventHandler

Remove an event handler, or change the conditions under which it is called. This function stops the *proc/client_data* event handler pair registered with XtAddEventHandler or XtInsertEventHandler from being called from widget *w* in response to the events specified in *event_mask*. In addition, if *nonmaskable* is True, the handler will no longer be called in response to the nonmaskable events. A handler is removed only if both the procedure *proc* and *client_data* match a previously registered handler/data pair.

```
void XtRemoveEventHandler( w, event_mask, nonmaskable, proc, client_data)
    Widget w;
    EventMask event_mask;          /* events for which to unregister handler */
    Boolean nonmaskable;           /* whether event handler should be removed */
                                   /* for nonmaskable events */
    XtEventHandler proc;           /* handler procedure to be removed */
    XtPointer client_data;         /* data registered with procedure */
```

XtRemoveGrab

Redirect user input from modal widget back to normal destination.

```
void XtRemoveGrab( w)
    Widget w;
```

XtRemoveInput

Cause the Intrinsics to stop calling a callback procedure registered with XtAppAddInput. The *id* argument is a handle returned by the call to XtAppAddInput that registered the input callback.

```
void XtRemoveInput( id)
    XtInputId id;                  /* IDs input source and callback procedure */
```

XtRemoveRawEventHandler

Remove a raw event handler, or change the conditions under which it is called. This function stops the *proc/client_data* event handler pair registered with XtAdd-RawEventHandler or XtInsertRawEventHandler from being called from widget *w* in response to the events specified in *event_mask*. In addition, if *nonmaskable* is True, then the handler will no longer be called in response to the nonmaskable events. A handler is removed only if both the procedure *proc* and *client_data* match a previously registered handler/data pair.

```
void XtRemoveRawEventHandler(w, event_mask, nonmaskable, proc, client_data)
    Widget w;
    EventMask event_mask;          /* events for which to unregister handler */
    Boolean nonmaskable;           /* whether handler should be removed for nonmaskable */
                                   /* events */
    XtEventHandler proc;/          /* handler procedure */
    XtPointer client_data;         /* client data with which procedure registered */
```

XtRemoveTimeOut

Unregister a timeout procedure registered with XtAppAddTimeout. The *timer* argument is the handle returned by the call which registered the timeout procedure.

```
void XtRemoveTimeOut(timer)
    XtIntervalId timer;
```

XtRemoveWorkProc

Unregister a work procedure. The *id* argument is the handle returned by XtApp-AddWorkProc when the procedure was registered.

```
void XtRemoveWorkProc(id)
    XtWorkProcId id;
```

XtResizeWidget

Change the width, height, and border width of *w* as specified. If the widget is realized, this function calls XConfigureWindow to change the size of the widget's window. It calls the widget's resize method to notify it of the size changes, whether the widget is realized or not.

```
void XtResizeWidget(w, width, height, border_width)
    Widget w;
    Dimension width, height, border_width;/* new widget size and border width */
```

XtResizeWindow

Resize a widget's window by calling the Xlib function XConfigureWindow to make the window of the specified widget match its Core width, height, and border_width fields. XtResizeWindow does not call the widget's resize method.

```
void XtResizeWindow(w)
    Widget w;
```

XtResolvePathname

Search for a file using standard substitutions in a path list. The caller must free the returned string.

```
String XtResolvePathname(display, type, filename, suffix, path, substitutions, num_substitutions,
            predicate)
    Display *display;
    String type;                        /* type of file; substituted for %T */
    String filename;                    /* name of file; substituted for %N */
    String suffix;                      /* suffix of file; substituted for %S */
    String path;                        /* path of file specifications to test */
    Substitution substitutions;         /* additional substitutions for path */
    Cardinal num_substitutions;         /* number of entries in substitutions */
    XtFilePredicate predicate;          /* procedure to be called to test each file name */
```

XtScreen

Return the screen pointer for the specified widget.

```
Screen *XtScreen(w)
    Widget w;
```

XtScreenDatabase

Obtain the resource database for a screen. (New in R5.)

```
XrmDatabase* XtScreenDatabase(screen)
    Screen *screen;
```

XtScreenOfObject

Return the screen pointer of a non-widget object. This function is identical to XtScreen if the object is a widget; otherwise it returns the screen pointer for the nearest ancestor of *object* that has a window.

```
Screen *XtScreenOfObject(object)
    Widget object;
```

Xt Routines

XtSetArg

Set a resource name and value in an argument list.

```
void XtSetArg( arg, resource_name, value)
    Arg arg;
    String resource_name;
    XtArgVal value;
```

XtSetErrorHandler

Set the low-level error handler procedure. This function has been superseded by XtAppSetErrorHandler, which performs the same function on a per-application context basis.

```
void XtSetErrorHandler( handler)
    XtErrorHandler handler;            /* new low-level fatal error procedure; should not return */
```

XtSetErrorMsgHandler

Set the high-level error handler procedure. This function has been superseded by XtAppSetErrorMsgHandler, which performs the same function on a per-application context basis.

```
void XtSetErrorMsgHandler( msg_handler)
    XtErrorMsgHandler msg_handler;     /* new high-level fatal error procedure—should not return */
```

XtSetKeyTranslator

Register a key translator. The default translator is XtTranslateKey, an XtKeyProc that uses the Shift, Lock, and group modifiers with the interpretations defined by the X11 protocol.

```
void XtSetKeyTranslator( display, proc)
    Display *display;
    XtKeyProc proc;                    /* procedure to perform key translations */
```

XtSetKeyboardFocus

Redirect keyboard input to a widget—cause XtDispatchEvent to remap keyboard events that occur within the widget hierarchy rooted at *subtree* and dispatch them to *descendant.*

```
void XtSetKeyboardFocus( subtree, descendant)
    Widget subtree, descendant;
```

XtSetLanguageProc

Register the language procedure that will be called to set the locale. (New in R5.)

```
XtLanguageProc XtSetLanguageProc(app_context, proc, client_data)
    XtAppContext app_context;           /* application context in which language procedure to */
                                        /* be used, or NULL */
    XtLanguageProc proc;                /* language procedure */
    XtPointer client_data;              /* additional data passed to language procedure */
```

XtSetMappedWhenManaged

Set the value of a widget's XtNmappedWhenManaged resource and map or unmap the widget's window.

```
void XtSetMappedWhenManaged(w, map_when_managed)
    Widget w;
    Boolean map_when_managed;           /* new value of map_when_managed field */
```

XtSetMultiClickTime

Set the multi-click time—the time interval used by the translation manager to determine when multiple events are interpreted as a repeated event.

```
void XtSetMultiClickTime(dpy, time)
    Display *display;
    int time;                           /* multi-click time in milliseconds */
```

XtSetSelectionTimeout

Set the Intrinsics selection timeout value. This function has been superseded by XtAppSetSelectionTimeout, which performs the same function on a per-application context basis.

```
void XtSetSelectionTimeout(timeout)
    unsigned long timeout;              /* selection timeout in milliseconds */
```

XtSetSensitive

Set the sensitivity state of a widget. An insensitive widget does not receive any user input events.

```
void XtSetSensitive(w, sensitive)
    Widget w;
    Boolean sensitive;                  /* whether widget should receive keyboard, pointer, */
        /* and focus events */
```

XtSetSubvalues

Copy resource settings from an ArgList to a subpart resource structure pointed to by *base*. The resource list resources specifies the size of each resource in this structure, and its offset from base. The name of each resource in args is looked up in this resource list, and the resource's specified size and offset are used to copy the resource value into the subpart structure.

```
void XtSetSubvalues(base, resources, num_resources, args, num_args)
    XtPointer base;                 /* base address of subpart data structure */
    XtResourceList resources;       /* subpart resource list */
    Cardinal num_resources;         /* number of resources in XtResourceList */
    ArgList args;                   /* argument list of name/value pairs */
    Cardinal num_args;              /* number of arguments in ArgList */
```

XtSetTypeConverter

Register a "new-style" type converter for all application contexts in a process. *converter* converts data of resource type *from_type* to resource type *to_type*. The *convert_args* array describes a list of additional arguments that will be computed and passed to the converter when it is invoked. *cache_type* specifies how converted values should be cached, and *destructor* optionally specifies a procedure to be called to free up resources when a cached value is no longer needed.

```
void XtSetTypeConverter(from_type, to_type, converter, convert_args, num_args, cache_type,
        destructor)
    String from_type, to_type;      /* source and destination type */
    XtTypeConverter converter;
    XtConvertArgList convert_args;  /* additional conversion arguments, or NULL */
    Cardinal num_args;              /* count of XtConvertArgList */
    XtCacheType cache_type;         /* whether resources are shareable or display-specific */
                                    /* and when they should be freed */
    XtDestructor destructor;        /* destroy procedure for resources produced by */
        /* conversion, or NULL */
```

XtSetValues

Set widget resources from an argument list.

```
void XtSetValues(object, args, num_args)
    Widget object;
    ArgList args;                   /* array of name/value pairs */
    Cardinal num_args;              /* number of elements in ArgList */
```

XtSetWMColormapWindows

Set WM_COLORMAP_WINDOWS property to inform window manager of custom colormaps.

```
void XtSetWMColormapWindows(widget, list, count)
    Widget widget;                    /* widget on whose window the property will be stored */
    Widget* list;                     /* widgets whose windows are to be listed in property */
    Cardinal count;                   /* number of widgets in list */
```

XtSetWarningHandler

Set the low-level warning handler procedure. This function has been superseded by XtAppSetWarningHandler, which performs the same function on a per-application context basis.

```
void XtSetWarningHandler(handler)
    XtErrorHandler handler;           /* new low-level warning procedure */
```

XtSetWarningMsgHandler

Set the high-level warning handler procedure. This function has been superseded by XtAppSetWarningMsgHandler, which performs the same function on a per-application context basis.

```
void XtSetWarningMsgHandler(msg_handler)
    XtErrorMsgHandler msg_handler;    /* new high-level nonfatal error procedure */
```

XtStringConversionWarning

Emit boilerplate string conversion error message. This function is a convenience routine for use in old-style resource converters that convert from strings. It issues a warning message with the name "conversionError", type "string", class "XtToolkitError", and default message string: "Cannot convert *src* to type *dst_type*"

```
void XtStringConversionWarning(src, dst_type)
    String src;                       /* string that could not be converted */
    String dst_type;                  /* type to which string could not be converted */
```

XtSuperclass

Obtain a widget's superclass.

```
WidgetClass XtSuperclass(w)
    Widget w;
```

XtToolkitInitialize

Initialize the X Toolkit internals. This function does not set up an application context or open a display. It is called by XtAppInitialize in the course of its initialization.

```
void XtToolkitInitialize()
```

XtTranslateCoords

Translate an x-y coordinate pair from widget coordinates to root coordinates. The transformed coordinates are returned in *root_x_return* and *root_y_return*.

```
void XtTranslateCoords(w, x, y, rootx_return, rooty_return)
    Widget w;
    Position x, y;                          /* x and y coordinates, relative to w */
    Position *rootx_return, *rooty_return;  /* return coordinates, relative to root window */
```

XtTranslateKey

The default keycode-to-keysym translator. This function takes a keycode and returns the corresponding keysym, recognizing Shift, Lock, and group modifiers. It handles all the keysyms defined by the X Protocol.

```
void XtTranslateKey(display, keycode, modifiers, modifiers_return, keysym_return)
    Display *display;
    KeyCode keycode;                 /* keycode to translate */
    Modifiers modifiers;             /* modifiers to be applied to keycode */
    Modifiers *modifiers_return;     /* modifiers examined by key translator */
    KeySym *keysym_return;
```

XtTranslateKeycode

Invoke the currently registered keycode-to-keysym translator.

```
void XtTranslateKeycode(display, keycode, modifiers, modifiers_return, keysym_return)
    Display *display;
    KeyCode keycode;                 /* keycode to translate */
    Modifiers modifiers;             /* modifiers to be applied to keycode */
    Modifiers *modifiers_return;     /* returns mask of modifiers used to generate keysym */
    KeySym *keysym_return;           /* returns resulting keysym */
```

XtUngrabButton

Cancel a passive button grab. If w is realized, XUngrabButton is called, specifying the widget's window as the ungrab window and passing the remaining arguments unmodified. If w is not realized, the deferred XtGrabButton request, if any, is removed.

```
void XtUngrabButton(widget, button, modifiers)
    Widget widget;
    unsigned int button;        /* mouse button to be released */
    Modifiers modifiers;        /* modifier keys to be ungrabbed */
```

XtUngrabKey

Cancel a passive key grab. If w is realized, XUngrabKey is called, specifying the widget's window as the ungrab window and passing the remaining argument unmodified. If the widget is not realized, the deferred XtGrabKey request for the the specified widget, keycode and modifiers, if any, is removed.

```
void XtUngrabKey(widget, keycode, modifiers)
    Widget widget;
    KeyCode keycode;                    /* keycode to be ungrabbed */
    Modifiers modifiers;                /* modifiers to be ungrabbed */
```

XtUngrabKeyboard

Release an active keyboard grab, by calling XUngrabKeyboard, passing the display of *widget* and *time*.

```
void XtUngrabKeyboard(widget, time)
    Widget widget;
    Time time;                          /* timestamp or CurrentTime */
```

XtUngrabPointer

Release an active pointer grab, by calling XUngrabPointer with the display of w and *time*.

```
void XtUngrabPointer(widget, time)
    Widget widget;
    Time time;                          /* timestamp or CurrentTime */
```

XtUninstallTranslations

Remove all existing translations from a widget. To completely replace a widget's translations, set a new translation table on the XtNtranslations resource of the widget. New translations can be merged with existing translations by using XtAugmentTranslations and XtOverrideTranslations.

```
void XtUninstallTranslations(w)
    Widget w;
```

XtUnmanageChild

Remove a widget from its parent's managed list. Unmanaged children are always unmapped.

```
void XtUnmanageChild(w)
    Widget w;                           /* child widget to be unmanaged */
```

XtUnmanageChildren

Remove a list of children from a parent widget's managed list. Unmanaged children are always unmapped.

```
void XtUnmanageChildren(children, num_children)
    WidgetList children;            /* array of child widgets */
    Cardinal num_children;          /* number of elements in children */
```

XtUnmapWidget

Unmap a widget explicitly. The widget remains under the geometry management of its parent, and will continue to have screen space allocated for it.

```
XtUnmapWidget(w)
    Widget w;
```

XtUnrealizeWidget

Destroy the windows associated with a widget and its descendants. The widget instances themselves remain intact. Use XtDestroyWidget to destroy the widgets themselves.

```
void XtUnrealizeWidget(w)
    Widget w;
```

XtVaAppCreateShell

Create a top-level widget that is the root of a widget tree, using varargs argument style. This function is identical to XtAppCreateShell except that the *args* array of resource names and values and the *num_args* argument of that function are replaced with a NULL-terminated variable-length argument list.

```
Widget XtVaAppCreateShell(application_name, application_class, widget_class, display, ...,
        NULL)
    String application_name;        /* name for this instance of application */
    String application_class;       /* class name for application */ .
    WidgetClass widget_class;       /* widget class for top-level widget */
    Display *display;
    ..., NULL;                      /* NULL-terminated variable length arg list */
```

XtVaAppInitialize

Initialize the X Toolkit internals, using varargs argument style. This function is identical to XtAppInitialize except that the *args* array of resource names and values and the *num_args* argument of that function are replaced with a NULL-terminated variable-length argument list.

```
Widget XtVaAppInitialize(app_context_return, application_class, options, num_options,
        argc_in_out, argv_in_out, fallback_resources, ..., NULL)
```

```
XtAppContext *app_context_return;      /* return application context, if non-NULL */
String application_class;              /* class name of application */
XrmOptionDescList options;             /* command line options table */
Cardinal num_options;                  /* number of entries in option list */
int *argc_in_out;                      /* pointer to number of command line arguments; */
                                       /* (type Cardinal * in R4) */
String *argv_in_out;                   /* command line arguments array */
String *fallback_resources;
    ..., NULL;                         /* variable-length list of name/value pairs */
```

XtVaCreateArgsList

Create a varargs list for use with the XtVaNestedList symbol. This function allocates, copies its arguments into, and returns a pointer to a structure that can be used in future calls to XtVa functions using the XtVaNestedList symbol. The caller must free the returned value.

```
typedef XtPointer XtVarArgsList;
XtVarArgsList XtVaCreateArgsList(unused, ..., NULL)
    XtPointer unused;
    ..., NULL;                         /* variable-length argument list */
```

XtVaCreateManagedWidget

Create and manage a widget, specifying resources with a varargs list. This function creates a widget or object named *name*, of class *widget_class*, as a child of *parent*, and with resource values as specified in the remaining arguments. It is identical to XtCreateManagedWidget except that the *args* array of resource names and values and the *num_args* argument of that function are replaced with a NULL-terminated variable-length argument list.

```
Widget XtVaCreateManagedWidget(name, widget_class, parent, ..., NULL)
    String name;
    WidgetClass widget_class;
    Widget parent;
    ..., NULL;                         /* variable-length argument list */
```

XtVaCreatePopupShell

Create a pop-up shell, specifying resources with a varargs list. This function creates and returns a shell widget of class *widget_class* and name *name*, as a popup child of *parent*. It is identical to XtCreatePopupShell except that the *args* array of resource names and values and the *num_args* argument of that function are replaced with a NULL-terminated variable-length argument list.

```
Widget XtVaCreatePopupShell(name, widget_class, parent, ..., NULL)
    String name;
    WidgetClass widget_class;
```

Widget *parent*;
    . . . ,NULL;   /* variable-length argument list */

XtVaCreateWidget

Create a widget, specifying resources with a varargs list. This function creates
and returns a widget or object of class *widget_class* with name *name*, as a child of
parent. It is identical to XtCreateWidget except that the *args* array of resource
names and values and the *num_args* argument of that function are replaced with a
NULL-terminated variable-length argument list.

Widget XtVaCreateWidget(*name, object_class, parent*, . . . , NULL)
    String *name*;
    WidgetClass *object_class*;
    Widget *parent*;
        . . . ,NULL;   /* variable-length argument list */

XtVaGetApplicationResources

Retrieve resources for the overall application using varargs argument style. This
function obtains values for the resources described by *resources*, from the variable-length argument list, the resource database, or from the default values associated with each resource, and stores these values into the structure pointed to by
base. It is identical to XtGetApplicationResources except that the *args* array of
resource names and values and the *num_args* argument of that function are
replaced with a NULL-terminated variable-length argument list.

void XtVaGetApplicationResources(*object, base, resources, num_resources*, . . .)
    Widget *object*;
    XtPointer *base*;   /* address of structure where resources to be written */
    XtResourceList *resources*;
    Cardinal *num_resources*;
        . . . , NULL;   /* variable-length argument list */

XtVaGetSubresources

Fetch resources for widget subparts using varargs argument style. This function
gets values for each of the resources described in *resources* from the variable
length argument list, the resource database, or the default values associated with
each resource, and stores these values into the structure pointed to by *base*. It is
identical to XtGetSubresources except that the *args* array of resource names and
values and the *num_args* argument of that function are replaced with a NULL-
terminated variable-length argument list.

void XtVaGetSubresources(*object, base, name, class, resources, num_resources*, . . . , NULL)
    Widget *object*;
    XtPointer *base*;   /* address of structure into which resources to be written */

```
String name;
String class;
XtResourceList resources;
Cardinal num_resources;
    ..., NULL;                          /* variable-length argument list */
```

XtVaGetSubvalues

Retrieve the current values of subpart resources, using varargs argument style.
This function obtains the values of the resources named in the variable-length
argument list (and described in the resource list *resources*) from the subpart structure pointed to by *base*, and stores those values at the addresses specified in the
variable length argument list. XtVaGetSubvalues is identical to XtGetSubvalues
except that the *args* array of resource names and values and the *num_args* argument of that function are replaced with a NULL-terminated variable-length argument list.

```
void XtVaGetSubvalues(base, resources, num_resources, ..., NULL)
    XtPointer base;
    XtResourceList resources;
    Cardinal num_resources;
    ..., NULL;                          /* variable-length argument list */
```

XtVaGetValues

Retrieve the current values of widget resources, using varargs argument style.
This function gets the values of the resources named in the variable length argument list from the specified widget or object and stores those values at the
addresses specified in the argument list. XtVaGetValues is identical to XtGetValues
except that the *args* array of resource names and values and the *num_args* argument of that function are replaced with a NULL-terminated variable-length argument list.

```
void XtVaGetValues(object, ..., NULL)
    Widget object;
    ..., NULL;                          /* variable-length argument list */
```

XtVaSetSubvalues

Set the current values of subpart resources, using varargs argument style. The
values are copied into the structure pointed to by *base* at the offset specified by
the resource descriptions in *resources*. This function is identical to XtSetSubvalues
except that the *args* array of resource names and values and the *num_args* argument of that function are replaced with a NULL-terminated variable-length argument list.

```
void XtVaSetSubvalues(base, resources, num_resources, ..., NULL)
    XtPointer base;
    XtResourceList resources;
    Cardinal num_resources;
    ...,NULL;
```

XtVaSetValues

Set resource values for a widget, using varargs argument style. This function is identical to XtSetValues except that the *args* array of resource names and values and the *num_args* argument of that function are replaced with a NULL-terminated variable-length argument list.

```
void XtVaSetValues(object, ..., NULL)
    Widget object;
    ..., NULL;                          /* variable-length argument list */
```

XtWarning

Call the low-level warning handler. In R4 and later releases, XtWarning has been superseded by XtAppWarning, which performs the same function on a per-application basis, and now calls that function, passing the default application context created by XtInitialize.

```
void XtWarning(message)
    String message;
```

XtWarningMsg

Call the high-level warning handler. In R4 and later releases, this function has been superseded by XtAppWarningMsg, which performs the same function on a per-application context basis.

```
void XtWarningMsg(name, type, class, default, params, num_params)
    String name;                        /* general kind of error */
    String type;                        /* detailed name of error */
    String class;                       /* resource class of error */
    String default;                     /* default message to use */
    String *params;                     /* array of values to be inserted in message */
    Cardinal *num_params;               /* number of elements in params */
```

XtWidgetToApplicationContext

Get the application context for a given widget.

```
XtAppContext XtWidgetToApplicationContext(w)
    Widget w;
```

XtWindow

Return the window of the specified widget.

```
Window XtWindow(w)
    Widget w;
```

XtWindowOfObject

Return the window for the nearest ancestor of an object that is of class Core. If the object is a widget, this function performs identically to XtWindow, and returns the window of that widget.

```
Window XtWindowOfObject(object)
    Widget object;
```

XtWindowToWidget

Translate a window and display pointer into a widget ID.

```
Widget XtWindowToWidget(display, window)
    Display *display;
    Window window;
```

5
Xt Data Types

This section alphabetically summarizes the data types used as arguments or return values in Xt Intrinsics functions. Defined symbols (for example, constants used to specify the value of a mask or a field in a structure) or other data types used only to set structure members are listed with the data type in which they are used.

Unless otherwise noted, data types and associated symbols are defined in the header file *<X11/Intrinsic.h>*.

Note that in order to increase the portability of widget and application source code between different system environments, Xt defines several data types whose precise representation is explicitly dependent upon, and chosen by, each individual implementation of the Xt Intrinsics. While we give information from the MIT sample implementation in describing various data types, be aware that the underlying values may differ in other versions of the Xt Intrinsics.

Note also that in this section, we describe the function prototypes for various user-supplied functions such as callbacks, resource converters, selection conversion procedures, and so forth, but not for widget methods. For more information on widget methods, see Section 6, *Inside a Widget*.

Arg
See ArgList.

ArgList
An ArgList is used for setting resources in calls to create a widget (XtCreateWidget, XtCreateManagedWidget, XtCreatePopupShell) as well as in calls to set or get resources (XtSetValues, XtGetValues, XtSetSubvalues, XtGetSubvalues, XtSetSubresources, XtGetSubresources). It is defined as follows:

```
typedef struct {
    String name;            /* resource name */
    XtArgVal value;         /* resource value */
} Arg, *ArgList;
```

The name member is typically a defined constant of the form XtN*resourcename* from either *<X11/StringDefs.h>* or a widget public header file. It identifies the name of the argument to be set. The value member is an XtArgVal, a system-dependent typedef chosen to be large enough to hold an XtPointer, Cardinal, Position or Dimension value.

Atom

To optimize communication with the server, a property is never referenced by name, but by a unique integer ID called an Atom. Standard atoms are defined in *<X11/Xatom.h>* using defined symbols beginning with XA_; nonstandard atoms can be obtained from the server by calling the Xlib function XInternAtom. The Xmu library supports an atom-caching mechanism to reduce the number of XInternAtom calls that may be required. See Section 2, *Xlib Data Types*, for a list of standard atoms from *<X11/Xatom.h>*.

Boolean

A datum that contains a zero or non-zero value. Use the symbols TRUE or FALSE, defined in *<X11/Intrinsic.h>*. Unless explicitly stated, clients should not assume that the non-zero value is equal to the symbolic value TRUE.

Cardinal

An unsigned numeric value with a minimum range of $[0..2^{16}-1]$, used to represent any numeric value.

Cursor

An XID (server resource ID) that identifies a cursor resource (hardware or software) maintained by the server. A Cursor can be returned from any of the Xlib calls XCreateFontCursor (which creates a cursor from the set of standard cursors contained in the cursor font), XCreateGlyphCursor (which creates a cursor from any other font glyph), or XCreatePixmapCursor (which creates a cursor from a bitmap image.) In Xt, the only occasion when you specify a Cursor is in a call to XtGrabButton or XtGrabPointer (new in R4), as the cursor to be displayed during a grab. The cursor resource must already be allocated by an Xlib call.

Dimension

A typedef used to specify window sizes. The Dimension data type was introduced in R3 to increase portability. R2 applications that specified dimensions as int should use Dimension instead. It represents an unsigned value with a minimum range of $[0..2^{16}-1]$.

Display

A structure defined in *<X11/Xlib.h>* that contains information about the display the program is running on. Display structure members should not be accessed directly; Xlib provides a number of macros to return essential values. In Xt, a pointer to the current Display is returned by a call to XtDisplay. XtOpenDisplay can be used to explicitly open more than one Display. See Section 2, *Xlib Data Types*, for more information.

EventMask

A mask used to specify which events are selected by an event handler. Specify the value as the bitwise OR of any of the following symbols defined in *<X11/X.h>*:

```
#define NoEventMask              0L          /* no events */
#define KeyPressMask             (1L<<0)     /* keyboard up events */
#define KeyReleaseMask           (1L<<1)     /* keyboard down events */
#define ButtonPressMask          (1L<<2)     /* pointer button down events */
#define ButtonReleaseMask        (1L<<3)     /* pointer button up events */
#define EnterWindowMask          (1L<<4)     /* pointer window entry events */
#define LeaveWindowMask          (1L<<5)     /* pointer window leave events */
#define PointerMotionMask        (1L<<6)     /* all pointer motion events */
#define PointerMotionHintMask    (1L<<7)     /* fewer pointer motion events */
#define Button1MotionMask        (1L<<8)     /* pointer motion while button 1 down */
#define Button2MotionMask        (1L<<9)     /* pointer motion while button 2 down */
#define Button3MotionMask        (1L<<10)    /* pointer motion while button 3 down */
#define Button4MotionMask        (1L<<11)    /* pointer motion while button 4 down */
#define Button5MotionMask        (1L<<12)    /* pointer motion while button 5 down */
#define ButtonMotionMask         (1L<<13)    /* pointer motion while any button down */
#define KeymapStateMask          (1L<<14)    /* any keyboard state change on Notify */
                                             /* or Focus events */
#define ExposureMask             (1L<<15)    /* any exposure (except GraphicsExpose */
                                             /* and NoExpose) */
#define VisibilityChangeMask     (1L<<16)    /* any change in visibility */
#define StructureNotifyMask      (1L<<17)    /* any change in window configuration */
#define ResizeRedirectMask       (1L<<18)    /* redirect resize of this window */
#define SubstructureNotifyMask   (1L<<19)    /* notify about reconfiguration of children */
#define SubstructureRedirectMask (1L<<20)    /* redirect reconfiguration of children */
#define FocusChangeMask          (1L<<21)    /* any change in keyboard focus */
#define PropertyChangeMask       (1L<<22)    /* any change in property */
#define ColormapChangeMask       (1L<<23)    /* any change in colormap */
#define OwnerGrabButtonMask      (1L<<24)    /* modifies handling of pointer events */
```

plus the following symbol defined in *<X11/Intrinsic.h>*:

```
#define XtAllEvents              ((EventMask) -1L)/* all of the above */
```

The XtBuildEventMask function returns the event mask representing the logical OR of all event masks registered on the widget with XtAddEventHandler, as well as event masks registered as a result of translations and accelerators installed on the widget.

GC

A Graphics Context. A pointer to a structure of this type is returned by the Xlib call XCreateGC or the Xt call XtGetGC. (The latter call does client-side caching of GCs to reduce the number of identical GCs that are created.) GCs are used by all Xlib drawing calls. The members of this structure should not be accessed directly. Values can be changed by passing an XGCValues structure to XtGetGC or the Xlib XCreateGC or XChangeGC. Values can be read with XGetGCValues. See Section 2, *Xlib Data Types*, for more information.

KeyCode

A value in the range 8-255, inclusive, that represents a physical or logical key on the keyboard. The mapping between keys and keycodes is defined for each server, and cannot be changed. A typedef from *<X11/X.h>* for an unsigned char. In Xt, the Translation Manager provides support for automatically translating Key-Codes in incoming key events into KeySyms. The translation can be invoked directly by a call to XtTranslateKeycode.

KeySym

A portable representation of the symbol on the cap of a key. Individual KeySyms are symbols defined in *<X11/keysymdef.h>*. In R4, Xt maintains a copy of the KeySym-to-Keycode mapping table for a particular display, which can be returned by a call to XtGetKeysmTable. Any KeyCodes in the table that have no KeySyms associated with them contain the value NoSymbol, which is defined as follows in *<X11/X.h>*:

```
#define NoSymbol          0L      /* special KeySym */
```

Modifiers

A typedef for an unsigned int, used to identify the state of the modifier keys. It is made up of a bitwise OR of the following symbols defined in *<X11/X.h>*:

```
#define ShiftMask           (1<<0)  /* Shift key is down */
#define LockMask            (1<<1)  /* Shift Lock key is down */
#define ControlMask         (1<<2)  /* Control key is down */
#define Mod1Mask            (1<<3)  /* Mod1 key is down */
#define Mod2Mask            (1<<4)  /* Mod2 key is down */
#define Mod3Mask            (1<<5)  /* Mod3 key is down */
#define Mod4Mask            (1<<6)  /* Mod4 key is down */
#define Mod5Mask            (1<<7)  /* Mod5 key is down */
```

Opaque

As its name implies, a typedef designed for portability, whose contents are not to be used.

Position

A typedef used to specify x and y coordinates. The Position data type was introduced in R3 to increase portability. R2 applications that specified coordinates as int should use Position instead. It represents a signed value with a minimum range of $[-2^{15}..2^{15}-1]$.

Region

An arbitrary set of pixels on the screen. Usually, a region is either a rectangular area, several overlapping or adjacent rectangular areas, or a general polygon. A Region is actually a typedef from *<X11/Xutil.h>* pointing to an internal data structure called an _XRegion. There are a number of Xlib functions for creating and manipulating regions; the members of the structure should not be accessed directly. For more information, see Volume Two, *Xlib Reference Manual*. In Xt, the only use is in the call XtAddExposureToRegion.

Screen

A structure that describes the characteristics of a screen (one or more of which make up a display). A pointer to a list of these structures is a member of the Display structure. The XtScreen macro can be used in Xt to return the current screen. A pointer to a structure of this type is also returned by the Xlib XGetWindowAttributes function. Xlib Macros are provided to access most members of this structure.

String

A typedef for char *.

Substitution

A structure used in XtFindFile and XtResolvePathname to specify substitution characters. In the *path* argument to XtFindFile, each character prefixed by a percent sign (%) is compared to the match member of a Substitution, and if found, is replaced with the string in the substitution member of the same structure. This allows for OS-independent filename searches, where substitutions can identify possible pathname separators.

It is defined as follows:

```
typedef struct {
      char match;                   /* character to match */
      String substitution;          /* string to substitute */
} SubstitutionRec, *Substitution;
```

SubstitutionRec

See Substitution.

Time

An unsigned long value containing a time value, expressed in milliseconds since the server was started. The constant CurrentTime is interpreted as the current time in milliseconds since the server was started. The Time data type is used in event structures and as an argument to XtAddTimeOut.

Visual

A structure that defines a way of using color resources on a particular screen. See Section 2, *Xlib Data Types*, for more information.

Widget

A structure returned by calls to create a widget, such as XtInitialize, XtCreateWidget, XtCreateManagedWidget, and XtCreatePopupShell. The members of this structure should not be accessed directly from applications; applications should regard it as an opaque pointer. Type Widget is actually a pointer to a widget instance structure. Widget code accesses instance variables from this structure. See Section 6, *Inside a Widget*, for more information.

WidgetClass

A pointer to the widget class structure, used to identify the widget class in various Xt calls that return information about widgets. Widget class names have the form nameWidgetClass, with the exception of the Intrinsic-mandated Core widget class, which has the class pointer widgetClass, and the widget-precursor classes, Object and RectObj, which have the class pointers objectClass and rectObjClass, respectively. See Section 6, *Inside a Widget*, for more information.

WidgetList

A pointer to a list of Widgets, used in calls to XtManageChildren and XtUnManageChildren.

Window

A structure maintained by the server, and known on the client side only by an integer ID. In Xt, a widget's window can be returned by the XtWindow macro. Given the window, the corresponding widget can be returned by XtWindowToWidget.

XEvent

A union of all thirty event structures. See Section 3, *Events*, for details on the individual event structures. However, note that the first member of each event structure is always the type, so it is possible to branch on the type, and do event-specific processing in each branch. The valid event types are identified by the following symbols defined in *<X11/X.h>*:

```
#define KeyPress          2
#define KeyRelease        3
```

```
#define ButtonPress          4
#define ButtonRelease        5
#define MotionNotify         6
#define EnterNotify          7
#define LeaveNotify          8
#define FocusIn              9
#define FocusOut            10
#define KeymapNotify        11
#define Expose              12
#define GraphicsExpose      13
#define NoExpose            14
#define VisibilityNotify    15
#define CreateNotify        16
#define DestroyNotify       17
#define UnmapNotify         18
#define MapNotify           19
#define MapRequest          20
#define ReparentNotify      21
#define ConfigureNotify     22
#define ConfigureRequest    23
#define GravityNotify       24
#define ResizeRequest       25
#define CirculateNotify     26
#define CirculateRequest    27
#define PropertyNotify      28
#define SelectionClear      29
#define SelectionRequest    30
#define SelectionNotify     31
#define ColormapNotify      32
#define ClientMessage       33
#define MappingNotify       34
#define LASTEvent           35    /* must be bigger than any event # */
```

Note that numbering of event types starts at 2, since 0 and 1 are reserved in the X Protocol for errors and replies. Note also that even though there are thirty-three event type symbols, there are only thirty event structures, since several pairs of event types (for example FocusIn and FocusOut) actually refer to the same event structure.

Be sure not to confuse these event type symbols with the event mask symbols used to select events in the XSetWindowAttributes structure.

XGCValues

A structure defined in *<X11/Xlib.h>* that is used to set the values in a Graphics Context using the XtGetGC function, or the Xlib functions XCreateGC, XChangeGC, or XGetGCValues. See Section 2, *Xlib Data Types*, for more information. The second argument of XtGetGC is a mask that specifies which members of the XGCValues structure are being set. See XtGCMask below for details.

XrmDatabase

A pointer to an internal resource manager structure. Members of this structure should not be accessed directly. An XrmDatabase can be returned by XtDatabase (a resource database) or XtGetErrorDatabase (an error message database).

XrmOptionDescList

See XrmOptionDescRec.

XrmOptionDescRec

A structure used to define command-line options, passed to XtInitialize, XtDisplay-Initialize, or XtOpenDisplay. The structure is defined as follows in *<X11/Xresource.h>*:

```
typedef struct {
    char *option;                /* option abbreviation in argv */
    char *specifier;             /* resource specifier */
    XrmOptionKind argKind;       /* which style of option it is */
    XtPointer value;             /* value to provide if XrmOptionNoArg */
} XrmOptionDescRec, *XrmOptionDescList;
```

The value for the argKind member is specified by one of the following enum values, defined in the same file:

```
typedef enum {
    XrmoptionNoArg,              /* value specified in OptionDescRec.value */
    XrmoptionIsArg,              /* value is the option string itself */
    XrmoptionStickyArg,          /* value immediately follows option */
    XrmoptionSepArg,             /* value is next argument in argv */
    XrmoptionResArg,             /* resource and value in next arg in argv */
    XrmoptionSkipArg,            /* ignore this opt and next arg in argv */
    XrmoptionSkipLine            /* ignore this opt and rest of argv */
} XrmOptionKind;
```

XrmOptionKind

See XrmOptionDescRec.

XrmValue

A structure defined in *<X11/Xresource.h>*, used in XtConvert and other resource conversion routines.

```
typedef struct {
    unsigned int size;           /* size of resource */
    XtPointer addr;              /* address of value */
} XrmValue, *XrmValuePtr;
```

XrmValuePtr

See XrmValue.

XtAccelerators

A pointer to an opaque internal type, a compiled accelerator table. A pointer to an XtAccelerators structure is returned by a call to XtParseAcceleratorTable. Usually, the compiled accelerator table is produced automatically by resource conversion of a string accelerator table stored in a resource file.

XtActionHookId

An opaque identifier returned by a call to XtAppAddActionHook, and used thereafter to refer to a particular action hook procedure.

XtActionHookProc

An application can specify a procedure that will be called just before every action routine is dispatched by the Translation Manager. To do so, the application supplies a procedure pointer of type XtActionHookProc. The function prototype for the procedure is as follows:

```
typedef void (*XtActionHookProc)(Widget, XtPointer, String, XEvent *, String *, Cardinal *)
    Widget widget;               /* widget whose action about to be dispatched */
    XtPointer client_data;       /* client-specific data passed to XtAppAddActionHook */
    String action_name;          /* name of action to be dispatched */
    XEvent *event;               /* event to be passed to action */
    String *params;              /* parameters to be passed to action*/
    Cardinal *num_params;
```

Action hooks should not modify any of the data pointed to by the arguments other than the *client_data* argument.

XtActionList

A typedef for _XtActionsRec, defined as follows:

```
typedef struct _XtActionsRec *XtActionList;
typedef struct _XtActionsRec{
    string *string;              /* string name of action proc */
    XtActionProc proc;           /* actual function pointer */
} XtActionsRec;
```

Actions are added by calls to XtAddActions or XtAppAddActions. By convention, the string and the function name are identical, except that the function name begins with an upper-case letter, as in the example:

```
static XtActionsRec two_quits[ ] = {
    {"confirm", Confirm},
    {"quit", Quit},
};
```

This mapping from strings to function pointers is necessary to allow translation tables to be specified in resource files, which are made up entirely of strings.

XtActionProc

The typedef for an action procedure.

```
typedef void (*XtActionProc)(Widget, XEvent *, String *, Cardinal *)
    Widget widget;              /* widget that caused action to be called */
    XEvent *event ;             /* event that caused action to be called */
    String *params;             /* pointer to list of strings specified as action arguments */
    Cardinal *num_params;
```

XtAddressMode

An enumerated type that specifies the possible values for the address_mode member of an XtConvertArgRec. See XtConvertArgRec below for details.

XtAppContext

A pointer to an internal structure used to hold data specific to a particular application context. An XtAppContext can be returned by a call to XtCreateApplication-Context. The application context being used by a widget can be returned by XtWidgetToApplicationContext. All standard Xt routines use a default application context; routines for handling explicit application contexts almost all have names containing the string *App*.

XtArgVal

See ArgList.

XtCacheRef

An opaque converter cache identifier returned in the *cache_ref_return* argument of XtCallConverter. The identifier reference count is decremented whenever the cached resource is released by a client.

XtCacheType

Identifies the type and amount of type converter caching to be used; specified in calls to XtAppSetTypeConverter and XtSetTypeConverter. Possible values are given by the following symbols:

```
#define XtCacheNone       0x001    /* never cache; always call converter */
#define XtCacheAll        0x002    /* reuse results of previous conversions if they match */
#define XtCacheByDisplay  0x003    /* reuse results; remove value from cache if display closed */
#define XtCacheRefCount   0x100    /* OR with above values; count times conversion used */
```

XtCallbackList

A structure used to hold callback function pointers. Callbacks are added with XtAddCallback or XtAddCallbacks.

```
typedef struct _XtCallbackRec*        XtCallbackList;

typedef struct _XtCallbackRec {
    XtCallbackProc  callback;
    XtPointer closure;
} XtCallbackRec;
```

An XtCallbackList is statically defined just after the callback function itself is declared or defined. Then the callback list is used to set a callback resource with any of the calls that set resources, including XtCreateWidget. In most documentation, the closure member is referred to as client_data. In application code, when XtAddCallback and XtRemoveCallback are used, an XtCallbackList is not required.

XtCallbackProc

The prototype for callback functions.

```
typedef void (*XtCallbackProc)(Widget, XtPointer, XtPointer)
    Widget widget;
    XtPointer closure;              /* data to be passed back to client */
    XtPointer call_data;            /* callback-specific data to be passed to client */
```

XtCallbackStatus

An enumerated type that defines the return values from XtHasCallbacks:

```
typedef enum {
    XtCallbackNoList,               /* callback resource doesn't exist */
    XtCallbackHasNone,              /* resource exists, but no callbacks on it */
    XtCallbackHasSome               /* resource exists--callbacks are registered for it */
} XtCallbackStatus;
```

XtCancelConvertSelectionProc

The prototype for the cancel selection conversion procedure registered by a call to XtOwnSelectionIncremental. This procedure is called when it has been determined (e.g., because of a timeout) that remaining segments of an incremental selection are no longer needed. The prototype is defined as follows:

```
typedef void (*XtCancelConvertSelectionProc)(Widget, Atom *, Atom *, XtRequestId *, XtPointer)
    Widget widget;                  /* widget owning the selection */
    Atom *selection;                /* atom that names selection being transferred */
    Atom *target;                   /* target type of conversion */
    XtRequestId *receiver_id;       /* opaque identification for a specific request */
    XtPointer client_data;          /* value passed in by widget when taking ownership */
```

XtCaseProc

The prototype for the case conversion procedure registered by a call to XtRegister-CaseConverter. The procedure should return upper and lowercase equivalents for a given KeySym. If there is no case distinction, this procedure should store the KeySym into both return values.

```
typedef void (*XtCaseProc)(Display *, KeySym *, KeySym *, KeySym *)
    Display *display;
    KeySym *keysym;             /* keysym to convert */
    KeySym *lower_return;       /* lower-case equivalent for keysym */
    KeySym *upper_return;       /* upper-case equivalent for keysym */
```

XtConvertArgList

A structure used in calls to XtAddConverter to specify how the converter will access the values to be converted. The structure is defined as follows:

```
typedef struct {
    XtAddressMode address_mode;     /* how to interpret address */
    XtPointer address_id;           /* the address */
    Cardinal size;                  /* size of the resource */
} XtConvertArgRec, *XtConvertArgList;
```

The enumerated type XtAddressMode specifies the possible values for the address_mode member, which controls how the address_id member should be interpreted.

```
typedef enum {
    XtAddress,              /* address */
    XtBaseOffset,           /* offset */
    XtImmediate,            /* constant */
    XtResourceString,       /* resource name string */
    XtResourceQuark         /* resource name quark */
} XtAddressMode;
```

By specifying the address mode as XtBaseOffset, you can use XtOffset to find the appropriate widget resource, much as you do in a resource list.

XtConvertArgRec

See XtConvertArgList.

XtConverter

The prototype for resource converters. Note that in R4, a new interface declaration for resource type converters was defined. (See XtTypeConverter for details.) XtConverter has been kept for compatibility only.

```
typedef void (*XtConverter)(XrmValue *, Cardinal *, XrmValue *, Xrmvalue *)
    XrmValue *args;             /* additional Xrm arguments, or NULL */
    Cardinal *num_args;
```

```
XrmValue *from;                /* value to convert */
Xrmvalue *to;                  /* descriptor to use to return converted value */
```

Be sure to return the size of the converted value as well as its address in the *to* parameter.

XtConvertSelectionIncrProc

The prototype for the incremental selection conversion procedure. This procedure is called repeatedly by Xt to get the next incremental chunk of data from a selection owner who has called XtOwnSelectionIncremental.

```
typedef Boolean (*XtConvertSelectionIncrProc)(Widget, Atom *, Atom *, Atom *, XtPointer *,
        unsigned long *, int *, unsigned long *, XtPointer, XtRequestId *)
    Widget widget;                      /* widget which currently owns selection */
    Atom *selection;                    /* atom naming selection requested */
    Atom *target;                       /* target type of selection requested */
    Atom *type_return;                  /* pointer to atom containing selection property type */
    XtPointer * value_return;           /* pointer to converted value of selection */
    unsigned long * length_return;      /* where number of value elements stored */
    int * format_return;                /* pointer where size of value data elements to be stored */
    unsigned long * max_length;         /* max. number of bytes that can be transferred */
    XtPointer  client_data;             /* value passed when widget took selection ownership*/
    XtRequestId * receiver_id;          /* opaque identification value for a specific request */
```

selection specifies the atom that names the selection requested (for example, XA_PRIMARY or XA_SECONDARY).

target specifies the type of information required about the selection; for example, FILENAME, TEXT, XA_WINDOW.

type_return specifies a pointer to an atom into which the property type of the converted value of the selection is to be stored. For instance, both file name and text might have property type XA_STRING.

value_return specifies a pointer into which a pointer to the converted value of the selection is to be stored. The selection owner is responsible for allocating this storage.

length_return specifies a pointer into which the number of elements in value (each of size indicated by format) is to be stored.

format_return specifies a pointer into which the size in bits of the data elements of the selection value is to be stored.

max_length specifies the maximum number of bytes which may be transferred at any one time.

client_data specifies the value passed in by the widget when it took ownership of the selection.

request_id specifies an opaque identification for a specific request.

XtConvertSelectionProc

The prototype for the selection conversion procedure registered by a call to XtOwnSelection:

```
typedef Boolean (*XtConvertSelectionProc)(Widget, Atom *, Atom *, Atom *, XtPointer *,
                                          unsigned long *, int *)
    Widget widget;
    Atom *selection;              /* atom describing type of selection requested */
    Atom *target;                 /* target type of selection requested */
    Atom *type_return;            /* atom containing property type of converted value */
    XtPointer *value_return;      /* pointer to pointer containing converted value */
    unsigned long *length_return; /* pointer storing number of elements in value */
    int *format_return;           /* pointer storing size of selection value data elements */
```

See XtConvertSelectionIncrProc for a more detailed description of the parameters.

XtDestructor

The prototype for a resource destroy procedure registered by a call to XtAppSet-TypeConverter or XtSetTypeConverter.

```
typedef void (*XtDestructor)(XtAppContext, XrmValue *, XtPointer,
XrmValue *, Cardinal *)
    XtAppContext app;             /* context in which resource is to be freed */
    XrmValue *to;                 /* descriptor for resource being converted */
    XtPointer converter_data;     /* converter data returned by type converter */
    XrmValue *args;               /* pointer to list of additional XrmValue arguments */
    Cardinal *num_args;
```

The destructor procedure is responsible for freeing the resource specified by the *to* argument, including any auxiliary storage associated with that resource, but not the memory directly addressed by the size and location in the *to* argument nor the memory specified by the args.

XtEnum

A datum large enough to encode at least 128 distinct values, two of which are the symbolic values TRUE and FALSE.

XtErrorHandler

The prototype for low-level error or warning handlers.

```
typedef void (*XtErrorHandler)(String)
    String message;               /* msg to be printed */
```

XtErrorMsgHandler

The prototype for high-level error or warning message handlers that use a resource-type database for error messages.

```
typedef void (*XtErrorMsgHandler)(String, String, String, String, String *, Cardinal *)
    String name;                /* string indicating general error name */
    String type;                /* string containing detailed error type */
    String class;               /* resource class to use in obtaining error message */
    String default;             /* message to use if not found in database */
    String *params;             /* pointer to list of values to be substituted in message */
    Cardinal *num_params;
```

XtEventHandler

The prototype for event handlers. The *client_data* argument specifies client-specific information registered with the event handler. It is usually NULL if the event handler is registered by the widget itself. The *continue_to_dispatch* argument specifies whether or not any remaining event handlers registered for the current event should be called.

```
typedef void (*XtEventHandler)(Widget, XtPointer, XEvent *, Boolean *)
    Widget widget;
    XtPointer client_data;            */ client-specific data passed to handler */
    XEvent *event;                    /* event that triggers handler */
    Boolean *continue_to_dispatch;    /* call remaining handlers registered for event? */
```

XtFilePredicate

The prototype for a filename evaluation procedure registered by the call to XtFindFile. The procedure will be called with a string that is potentially a file name. It should return TRUE if this string specifies a file that is appropriate for the intended use and FALSE otherwise.

```
typedef Boolean (*XtFilePredicate)(String);
    String filename;
```

XtGCMask

A mask used in calls to XtGetGC that indicates which fields in the XGCValues structure are to be used. The mask consists of a bitwise OR of the following mask symbols defined in <X11/X.h>. (The mask symbols are shown here in tabular format, along with the members of the XGCValues structure they specify, and the default value for each member. For the actual value of each mask symbol, see the discussion of XGCValues in Section 2, *Xlib Data Types*).

Member	Mask	Default
function	GCFunction	GXcopy
plane_mask	GCPlaneMask	all 1's
foreground	GCForeground	0
background	GCBackground	1
line_width	GCLineWidth	0
line_style	GCLineStyle	LineSolid
cap_style	GCCapStyle	CapButt
join_style	GCJoinStyle	JoinMiter
fill_style	GCFillStyle	FillSolid
fill_rule	GCFillRule	EvenOddRule
tile	GCTile	pixmap filled with foreground pixel
stipple	GCStipple	pixmap filled with 1's
ts_x_origin	GCTileStipXOrigin	0
ts_y_origin	GCTileStipYOrigin	0
font	GCFont	(implementation-dependent)
subwindow_mode	GCSubwindowMode	ClipByChildren
graphics_exposures	GCGraphicsExposures	TRUE
clip_x_origin	GCClipXOrigin	0
clip_y_origin	GCClipYOrigin	0
clip_mask	GCClipMask	None
dash_offset	GCDashOffset	0
dashes	GCDashList	4 (i.e., the list [4, 4])
arc_mode	GCArcMode	ArcPieSlice

XtGeometryMask

See XtWidgetGeometry.

XtGeometryResult

An enumerated type used as the return value of the XtQueryGeometry, XtMake-GeometryRequest, and XtMakeResizeRequest functions. It is defined as follows:

```
typedef enum {
    XtGeometryYes,          /* request accepted */
    XtGeometryNo,           /* request denied */
    XtGeometryAlmost        /* request denied but willing to take reply */
    XtGeometryDone          /* request accepted and done */
} XtGeometryResult;
```

XtGrabKind

An enumerated type used in calls to XtPopup to specify the nature of the grab to be asserted by the pop-up widget.

```
typedef enum {
    XtGrabNone,
    XtGrabNonexclusive,
    XtGrabExclusive
} XtGrabKind;
```

An exclusive grab constrains input to the widget actually making the grab (the latest widget in a pop-up cascade), while a non-exclusive grab allows input to any widget in the cascade.

XtInputCallbackProc

The prototype for the procedure registered by a call to XtAddInput, which adds file input or output to the event stream. This procedure is called when file events occur.

```
typedef void (*XtInputCallbackProc)(XtPointer, int *, XtInputId *)
    XtPointer client_data;      /* if any */
    int *source;                /* for input */
    XtInputId *id;              /* returned from XtAddInput */
```

XtInputId

A unique ID returned by a call to XtAddInput; used to remove an input source with XtRemoveInput.

XtInputMask

A mask used in calls to XtProcessEvent to indicate which types of events should be processed. An XtInputMask is also returned by XtPending to indicate what type of events are in the event queue. This mask is made up of a bitwise OR of the following symbols:

```
#define XtIMXEvent              1    /* a true X event */
#define XtIMTimer               2    /* timeouts from XtAddTimeout */
#define XtIMAlternateInput      4    /* file I/O registered by XtAddInput */
#define XtIMAll (XtIMXEvent | XtIMTimer | XtIMAlternateInput)
```

Don't confuse these values with XtInputNoneMask, XtInputWriteMask, XtInputRead-Mask, and XtInputExceptMask, which are used in calls to XtAddInput to indicate whether the file should be monitored for reads, writes, or exception conditions. It is particularly confusing that the latter symbols are defined in *<X11/Intrinsic.h>* immediately following the typedef for XtInputMask, even though they have nothing to do with it.

XtIntervalId

A unique ID returned by a call to XtAddTimeout; used to remove a timeout with XtRemoveTimeout. Remember that timeouts are automatically removed when the time expires.

XtKeyProc

The prototype for the keycode-to-keysym translation procedure registered in a call to XtSetKeyTranslator. The default key translator is the Xt Intrinsics function XtTranslateKey.

```
typedef void (*XtKeyProc)(Display *, KeyCode *, Modifiers *, Modifiers *, KeySym *)
    Display *dpy;
    KeyCode *keycode;              /* keycode to be translated */
    Modifiers *modifiers;          /* mask indicating modifier keys pressed */
    Modifiers *modifiers_return;   /* mask of function keys evaluated during conversion */
    KeySym *keysym_return;         /* resulting keysym */
```

XtListPosition

Used in calls to XtInsertEventHandler and XtInsertRawEventHandler to specify when the event handler is to be called relative to other previously registered handlers. This enumerated type is defined as follows:

```
typedef enum {XtListHead, XtListTail} XtListPosition;
```

XtLoseSelectionIncrProc

The prototype for the lose selection procedure registered by a call to XtOwnSelectionIncremental. This optional procedure is called by Xt to inform the specified widget that it has lost the given selection.

```
typedef void (*XtLoseSelectionIncrProc)(Widget, Atom *, XtPointer)
    Widget widget;
    Atom *selection;
    XtPointer client_data;
```

XtLoseSelectionProc

The typedef for the incremental lose selection procedure registered by a call to XtOwnSelection. This optional procedure is called by Xt to inform the specified widget that it has lost the given selection.

```
typedef void (*XtLoseSelectionProc)(Widget, Atom *)
    Widget widget;
    Atom *selection;
```

XtPointer

A datum large enough to contain the largest of a char*, int*, function pointer, structure pointer, or long value. A pointer to any type or function, or a long, may be converted to an XtPointer and back again and the result will compare equal to the original value. In ANSI C environments, it is expected that XtPointer will be defined as void*.

XtRequestId

An opaque identifier for a particular incremental selection transfer request.

XtResourceList

A structure used to declare widget or application resources, and to retrieve the current value of resources using XtGetSubresources, XtGetSubvalues, or XtGetResourceList. It is defined as follows:

```
typedef struct _XtResource {
        String resource_name;           /* specify using XtN symbol */
        String resource_class;          /* specify using XtC symbol */
        String resource_type;           /* actual data type of variable */
        Cardinal resource_size;         /* specify using sizeof() */
        Cardinal resource_offset;       /* specify using XtOffset() */
        String default_type;            /* will be converted to resource_type */
        XtPointer default_address;      /* address of default value */
} XtResource;

typedef struct _XtResource *XtResourceList;
```

XtSelectionCallbackProc

The prototype for the selection callback procedure registered by a call to XtGet-SelectionValue, XtGetSelectionValues, or XtGetSelectionValueIncremental. This is the procedure that is called to receive the data.

```
typedef void (*XtSelectionCallbackProc)(Widget, XtPointer, Atom *,
Atom *, XtPointer,
        unsigned long *, int *)
        Widget widget;
        XtPointer client_data;
        Atom *selection;
        Atom *type;                     /* e.g., XA_STRING */
        XtPointer value;                /* client storage for converted data */
        unsigned long *length;          /* number of elements in value */
        int *format;                    /* size in bits of data element in value */
```

The special atom XT_CONVERT_FAIL is passed in the *type* argument to indicate that the selection conversion failed because the selection owner did not respond within Xt's selection timeout interval.

XtSelectionDoneIncrProc

The prototype for the selection completion procedure registered by a call to XtOwnSelectionIncremental. This procedure informs the selection owner when a selection requestor has successfully retrieved the entire incremental selection value.

```
typedef void (*XtSelectionDoneIncrProc)(Widget, Atom *, Atom *, XtRequestId *, XtPointer)
    Widget widget;
    Atom *selection;
    Atom *target;              /* target type to which conversion done */
    XtRequestId *request_id;   /* opaque identification for specific request */
    XtPointer client_data;     /* value passed in when widget takes selection ownership */
```

XtSelectionDoneProc

The prototype for the selection completion procedure registered by a call to XtOwnSelection. This procedure informs the selection owner when a selection requestor has successfully retrieved the selection value.

```
typedef void (*XtSelectionDoneProc)(Widget, Atom *, Atom *)
    Widget widget;
    Atom *selection;    /* atom describing selection type that was converted */
    Atom *target;       /* target type to which conversion done */
```

XtTimerCallbackProc

The prototype for a procedure to be invoked after a timeout registered by a call to XtAddTimeout.

```
typedef void (*XtTimerCallbackProc)(XtPointer, XtIntervalId *)
    XtPointer client_data;
    XtIntervalId *id;    /* returned by XtAddTimeout */
```

XtTranslations

A pointer to an opaque internal type, a compiled translation table. A pointer to an XtTranslations structure is returned by a call to XtParseTranslationTable. Usually, the compiled translation table is produced automatically by resource conversion of a string translation table stored in a resource file. See Section 9, *Translations*, for the format of a string translation table (before conversion).

XtTypeConverter

The prototype for type converters.

```
typedef Boolean (*XtTypeConverter)(Display *, XrmValue *, Cardinal *, XrmValue *, XrmValue *,
                    XtPointer *)
    Display *dpy;
    XrmValue *args;
    Cardinal *num_args;
```

```
XrmValue *from;
XrmValue *to;
XtPointer *converter_data;
```

args specifies NULL, or a list of additional XrmValue arguments to the converter, if additional context is needed to perform the conversion. For example, the string-to-font converter needs the widget's screen, or the string-to-pixel converter needs the widget's screen and color map.

The *converter_data* argument specifies a location into which the converter may store converter-specific data that is associated with this conversion.

The *to* argument specifies the size and location into which the converter should store the converted value.

XtValueMask

A mask used in calls to XtCreateWindow to indicate which window attribute fields to use. See the discussion of XSetWindowAttributies in Section 2, *Xlib Data Types*, for more information.

XtWidgetGeometry

A structure used to pass in and return data about widget geometry in calls to XtQueryGeometry and XtMakeGeometryRequest. It is defined as follows:

```
typedef struct {
    XtGeometryMask request_mode;
    Position x, y;
    Dimension width, height, border_width;
    Widget sibling;
    int stack_mode;
} XtWidgetGeometry;
```

The request_mode member specifies which of the other fields are to be used, or (for returned structures) contain valid values. It is made up of a bitwise OR of the following symbols defined in *<X11/X.h>*:

```
#define CWX                 (1<<0)
#define CWY                 (1<<1)
#define CWWidth             (1<<2)
#define CWHeight            (1<<3)
#define CWBorderWidth       (1<<4)
#define CWSibling           (1<<5)
#define CWStackMode         (1<<6)
```

plus the following symbol from *<X11/Intrinsic.h>*:

```
#define XtCWQueryOnly       (1 << 7)
```

which means that this call is a query only, and none of the values should be used; the return value should show what would happen if the geometry request were made. (In case you're wondering, the *CW* prefix stands for *ConfigureWindow*—these symbols are also used by the Xlib XConfigureWindow call.)

The stack_mode member specifies the relationship between the current widget and a *sibling* widget specified in the same call. It is specified using one of the following symbols defined in *<X11/X.h>*:

```
#define Below          1
#define TopIf          2
#define BottomIf       3
#define Opposite       4
```

plus the following symbol from *<X11/Intrinsic.h>*:

```
#define XtSMDontChange      5
```

If no sibling widget is specified in the call, the stacking order is relative to any sibling.

XtWorkProc

The prototype for the work procedure registered by a call to XtAddWorkProc. This procedure is called in idle time when a client is waiting for events.

```
typedef Boolean (*XtWorkProc)(XtPointer)
    XtPointer client_data;          /* data the application registered */
```

XtWorkProcId

The unique identifier returned by a call to XtAddWorkProc and used as an argument in XtRemoveWorkProc.

6

Inside a Widget

The fundamental abstraction and data type of the X Toolkit is the *widget*, which is a combination of an X window and its associated input and display semantics. A widget is dynamically allocated and contains state information. Some widgets display information (for example, text or graphics), and others are merely containers for other widgets (for example, a menu box). Some widgets are output-only and do not react to pointer or keyboard input, and others change their display in response to input and can invoke functions that an application has attached to them.

Every widget belongs to exactly one widget class that is statically allocated and initialized and that contains the operations allowable on widgets of that class. Logically, a widget class is the procedures and data that are associated with all widgets belonging to that class. These procedures and data can be inherited by subclasses.

Physically, a widget class is a pointer to a structure. The contents of this structure are constant for all widgets of the widget class but will vary from class to class. (Here, constant means the class structure is initialized at compile-time and never changed, except for a one-time class initialization and in-place compilation of resource lists, which takes place when the first widget of the class or subclass is created.)

All MIT-supplied widgets have three separate files associated with them:

- A "private" header file (usually called **WidgetnameP**.*h*) containing declarations needed by the widget and any subclasses.

- A "public" header file (usually called **Widgetname**.*h*) containing declarations needed by applications programmers.

- A source code file (usually called **Widgetname**.*c*) that initializes the widget data structures and provides the widget procedures that give the widget its unique behavior.

This separation of functions into three files is suggested for all widgets, but nothing in the Toolkit actually requires this format. In particular, a private widget created for a single application may easily combine the "public" and "private" header files into a single file, or merge the contents into another application header file. Similarly, the widget implementation can be merged into other application code.

To demonstrate the structure of a typical widget, we show here the contents of these files for the Athena Template widget—a stripped-down widget that can be used as the basis for new widgets.

Private Header File

The private header file contains the complete declaration of the class and instance structures for the widget and any additional private data that will be required by anticipated subclasses of the widget. Information in the private header file is normally hidden from the application and is designed to be accessed only through other public procedures, for example, XtSetValues.

Here are the contents of *<X11/Xaw/TemplateP.h>*, the Template private header file:

```
#include <X11/copyright.h>

/* XConsortium: TemplateP.h,v 1.2 88/10/25 17:31:47 swick Exp $ */
/* Copyright Massachusetts Institute of Technology 1987, 1988 */

#ifndef _TemplateP_h
#define _TemplateP_h

#include "Template.h"
/* include superclass private header file */
#include <X11/CoreP.h>

/* define unique representation types not found in <X11/StringDefs.h> */

#define XtRTemplateResource "TemplateResource"

typedef struct {
        int empty;                              /* no class fields necessary */
} TemplateClassPart;

typedef struct _TemplateClassRec {
        CoreClassPart       core_class;         /* include superclass class parts */
```

```
        TemplateClassPart    template_class;      /* the new class part above */
} TemplateClassRec;

extern TemplateClassRec templateClassRec;

typedef struct {
        /* resources, if we add any */
        char* resource;
        /* private state variables, if any */
} TemplatePart;

typedef struct _TemplateRec {
        CorePart              core;                /* superclass instance parts */
        TemplatePart          template;           /* the new instance part above */
} TemplateRec;

#endif  _TemplateP_h
```

The various parts of this file are summarized below.

Representation Types

If a widget defines any special representation types to be used for resource conversion, the constants used to represent them should be defined here. Standard representation types are defined in *<X11/StringDefs.h>*.

Class and Instance Structures

A widget instance is composed of two parts:

- A data structure that contains instance-specific values (such as widget resources and private state data).

- A class structure that contains information that is applicable to all widgets of that class (such as pointers to the widget's internal functions, or *methods*).

Each of these structures is built up incrementally out of the corresponding structures in each of its superclasses. Thus, a given widget must declare a total of four new structures:

- The *widget*ClassPart (referred to colloquially as the Class Part), which contains any new fields that will be used by all members of the new class. Most widgets will not need new class part fields (since most of these contain pointers to information used only by the Xt Intrinsics), but will just declare a dummy field to keep the C compiler happy.

- The *widget*ClassRec (the Class Record), which includes the new *widget*ClassPart, plus the corresponding structures in each of the widget's superclasses. The contents of the three base classes from which most widgets are descended, Core, Composite, and Constraint, are described later in this section.

- The *widget*Part (the Instance Part), which contains any new fields that will contain widget instance data. For example, a widget wanting to do drawing might declare resources (publicly accessible variables) to hold colors; instance fields might also hold private state data.

- The *widget*Record (the Instance Record), which includes the new *widget*Part, plus the corresponding structures in each of the widget's superclasses.

Public Header File

The public header file contains declarations that will be required by any application module that needs to refer to the widget; whether to create an instance of the class, to perform an XtSetValues operation, or to call a public routine implemented by the widget class.

Here are the contents of *<X11/Xaw/Template.h>*, the Template public header file:

```
#include <X11/copyright.h>

/* XConsortium: Template.h,v 1.2 88/10/25 17:22:09 swick Exp $ */
/* Copyright Massachusetts Institute of Technology 1987, 1988 */

#ifndef _Template_h
#define _Template_h
/****************************************************************
*
* Template widget
*
****************************************************************/

/* Resources:

Name                Class           RepType         Default Value
--------            --------        ----------      -----------------
background          Background      Pixel           XtDefaultBackground
border              BorderColor     Pixel           XtDefaultForeground
borderWidth         BorderWidth     Dimension       1
destroyCallback     Callback        Pointer         NULL
height              Height          Dimension       0
mappedWhenManaged                   MappedWhenManagedBooleanTrue
sensitive           Sensitive       Boolean         True
width               Width           Dimension       0
```

```
x                          Position        Position0
y                          Position        Position0

*/

/* define any special resource names here that are not in <X11/StringDefs.h> */

#define XtNtemplateResource             "templateResource"

#define XtCTemplateResource             "TemplateResource"

/* declare specific TemplateWidget class and instance datatypes */

typedef struct _TemplateClassRec*       TemplateWidgetClass;
typedef struct _TemplateRec*            TemplateWidget;

/* declare the class constant */

extern WidgetClass templateWidgetClass;

#endif _Template_h
```

You will notice that most of this file is documentation. The crucial parts are the last eight lines, where symbols for any private resource names and classes are defined and where the widget class data types and class record pointer are declared.

Widget Source File

The source code file implements the widget class itself. The unique part of this file is the declaration and initialization of the widget class record structure and the declaration of all resources and action routines added by the widget class.

Here are the contents of *<X11/Xaw/Template.c>*, the Template implementation file:

```
#include <X11/copyright.h>

/* XConsortium: Template.c,v 1.2 88/10/25 17:40:25 swick Exp $ */
/* Copyright Massachusetts Institute of Technology 1987, 1988 */

#include <X11/IntrinsicP.h>
#include <X11/StringDefs.h>
#include "TemplateP.h"

static XtResource resources[ ] = {
#define offset(field) XtOffset(TemplateWidget, template.field)
    /* {name, class, type, size, offset, default_type, default_addr}, */
```

```
        { XtNtemplateResource, XtCTemplateResource, XtRTemplateResource,
                                sizeof(char*), offset(resource), XtRString, "default" },
#undef offset
};

static void TemplateAction(/* Widget, XEvent*, String*, Cardinal* */);

static XtActionsRec actions[ ] =
{
    /* {name,                procedure}, */
    {"template",             TemplateAction},
};

static char translations[ ] =
"     <Key>:                 template( ) \n\
";

TemplateClassRec templateClassRec = {
  { /* core fields */
        /* superclass          */  (WidgetClass) &widgetClassRec,
        /* class_name          */  "Template",
        /* widget_size         */  sizeof(TemplateRec),
        /* class_initialize    */  NULL,
        /* class_part_initialize */  NULL,
        /* class_inited        */  FALSE,
        /* initialize          */  NULL,
        /* initialize_hook     */  NULL,
        /* realize             */  XtInheritRealize,
        /* actions             */  actions,
        /* num_actions         */  XtNumber(actions),
        /* resources           */  resources,
        /* num_resources       */  XtNumber(resources),
        /* xrm_class           */  NULLQUARK,
        /* compress_motion     */  TRUE,
        /* compress_exposure   */  TRUE,
        /* compress_enterleave */  TRUE,
        /* visible_interest    */  FALSE,
        /* destroy             */  NULL,
        /* resize              */  NULL,
        /* expose              */  NULL,
        /* set_values          */  NULL,
        /* set_values_hook     */  NULL,
        /* set_values_almost   */  XtInheritSetValuesAlmost,
        /* get_values_hook     */  NULL,
        /* accept_focus        */  NULL,
        /* version             */  XtVersion,
        /* callback_private    */  NULL,
        /* tm_table            */  translations,
```

```
        /* query_geometry      */  XtInheritQueryGeometry,
        /* display_accelerator  */  XtInheritDisplayAccelerator,
        /* extension            */  NULL
    },
    {   /* template fields */
        /* empty               */   0
    }
};
```

WidgetClass templateWidgetClass = (WidgetClass)&templateClassRec;

The various elements of this file are described below.

Resource Declarations

The XtResource list declares any resources that will be used by the widget.

The name, class, and representation type of resources are specified in the resource list (and elsewhere in Xt code, but not in user database files) using symbolic constants defined in *<X11/StringDefs.h>*, and consist of the actual name, class, or type preceded by the characters XtN, XtC, or XtR, respectively. Use of these constants provides compile-time checking of resource names, classes, and types.

The resource name is usually similar to the name of the variable being set by the resource; by convention, it begins with a lower-case letter, and no underscores are used to separate multiple words. Instead, the initial character of subsequent words is given in upper case. For example, the resource name for a variable named border_width would be borderWidth, and the defined constant used to refer to this name would be XtNborderWidth.

The representation type of the resource is specified by the resource_type field of the resource list, using a symbolic constant prefixed by XtR. The correspondences between the XtR symbols defined by Xt, and actual C data types or X data types and structures is show below:

Resource Type	Data Type
XtRAccelerator Table	XTAccelerators
XtRBoolean	Boolean
XtRBool	Bool
XtRCallback	XtCallbackList
XtRColor	XColor
XtRCursor	Cursor
XtRDimension	Dimension
XtRDisplay	Display*
XtRFile	FILE*
XtRFloat	float

Resource Type	Data Type
XtRFont	Font
XtRFontStruct	XFontStruct *
XtRFunction	(*) ()
XtRInt	int
XtRPixel	Pixel
XtRPixmap	Pixmap
XtRPointer	caddr_t
XtRPosition	Position
XtRShort	short
XtRString	char*
XtRTranslationTable	XtTranslations
XtRUnsignedChar	unsigned char
XtRWidget	Widget
XtRWindow	Window

The resource_size field is the size of the resource's actual representation in bytes; it is normally specified as sizeof(*type*) (where *type* is the C-language type of the resource) so that the compiler fills in the value.

The resource_offset field is the offset in bytes of the field within the widget instance structure or application data structure. The XtOffset macro is normally used to obtain this value. This macro takes as arguments a pointer to the data structure, and the name of the structure field to be set by the resource.

If no value is found in the resource database, the value pointed to by the default_address field will be used instead. The type of this default is given by the default_type field. If the default_type is different from the resource_type, a conversion will be performed automatically in this case as well.

There are two special resource types that can be used only in the default_type. XtRImmediate means that the value in the default_address field is to be used as the actual resource value, rather than as a pointer to it. XtRCallProc is a pointer to a function that will supply the default value at run time.

For more information on widget resources, see the *listres* client, which generates a list of a widget's resource database, including the class in which each resource is first defined, the instance and class name, and the type of each resource.

Actions and Translations

If the widget provides any actions (functions that can be invoked by user events), it must define an action list and translation table to allow the user to configure the events that will call the action.

An ActionList is simply a structure that maps string names to actual function pointers. The translation table maps event specifications to actions; this default table can be overridden by the user. See Section 9, *Translations*, for more information.

Class Record Initialization

Since all widgets are subclassed from Core, it is necessary, at minimum, to initialize the Core Class Part. In many cases, the Core class record can be initialized just as shown in the Template widget code above. Here is a brief description of each of the fields:

- The superclass defines a pointer to the superclass's class structure. This defines which widgets this class can inherit from. For a subclass of Core this would be &widgetClassRec; for a subclass of Composite, &compositeClassRec; for a subclass of Constraint, &constraintClassRec, and so on.

- The next field, class_name, contains the name that will be used to set resources by class. In other words, this is the string that you want to appear in the resource database when setting resources for all instances of this class.

- The widget_size field is the size of the instance record. This should always be specified using sizeof with the complete instance record declaration for this class, defined in *BitmapEditP.h*, as an argument. In this case the field is initialized to sizeof(BitmapEditRec). Xt uses this field to allocate memory for instance records at run-time.

- The next field, class_initialize, is the first of many pointers to widget methods. There are several issues regarding methods that require separate treatment so they will be described after the other fields rather than in order. The complete list of methods in the Core part structure is as follows: class_initialize, class_part_init, initialize, realize, destroy, resize, expose, set_values, set_values_almost, query_geometry, and accept_focus.

- The display_accelerator field is used in conjunction with accelerators, which are a way of redirecting events to actions in different widgets.

- The class_inited field is used internally by Xt to indicate whether this class has been initialized before. Always initialize it to FALSE.

- The initialize_hook, set_values_hook, and get_values_hook fields are for use in widgets that have subparts that are not widgets. Subparts can have their own resources, and can load them from the resource databases like a widget can. These methods are called immediately after the method of the same name without _hook, and are for performing the same operations except on subparts.

- The fields relating to resources, the default translation table, and the actions table have already been described. The only one of these fields without an obvious name is the tm_table field, in which you place the default translation table.

- The xrm_class field is used internally by Xt, and must always be initialized to NULLQUARK. This is a fixed initialization value.

- The compress_motion, compress_exposure, and compress_enterleave fields control the Toolkit's *event filters*. Basically, these filters remove events that some widgets can do without, thus improving performance. Unless a widget performs complicated drawing or tracks the pointer, these fields should usually be TRUE.

- The visible_interest field can be set to TRUE if your widget wishes to get VisibilityNotify events, which signal changes in the visibility of your widget. Normally this is set to FALSE, because Expose events cause the widget to be redrawn at the proper times. For some widgets, however, Expose events are not enough. If your widget draws continuously, as in a game, it can stop computing output for areas that are no longer visible. There are other cases where VisibilityNotify events are useful.

- Xt uses the version field to check the compiled widget code against the library the widget is linked against. If you specify the constant XtVersion and it is different from the version used by the libraries, then Xt displays a run-time warning message. However, if you have intentionally designed a widget to run under more than one version of Xt, you can specify the constant XtVersion-DontCheck.

- The callback_private field is, as it says, private to Xt, and you always initialize it to NULL.

- The extension field is unused. It is for extending the Core widget in later releases while maintaining binary compatibility with the current release.

Core Widget Methods

A widget's methods are the procedures that handle basic widget "housekeeping" such as initialization, updating resources, redisplay, and destruction. Methods are called by the Xt Intrinsics at defined times; it is not possible to add new types of methods. (For user interface behavior, add callbacks or actions.)

All of the essential widget methods are defined as part of the Core widget class. Other methods that have to do with managing subwidgets are defined by the Composite and Constraint widget classes.

The methods provided by superclasses can be inherited by any widget class. However, there are two types of methods: chained and self-contained.

Chained methods are always inherited; you cannot replace them, but can only add to them, by writing a function in your own widget, and placing a pointer to your function in the appropriate field in the widget class structure. To simply inherit the superclass method(s), specify NULL for that method in your own widget. Some methods are downward-chained (superclass methods are called first) while others are upward-chained (subclass methods are called first).

Self-contained methods are called alone. If you define a self-contained method, it replaces the corresponding methods in all superclasses. To inherit the methods from the superclasses, you must specify a constant of the form XtInherit*method*. (If you specify NULL, no method would be called.)

The following list briefly describes each of the Core methods, and whether it is self-contained, or upward- or downward-chained.

- initialize sets initial values for all the fields in the instance part structure. This method is responsible for checking that all public fields have been set to reasonable values. This method is downward-chained, so each class's initialize method sets the initial values for its own instance part structure.

- initialize_hook is called immediately after the initialize method of the same class. It allows the widget to initialize subparts, and is used only in widgets that have subparts, like the Athena Text widget. Subparts have their own resources. initialize_hook is downward-chained.

- class_initialize is called once, the first time an instance of a class is created by the application. The widget registers type converters here, if it has defined any nonstandard ones. class_initialize is self-sufficient.

- class_part_init is called once the first time an instance of a class is created by the application. It is different from class_initialize only in that it is downward-chained. This method resolves inheritance of self-sufficient methods from the immediate superclass. It is needed only in classes that define their own methods in their class part (but is not present in Core, Composite, or Constraint, because Xt handles inheritance in these).

- realize is called when the application calls XtRealizeWidget. This method is responsible for setting window attributes and for creating the window for the widget. It is self-sufficient.

- expose redraws a widget whenever an Expose event arrives from the server (but note that Xt can coalesce consecutive Expose events to minimize the number of times it is called). This method is responsible for making Xlib calls to draw in the widget's window. The widget's instance variables are often used in the expose method to guide the drawing. This method is self-sufficient.

- resize is called when the parent widget resizes the widget. It recalculates the instance variables based on the new position and size of its window, which are passed into the method. This method is self-sufficient.

- set_values is called whenever the application calls XtSetValues to set the resources of the widget. This method recalculates private instance variables based on the new public instance variable values. It contains similar code to the initialize method, but is called at different, and perhaps multiple, times. The set_values method is downward-chained.

- set_values_almost is used to process application requests to change this widget's size. This field should never be NULL. Unless you've written your own set_values_almost method, this field should be set to XtInheritSetValuesAlmost. Most classes inherit this procedure from their superclass. This method is self-contained.

- set_values_hook sets resource values in subparts. This method is used only in widgets that have subparts. It is downward-chained.

- accept_focus is NULL for most widgets (or, at least, for all the Athena widgets). When it is present, this method should set the keyboard focus to a subwidget of this widget. This would be used, for example, to allow the application to set the input focus to the Text widget within a Dialog widget. This method is invoked when the application calls XtCallAcceptFocus. This method is self-contained.

- get_values_hook is called just after get_values and is used to return the resources of subparts. This method is downward-chained.

- destroy deallocates local and server memory allocated by this widget. This is called when an application destroys a widget but remains running.

- query_geometry may be called when the parent widget is about to resize the widget. The method is passed the proposed new size, and is allowed to suggest a compromise size, or to agree to the change as specified. This method is self-contained.

The Class Pointer

The last essential step in the code file is to provide a pointer to the class record that can be used by applications that wish to use this widget. This pointer is usually of the form *widget*WidgetClass (e.g., templateWidgetClass.)

7
Clients

This section lists the X clients in the standard MIT X11.5 release.

For each client, we give a syntax line, followed by a brief description and a listing of the unique resources and command-line options recognized by that client.

Some clients take only command-line options, which are specific to the individual program.* However, many clients are based on the X Toolkit, and take standard options and resources, which are described later in this introduction. In these cases, only the additional non-standard options and resources are listed following the client.

In X Toolkit-based clients, most command-line options have a corresponding resource (and vice versa). This means that instead of enabling a feature by specifying an option on the command-line, you can enable it by setting the corresponding resource in a resource database. The customary name for the resource file is *$HOME/.Xresources* (*$HOME/.Xdefaults* is generally no longer used). The contents of your resource file are made available to clients with the program *xrdb*, which is automatically invoked by *xdm*. If you use *xinit* or start up X in some other way, you will have to invoke *xrdb* by hand or in your custom startup script.

Clients

---

*Most such programs do not create any windows. They either have no output, or else display using standard output to a tty (i.e., to an *xterm* window).

Resource File Format

A resource file contains text representing the default resource values for an application or set of applications. The resource file is an ASCII text file that consists of a number of lines with the following EBNF syntax:

resourcefile	= {line "\n"}
line	= (comment | production)
comment	= "!" string
production	= resourcename ":" string
resourcename	= ["*"] name {("." | "*") name}
string	= {<any character not including eol>}
name	= {"A"-"Z" | "a"-"z" | "0"-"9"}

If the last character on a line is a backslash (\\), that line is assumed to continue onto the next line. To include a newline character in a string, use \\en.

In plain English, you can think of a resource specification as having the following format:

program.widget[.widget...].resource: value

where:

program   is the client program, or a specific instance of the program.

widget   corresponds to one of the levels of the widget hierarchy (usually the major structures within an application, such as windows, menus, scrollbars, etc.).

resource   is a feature of the last *widget* (perhaps a command button), such as background color or a label that appears on it.

value   is the actual setting of *resource*; i.e., the label text, color, or other feature.

The type of *value* to supply should usually be evident from the name of the resource or from the description of the corresponding option. For example, various resources, such as borderColor or background, take color specifications; geometry takes a geometry string, font takes a font name, and so on. Boolean values are specified as either on or off, yes or no, or true or false. Usually, a command-line option without accompanying options is equivalent to setting a Boolean to true (though occasionally, there is a corresponding option to set it to false).

Wildcarding Resource Component Names

The character ? can be used to wildcard a single component (name or class) in a resource specification. Thus the specification:

xmail.?.?.Background: antique white

sets the background color for all widgets (and only those widgets) that are grandchildren of the top-level shell of the application xmail. And the specification:

xmail.?.?*Background: brick red

sets the background color of the grandchildren of the shell and all of their descendants.

There is one obvious restriction on the use of the ? wildcard: it cannot be used as the final component in a resource specification—you can wildcard widget names, but not the resource name itself. When there is more than one possible match for a component name, the following rules are applied:

1. A resource that matches the current component by name, by class, or with the ? wildcard takes precedence over a resource that omits the current component by using a *.

2. A resource that matches the current component by name takes precedence over a resource that matches it by class, and both take precedence over a resource that matches it with the ? wildcard.

3. A resource in which the current component is preceded by a dot (.) takes precedence over a resource in which the current component is preceded by a *.

Including Files in a Resource File

The Xrm functions that read resources from files, XrmGetFileDatabase and XrmCombineFileDatabase (new in R5), recognize a line of the form:

#include "filename"

as a command to include the named file at that point. The directory of the included file is interpreted relative to the directory of the file in which the include statement occurred. Included files may themselves contain #include directives, and there is no specified limit to the depth of this nesting. Note that the C syntax #include <filename> is not supported; neither Xlib nor Xt defines a search path for included files.

Tight Bindings and Loose Bindings

Components of a resource specification can be linked in two ways:

- By a *tight* binding, represented by a dot (.).

- By a *loose* binding, represented by an asterisk (*).

A tight binding means that the components on either side of the dot must be next to one another in the widget hierarchy. A loose binding is signalled by an asterisk, a wildcard character. A loose binding means there can be any number of levels in the hierarchy between the two surrounding components.

The most general specification is of the form:

resource: value

However, this can be overridden by more specific entries elsewhere in the resource database.

In the resource database, you can set either the resource instance name—which affects a specific resource—or the resource class—which will affect all related resources. For example, the *oclock* client has three separate resources that control the color of portions of the clock. All three have the same class—Foreground—so setting the Foreground class resource will set all three to the same color. However, since instance settings take precedence over class settings, any or all could also be set individually by resource name.

Format of the Client Entries

In presenting the X clients, we have chosen to key alphabetically on the resources, rather than on the command-line option. So, for example, the first option listed under the *xload* client reads as follows:

*load.minScale (class **Scale**, option **−scale** *integer*)
    Produce histogram with at least *integer* tick marks in the histogram. If the load goes above *integer*, *xload* will create more divisions, but it will never use fewer than this number. Default is 1.

What this line tells you is that minScale is a resource of the load widget, that its resource class is Scale, and that the corresponding command-line option is −scale. In other words, you could set the scaling factor to 2 by either of the resource settings:

*load.minScale: 2   ! set the minScale resource to 2

or

*load.Scale: 2   ! set all Scale type resources to 2 or the command-line option:

    –scale 2

If a resource is shown with no option in parentheses, then there is no corresponding command-line option. If an option is shown, but no resources, only the option is valid. Also, some older X clients may have a resource without a corresponding class.

See the section "X Toolkit Options and Resources" for more information.

Symbol Conventions

The following symbols are used in describing the clients:

	surround an optional field in a command-line or file entry.
[ ]	surround an optional field in a command-line or file entry.
|	separate values when only one of them should be chosen.
$	standard prompt from the Bourne shell, *sh*(1).
%	standard prompt from the C shell, *csh*(1).
name(1)	reference to a command called *name* in Section 1 of the *UNIX Reference Manual* (which may have a different name depending on the version of UNIX you use).

X Toolkit Options and Resources

All applications written with the X Toolkit Intrinsics automatically accept a standard set of options and resources. Rather than repeat them for each client, they are summarized here. However, any standard options that have special meaning in a particular client are listed with the client.

Of course, some standard options are more appropriate for some clients than for others. For example, –fn or *font makes no sense with *xbiff*, since *xbiff* doesn't display any text. And so, while standard options and resources won't result in an error message, they might also have no effect.

Here, then, are the standard options and resource settings for X Toolkit-based clients. Some options accept an abbreviated syntax. This short form, when it exists, is mentioned in the description.

–display [*host*]:*server*[.*screen*]
    The name of the X server to use. *host* specifies the machine; *server* specifies the display server number; and *screen* specifies the screen number. Either or both the *host* and *screen* elements to the display specification can be omitted. If *host* is omitted, the local machine is assumed. If *screen* is omitted, screen 0

is assumed (and the period is unnecessary). The colon and display *server* number are necessary in all cases.

–geometry *geometry*

The initial size and location of the application window. This option can be abbreviated to **–g**, unless a conflicting option begins with "g." The argument *geometry* is referred to as a "standard geometry string," and has the form *width*x*height*±*xoff*±*yoff*. These values are in pixels. Offsets are defined as follows:

+*xoff*	Distance of window's left edge from screen's left edge.
–*xoff*	Distance of window's right edge from screen's right edge.
+*yoff*	Distance of window's top edge from screen's top edge.
–*yoff*	Distance of window's bottom edge from screen's bottom edge.

*background (class **Background**, option **–background** *color*)

The color to use for the window background. (Short form: **–bg**.)

*borderColor (class **BorderColor**, option **–bordercolor** *color*)

The color to use for the window border. (Short form: **–bd**.)

*borderWidth (class **BorderWidth**, option **–borderwidth** *pixels*)

The width in pixels of the window border. (Short form: **–bw**.)

*foreground (class **Foreground**, option **–foreground** *color*)

The color to use for text or graphics. (Short form: **–fg**.)

*font (class **Font**, option **–font** *font*)

The font to use for displaying text. (Short form: **–fn**.)

–iconic

Start the application in iconified form. Window managers may choose not to honor the application's request.

–name

The name of the application being run. This option is useful in shell aliases to distinguish between invocations of an application, without resorting to creating links to alter the executable filename.

*reverseVideo (class **ReverseVideo**, option **–reverse**)

Reverse foreground and background colors. Not all programs honor this or implement it correctly. It is usually only used on monochrome displays. (Short form: **–rv**.)

+rv Do not reverse foreground and background colors. This is used to override any defaults, since reverse video doesn't always work.

*selectionTimeout (class **SelectionTimeout**, option **–selectionTimeout**)

The timeout in milliseconds within which two communicating applications must respond to one another for a selection request.

*synchronous (class ***Synchronous**, option **–synchronous**)

Send requests to the X server synchronously. Since Xlib normally buffers requests to the server, errors do not necessarily get reported immediately after they occur. This option turns off the buffering so that the application can be debugged. It should never be used with a working program.

+synchronous

Do not send requests to the X server synchronously.

*title (class **Title**, option **–title** *string*)

The title to be used for this window. This information is sometimes used by a window manager to provide some sort of header identifying the window.

*xnlLanguage (class **XnlLanguage**)

(option **–xnllanguage** *language*[*_territory*][*.codeset*])

The *language*, *territory*, and *codeset* for use in resolving resource and other filenames.

–xrm *resourcestring*

A resource name and value to override any defaults. This option is useful for setting resources that don't have explicit command-line arguments.

Alphabetical Listing

The rest of this section presents the X clients in alphabetical order. (Contributed software has not been included here.)

appres

appres [[*classname* [*instancename*]] [*options*]

Print the resources seen by an application of the specified *classname* and *instancename*. *appres* is used to determine which resources a particular program would load. For example:

% **appres XTerm**

would list the resources that any *xterm* program would load. To also match particular instance names, you can enter both an instance and class name, as in the following:

% **appres XTerm myxterm**

If no application class is specified, the class –AppResTest– is used. Without any arguments, *appres* returns those resources that might apply to any application (for example, those beginning with an asterisk in your *.Xresources* file).

As of Release 5, *appres* also accepts hierarchical class and instance names as input. This allows you to list the resources that match a particular sublevel of an application's widget hierarchy. To list the resources that may apply to part of the widget hierarchy, you provide F*(F8appres with both a hierarchical class and instance name. The number of class and instance components must be equal. (Note that the instance name should not be specified with the toolkit -name option.) For example, the command:

% appres Xman.TopLevelShell.Form xman.topBox.form

will list the resources that may apply to widgets within (F8xman's topBox hierarchy.

appres takes the following non-standard option:

−1   Limits the matching to a specific widget in the hierarchy (the widget given on the command line). For example, the command: **appres XTerm.VT100 xterm.vt100 -1** will list the resources that match the *xterm* **vt100** widget.

The two useful standard options for this client are: −xrm, which returns an additional *resource* if it applies to the given *classname* and *instancename*; and −name which can be used preceding the *instancename* (unless hierarchical class and instance names are given).

atobm

atobm [*options*] *filename*

Filter to convert an array of ASCII characters in *filename* to a bitmap. *atobm* takes the following non-standard options:

−chars *cc*

Use *cc* character pair when converting string bitmaps into arrays of numbers. The first character is used for 0 bits and the second character is used for 1 bits. Default is to use dashes (−) for 0's and number signs (#) for 1's.

−xhot *coord*

Specify the x-coordinate of the hot spot. Positive only.

−yhot *coord*

Specify the y-coordinate of the hot spot. Positive only.

−name *bitmap_file*

Use *bitmap_file* when writing out the bitmap file. Default is to use the basename of the *filename* command-line argument.

bdftopcf

bdftopcf [*options*] *font-file.bdf*

Release 5 font compiler. Fonts in Portable Compiled Format can be read by any architecture, although the file is structured to allow one particular architecture to read them directly without reformatting. This allows fast reading on the appropriate machine, but the files are still portable (but read more slowly) on other machines.

-p*n*
> Set the font glyph padding.

-u*n*
> Set the font scanline unit.

-m Set the font bit order to MSB (most significant bit) first.

-l Set the font bit order to LSB (least significant bit) first.

-M Set the font byte order to MSB first.

-L Set the font byte order to LSB first.

-t Convert fonts into "terminal" fonts when possible. A terminal font has each glyph image padded to the same size; the X server can usually render these types of fonts more quickly.

-i Inhibit the normal computation of ink metrics.

-o *<output-file-name>*
> By default, *bdftopcf* writes the pcf file to standard output; this option gives the name of a file to be used instead.

bdftosnf

bdftosnf [*options*] *bdf_file*

Read a Bitmap Distribution Format (BDF) font from the specified *bdf_file* (or from standard input if no file is specified) and write an X11 Server Natural Format (SNF) font to standard output. This client has been replaced by *bdftopcf* for Release 5. *bdftosnf* takes the following non-standard options:

-p*number*
> Force glyph padding to *number*. Legal values are 1, 2, 4, and 8.

-u*number*
> Force scanline unit padding to *number*. Legal values are 1, 2, and 4.

-m Force bit order to most significant bit first.

-l Force bit order to least significant bit first.

-M Force byte order to most significant byte first.

-L Force byte order to least significant byte first.

-w Print warnings if the character bitmaps have bits set to one outside of their defined widths.

-W Print warnings for characters with an encoding of –1; the default is to silently ignore such characters.

-t Expand glyphs in "terminal-emulator" fonts to fill the bounding box.

-i Suppress computation of correct ink metrics for "terminal-emulator" fonts.

bitmap

bitmap [*options*] *filename basename*

Bitmap editor and converter utilities for the X Window System. Use *filename* when writing out the bitmap file. This client creates its own window. *bitmap* takes the following non-standard resources and options:

-size *WIDTHxHEIGHT*
: Size of grid in squares.

-sh *dimension*
: Height of each square in pixels.

-sw *dimension*
: Width of each square in pixels.

-gt *dimension*
: Grid tolerance. If square dimensions fall below specified value, grid will be automatically turned off.

-axes, +axes
: Turns major axes on (-) or off (+).

-grid, +grid
: Turns grid lines on (-) or off (+).

-dashed, +dashed
: Turns dashing for frame and grid lines on (-) or off (+).

-stippled, +stippled
: Turns stippling of highlighted squares on (-) or off (+).

-proportional, +proportional
> Turns proportional mode on (-) or off (+).

-dashes *filename*
> Bitmap to be used as a stipple for dashing.

-stipple *filename*
> Bitmap to be used as a stipple for highlighting.

-hl *color*
> Color used for highlighting.

-fr *color*
> Color used for frame and grid lines.

filename
> Bitmap to be initially loaded into program.

basename
> Basename to be used in C code output file.

bmtoa

> bmtoa [*options*] *filename*

Filter to convert the bitmap in *filename* to an array of ASCII characters. *bmtoa* takes the following non-standard options:

-chars *cc*
> Use *cc* character pair in the ASCII-string version of the bitmap. The first character is used for 0 bits and the second character is used for 1 bits. Default is to use dashes (–) for 0's and number signs (#) for 1's.

editres

> editres [*options*]

Dynamic resource editor for X Toolkit applications. This client allows users to view the full widget hierarchy of any X Toolkit client that speaks the *editres* protocol, construct resource specifications for that client, and apply those specificiations dynamically to the application. (New in R5.)

editres takes the following non-standard resources and options:

numFlashes (class **NumFlashes**)
> Number of times widgets in client application are flashed when Show Active Widgets command is invoked.

flashTime (class **FlashTime**)
Amount of time between flashes described above.

flashColor (class **FlashColor**)
Color used to flash client widgets.

saveResourcesFile (class **SaveResourcesFile**)
File to which resource line is appended when *Save* button in resource box is activated.

fs

fs [*options*]

fs is the X Window System font server. For more information about font server implementation, see the *X Window System Administrator's Guide*.

-config *configuration_file*
Configuration file used by font server.

-ls *listen_socket*
File descriptor already set up to be used as listen socket.

-port *tcp_port*
TCP port number on which server will listen for connections.

fsinfo

fsinfo [-server *servername*]

Utility for displaying information about an X font server. It is used to examine the capabilities of a server, the predefined values for various parameters used in communicating between clients and the server, and the font catalogues and alternate servers that are available.

fstobdf

fstobdf -fn *fontname* [-server *servername*]

BDF font generator. This client reads a font from a font server and prints a BDF file on the standard output that may be used to recreate the font. This is useful in testing servers, debugging font metrics, and reproducing lost BDF files.

-fn *fontname*
Font for which a BDF file should be generated.

-server *servername*
> Server from which the font should be read.

fslsfonts

> fslsfonts [*options*] [-fn *pattern*]

Server font list displayer for X font server. This client lists the fonts that match the given *pattern*. The wildcard character "*" may be used to match any sequence of characters (including none), and "?" to match any single character. If no pattern is given, "*" is assumed.

-server *host:port*
> X font server to contact.

-l[l[l]]
> Medium, long, and very long listings, respectively, should be generated for each font.

-m Long listings should also print the minimum and maximum bounds of each font.

-C Listings should use multiple columns. This is the same as **-n 0**.

-1 Listings should use a single column. This is the same as **-n 1**.

-w *width*
> Width in characters that should be used in figuring out how many columns to print. Default is 79.

-n *columns*
> Number of columns to use in displaying the output.

-u *columns*
> Output should be left unsorted.

listres

> listres [*options*]

Generate a list of a widget's resource database. The list includes the class in which each resource is first defined, the instance and class name, and the type of each resource. If no specific widgets or the -all option are given, a two-column list of widget names and their class hierarchies is printed. *listres* takes the following non-standard resources and options:

–all
> Print information for all known widgets and objects.

*showSuper (class **ShowSuper**, option **−nosuper**)
Don't list resources inherited from a superclass.

*showVariable (class **ShowVariable**, option **−variable**)
Identify widgets by the names of the class record variables rather than the class name given in the variable.

*topObject (class **TopObject**, option **−top** *name*)
Specify the *name* of the top-level widget. Default is Core.

*showTree (class **ShowTree**, option **−tree**)
Print the tree of objects traversed.

*resourceFormat (class **ResourceFormat**, option **−format** *printf_string*)
List the resource information in a specified format. Information includes the name, instance, class, and type of each resource. *printf_string* is a set of characters in the syntax of the UNIX *printf* command.

mkfontdir

mkfontdir [*directory_name1...*]

Create a *fonts.dir* file for each directory of font files. For each *directory_name*, *mkfontdir* reads all of the font files in the directory and searches for properties named "FONT" or, failing that, the name of the file stripped of its suffix. *mkfontdir* then creates a *fonts.dir* file containing all of these names in each directory listed.

oclock

oclock [*options*]

Display time of day in analog form. This client creates its own window. *oclock* takes the following non-standard resources and options:

*clock.transparent (class **Transparent**, option **-transparent**)
Clock consists of only jewel, hands, and border.

*clock.jewel (class **Foreground**, option **−jewel** *color*)
Jewel color.

*clock.minute (class **Foreground**, option **−minute** *color*)
Minute hand color.

*clock.hour (class **Foreground**, option **−hour** *color*)
Hour hand color.

*clock.backingStore (class **BackingStore**, option **–backing** *value*)

Select backing store level. *value* is one of WhenMapped, Always, or NotUseful.

*clock.shapeWindow (class **ShapeWindow**, option **–noshape**)

Do not reshape clock; clock will exactly fit window outline.

resize

resize [*options*]

Utility to set TERMCAP and terminal settings to current window size. For this output to take effect, *resize* must either be evaluated as part of the command line (usually done with a shell alias or function) or else redirected to a file which can then be read in. From the C shell (usually known as */bin/csh*), the following alias could be defined in the user's *.cshrc*:

% **alias rs 'set noglob; eval 'resize'; unset noglob'**

resize takes the following non-standard options:

–u   Generate Bourne shell commands regardless of user's current shell.

–c   Generate C shell commands regardless of user's current shell.

–s [*rows columns*]

Use Sun console escape sequences instead of *xterm* escape code. If *rows* and *columns* are given, *resize* asks the *xterm* window to resize itself. The window manager may choose, however, to disallow the change.

sessreg

sessreg [*options*] *user_name*

Manage utmp/wtmp entries for non-init clients. To manage BSD-style utmp files, *sessreg* has two strategies. In conjunction with *xdm*, the -x option counts the number of lines in */etc/ttys*, then adds to that the number of the line in the *Xservers* file which specifies the display. The display name must be specified as the *line_name*, using the -l option. This sum is used as the *slot_number* in */etc/utmp* at which this entry will be written. In the more general case, the -s option specifies the *slot_number* directly. *sessreg* takes the following non-standard options:

–w *wtmp_file*

Alternate wtmp file, instead of *usr/adm/wtmp* for BSD or */etc/wtmp* for System V. The special name "none" disables writing records to */usr/adm/wtmp*.

–u *utmp_file*

Alternate utmp file, instead of */etc/utmp*. The special name "none" disables writing records to */etc/utmp*.

Clients

–l *line_name*

Line name of entry. For terminal sessions, this is the final pathname segment of the terminal device filename. If none is specified, the terminal name will be determined with ttyname(3) and stripped of leading components.

–h *host_name*

Set for BSD hosts to indicate that the session was initiated from a remote host.

–s *slot_number*

Each potential session has a unique slot number in BSD systems; most are identified by the position of the *line_name* in the *etc/ttys* file. This option overrides the default position determined with *ttyslot(3)*; inappropriate for use with *xdm*.

–x *Xservers_file*

Set the *slot_number* to be the number of lines in the *ttys_file* plus the index into this file that the *line_name* is found.

–t *ttys_file*

Alternate file that the -x option will use to count the number of terminal sessions on a host.

–a   This session should be added to utmp/wtmp.

–d   This session should be deleted from utmp/wtmp. One of -a or -d must be specified.

showfont

showfont [*options*] [-fn *pattern*]

Font dumper for X font server. This client displays data about the font that matches the given *pattern*. The wildcard character "*" may be used to match any sequence of characters (including none), and "?" to match any single character. If no pattern is given, "*" is assumed. *showfont* is intended to be run with the font server. (New in R5.)

–server *host:port*

X font server to contact.

-l   Bit order of the font is LSBFirst (least significant bit first).

-m   Bit order of the font is MSBFirst (most significant bit first).

-L   Byte order of the font is LSBFirst (least significant byte first).

-M   Byte order of the font is MSBFirst (most significant byte first).

-extents_only
> Only the font's extents should be displayed.

-start #
> Start of the range of the characters to display. (# is a number.)

-end #
> End of the range of characters to display. (# is a number.)

-unit #
> Scanline unit of the font (1, 2, 4 or 8). (# is a number.)

-pad #, -unit #
> Bitmap padding unit of the font; 0, 1, or 2, where 0 is ImageRectMin, 1 is ImageRectMaxWidth and 2 is ImageRectMaxWidth.

bitmap_pad #
> Bitmap padding unit of the font; 0, 1, or 2, where 0 is ImageRectMin, 1 is ImageRectMaxWidth and 2 is ImageRectMaxWidth.

showsnf

> showsnf [*options*] *snf_file*

Print contents of an *snf_file* to standard output. This client has been removed from the standard distribution in R5. *showsnf* takes the following non-standard options:

−v   Print character bearings and sizes.

−g   Print character glyph bitmaps.

−m   Bit order of the font is most significant bit first.

−l   Bit order of the font is least significant bit first.

−M   Byte order of the font is most significant byte first.

−L   Byte order of the font is least significant byte first.

−p*number*
> Glyph padding of the font.

−u*number*
> Scanline unit of the font.

twm

twm [*options*]

Window manager for the X Window System. *twm* takes the following non-standard options:

−s Manage only the default screen (as specified by −display or by the DISPLAY environment variable). Default is to manage all screens on the display.

−f *filename*
> Name of startup file to use. By default, *twm* will look in the user's home directory for files named *.twmrc.num* (where **num** is a screen number) or *.twmrc*.

−v Print error messages whenever an unexpected X Error event is received.

twm startup files are logically broken up into three types of specifications: *variables*, *bindings*, and *menus*. Variable specifications must come first; they describe fonts, colors, cursors, border widths, icon and window placement, highlighting, autoraising, layout of titles, warping, and use of the icon manager. For example:

```
BorderColor  "gray50"
{
    "XTerm"  "red"
    "xmh"    "green"
}
```

Binding specifications usually come second; they specify functions to be invoked when keyboard and pointer buttons are pressed in icons, windows, titles, and frames. Binding specifications have the following syntax:

```
"FP1"      = modlist : context : function
Button1    = modlist : context : function
```

modlist is any combination of the modifier names shift, control, and meta (or s, c, m) separated by a vertical bar (|). *context* is any combination of window, title, icon, root, frame, iconmgr (or w, t, i, r, f, m), or all, separated by a vertical bar. *function* is any of the f. keywords.

A sample binding specification might look like this:

```
Button1 =   : root      : f.menu "TwmWindows"
Button1 = m : window | icon : f.function "move-or-lower"
Button2 = m : window | icon : f.iconify
Button3 = m : window | icon : f.function "move-or-raise"
Button1 =   : title     : f.function "move-or-raise"
Button2 =   : title     : f.raiselower
```

Menu specifications give any user-defined menus (containing functions to be invoked or commands to be executed). A special menu named TwmWindows contains the names of all of the client- and *twm*-supplied windows. Selecting an entry will cause the WindowFunction to be executed on that window. If WindowFunction hasn't been set, the window will be deiconified and raised.

viewres

>viewres [*options*]

Allow the user to view the class hierarchy and resource inheritance for the Athena Widget Set. (New in R5.)

viewres takes the following non-standard resources and options:

-top *name*
>Name of highest widget in hierarchy to display. Default is Object.

-variable
>Widget variable names (as declared in header files) should be displayed in nodes rather than widget class name.

-vertical
>Tree displays top to bottom rather than left to right.

xauth

>xauth [*options*] [*commands*]

Edit and display the authorization information used in connecting to the X server. *xauth* is usually used to extract authorization records from one machine and merge them in on another. *xauth* takes the following non-standard options:

−f *authfile*
>Use *authfile* as the name of the authority file. Default is file specified by the XAUTHORITY environment variable or *.Xauthority* in the user's home directory.

−q Do not print unsolicited status messages. This is the default when *xauth* is issued on the command line or if the standard output is not directed to a terminal.

−v Print status messages (verbose). This is the default if *xauth* is reading commands from standard input and its standard output is directed to a terminal.

−i Ignore authority file locks.

−b Break authority file locks before proceeding and clean up stale locks.

Commands may be entered interactively, on the *xauth* command line, or in scripts. *xauth* uses the following commands to manipulate authority files:

add *display protocol key*

Add to the authorization file an authorization entry for the indicated *display* using the given *protocol* and *key* data. The data is specified as an even-lengthed string of hexadecimal digits, each pair representing one octet.

[n]extract *file display ...*

Write authorization entries to the indicated *file* for each *display.* nextract writes entries in a numeric format suitable for non-binary transmission (such as secure electronic mail).

[n]list [*display ...*]

Print authorization entries on standard output for each *display* (or all if no displays are named). nlist shows entries in the numeric format used by nextract.

[n]merge [*file ...*]

Read authorization entries from each *file* and merge into the authorization database, superseding any matching existing entries. nmerge command uses numeric format.

remove *display ...*

Remove from the authority file any authorization entries matching a *display.*

source *file*

Treat *file* as a script containing *xauth* commands to execute. Blank lines and lines beginning with a sharp sign (#) are ignored.

info

List information describing the authorization file, whether changes have been made, and where *xauth* commands are being read from.

exit

If any modifications have been made, the authority file is written out (if allowed), and the program exits. An end of file is treated as an implicit exit command.

quit

The program exits, ignoring any modifications. This may also be accomplished by pressing the interrupt character.

help [*string*]

List all commands that begin with the given *string* (or all commands if no string is given).

?   Print a short list of valid commands.

xbiff

xbiff [*options*]

xbiff displays an image of a mailbox. When there is no mail, the flag on the mailbox is down. When mail arrives, the flag goes up and the mailbox beeps. This client creates its own window. *xbiff* takes the following non-standard resources and options:

–help

Display a usage summary of command-line options.

*update (class **Interval**, option **–update** *seconds*)

Update display after every number of *seconds*. Default is 60 seconds.

*file (class **File**, option **–file** *filename*)

Monitor *filename*. Default is */usr/spool/mail/username*, where *username* is your login name.

*volume (class **Volume**, option **–volume** *percentage*)

Set loudness of bell that rings when new mail comes in. Specify a *percentage* of maximum volume.

*shapeWindow (class **ShapeWindow**, option **–shape**)

Shape mailbox window if masks for the empty or full images are given.

*checkCommand (class **CheckCommand**)

Execute a shell command to check for new mail rather than examining the size of file. Uses the specified string value as the argument to a *system*(3) call and may therefore contain I/O redirection. An exit status of zero indicates that new mail is waiting, 1 indicates that there has been no change in size, and 2 indicates that the mail has been cleared.

*flip (class **Flip**)

If true (default), invert image shown when mail has arrived.

*fullPixmap (class **Pixmap**)

Show bitmap when new mail has arrived.

*fullPixmapMask (class **PixmapMask**)

Show mask for the bitmap when new mail has arrived.

*emptyPixmap (class **Pixmap**)
Show bitmap when no new mail is present.

*emptyPixmapMask (class **PixmapMask**)
Show mask for the bitmap when no new mail is present.

*width (class **Width**)
Set mailbox width.

*height (class **Height**)
Set mailbox height.

*onceOnly (class **Boolean**)
Ring bell the first time new mail is found.

xcalc

xcalc [*options*]

Scientific calculator for X. This client creates its own window. *xcalc* takes the following non-standard resources and options:

*stipple (class **Stipple**, option **–stipple**)
Draw background using a stipple of the foreground and background colors. On monochrome displays, this improves the appearance.

*rpn (class **Rpn**, option **–rpn**)
Use Reverse Polish Notation, as in an HP-10C. Default behavior is to emulate a TI-30.

*cursor (class **Cursor**)
The name of the symbol used to represent the pointer. Default is hand2.

xclipboard

xclipboard [*options*]

Collect and display text selections that are sent to the CLIPBOARD by other clients. This client creates its own window. *xclipboard* takes the following non-standard options:

–w Wrap lines of text that are too long.

–nw Do not wrap long lines of text (default).

xclock

xclock [*options*]

Continuously display time in either analog or digital form. This client creates its own window. *xclock* takes the following non-standard resources and options:

–help
Display a usage summary of command-line options.

*clock.analog (class **Boolean,** option **–analog**)
Draw a conventional 12-hour clock face with tick marks for each minute and stroke marks for each hour (default).

*clock.analog (class **Boolean,** option **–digital** or **–d**)
If this resource is false or the -digital or -d option is used, *xclock* displays date and time in digital format.

*clock.chime (class **Boolean,** option **–chime**)
Ring the clock chime once on the half hour and twice on the hour.

*clock.hands (class **Foreground,** option **–hd** *color*)
On analog clock, display hands in *color*. Default is black.

*clock.highlight (class **Foreground,** option **–hl** *color*)
On analog clock, display the edges of the hands in *color*. Useful on color displays. Default is black.

*clock.padding (class **Margin,** option **–padding** *pixels*)
Add the specified number of *pixels* of space between the window border and any portion of the *xclock* display. Default is 10 in digital mode, 8 in analog mode.

*clock.update (class **Interval,** option **–update** *seconds*)
Update display every number of *seconds*. If the *xclock* window is obscured and then exposed, *xclock* overrides this setting and redisplays immediately. A value below 30 seconds enables a second hand on an analog clock. Default is 60 seconds.

*width (class **Width**)
Set clock width.

*height (class **Height**)
Set clock height.

xcmsdb

xcmsdb [options] [filename]

Set screen color characterization data properties. (New in R5.)

xcmsdb takes the following non-standard options:

-query

Attempt to read the XDCCC properties off screen's root window. If successful, data is transformed into more readable format, then sent to standard out.

-remove

Attempt to remove XDCCC properties on screen's root window.

-color

Set the query and remove options to check only for the XDCCC_LINEAR_RGB_MATRICES and XDCCC_LINEAR_RGB_CORRECTION properties.

-format *property_format*

Property format (the number of bits per entry) for XDCCC_LINEAR_RGB_CORRECTION property. Legal values are 8, 16, and 32. Default is 32 bits per entry.

xconsole

Monitor system console messages. This client displays messages that are usually sent to */dev/console*. (New in R5.)

xconsole [options]

xconsole takes the following non-standard resources and options:

-file *filename*

Device name, when monitoring some other device. Does not work on regular files as they are always ready to be read from.

-notify, -nonotify

Appends "*" to new data received from console. *-notify* is default.

-daemon

Causes *xconsole* to place itself in the background, using fork/exit.

-verbose

Directs *xconsole* to display message in first line of the text buffer.

-exitOnFail

Directs *xconsole* to exit when unable to redirect console output.

xcutsel

xcutsel [*options*]

xcutsel allows you to copy the current selection into a cut buffer and to make a selection that contains the current contents of the cut buffer. This client acts as a bridge between applications that don't support selections and those that do. This client creates its own window. *xcutsel* takes the following non-standard resources and options:

*selection (class **Selection**, option **–selection** *name*)
Use selection with the specified *name*. Default is PRIMARY. The only supported abbreviations for this option are –select, –sel and –s, since the standard Toolkit option –selectionTimeout has a similar name.

*cutBuffer (class **CutBuffer**, option **–cutbuffer** *number*)
Use cut buffer *number*. Default is 0.

xditview

xditview [*options*] [*ditroff_file*]

Display *ditroff* output on an X display. *xditview* uses no special metrics; it automatically converts the printer coordinates into screen coordinates, using the user-specified screen resolution rather than the actual resolution so the appropriate fonts can be found.

% **ditroff** *myfile* | **xditview**

On servers that support scaled fonts, all requested font sizes will be accurately reflected on the screen. For servers that do not support scaled fonts, *xditview* will use the closest font from the same family. This client creates its own window. *xditview* takes the following non-standard resources and options:

*dvi.pageNumber (class **PageNumber**, option **–page**)
Display the page number of the document.

*dvi.backingStore (class **BackingStore**, option **–backingStore** *value*)
Save window contents. When scrolled around the viewport, the window will be painted from contents saved in backing store. *value* can be one of Always, WhenMapped, or NotUseful.

–noPolyText
Suppress PolyText with multiple strings per request.

-resolution *dots_per_inch*
Screen resolution. Used as resolution field in XLFD names.

*fontMap (class *FontMap*)

To associate the *ditroff* fonts with appropriate X fonts, this string resource contains a set of newline-separated specifications, each of which consists of a *ditroff* name, some white space and an XLFD pattern with wildcard (*) characters in appropriate places to allow all sizes to be listed. This resource has been added in Release 5. The default `fontMap` is:

```
R     -*-times-medium-r-normal--*-*-*-*-*-*-iso8859-1\n\
I     -*-times-medium-i-normal--*-*-*-*-*-*-iso8859-1\n\
B     -*-times-bold-r-normal--*-*-*-*-*-*-iso8859-1\n\
F     -*-times-bold-i-normal--*-*-*-*-*-*-iso8859-1\n\
BI    -*-times-bold-i-normal--*-*-*-*-*-*-iso8859-1\n\
C     -*-courier-medium-r-normal--*-*-*-*-*-*-iso8859-1\n\
CO    -*-courier-medium-o-normal--*-*-*-*-*-*-iso8859-1\n\
CB    -*-courier-bold-r-normal--*-*-*-*-*-*-iso8859-1\n\
CF    -*-courier-bold-o-normal--*-*-*-*-*-*-iso8859-1\n\
H     -*-helvetica-medium-r-normal--*-*-*-*-*-*-iso8859-1\n\
HO    -*-helvetica-medium-o-normal--*-*-*-*-*-*-iso8859-1\n\
HB    -*-helvetica-bold-r-normal--*-*-*-*-*-*-iso8859-1\n\
HF    -*-helvetica-bold-o-normal--*-*-*-*-*-*-iso8859-1\n\
N     -*-new century schoolbook-medium-r-normal--*-*-*-*-*-*-iso8859-1\n\
NI    -*-new century schoolbook-medium-i-normal--*-*-*-*-*-*-iso8859-1\n\
NB    -*-new century schoolbook-bold-r-normal--*-*-*-*-*-*-iso8859-1\n\
NF    -*-new century schoolbook-bold-i-normal--*-*-*-*-*-*-iso8859-1\n\
A     -*-charter-medium-r-normal--*-*-*-*-*-*-iso8859-1\n\
AI    -*-charter-medium-i-normal--*-*-*-*-*-*-iso8859-1\n\
AB    -*-charter-bold-r-normal--*-*-*-*-*-*-iso8859-1\n\
AF    -*-charter-bold-i-normal--*-*-*-*-*-*-iso8859-1\n\
S     -*-symbol-medium-r-normal--*-*-*-*-*-*-adobe-fontspecific\n\
S2    -*-symbol-medium-r-normal--*-*-*-*-*-*-adobe-fontspecific\n
```

xdm

xdm [*options*]

xdm manages a collection of X displays, which may be on the local host or remote servers. This client creates its own window, and takes the following non-standard resources and options:

−config *configuration_file*

Names the configuration file, which specifies resources to control the behavior of *xdm*. Defaults to */usr/lib/X11/xdm/xdm-config*.

The X Window System in a Nutshell

−nodaemon

Specifies "false" as the value for the DisplayManager.daemonMode resource. This suppresses the normal daemon behavior, which is for *xdm* to close all file descriptors, disassociate the controlling terminal and put itself in the background when it first starts up. The default for the DisplayManage.daemon-Mode resource is True.

−debug *debug_level*

Numeric value of the DisplayManager.debugLevel resource. A non-zero value causes *xdm* to print piles of debugging statements to the terminal; it also disables the DisplayManager.daemonMode resource, forcing *xdm* to run synchronously.

−error *error_log_file*

Value for the DisplayManager.errorLogFile resource. This file contains errors from *xdm* as well as anything written to standard error by the various scripts and programs run during the progress of the session.

−resources *resource_file*

Value of the DisplayManager*resources resource. This file is loaded using *xrdb* to specify configuration parameters for the authentication widget.

−server *server_entry*

Value of the DisplayManager.servers resource.

−udpPort *port_number*

Value for the DisplayManager.requestPort resource. This sets the port number which XDM will monitor for XDMCP requests. As XDMCP uses the registered, well-known udp port 177, this resource should probably not be changed except for debugging.

−session *session_program*

Value for the DisplayManager*session resource. This indicates the program to run as the session after the user has logged in.

−xrm *resource_specification*

Allows an arbitrary resource to be specified, as in most X Toolkit applications.

xdpr

xdpr [*options*] [*filename*]

Dump an X window directly to the printer. *filename* is an existing file containing a window dump (created by *xwd*). *xdpr* takes the same options as *xwd*, *xpr*, and *lpr*. The most commonly used non-standard options are listed below:

–help

    Display a usage summary of command-line options.

–P*printer*

    Send output to alternate printer. If a printer name is not specified here, *xdpr* (really, *lpr*(1)) will send your output to the printer specified by the PRINTER environment variable. Printer type must match type specified with the –device option.

–device *printer_device*

    Print output on *printer_device*. The following printers currently are supported. Default is PostScript.

ln03   Digital LN03.

la100   Digital LA100.

ljet   HP LaserJet series and other monochrome PCL devices, such as ThinkJet, QuietJet, RuggedWriter, HP2560 series, and HP2930 series printers.

pjet   HP PaintJet (color mode).

pjetxl   HP PaintJet XL Color Graphics Printer (color mode).

pp   IBM PP3812.

ps   PostScript printer.

xdpyinfo

    xdpyinfo [–display *displayname*]

Display information about the X display *displayname*. Default is the current display.

xedit

    xedit [*standard_options*] [*filename*]

Simple text editor for X. *xedit* loads *filename* during start-up. This is the file that will be edited. Three commands are available when using *xedit*:

Load   Read in a new or existing file.

Save   Save the current file.

Quit   Exit *xedit*.

This client creates its own window. *xedit* takes the following non-standard resources:

*enableBackups (class **EnableBackups**)
Copy the original version of file to *filename* before saving the changes. Default value is off (no backups should be created). *filename* might include a prefix, a suffix, or both.

*backupNamePrefix (class **BackupNamePrefix**)
Prepend string to backup filename. Default is to not prepend string.

*backupNameSuffix (class **BackupNameSuffix**)
Append string to backup filename. Default is to append string *.BAK*.

xev

> xev [*standard_options*]

xev displays contents of X events. *xev* can be found in the *demos* directory. This client creates its own window. The most useful standard options are –display and –geometry.

xfd

> xfd [*options*] –fn *fontname*

xfd creates a window to display all of the characters of *fontname*. The window contains the name of the font being displayed, a row of command buttons, several lines of text for displaying character metrics, and a grid containing one glyph per cell. The characters are shown in increasing order from left to right, top to bottom. This client creates its own window. *xfd* takes the following non-standard resources and options:

*grid.boxChars (option **–box**)
Display a box filled with background color outlining the area by an ImageText request.

*grid.centerChars (option **–center**)
Center each glyph in its grid.

*startChar (option **–start** *char_num*)
Display, as first character, the character that has position *char_num*. This option is used for viewing characters at arbitrary locations in the font. Default is 0.

*grid.boxColor (option **–bc** *color*)
Use *color* for ImageText boxes.

*grid.cellRows (option **-rows** *num*)

Number of rows in grid.

*grid.cellColumns (option **-columns** *num*)

Number of columns in grid.

*selectFormat (class **SelectFormat**)

Define format that shows a selected character.

*metricsFormat (class **MetricsFormat**)

Define format that shows metrics of a selected character.

*rangeFormat (class **RangeFormat**)

Define format that shows range of a font.

*startFormat (class **StartFormat**)

Define format that shows a font's start point.

*nocharFormat (class **NocharFormat**)

Define format that shows that no such character exists.

xfontsel

xfontsel [*options*]

Point and click interface for selecting display font names. This client creates its own window. *xfontsel* takes the following non-standard resources and options:

*pattern (class **Pattern**, option **-pattern** *fontname*)

Specify a subset of available fonts, with names that contain *fontname*, which can be a partial or full name.

*printOnQuit (class **PrintOnQuit**, option **-print**)

Write selected font to standard output when the quit button is activated.

*sampleText.label (class **Text**, option **-sample** *text*)

Use sample *text* to display selected font. Default is lower-case and upper-case alphabet and the digits 0 through 9.

*cursor (class **Cursor**)

Set application's window cursor.

*showUnselectable (class **ShowUnselectable**)

For each field menu, specifies whether or not to show values that are not currently selectable, based upon previous field selections.

*pixelSizeList (class **PixelSizeList**)

List of pixel sizes to add to the pixel size menu, so that scalable fonts can be selected at those pixel sizes. Default pixelSizeList contains 7, 30, 40, 50, and 60.

*pointSizeList (class **PointSizeList**)

List of point sizes (in units of tenths of points) to add to the point size menu, so that scalable fonts can be selected at those point sizes. Default pointSizeList contains 250, 300, 350, and 400.

*sampleText16 (class **Text16**, option **-sample16 text16**)

Sample 2-byte text to use for matrix-encoded fonts. Each glyph index is two bytes, with a 1-byte newline separating lines.

*scaledFonts (class **ScaledFonts**)

If True, then selection of artibrary pixel and pints sizes for scalable fonts is enabled. The -noscaled option is equivalent to *scaledFonts: false.

xhost

xhost [*options*]

Add and delete hosts from the list of machines that are allowed to make connections to the X server. The current machine is allowed to be removed; however, further connections (including attempts to add it back) will not be permitted. Resetting the server (thereby breaking all connections) is the only way to allow local connections again. *xhost* takes the following non-standard options:

[+]hostname

Add *hostname* to the list of machines that are allowed to connect to the X server.

−hostname

Remove *hostname* from the list of machines that are allowed to connect to the server. Existing connections are not broken, but new connection attempts will be denied.

+   Access is granted to everyone, even if they aren't on the list of allowed hosts (i.e., access control is turned off).

−   Access is restricted to only those machines on the list of allowed hosts (i.e., access control is turned on).

If no command line arguments are given, a message indicating whether or not access control is enabled is printed, followed by the list of those allowed to connect.

xinit

xinit [[*client*] [*options*] [*-- server*] [*display*] [*options*]

X Window System initializer. This client creates its own window. *xinit* takes the following arguments:

client
Start *client* with the server.

server_program
Use the specified *server_program.*

xkill

xkill [*options*]

Kill a client by its X resource. *xkill* takes the following non-standard resources and options:

-id *resource*
Specify the X identifier for the *resource* whose creator is to be aborted. If *resource* is specified, *xkill* displays a cursor with which to select a window to be killed.

*Button (option **-button** *number*)
Set pointer button *number* as the button that selects the window to kill. If *number* is specified as any, then any button on the pointer can be used. Default is first button, usually the leftmost.

-all
Kill all clients with top-level windows on the screen. *xkill* will ask you to select the root window with each of the currently defined buttons to give you several chances to abort. Use of this option is highly discouraged.

-frame
Ignore the standard conventions for finding top-level client windows (which are typically nested inside a window manager window). *xkill* assumes that you want to kill direct children of the root.

xload

xload [*options*]

Display system load average. One *xload* division represents one load average point. This client creates its own window. *xload* takes the following non-standard resources and options:

*load.minScale (class **Scale**, option **−scale** *integer*)

Produce histogram with at least *integer* tick marks in the histogram. If the load goes above *integer*, *xload* will create more divisions, but it will never use fewer than this number. Default is 1.

*load.update (class **Interval**, option **−update** *seconds*)

Update the display every *seconds*. Default is 10. Minimum value is 1.

*load.highlight (class **Foreground**, option **−highlight** *color*)

Color of the scale lines.

*load.jumpScroll (class **JumpScroll**, option **−jumpscroll** *pixels*)

When the graph reaches the right edge of the window, specify the number of *pixels* to shift the graph to the left. Default value is 1/2 the width of current window. Smooth scrolling can be achieved by setting it to 1.

*label.label (class **String**, option **−label** *string*)

Place text *string* as a label above the load average. By default, the host name is used.

*showLabel (class **Boolean**, option **−nolabel**)

Setting this resource to false suppresses a label. Display current load average by using the keyboard LEDs. For an average of *n*, *xload* lights the first *n* keyboard LEDs. Turns off the usual screen display.

xlogo

xlogo [*standard_options*]

Display the X Window System logo. This client creates its own window. Window is shaped to the X logo (rather than being rectangular). Default is false.

xlsatoms

xlsatoms [*options*]

List interned atoms defined on server. *xlsatoms* takes the following non-standard resources and options:

−format *printf_string*

List each atom as a value-name pair with a specified format. *printf_string* is a set of characters in the syntax of the UNIX *printf* command. In each value-name pair, the value is an unsigned long and the name is a pointer to a char. *xlsatoms* will supply a newline at the end of each line. The default is %ld\t%s.

−range [*low*]−[*high*]

 Specify the range of atom values to check. If *low* is not given, a value of 1 assumed. If *high* is not given, *xlsatoms* will stop at the first undefined atom at or above *low*.

−name *string*

 List atom that has the name *string*. If atom does not exist, a message will be printed on the standard error.

xlsclients

 xlsclients [*options*]

List client applications running on a display. *xlsclients* takes the following non-standard options:

−a List clients that are on all screens instead of clients only on the default screen.

−l Show long listing: window name, icon name, and class hints (as well as machine name and command string in the default listing).

−m *maxlength*

 Display up to *maxlength* characters for each client listed. Default is 10000.

xlsfonts

 xlsfonts [*options*] [−fn *pattern*]

List available fonts that match the given *pattern*. The wildcard character "*" may be used to match any sequence of characters (including none), and "?" to match any single character. If no pattern is given, "*" is assumed. *xlsfonts* takes the following non-standard options:

−l[l[l]]

 Generate medium, long, and very long listings, respectively.

−m In long listings, print the minimum and maximum bounds of each font.

−C Produce list using multiple columns. Same as −n 0.

−1 Produce list using a single column. Same as −n 1.

−w *width*

 Set column *width* in characters that should be used in figuring out how many columns to print. Default is 79.

−n *columns*

Use number of *columns* in displaying the output. By default, it attempts to fit as many columns of font names into the number of characters specified by −w *width*.

−u   Output should be unsorted

−o   *xlsfonts* should do an OpenFont (and QueryFont, if appropriate) rather than a ListFonts. Useful if ListFonts or ListFontsWithInfo fail to list a known font (as is the case with some scaled font systems).

xlswins

xlswins [*options*] [*window_id*]

Lists the window tree. By default, the root window is used as the starting point, although another window may be specified using the *window_id* argument. This client has been replaced in R5 by *xwininfo -tree*. *xlswins* takes the following non-standard resources and options:

−l   Generate a long listing for each window: a number indicates the depth, the geometry relative to the parent, as well as the location relative to the root window.

−format *radix*

Use *radix* when printing out window IDs. Allowable values are: hex, octal, and decimal. Default is hex.

−indent *number*

Indent *number* of spaces for each level in the window tree. Default is 2.

xmag

xmag [-mag *magfactor*] [-source *geom*] [*options*]

Magnify parts of the screen. The size of the source is used with the desired magnification to compute the default enlargement window size. If no explicit region is specified, a square with the pointer in the upper left corner is displayed indicating the area to be enlarged. This client creates its own window. *xmag* takes the following non-standard resources and options:

*source (class **Source**, option **−source** *geometry*)

Set the size and/or location of the source region on the screen. Default is a 64x64 square centered about the pointer. Only one of −geometry *size* and −mag *magfactor* options may be specified if a source size is given with this option.

*magnification (class **Magnification,** option **–mag** *magfactor*)

Enlarge the source region by the integral *magfactor.* Default magnification is 5. Only one of –geometry *size* and –source *geom* options may be specified if a magnification factor is given with this option.

xman

xman [*options*]

Display manual pages. This client creates its own window. *xman* takes the following non-standard resources and options:

–helpfile *filename*

Use alternate *filename* for help.

*bothShown (class **Boolean,** option **–bothshown**)

Show both the manual page and manual directory on the screen.

*topBox (class **Boolean,** option **–notopbox**)

If false, start without the top menu with the three buttons in it.

*manualBrowser.geometry (class **Geometry,** option **–pagesize** *geometry*)

Set the size and location of all manual pages.

*manualFontNormal (class **Font**)

The font to use for normal text in the manual pages.

*manualFontBold (class **Font**)

The font to use for bold text in the manual pages.

*manualFontItalic (class **Font**)

The font to use for italic text in the manual pages.

*directoryFontNormal (class **Font**)

The font to use for the directory text.

*bothShown (class **Boolean**)

Either true or false: specifies whether or not you want both the directory and the manual page shown at start up.

*directoryHeight (class **DirectoryHeight**)

The height in pixels of the directory, when the directory and the manual page are shown simultaneously.

*topCursor (class **Cursor**)

The cursor to use in the top box.

*helpCursor (class **Cursor**)

The cursor to use in the help window.

*manpageCursor (class **Cursor**)

The cursor to use in the manual page window.

*searchEntryCursor (class **Cursor**)

The cursor to use in the search entry text widget.

*pointerColor (class **Foreground**)

The color of all the cursors (pointers) listed above. The name was chosen to be compatible with *xterm*. (Available as of R4.)

*helpFile (class **File**)

A filename to use instead of the system's default helpfile.

*verticalList (class **Boolean**)

Organize the directory listing vertically (true) or horizontally (false). Default is false.

xmh

xmh [–path *mailpath*] [–initial *foldername*] [–flag] [*options*]

X window interface to the Rand *mh* Message Handling System. This client creates its own window. *xmh* takes the following non-standard resources and options:

*mailPath (class **MailPath**, option –**path** *mailpath*)

Specify an alternate collection of mail folders in which to process mail. Default *mailpath* is the value of the Path component in *$HOME/.mh_profile*, or *$HOME/Mail*.

*initialFolder (class **InitialFolder**, option –**initial** *foldername*)

Specify an alternate folder that may receive new mail and is initially opened by *xmh*. Default *foldername* is *inbox*.

*mailWaitingFlag (class **MailWaitingFlag**, option –**flag**)

Change the appearance of *xmh* icon when new mail arrives.

*banner (class **Banner**)

A short string that is the default label of the folder, Table of Contents, and view. The default is:

```
xmh   MIT X Consortium   R5
```

*blockEventsOnBusy (class **BlockEventsOnBusy**)

Whether to disallow user input and show a busy cursor while *xmh* is busy processing a command. Default is true.

*busyCursor (class **BusyCursor**)

The name of the symbol used to represent the position of the pointer, displayed if BlockEventsOnBusy is true, when *xmh* is processing a time-consuming command. The default is watch.

*busyPointerColor (class **BusyPointerColor**)

The foreground color of the busy cursor. Default is XtDefaultForeground.

*checkFrequency (class **CheckFrequency**)

How often to check for new mail, make checkpoints, and rescan the Table of Contents, in minutes. If CheckNewMail is true, *xmh* checks to see if you have new mail each interval. If MakeCheckpoints is true, checkpoints are made every fifth interval. Also every fifth interval, the Table of Contents is checked for inconsistencies with the file system, and rescanned. To prevent all of these checks from occurring, set CheckFrequency to 0. The default is 1.

*checkpointInterval (class **Interval**)

Specify in minutes how often to make checkpoints of volatile state, if makeCheckpoints is true. The default is 5 times the value of checkFrequency.

*checkpointNameFormat

Specify how checkpointed files are to be named.

*checkNewMail (class **CheckNewMail**)

If true, *xmh* will check at regular intervals to see if new mail has arrived for any of the folders. Default is True. The interval can be adjusted with the CheckFrequency.

*commandButtonCount (class **CommandButtonCount**)

The number of command buttons to create in a button box in between the toc and the view areas of the main window. *xmh* will create these buttons with the names *button1*, *button2* and so on, in a box with the name *commandBox*. The user can specify labels and actions for the buttons in a private resource file. The default is 0.

*compGeometry (class **CompGeometry**)

Initial geometry for windows containing compositions.

*cursor (class **Cursor**)

The name of the symbol used to represent the pointer. Default is left_ptr.

*debug (class **Debug**, option **-debug**)

If true, *xmh* prints information to standard error. Default is false.

*draftsFolder (class **DraftsFolder**)

The folder used for message drafts. Default is drafts.

*hideBoringHeaders (class **HideBoringHeaders**)

If "on", *xmh* will attempt to skip uninteresting header lines within messages by scrolling them off. Default is on.

*initialIncFile (class **InitialIncFile**)

The filename of your incoming mail drop. *xmh* tries to construct a filename for the inc –file command, but in some installations (e.g., those using the Post Office Protocol) no file is appropriate. In this case, InitialIncFile should be specified as the empty string, and inc will be invoked without a –file argument. The default is to use the value of the environment variable MAIL, or if that is not set, to append the value of the environment variable USER to */usr/spool/mail/*.

*mailInterval (class **Interval**)

Specify interval in minutes at which mail should be checked if mailWaiting-Flag or checkNewMail is true; default is the value of checkFrequency.

*makeCheckpoints (class **MakeCheckpoints**)

If true, *xmh* will attempt to save checkpoints of volatile information. The frequency of checkpointing is controlled by the resource checkFrequency.

*mhPath (class **MhPath**)

Directory in which to find the *mh* commands. If a command isn't found here, then the directories in the user's path are searched. Default is */usr/local/mh6*.

*newMailBitmap (class **NewMailBitmap**)

Bitmap suggested to the window manager for the icon when any folder has new mail. Default is "flagup."

*newMailIconBitmap (class **NewMailBitmap**)

Bitmap suggested to the window manager for the icon when any folder has new mail. Default is "flagup."

*noMailBitmap (class **NoMailBitmap**)

Bitmap suggested to the window manager for the icon when no folders have new mail. Default is "flagdown."

noMailIconBitmap (class **NoMailBitmap**)

Bitmap suggested to the window manager for the icon when no folders have new mail. Default is "flagdown."

*pickGeometry (class **PickGeometry**)

Initial geometry for pick windows.

*pointerColor (class **PointerColor**)

The foreground color of the pointer. Default is XtDefaultForeground.

*prefixWmAndIconName (class PrefixWmAndIconName)

Whether to prefix the window and icon name with "xmh:". Default is true.

*printCommand (class PrintCommand)

An *sh* command to print a message. Note that standard output and standard error must be specifically redirected! If a message or range of messages is selected for printing, the full filename of each message file is appended to the specified print command. The default is *enscript >/dev/null 2>/dev/null*.

*replyInsertFilter (class ReplyInsertFilter)

A shell command to be executed when the Insert button is activated in a composition window. The full path and filename of the source message is added to the end of the command before being passed to *sh*(1). The default filter is *cat*; i.e., it inserts the entire message into the composition. Interesting filters are: *awk −e '{print "" $0}'* or *<mh directory>/lib/mhl −form mhl.body*.

*rescanInterval (class Interval)

How often to check the Table of Contents of currently viewed folders and of folders with messages currently being viewed, and to update the Table of Contents if *xmh* sees inconsistencies with the file system in these folders. Default is 5 times the value of checkFrequency.

*reverseReadOrder (class ReverseReadOrder)

When true, the next message will be the message prior to the current message in the table of contents, and the previous message will be the message after the current message in the table of contents. The default is false.

*sendBreakWidth (class SendBreakWidth)

When a message is sent from *xmh*, lines longer than this value will be split into multiple lines, each of which is no longer than SendWidth. This value may be overridden for a single message by inserting an additional line in the message header of the form SendBreakWidth: *value*. This line will be removed from the header before the message is sent. The default is 85.

*showOnInc

Whether to automatically show the current message after incorporating new mail. Default is true.

*sendWidth (class SendWidth)

When a message is sent from *xmh*, lines longer than *SendBreakWidth* characters will be split into multiple lines, each of which is no longer than this value. This value may be overridden for a single message by inserting an additional line in the message header of the form SendWidth: *value*. This line will be removed from the header before the message is sent. The default is 72.

*skipCopied (class SkipCopied)

Whether to skip over messages marked for copying when using View Next Message and View Previous Message. Default is true.

*skipDeleted (class SkipDeleted)

Whether to skip over messages marked for deletion when using View Next Message and View Previous Message. Default is true.

*skipMoved (class SkipMoved)

Whether to skip over messages marked for moving to other folders when using View Next Message and View Previous Message. Default is true.

*stickyMenu (class StickyMenu)

If true, when pop-up command menus are used, the most recently selected entry will be under the cursor when the menu pops up. Default is false. See the file *clients/xmh/Xmh.sample* for an example of how to specify resources for pop up command menus.

*tempDir (class TempDir)

Directory for *xmh* to store temporary directories. For privacy, a user might want to change this to a private directory. Default is */tmp*.

*tocGeometry (class TocGeometry)

Initial geometry for master *xmh* windows.

*tocPercentage (class TocPercentage)

The percentage of the main window that is used to display the Table of Contents. Default is 33.

*tocWidth (class TocWidth)

How many characters to generate for each message in a folder's table of contents. Default is 100. Use 80 if you plan to use *mhl* a lot, because it will be faster, and the extra 20 characters may not be useful.

*viewGeometry (class ViewGeometry)

Initial geometry for windows showing only a view of a message.

xmodmap

xmodmap [*options*] [*filename*]

Keyboard and pointer modifier utility. *filename* specifies a file containing *xmodmap* expressions to be executed. This file is usually kept in the user's home directory and has a name like *.xmodmaprc*. *xmodmap* takes the following non-standard options:

–help

Display a usage summary of command-line options. This also takes effect if an undefined argument is given.

Clients

–grammar

Print, on the standard error, a help message describing the expression grammar used in files and with –e expressions.

–verbose

Print logging information as it parses its input.

–quiet

Turn off the verbose logging (default).

–n   Display changes, but do not execute. (Cannot be used with expressions to change the pointer mapping.)

–e *expression*

Execute *expression*. Any number of expressions may be specified from the command line. Use –grammar to see the syntax of *xmodmap* expressions.

–pm

Print the current modifier map on the standard output.

–pk

Print the current keymap table on the standard output.

–pke

Print the current keymap table on the standard output in the form of expressions that can be fed back to *xmodmap*.

–pp

Print the current pointer map on the standard output.

–   A lone dash means that the standard input should be used as the input file. For compatibility with an older version, *xmodmap* also accepts the following obsolete single letter options:

–[SLC12345]

Remove all current keys for the Shift, Lock, Control, or Mod modifier sets from the modifier map. These are equivalent to clear expressions.

–[slc] *keysym*

Remove a *keysym* from the Shift, Lock, or Control modifier sets. These are equivalent to remove expressions.

+[slc12345] *keysym*

Add a *keysym* to the Shift, Lock, or Control modifier sets. These are equivalent to add expressions.

xpr

xpr [*options*] [*filename*]

Print an X window dump. By default, no header or trailer is printed, and the window is printed such that its longest side follows the long side of the paper (portrait mode). *xpr* takes the following non-standard resources and options:

−device *printer_device*
> Print *filename* on *printer_device*. See *xdpr* for supported printers. The default is PostScript. −device lw (Apple LaserWriter) is equivalent to −device ps and is provided only for backwards compatibility.

−scale *scale*
> Affects the size of the window on the page. The PostScript, LN03, and HP printers are able to translate each bit in a window pixel map into a grid of a specified size. For example, each bit might translate into a 3x3 grid. This is specified by −scale 3. By default, a window is printed with the largest scale that fits onto the page for the specified orientation.

−height *inches*
> Maximum page height, in *inches*.

−width *inches*
> Maximum page width, in *inches*.

−left *inches*
> Left margin, in *inches*. Fractions are allowed. Default is centered on the page.

−top *inches*
> Top margin for the picture, in *inches*. Fractions are allowed. By default, the window is centered on the page.

−header *header*
> Print a *header* string above the window. Default is no header.

−trailer *trailer*
> Print a *trailer* string below the window. Default is no trailer.

−landscape
> Print windows in landscape mode.

−portrait
> Print window in portrait mode.

−compact
> Compress encoding of white pixels on PostScript printers.

–output *filename*

Send output to *filename*. Normally, standard output is used.

–append *filename*

Append the window contents to a *filename* previously produced by *xpr*.

–noff

In conjunction with –append, place window on the same page as the previous window.

–split *n*

Split a window onto several pages. This might be necessary for large windows that would otherwise cause the printer to overload and print the page in an obscure manner.

–plane *number*

Specify the bit plane to use in an image. The default is to use the entire image and map values into black and white based on color intensities.

–gray 2│3│4

Use a simple 2x2, 3x3, or 4x4 gray scale conversion on a color image, rather than mapping to strictly black and white. This doubles, triples, or quadruples the effective width and height of the image. This option is not supported for HP or IBM printers.

–rv Forces the window to be printed in reverse video.

–psfig

Suppress translation of the PostScript picture to the center of the page.

–density *dpi*

Use the specified dot-per-inch density for the HP printer.

–cutoff *level*

Change the intensity level where colors are mapped to either black or white for monochrome output on a LaserJet printer. *level* is expressed as a percentage of full brightness. Fractions are allowed.

–noposition

Bypass command generation of header, trailer, and image positioning for LaserJet, PaintJet, and PaintJet XL printers.

–gamma *correction*

Change the intensity of the colors printed by PaintJet XL printer. *correction* is a floating point value in the range 0.00 to 3.00. Consult an operator's manual to determine the correct value for the specific printer.

–render *algorithm*

For the PaintJet XL printer, render the image with the best quality-versus-performance tradeoff. Consult the operator's manual to determine which *algorithm*s are available.

–slide

Print overhead transparencies using the PaintJet and PaintJet XL printers.

xprop

xprop [*options*]

Display window and font properties for X. One window or font is selected using the command-line arguments or, in the case of a window, by clicking on the desired window. *xprop* takes the following non-standard options:

–help

Display a usage summary of command-line options.

–grammar

Print a detailed grammar for all command line options.

–id *id*

Select window *id* on the command line rather than using the pointer to select the target window. This is very useful in debugging X applications where the target window is not mapped to the screen or where the use of the pointer might be impossible or might interfere with the application.

–name *name*

Use the command line (rather than the pointer) to select *name* as the target window.

–font *font*

Display properties of *font*.

–root

Set the root window as the target window. Useful when the root window is completely obscured.

–len *n*

Read or display at most *n* bytes of any property.

–notype

Do not display the type of each property.

–fs *file*

Use *file* as a source of more formats for properties.

-remove *propname*

Remove the specified property name from the indicated window.

-f *propname format* [*dformat*]

Use the specified *format* and *dformat* for a property name. A sample *format* is
32ica. If *dformat* is missing, " = $0+\n" is assumed. This option is rarely
needed, since it is useful only when you are adding a property to the X Window System.

-frame

When selecting a window by hand (i.e., if none of –name, –root, or –id are
given), look at the window manager frame (if any) instead of looking for the
client window.

-spy

Examine window properties forever, looking for property change events.

xrdb

xrdb [*options*] [*filename*]

X server resource database utility. *xrdb* gets or sets the contents of the
RESOURCE_MANAGER property on the root window of screen 0. *xrdb* also
allows you to print or edit the contents of this property. You would normally run
this program from your X startup file. The *filename* (or standard input) is optionally passed through the C preprocessor. *xrdb* takes the following non-standard
options:

-all

Operation should be performed on the screen-independent resource property
(RESOURCE_MANAGER), as well as the screen-specific property
(SCREEN_RESOURCES) on every screen of the display. For *-load* and
-merge, the input file is processed once for each screen.

-global

Operation should only be performed on the screen-independent
RESOURCE_MANAGER property.

-help

Display a usage summary of command-line options. Using any unsupported
option has the same effect.

-cpp *filename*

Use *filename* as the C preprocessor program. Although *xrdb* was designed to
use CPP, any program that acts as a filter and accepts the –D, –I, and –U
options may be used.

−nocpp

Do not run the input file through a preprocessor before loading it into the RESOURCE_MANAGER property.

−symbols

Print to the standard output the symbols that are defined for the preprocessor. This option can be used in conjunction with −query, but not with the options that change the RESOURCE_MANAGER property.

−query

Print to the standard output the current contents of the RESOURCE_MANAGER property.

−load

Load the input as the new value of the RESOURCE_MANAGER property, replacing what was there (i.e., the old contents are removed). This is the default action.

−merge

Merge the input with, instead of replacing, the current contents of the RESOURCE_MANAGER property. This option does a lexicographic sorted merge of the two inputs, which is almost certainly not what you want, but remains for backward compatibility.

−n

Echo, but don't execute, changes to the property (when used with −load) or to the resource file (when used with −edit).

−quiet

Do not warn about duplicate entries.

−remove

Remove the RESOURCE_MANAGER property from its window.

−retain

Instruct the server not to reset if *xrdb* is the first client.

−screen

Operation should only be performed on the SCREEN_RESOURCES property of the default screen of the display.

−screens

Operation should be performed on the SCREEN_RESOURCES property of each screen of the display. For -*load* and -*merge*, the input file is processed for each screen.

−edit *filename*

Edit the RESOURCE_MANAGER property into *filename*, replacing any values already listed there. This allows you to put changes that you have made to your defaults back into your resource file, preserving any comments or preprocessor lines.

−backup *string*

Generate a backup file appending a suffix *string* to the filename used with −edit.

−D*name*[*=value*]

Pass *name* and *value* to the preprocessor to define symbols for use with conditionals such as #ifdef.

−U*name*

Pass *name* to the preprocessor to remove any definitions of this symbol.

−I*directory*

Pass *directory* to the preprocessor to search this directory for files that are referenced with #include.

xrefresh

xrefresh [*options*]

Refresh all or part of an X screen. This client uses the Xlib routine XGetDefault rather than the X Toolkit to read defaults, so its resource names are all capitalized. *refresh* takes the following non-standard resources and options:

*White (option **−white**)

Use a white background. The screen flashes quickly and then repaints.

*Black (option **−black**)

Use a black background.

*Solid (option **−solid** *color*)

Use a solid background of the specified *color*. Try green.

*Root (option **−root**)

Use the root window background.

*None (option **−none**)

Repaint all windows (default).

*Geometry (option **−geometry** *widthxheight±xoff±yoff*)

Set area to refresh. Not very useful. Offset variables are defined with the standard −geometry option in the introduction of this section.

Xserver

Xserver [: *displaynumber*] [*options*] [*ttyname*]

X Window System server. This client is not usually invoked explicitly as a user command. *displaynumber* identifies a particular display. *Xserver* takes the following non-standard options:

−a *number*
Set pointer acceleration to *number*.

−auth *authorization_file*
Authenticate access using the collection of authorization records found in the specified *authorization_file*.

bc Disable certain kinds of error checking, for bug compatibility with previous releases. Use of this option is discouraged.

−bs Disable backing store support on all screens.

−c Turn off key-click.

c *volume*
Set key-click *volume* (allowable range: 0–8).

−cc *class*
Set the visual *class* for the root window of color screens. The *class* numbers are as specified in the X protocol. Not obeyed by all servers.

−dpi *resolution*
Set the *resolution* of the screen, in dots per inch. Use when the server cannot determine the screen size from the hardware.

−f *volume*
Set beep (bell) *volume* (allowable range: 0–7).

−l Ignore all remaining command line arguments.

−lf *files*
Limit number of open files of the server to the specified number of *files*. Zero makes the limit as large as possible. Default of -1 leaves the limit unchanged. Not available on all operating systems.

−ld *kilobytes*
Limit the data space of the server to the specified number of *kilobytes*. The default of 0 makes the data size as large as possible. A value of −1 leaves the data space limit unchanged. (not available in all operating systems.)

−ls *kilobytes*
Limit the stack space of the server to the specified number of *kilobytes*. The default value is zero, making the stack size as large as possible. A value of

−1 leaves the stack space limit unchanged. (not available in all operating systems.)

−logo
>Turn on the X Window System logo display in the screen-saver. There is currently no way to change this from a client.

nologo
>Turn off the X Window System logo display in the screen-saver. There is currently no way to change this from a client.

−p *minutes*
>Set screen-saver pattern cycle time in *minutes*.

−r   Turn off auto-repeat.

r   Turn on auto-repeat.

−s *minutes*
>Set screen-saver timeout in *minutes*.

−su   Disable save under support on all screens.

−t *pixels*
>Set pointer acceleration threshold in *pixels* (i.e., after how many pixels pointer acceleration should take effect).

−to *seconds*
>Set default screen-saver timeout in *seconds*.

−tty *xx*
>Server started from init on tty*xx*.

v   Set video-on screen-saver preference.

−v   Set video-off screen-saver preference.

−co *filename*
>Use *filename* as the name of the RGB color database.

−help
>Display a usage summary of command-line options.

−fp *font_path*
>Set the search path for fonts. *font_path* is a comma-separated list of directories the server searches for font databases.

−fc *cursor_font*
>Set the default *cursor_font*.

−wm

Force the default backing-store of all windows to be WhenMapped; this is a cheap trick way of getting backing-store to apply to all windows.

−x *extension*

Load the specified extension at init. (not supported in most implementations.)

You can also have the X server connect to *xdm* using XDMCP. The following options control the behavior of XDMCP:

−query *hostname*

Enable XDMCP and sends Query packets to the specified *hostname*.

−broadcast

Enable XDMCP and broadcast BroadcastQuery packets to the network. The first responding display manager will be chosen for the session.

−indirect *hostname*

Enable XDMCP and send IndirectQuery packets to the specified *hostname*.

−port *port_number*

Specify an alternate *port_number* for XDMCP packets. Must be specified before any −query, −broadcast or −indirect options.

−once

Make the server exit after the first session is over. Normally, the server keeps starting sessions, one after the other.

−class *display-class*

XDMCP has an additional display qualifier used in resource lookup for display-specific options. This option sets that qualifier to *display_class*; by default it is "MIT-Unspecified" (not a very useful value).

−cookie *xdm_auth_bits*

When testing XDM-AUTHENTICATION, a private key is shared between the server and the manager. This option sets the value of that private data to *xdm-auth-bits* (not that it's very private, being on the command line).

−displayID *xdm-auth-bits*

An XDMCP-specific value; allows the display manager to identify each display so that it can locate the shared key.

Clients

xset

xset [*options*]

User preference utility for X. *xset* allows you to customize session characteristics such as bell volume, key click, and screen saving. All settings reset to default values when you log out. *xset* takes the following non-standard options:

[–]b [*volume* [*pitch* [*duration*]]] [on | off]

Control bell volume, pitch, and duration. The b option accepts up to three numerical parameters (*volume*, *pitch*, and *duration*), a preceding dash (–), or an on/off flag. If no parameters are given, or the on flag is used, the system defaults will be used. If the dash or off are given, the bell will be turned off. If only one numerical parameter is given, the bell *volume* will be set to that value, as a percentage of its maximum. Likewise, the second numerical parameter specifies the bell *pitch*, in hertz, and the third numerical parameter specifies the *duration* in milliseconds.

–bc or bc

Control **b**ug **c**ompatibility mode in the server, if possible. A preceding dash (–) disables the mode; no dash enables the mode.

[–]c [*value*] [on | off]

Control key click. The c option accepts an optional *value*, a preceding dash (–), or an on/off flag. If no parameter or the on flag is given, the system defaults are used. If the dash or off flag is used, keyclick is disabled. A *value* from 0 to 100 indicates volume as a percentage of maximum.

fp= *path*

Set the font path used by the server. *path* must be a directory or a comma-separated list of directories. The directories are interpreted by the server, not the client, and are server-dependent.

fp default

Restore the default font path.

fp rehash

Reread the font databases in the current font path. This is generally only used when adding new fonts to a font directory (after running *mkfontdir* to recreate the font database).

–fp *path* or fp– *path*

Remove elements from the current font path. *path* must be a directory or comma-separated list of directories.

+fp *path* or fp+ *path*

Prepend and append elements to the current font path, respectively. *path* must be a directory or comma-separated list of directories.

[–] led [*integer*] [on | off]

Turn LEDs on or off. With no *integer* or with the flag on, turn LEDs on. With a preceding dash or flag off, turn LEDs off. With an *integer* between 1 and 32 and with the on/off flag, turn the respective LED on or off.

m [*acceleration* [*threshold*]] [default]

Set mouse parameters. The mouse will go *acceleration* times as fast when it travels more than *threshold* pixels in a short time. The acceleration can be specified as an integer or as a simple fraction. If no parameters or the flag default is used, the system defaults will be set.

p [*colormap_entry color*]

Set pixel color values, using a decimal *colormap_entry* number and a *color*. The root background colors may be changed on some servers by altering the entries for BlackPixel and WhitePixel.

[–]r [on | off]

Control the autorepeat. Disable (off flag or preceding dash); or enable (on flag or no parameters).

s [*time* [*cycle*]] [blank | noblank] [expose | noexpose] [on | off] [default]

Control the screen saver parameters. If no parameters or the default flag is used, the system is set to its default screen saver characteristics. The on/off flags simply turn the screen saver functions on or off. The blank flag sets the preference to blank the video (if the hardware can do so) rather than display a background pattern, while noblank sets the preference to display a pattern rather than blank the video. The expose flag sets the preference to allow window exposures (the server can freely discard window contents), while noexpose sets the preference to disable screen saver unless the server can regenerate the screens without causing exposure events. *time* and *cycle* (in seconds) determine how long the server must be inactive for screen saving to activate, and the period to change the background pattern to avoid burn in, respectively.

q

Gives you information on the current settings.

xsetroot

xsetroot [*options*]

Set the appearance of the root (background) window on a display. If you specify no options or the option –def, the window resets to its defaults. If you specify def and other options, only the non-specified options are reset to their defaults. *xsetroot* takes the following non-standard options:

-help

Display a usage summary of command-line options.

-def

Reset unspecified attributes to default values: the background to gray mesh, and the pointer to the hollow X pointer.

-cursor *cursorfile maskfile*

Set cursor shape for the root window pointer. The *cursorfile* and *maskfile* are bitmaps made with the *bitmap* client. The default root window pointer is an X cursor.

-cursor_name *standard_cursor_name*

Change the root window cursor to one of the standard cursors. Specify *standard_cursor_name* by stripping the XC_ prefix from the name.

-bitmap *filename*

Use the bitmap specified in *filename* to set the window pattern. Default is gray mesh.

-mod *x y*

Make a plaid-like grid pattern on the screen. *x* and *y* are integers ranging from 1 to 16. Zero and negative numbers are taken as 1.

-gray or **-grey**

Create a grey background.

-solid *color*

Set root window color. Default is gray mesh.

xstdcmap

xstdcmap [*options*]

Selectively define standard colormap properties. It should be run from a user's X startup script. Where at all possible, colormaps are created with read-only allocations. *xstdcmap* takes the following non-standard options:

-all

Define all six standard colormap properties on each screen of the display.

-best

Define the RGB_BEST_MAP.

-blue

Define the RGB_BLUE_MAP.

-default

Define the RGB_DEFAULT_MAP.

–delete *map*

Remove a standard colormap property. *map* may be one of: *default, best, red, green, blue,* or *gray.*

–gray

Define the RGB_GRAY_MAP.

–green

Define the RGB_GREEN_MAP.

–help

Display a usage summary of command-line options. This help message also prints whenever an undefined option is given.

–red

Define the RGB_RED_MAP.

–verbose

Print logging information as *xstdcmap* parses its input and defines the standard colormap properties.

xterm

xterm [*options*]

Window terminal emulator. Many features of *xterm* can be enabled with Boolean resources that (when true) correspond to an option that has a leading minus sign (–). To override a resource setting, use the corresponding option with the appropriate sign. This client creates its own window. *xterm* takes the following non-standard resources and options.

–help

Display a verbose message describing *xterm* options.

*vt100.c132 (class C132, option –132)

Use the VT102 DECCOLM escape sequence that switches between 80- and 132-column mode. Enables the *xterm* window to resize properly. Default is to ignore the DECCOLM escape sequence.

*vt100.alwaysHighlight (class AlwaysHighlight, option –ah/+ah)

Whether to always highlight the text cursor and window borders. By default, *xterm* displays a hollow text cursor whenever the focus is lost or the pointer leaves the window. (+ah resets the default.)

*appcursorDefault (class AppcursorDefault)

If 'true," the cursor keys are initially in application mode. Default is 'false."

*appkeypadDefault (class **AppkeypadDefault**)

If 'true," the keypad keys are initially in application mode. Default is 'false."

*bellSuppressTime (class **BellSuppressTime**)

Number of milliseconds after a bell command is sent during which additional bells will be suppressed. Default is 200.

*autoWrap (class **AutoWrap**, option −aw/+aw)

Whether or not auto-wraparound should be enabled. The default is true.

*vt100.internalBorder (class **BorderWidth**, option −b *innerborder*)

Set the inner border width (distance between the outer edge of the characters and the window border) in pixels. Default is 2 pixels.

−C Direct the *xterm* window to receive console output. Not supported on all systems.

*vt100.charClass (class **CharClass**, option −cc *range*:*value*[,...])

Specify comma-separated lists of character class bindings of the form [*low−*]*high*:*value* for use in selecting by words.

*vt100.cutNewline (class **CutNewline**, option -cn/+cn)

If resource is false or -cn is given, does not cut newlines in line mode selections.

*vt100.cursorColor (class **Foreground**, option −cr *color*)

Set text cursor to *color*. Default is to use the text foreground color.

*vt100.curses (class **Curses**, option −cu/+cu)

Whether to enable the *curses* fix. Several programs that use the *curses*(3x) cursor motion package have some difficulties with VT102-compatible terminals. The bug occurs when you run the *more* program on a file containing a line that is exactly the width of the window and which is followed by a line beginning with a tab. The leading tabs are not displayed. −cu causes the tabs to be displayed correctly. (+cu disables the fix.)

−e *command* [*arguments*]

Run *command* (and its *arguments*) in the *xterm* window. It also sets the window title and icon name to be the name of the program being executed if neither −T nor −n are given on the command line. The −e option must appear last on the *xterm* command line; e.g., xterm −rv −e more bigfile &.

*vt100.boldFont (class **Font**, option −fb *font*)

Use *font* as the bold font. This font must be the same height and width as the normal font. If only one font (normal or bold) is specified, it is used as the normal font and the bold font is produced by overstriking this font. Default is to overstrike the normal font.

*vt100.jumpScroll (class **JumpScroll**, option **−j/+j**)

Whether to perform jump scrolling. When *xterm* falls behind scrolling the screen, it moves lines up several at a time. The VT100 escape sequences for smooth scroll can be used to enable/disable this feature from a program. (+j disables jump scrolling.)

*vt100.logging (class **Logging**, option **−l/+l**)

Whether to log *xterm* input/output into a file called *XtermLog.xxxx*, where *xxxx* represents the process ID number. (+l disables logging.)

*vt100.logFile (class **LogFile**, option **−lf** *file*)

Write data to *file* rather than to the default *XtermLog.xxxx*, where *xxxx* is the process ID of *xterm*. (The file is created in the directory in which *xterm* is started or in the home directory for a login *xterm*). If *file* begins with a " | ", the rest of the string is assumed to be a command to be executed by the shell and a pipe is opened to the process.

*vt100.logInhibit (class **LogInhibit**)

Whether or not terminal session logging should be inhibited. Default is false.

*vt100.cutToBeggingOfLine (class **CutToBeginningOfLine**, option **-cb/+cb**)

If resource is false, or -cb is given, triple checking to select a line does not include the newline at the end of the line. Default is true.

*useInsertMode (class **UseInsertMode**, option **-im/+im**)

Force use of insert mode by adding appropriate entries to the Termcap environment variable. Default is false.

*vt100.loginShell (class **LoginShell**, option **−ls/+ls**)

Whether to use the shell started in the *xterm* window as the login shell; that is, the first character of argv[0] will be a dash, indicating to the shell that it should read the user's *.login* or *.profile*. (+ls does not start a login shell; that is, the shell will be a normal "subshell.")

*vt100.marginBell (class **MarginBell**, option **−mb/+mb**)

Whether to turn the margin bell on. (+mb turns it off, which is the default.)

*vt100.multiClickTime (class **MultiClickTime**, option **−mc** *milliseconds*)

Set the maximum time between multi-click selections. (New in R4.)

*vt100.pointerColor (class **Foreground**, option **−ms** *color*)

Set pointer to *color*. Default is to use foreground color.

*vt100.nMarginBell (class **Column**, option **−nb** *number*)

Set the distance at which the margin bell rings for the right margin. Default is 10 characters.

Clients

Clients

*resizeGravity (class ResizeGravity)

Affects the behavior when the window is resized to be taller or shorter. NorthWest specifies that the top line of text on the screen stay fixed. South-West (default) specifies that the bottom line of text on the screen stay fixed.

*vt100.reverseWrap (class ReverseWrap, option –rw/+rw)

Whether to turn on reverse-wraparound mode, allowing the cursor to wrap around from the leftmost column to the rightmost column of the previous line. When set, this allows you to backspace to the previous line and over-strike data or erase data with the spacebar. (+rw turns off this mode.)

–Sccn

Set the last two letters of the name of a pseudo-terminal to use in slave mode, plus the number of the inherited file descriptor. The option is parsed "%c%c%d". This allows *xterm* to be used as an input and output channel for an existing program and is sometimes used in specialized applications.

*vt100.multiScroll (class MultiScroll, option –s/+s)

Whether to scroll asynchronously with the display. This means that the screen does not have to be kept completely up to date while *xterm* saves data in memory that is displayed later. This allows *xterm* to run faster when network latencies are high and is useful when running *xterm* across a large internet or many gateways. (+s produces synchronous scrolling.)

*vt100.scrollBar (class ScrollBar, option –sb/+sb)

Whether to save some number of lines scrolled off the top of the window and display a scrollbar at startup to view those lines. (+sb does *not* display a scrollbar.)

*sunFunctionKeys (class SunFunctionKeys, option –sf/+sf)

For function keys, specify whether to generate Sun function key escape codes. (+sf generates standard escape codes.)

*vt100.scrollTtyOutput (class ScrollCond, option –si/+si)

Whether to disable repositioning of the cursor at the bottom of the scroll region when the process sends output. (+si enables repositioning.)

*vt100.scrollKey (class ScrollCond, option –sk/+sk)

Whether to reposition the cursor at the bottom of the scroll region when a key is pressed. (+sk means don't reposition.)

*vt100.saveLines (class SaveLines, option –sl *number*)

Set the maximum number of lines to be saved that are scrolled off the top of the window. Default is 64 lines.

*vt100.tekStartup (class TekStartup, option –t/+t)

Whether to use the Tektronix window as the startup *xterm* window. (+t resets the startup window to the default—a VT102 window.)

*ttyModes (class **TtyModes**, option **−tm** *string*)

Set a series of terminal-setting keywords followed by the characters that should be bound to those functions, similar to the *stty* program. (In R3, this is ignored when −L is given since *getty* resets the terminal. The −L option is not supported in R4.) Allowable keywords include: intr, quit, erase, kill, eof, eol, swtch, start, stop, brk, susp, dsusp, rprnt, flush, weras, and lnext. Control characters may be specified as ˆ*char* (e.g., ˆc or ˆu), and ˆ? may be used to indicate delete.

*termName (class **TermName**, option **−tn** *type*)

Set the terminal *type* to be set in the TERM environment variable. This terminal type must exist in the *termcap*(5) database and should have li# and co# entries.

*utmpInhibit (class **UtmpInhibit**, option **−ut/+ut**)

Whether *xterm* should not write a record into the the system log file */etc/utmp*. (+ut means to write the record.)

*vt100.visualBell (class **VisualBell**, option **−vb/+vb**)

Whether to flash terminal window (rather than ringing terminal bell) whenever an event occurs. (+vb means not to use "visual" bell.)

*vt100.waitForMap (class **WaitForMap**, option **−wf/+wf**)

Whether *xterm* should wait for the window to be mapped the first time before starting the subprocess. This is so that initial terminal size settings and environment variables are correct. It is the application's responsibility to catch subsequent terminal size changes. (+wf means not to wait.)

−L Start *xterm* by *init*. In this mode, *xterm* does not try to allocate a new pseudo-terminal as *init* has already done so. (*xterm* presumes that its file descriptors are already open on a slave pseudo-terminal.) In addition, the system program *getty* is run rather than the user's shell. This option is only used by *init*.

This option has been superseded by the *xdm* program. Furthermore, −L should never be specified by users when starting terminal windows. This option has been eliminated in R4.

*vt100.tekGeometry (class **Geometry**, option **%geometry**)

Set the preferred size and location of the Tektronix window. Shorthand for specifying the tekGeometry resource.

*iconGeometry (class **IconGeometry**, option **#geometry**)

Set the preferred icon position.

*iconName (class **IconName**, option **−n** *string*)

Set the *xterm* window icon name. This is *not equivalent* to the Toolkit option −name. Default icon name is the name of a program run with the −e option, if any. Otherwise it is the application name.

*vt100.reverseVideo (class **ReverseVideo**, option **−r**)

Simulate reverse video by swapping foreground and background colors. Equivalent to −rv.

*vt100.allowSendEvents (class **AllowSendEvents**)

Whether synthetic key and button events (generated using the X protocol SendEvent request) should be interpreted or discarded. The default is false meaning they are discarded. Note that allowing such events creates a very large security hole.

*vt100.eightBitInput (class **EightBitInput**)

Whether eight-bit characters should be accepted. The default is true.

*vt100.eightBitOutput (class **EightBitOutput**)

Whether eight-bit characters sent from the host should be accepted as is or stripped when printed. The default is true.

*vt100.font1 (class **Font1**)

Specify the name of the first alternative font. This font is toggled using the Unreadable menu item on the VT Fonts menu.

*vt100.font2 (class **Font2**)

Specify the name of the second alternative font. This font is toggled using the Tiny menu item on the VT Fonts menu.

*vt100.font3 (class **Font3**)

Specify the name of the third alternative font. This font is toggled using the Small menu item on the VT Fonts menu.

*vt100.font4 (class **Font4**)

Specify the name of the fourth alternative font. This font is toggled using the Medium menu item on the VT Fonts menu.

*vt100.font5 (class **Font5**)

Specify the name of the fifth alternative font. This font is toggled using the Large menu item on the VT Fonts menu.

*vt100.font6 (class **Font6**)

Specify the name of the sixth alternative font. This font is toggled using the Huge menu item on the VT Fonts menu.

*vt100.pointerColorBackground (class **Background**)

Specify the background color of the pointer. The default is XtDefaultBackground color.

*vt100.pointerShape (class **Cursor**)

Specify the name of the shape of the pointer. The default is "xterm."

*vt100.scrollLines (class **ScrollLines**)

Specify the number of lines that the scroll-back and scroll-forw actions should use as a default. The default value is 1.

*vt100.signalInhibit (class **SignalInhibit**)

Whether the entries in the Main Options menu for sending signals to *xterm* should be disallowed. The default is false.

*vt100.tekInhibit (class **TekInhibit**)

Whether Tektronix mode should be disallowed. The default is false.

*vt100.tekSmall (class **TekSmall**)

Whether the Tektronix mode window should start in its smallest size if no explicit geometry is given. This is useful when running *xterm* on displays with small screens. The default is false. (Available as of R4.)

*vt100.titleInhibit (class **TitleInhibit**)

Whether *xterm* should remove ti or te termcap entries (used to switch between alternate screens on startup of many screen-oriented programs) from the TERMCAP string.

*vt100.translations (class **Translations**)

Specify the key and button bindings for menus, selections, "programmed strings," etc.

*tek4014.width (class **Width**)

Specify the width of the Tektronix window in pixels.

*tek4014.height (class **Height**)

Specify the height of the Tektronix window in pixels.

*tek4014.fontLarge (class **Font**)

Specify the large font to use in the Tektronix window. This font is toggled using the Large Characters item on the Tek Options menu.

*tek4014.font2 (class **Font**)

Specify font number 2 to use in the Tektronix window. This font is toggled using the #2 Size Characters item on the Tek Options menu.

*tek4014.font3 (class **Font**)

Specify font number 3 font to use in the Tektronix window. This font is toggled using the #3 Size Characters item on the Tek Options menu.

*tek4014.fontSmall (class **Font**)

Specify the small font to use in the Tektronix window. This font is toggled using the Small Characters item on the Tek Options menu.

*tek4014.ginTerminator (class **GinTerminator**)

Specifies what character(s) should follow a GIN report or status report. The possibilities are 'none," which sends no terminating characters, 'CRonly," which sends CR, and 'CR&EOT," which sends both CR and EOT. The default is 'none."

*tek4014.initialFont (class **InitialFont**)

Specifies which of the four Tektronix fonts to use initially. Default is 'large."

*mainMenu.securekbd (class **SmeBSB**)

Invoke the secure() action.

*mainMenu.allowsends (class **SmeBSB**)

Invoke the allow-send-events(toggle) action.

*mainMenu.logging (class **SmeBSB**)

Invoke the set-logging(toggle) action.

*mainMenu.redraw (class **SmeBSB**)

Invoke the redraw() action.

*mainMenu.line1 (class **SmeLine**)

A separator.

*mainMenu.suspend (class **SmeBSB**)

Invoke the send-signal(suspend) action on systems that support job control.

*mainMenu.continue (class **SmeBSB**)

Invoke the send-signal(cont) action on systems that support job control.

*mainMenu.interrupt (class **SmeBSB**)

Invoke the send-signal(int) action.

*mainMenu.hangup (class **SmeBSB**)

Invoke the send-signal(hup) action.

*mainMenu.terminate (class **SmeBSB**)

Invoke the send-signal(term) action.

*mainMenu.kill (class **SmeBSB**)

Invoke the send-signal(kill) action.

*vtMenu.clearsavedlines (class **SmeBSB**)

Invoke the clear-saved-lines() action.

*mainMenu.line2 (class **SmeLine**)

A separator.

*mainMenu.quit (class **SmeBSB**)

Invoke the quit() action.

*vtMenu.scrollbar (class **SmeBSB**)

Invoke the set-scrollbar(toggle) action.

*vtMenu.jumpscroll (class **SmeBSB**)

Invoke the set-jumpscroll(toggle) action.

*vtMenu.reversevideo (class **SmeBSB**)

Invoke the set-reverse-video(toggle) action.

*vtMenu.autowrap (class **SmeBSB**)

Invoke the set-autowrap(toggle) action.

*vtMenu.reversewrap (class **SmeBSB**)

Invoke the set-reversewrap(toggle) action.

*vtMenu.autolinefeed (class **SmeBSB**)

Invoke the set-autolinefeed(toggle) action.

*vtMenu.appcursor (class **SmeBSB**)

Invoke the set-appcursor(toggle) action.

*vtMenu.appkeypad (class **SmeBSB**)

Invoke the set-appkeypad(toggle) action.

*vtMenu.scrollkey (class **SmeBSB**)

Invoke the set-scroll-on-key(toggle) action.

*vtMenu.scrollttyoutput (class **SmeBSB**)

Invoke the set-scroll-on-tty-output(toggle) action.

*vtMenu.allow132 (class **SmeBSB**)

Invoke the set-allow132(toggle) action.

*vtMenu.cursesemul (class **SmeBSB**)

Invoke the set-cursesemul(toggle) action.

*vtMenu.visualbell (class **SmeBSB**)

Invoke the set-visualbell(toggle) action.

*vtMenu.marginbell (class **SmeBSB**)

Invoke the set-marginbell(toggle) action.

*vtMenu.altscreen (class **SmeBSB**)

This entry is currently disabled.

*vtMenu.line1 (class **SmeLine**)

A separator.

*vtMenu.softreset (class **SmeBSB**)
Invoke the soft-reset() action.

*vtMenu.hardreset (class **SmeBSB**)
Invoke the hard-reset() action.

*vtMenu.line2 (class **SmeLine**)
A separator.

*vtMenu.tekshow (class **SmeBSB**)
Invoke the set-visibility(tek,toggle) action.

*vtMenu.tekmode (class **SmeBSB**)
Invoke the set-terminal-type(tek) action.

*vtMenu.vthide (class **SmeBSB**)
Invoke the set-visibility(vt,off) action.

*fontMenu.fontdefault (class **SmeBSB**)
Invoke the set-vt-font(d) action.

*fontMenu.font1 (class **SmeBSB**)
Invoke the set-vt-font(1) action.

*fontMenu.font2 (class **SmeBSB**)
Invoke the set-vt-font(2) action.

*fontMenu.font3 (class **SmeBSB**)
Invoke the set-vt-font(3) action.

*fontMenu.font4 (class **SmeBSB**)
Invoke the set-vt-font(4) action.

*fontMenu.font5 (class **SmeBSB**)
Invoke the set-vt-font(5) action.

*fontMenu.font(6) (class **SmeBSB**)
Invoke the set-vt-font(6) action.

*fontMenu.fontescape (class **SmeBSB**)
Invoke the set-vt-font(e) action.

*fontMenu.fontsel (class **SmeBSB**)
Invoke the set-vt-font(s) action.

*tekMenu.tektextlarge (class **SmeBSB**)
Invoke the set-tek-text(l) action.

*tekMenu.tektext2 (class **SmeBSB**)
Invoke the set-tek-text(2) action.

*tekMenu.tektext3 (class **SmeBSB**)

Invoke the set-tek-text(3) action.

*tekMenu.tektextsmall (class **SmeBSB**)

Invoke the set-tek-text(s) action.

*tekMenu.line1 (class **SmeLine**)

A separator.

*tekMenu.tekpage (class **SmeBSB**)

Invoke the tek-page() action.

*tekMenu.tekreset (class **SmeBSB**)

Invoke the tek-reset() action.

*tekMenu.tekcopy (class **SmeBSB**)

Invoke the tek-copy() action.

*tekMenu.line2 (class **SmeLine**)

A separator.

*tekMenu.vtshow (class **SmeBSB**)

Invoke the set-visibility(vt,toggle) action.

*tekMenu.vtmode (class **SmeBSB**)

Invoke the set-terminal-type(vt) action.

*tekMenu.tekhide (class **SmeBSB**)

Invoke the set-visibility(tek,toggle) action.

*scrollBar.thickness (class Thickness)

Specify the width in pixels of the scrollbar.

*scrollBar.background (class Background)

Specify the color to use for the background of the scrollbar.

*scrollBar.foreground (class Foreground)

Specify the color to use for the foreground of the scrollbar. The "thumb" of the scrollbar is a simple checkerboard pattern alternating pixels for foreground and background color.

xwd

xwd [*options*]

Store window images in a specially formatted window dump file. This file can then be read by various other X utilities for redisplay, printing, editing, formatting, archiving, image processing, etc. The target window is selected by clicking the mouse in the desired window. The keyboard bell is rung once at the beginning of the dump and twice when the dump is completed. *xwd* takes the following non-standard options:

−icmap

Normally the colormap of the chosen window is used to obtain RGB values. This option forces the first installed colormap of the screen to be used instead.

−screen

The GetImage request used to obtain the image should be done on the root window rather than directly on the specified window.

−id *window*

Specify a target window id on the command line rather than using the mouse.

−help

Display a usage summary of command-line options.

−name *name*

Specify a target window name rather than using the mouse to select the target window.

−nobdrs

Exclude window border from the dumped window; useful when the window contents are included in a document as an illustration.

−out *file*

Specify *file* as the output. Default output is *stdout*.

−xy

For color displays only, select "XY" pixmap format dumping instead of the default 'Z' pixmap format.

−root

Dump the entire root window.

−add *value*

Add a signed *value* to every pixel.

−frame

Include the window manager frame when manually selecting a window.

xwininfo

xwininfo [*options*]

Window information utility for X. You may select the target window with the mouse, or by specifying its window ID or name on the command line. There is also a special –root option to quickly obtain information on the root window. *xwininfo* takes the following non-standard options:

–help
> Display a usage summary of command-line options.

–id *id*
> Specify a target window *id* on the command line rather than using the mouse to select the target window. This is useful in debugging X applications where the target window is not mapped to the screen or where the use of the mouse might be impossible or interfere with the application.

–name *name*
> Specify a target window *name* rather than using the mouse to select the target window.

–root
> Specify the root window as the target window. This is useful when the root window is completely obscured.

–frame
> Do not ignore window manager frames when manually selecting windows.

–int
> Display all X window IDs as integer values. Default is to display them as hexadecimal values.

–children
> For the selected window, display the root, parent and children windows' IDs and names.

–tree
> Like -children, but displays all children recursively. Replaces *xlswins* client.

–stats
> Display information for the selected window. Information includes the location of the window, its width, height, depth, border width, class, and map state, colormap ID (if any), backing-store hint, and the location of its corners. If *xwininfo* is run with no options, –stats is assumed.

–bits
> Display information pertaining to the selected window's raw bits. Information includes the selected window's bit gravity, window gravity, backing

store hint, backing_planes value, backing pixel, and whether or not the window has save-under set.

–events

Display the selected window's event masks, including the mask of events a client wants and of events that do not propagate.

–size

Display the selected window's sizing hints, if they exist. Information includes: for normal size hints and zoom size hints, the user-supplied location; the program-supplied location; the user-supplied size; the program-supplied size; the minimum size; the maximum size; the resize increments; and the minimum and maximum aspect ratios.

–wm

Display the window manager hints for the selected window. Information may include whether or not the application accepts input, what the window's icon window # and name is, where the window's icon should go, and what the window's initial state should be.

–shape

For the selected window, display the window and border shape extents.

–metric

Display all individual height, width, and x and y positions in millimeters, as well as number of pixels, based on what the server thinks the resolution is. Geometry specifications that are in +x+y form are not changed.

–english

Display all individual height, width, and x and y positions to be displayed in inches (and feet, yards, and miles if necessary), as well as number of pixels. –metric and–english may be used at the same time.

–all Ask for all information possible.

xwud

xwud [*options*]

Display a window image saved in a specially formatted dump file, such as one produced by *xwd*. *xwud* takes the following non-standard options:

–help

Display a usage summary of command-line options.

–in *file*

Specify the input *file* on the command line. Default is to take input from standard input.

–new

    Force creation of a new colormap for displaying the image. If the image characteristics happen to match those of the display, this can get the image on the screen faster, but at the cost of using a new colormap (which on most displays will cause other windows to go technicolor).

–noclick

    Unless this option is specified, clicking any button in the window will terminate the application. Termination can always be achieved by typing q, Q, or Ctrl-C.

–plane *number*

    Select a single bit plane of the image to display. Planes are numbered with zero being the least significant bit. This option can be used to figure out which plane to pass to *xpr* for printing.

–raw

    Force the image to be displayed with whatever color values happen to currently exist on the screen. This option is mostly useful when undumping an image back onto the same screen that the image originally came from, while the original windows are still on the screen, and results in getting the image on the screen faster.

–std *type*

    Display the image using the specified standard colormap. The property name is obtained by converting *type* to uppercase, prepending "RGB_", and appending "_MAP". Typical types are best, default, and gray. See *xstdcmap* for one way of creating standard colormaps.

–vis [*class* | *ID*]

    Specify a particular visual *class* or visual *ID*. Default is to pick the "best" one. *class* can be one of the classes: StaticGray, GrayScale, StaticColor, PseudoColor, DirectColor, or TrueColor. *class* can also be specified as Match (use the same class as the source image) or Default (use the same class as the colormap of the root window). Case is not significant in any of these strings. Alternatively, an exact visual ID (specific to the server) can be specified, either as a hexadecimal number (prefixed with "0x") or as a decimal number.

8

Fonts, Colors, Cursors, and Bitmaps

The X Window System provides several features that allow you to customize your X environment. Six of these features are presented here. Section 8 consists of the following parts:

Fonts   Describes the directories, utilities, and naming conventions for fonts.

Font Service and   Describes networked font service and font scaling.
Scalable Fonts

Color   Describes how to specify colors on the command line, lists available color names, and describes device-independent and hexadecimal color specifications.

Cursors   Lists the cursor symbols and displays the cursor font.

Bitmaps   Shows the standard bitmaps available in R5.

Customizing X

Fonts

Standard fonts are stored in three directories:

Directory	Contents
/usr/lib/X11/fonts/misc	Six fixed-width fonts, the cursor font, other miscellaneous fonts.
/usr/lib/X11/fonts/75dpi	Fixed- and variable-width fonts, 75 dots per inch.
/usr/lib/X11/fonts/100dpi	Fixed- and variable-width fonts, 100 dots per inch.

X provides three utilities that deal with fonts:

xlsfonts   Lists the names of the fonts available on your server, as well as any aliases.

xfd   Displays the character set for any individual font you specify on the command line.

xfontsel   Lets you preview and then select the name of a font.

To display an *xterm* window in (for example) 14-point Courier bold, the font specification on your command line might include:

- Full names
- Wildcards
- Aliases

These are demonstrated, respectively, below:

```
% xterm –fn –adobe–courier–bold–r–normal––14–140–75–75–m–90–iso8859–1
% xterm –fn '*courier–bold–r*140*'
% xterm –fn courierB14
```

A font's full name can be intimidating. The following figure explains the fields in a complete font name.

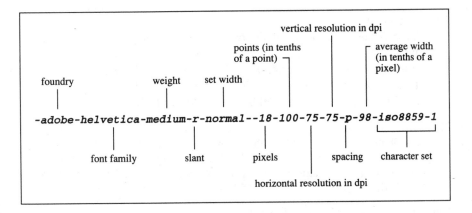

These fields are defined as follows:

Foundry

    The type foundry (in this case, Adobe) that digitized and supplied the font.

Font Family

    A group of related fonts. The major families available are shown below, printed in the font they represent (note the line in Greek).

```
-adobe-courier-medium-r-normal--18-180-75-75-m-110-
-adobe-helvetica-medium-r-normal--18-180-75-75-p-98-iso8859-
-adobe-new century schoolbook-medium-r-normal--18-180-75-
-αδοβε-σψμβολ-μεδιυμ-ρ-νορμαλ--18-180-75-75-π-107-αδοβε-φο\
-adobe-times-medium-r-normal--18-180-75-75-p-94-iso8859-1
-b&h-lucida-medium-r-normal-sans-18-180-75-75-p-1(
-b&h-lucidabright-medium-r-normal--18-180-75-75-p-103
-b&h-lucidatypewriter-medium-r-normal-sans-18-180-7
-bitstream-charter-medium-r-normal--19-180-75-75-p-106-iso8859-1
```

Weight and Slant

    Modify the appearance and orientation within a font family. Stroke weight is usually medium or bold. Slant is usually roman (upright), italic, or oblique.

Set Width

    A value describing a font's proportionate width, according to the foundry. Typical set widths include: normal, condensed, narrow, double width. All of the R3 fonts and most of the R4 fonts have the set width *normal*. A few of the R4 fonts have the set width *semi-condensed*.

Pixels and Points

> Type is normally measured in points, a printer's unit equal to 1/72 of an inch. The size of a font in pixels depends on the resolution of the display font in pixels. For example, if the display font has 100 dots per inch (dpi) resolution, a 12-point font will have a pixel size of 17, while with 75 dpi resolution, a 12-point font will have a pixel size of 12.

Spacing

> All standard R3 fonts are either *m* (monospace, i.e., fixed-width) or *p* (proportional, i.e., variable-width). In R4, fonts may also have the spacing characteristic *c*, (character cell, a fixed-width font based on the traditional typewriter model).

Horizontal and Vertical Resolution

> The resolution in dots per inch that a font is designed for. Horizontal and vertical figures are required because a screen may have different capacities for horizontal and vertical resolution.

Average Width

> Mean width of all font characters, measured in tenths of a pixel.

Character Set

> ISO, the International Standards Organization, has defined character set standards for various languages. iso8859-1 represents the ISO Latin 1 character set, which is used by most fonts in the standard X distribution.

Color

This section describes how to specify colors on the command line. Color names are listed, along with color databases. Lastly, the X Color Management System (Xcms) is introduced.

Color Names

Many X clients use options of the form:

–bg *color*	Set the window's background color.
–fg *color*	Set the window's foreground color.
–bd *color*	Set the window's border color.

For example, you could specify an *xterm* window using either of these command lines:

```
% xterm –bg lightblue –fg darkslategrey –bd plum &
% xterm –bg "light blue" –fg "dark slate grey" –bd plum &
```

Color names are found in the database */usr/lib/X11/rgb.txt*. For convenience, names are grouped by simple color families, and trivial names are omitted. Because of these omissions, note the following:

- Compound names can be specified as lower-case words separated by a space. For example, LightSeaGreen can also be specified as light sea green.

- Colors with varying intensities can be specified. These colors are listed with the suffix n, where n is a value from 1 to 4. For example, blue$n$ indicates that you can specify either blue1 (brightest), blue2, blue3, or blue4 (dimmest). In this case, blue and blue1 are equivalent; however, this isn't true for every color. (Compound names with intensities have no lower-case equivalent.)

- The words *gray* or *Gray* may also be spelled *grey* or *Grey*. In addition, the color gray has special use. You can specify over 100 intensities, known as grayscales.

Unfortunately, the RGB values in the color database provided by MIT are correct for only one type of display. You might find that the color you get is not exactly what you expect, given the name; however, vendors might have corrected the RGB values to produce colors closer to what the name implies.

To see the specific RGB value assigned to any color, type:

```
% showrgb | more
```

showrgb displays the *rgb.txt* file to your screen. Following is a list of color names found in the */usr/lib/X11/rgt.txt* database.

Off-whites
snow
snow$n$
GhostWhite
WhiteSmoke
gainsboro
FloralWhite
OldLace
linen
AntiqueWhite
AntiqueWhite$n$
PapayaWhip
BlanchedAlmond
bisque
bisque$n$
PeachPuff
PeachPuff$n$
NavajoWhite

NavajoWhite$n$
moccasin
cornsilk
cornsilk$n$
ivory
ivory$n$
LemonChiffon
LemonChiffon$n$
seashell
seashell$n$
honeydew
honeydew$n$
MintCream

Shades of Gray
white
black
gray

Customizing X

gray$n$ (n = 0–100)
DarkSlateGray
DarkSlateGray$n$
DimGray
SlateGray
SlateGray$n$
LightSlateGray
LightGray

Blues

azure
azure$n$
AliceBlue
lavender
LavenderBlush
LavenderBlush$n$
MistyRose
MistyRose$n$
MidnightBlue
navy
NavyBlue
CornflowerBlue
DarkSlateBlue
SlateBlue
SlateBlue$n$
MediumSlateBlue
LightSlateBlue
MediumBlue
RoyalBlue
RoyalBlue$n$
blue
blue$n$
DodgerBlue
DodgerBlue$n$
DeepSkyBlue
DeepSkyBlue$n$
SkyBlue
SkyBlue$n$
LightSkyBlue
LightSkyBlue$n$
SteelBlue
SteelBlue$n$
LightSteelBlue
LightSteelBlue$n$

LightBlue
LightBlue$n$
PowderBlue
PaleTurquoise
PaleTurquoise$n$
DarkTurquoise
MediumTurquoise
turquoise
turquoise$n$
cyan
cyan$n$
LightCyan
LightCyan$n$
CadetBlue
CadetBlue$n$
MediumAquamarine
aquamarine
aquamarine$n$

Greens

DarkGreen
DarkOliveGreen
DarkOliveGreen$n$
DarkSeaGreen
DarkSeaGreen$n$
SeaGreen
SeaGreen$n$
MediumSeaGreen
LightSeaGreen
PaleGreen
PaleGreen$n$
SpringGreen
SpringGreen$n$
LawnGreen
green
green$n$
chartreuse
chartreuse$n$
MediumSpringGreen
GreenYellow
LimeGreen
YellowGreen
ForestGreen
OliveDrab

OliveDrab$n$
DarkKhaki
khaki
khaki$n$

Yellows

PaleGoldenrod
LightGoldenrodYellow
LightYellow
LightYellow$n$
yellow
yellow$n$
gold
gold$n$
LightGoldenrod
LightGoldenrod$n$
goldenrod
goldenrod$n$
DarkGoldenrod
DarkGoldenrod$n$

Reds/Browns/Oranges

RosyBrown
RosyBrown$n$
IndianRed
IndianRed$n$
SaddleBrown
sienna
sienna$n$
peru
burlywood
burlywood$n$
beige
wheat
wheat$n$
SandyBrown
tan
tan$n$
chocolate
chocolate$n$
firebrick
firebrick$n$
brown
brown$n$

DarkSalmon
salmon
salmon$n$
LightSalmon
LightSalmon$n$
orange
orange$n$
DarkOrange
DarkOrange$n$
coral
coral$n$
LightCoral
tomato
tomato$n$
OrangeRed
OrangeRed$n$
red
red$n$
HotPink
HotPink$n$
DeepPink
DeepPink$n$
pink
pink$n$
LightPink
LightPink$n$
maroon
maroon$n$

Purples

PaleVioletRed
PaleVioletRed$n$
MediumVioletRed
VioletRed
VioletRed$n$
magenta
magenta$n$
violet
plum
plum$n$
orchid
orchid$n$
MediumOrchid
MediumOrchid$n$

DarkOrchid
DarkOrchid$n$
DarkViolet
BlueViolet
purple
purple$n$
MediumPurple
MediumPurple$n$
thistle
thistle$n$

Alternative R4 Color Databases

In addition to the standard color database *rgb.txt*, R4 includes three other databases that can be compiled by your system administrator. These files can be found in the general release in the directory *./rgb/others*.

raveling.txt   Rivals the default database in size and scope, but has been tuned to display optimally on Hewlett-Packard monitors. Designed by Paul Raveling.

thomas.txt   Based on the R3 database, but approximates the colors in a box of Crayola Crayons. Modified by John Thomas of Tektronix.

old-rgb.txt   Nothing more than the R3 database.

The Client-side Color Name Database

Support for device-independent colors is, by design, kept entirely on the client side. The X protocol and the X server itself still use device-dependent RGB colors exclusively, so it is not possible to use the new device-independent color specifications in the color name database read by the server. Because it is sometimes useful to give symbolic names to device-independent colors, R5 supports a client-side color database that maps names to device-independent or device-dependent color specifications.

X clients (on most UNIX systems) look for the client-side database in the file */usr/lib/X11/Xcms.txt* by default, but the MIT sample implementation allows a different file to be specified with the XCMSDB environment variable. The format of the database is implementation-dependent. Note that R5 is not shipped with a device-independent color database. Some sites (or users) may choose to define their own. Following is an example of entries from a client color database in the format supported by the MIT distribution.

```
XCMS_COLORDB_START 0.1
device red           RGBi:1.0/0/0
device blue          RGB:00/00/ff
navy blue            CIEXYZ:0.0671/0.0337/0.3130
gray0                CIELab:0.0/0.0/0.0
gray50               CIELuv:50.0/0.0/0.0
grey100              TekHVC:0.0/100.0/0.0
rouge                red
roja rouge
XCMS_COLORDB_END
```

Numeric Color Specifications

To address the problem of color databases and displays, R5 has introduced the X Color Management System (Xcms). Xcms supports device-independent color specifications. It defines a new syntax for the color strings used throughout Xlib, and provides a programming interface that allows extremely precise control over the allocation of colors. Device-independent color specification results in identically displayed colors regardless of the device used.

The device-independent color representations supported by R5 are based on an international standard color representation model known as CIEXYZ. In CIEXYZ and related color spaces, a color is described by the value of three coordinates (as is the case with RGB), and the color space itself is commonly referred to by the names of its coordinates. R5 supports the CIEXYZ color space; related spaces known as CIExyY, CIExyY, CIEuvY, CIELuv, and CIELab; and a color space designed by Tektronix known as TekHVC.

R5 supports an additional device-independent color space, called RGBi, in which each red, green, and blue integer value is replaced with a floating-point intensity between 0.0 and 1.0. A color specification for RGBi has the following form:

> RGBi:*<red>*/*<green>*/*<blue>*

where *<red>*, *<green>*, and *<blue>* are floating-point numbers between 0.0 and 1.0, inclusive.

Device-independent color specifications follow the same syntax—a color space name followed by a colon and slash-separated color space values. The following forms are recognized:

> CIEXYZ:*<X>*/*<Y>*/*<Z>*
> CIEuvY:*<u>*/*<v>*/*<Y>*
> CIExyY:*<x>*/*<y>*/*<Y>*
> CIELab:*<L>*/*<a>*/*<b>*
> CIELuv:*<L>*/*<u>*/*<v>*

Color Conversion

In R5, each colormap has a color conversion context (CCC) automatically associated with it. A CCC is an opaque structure of type XcmsCCC. It contains the attributes that control the details of color conversion from one color space to another. These attributes include the procedure that is called to perform gamut compression when a device-independent color specification is outside the range of displayable colors for a particular device.

Hexadecimal Color Specifications

It is also possible to specify colors using a hexadecimal string. The hexadecimal form of color specification is necessary since you may want the user to be able to specify an exact color, not just the rough approximation allowed by an string name. The hexadecimal specification must be in one of the following formats:

#RGB	*(4 bits each of red, green, and blue)*
#RRGGBB	*(8 bits each of red, green, and blue)*
#RRRGGGBBB	*(12 bits each of red, green, and blue)*
#RRRRGGGGBBBB	*(16 bits each of red, green, and blue)*

Each of the letters represents a hexadecimal digit. In the shorter formats, the specified values are interpreted as the most significant bits of a 16-bit value. For example, #3a7 and #3000a0007000 are equivalent. For more detail on device-independent color, see the Xcms manpages in the Xlib routines section, and *xcmsdb* in the client section.

Cursors

A standard font consisting of cursor shapes is available (see figure on page 269).

Cursor Specifications

To specify a cursor as an argument to a command line option, as the value of a resource variable, etc., strip the XC_ prefix from the symbol name. For example, to specify the XC_sailboat cursor as the *xterm* pointer, you could enter the command:

% **xterm –xrm 'xterm*pointerShape: sailboat'**

Calling XCreateFontCursor loads the standard cursor font automatically. To specify a cursor shape from the standard font, use one of the symbols defined in *<X11/cursorfont.h>* by including this file in your source code.

Cursor Symbols

Each cursor symbol has an associated numeric value. Notice that the values skip the odd numbers. Each cursor is really two font characters: one that defines the shape, and a mask character (not shown) that selects which surrounding pixels are disturbed by the cursor. The mask is generally the same shape as the character it underlies, but is one pixel wider in all directions.

To get an idea of what masks look like, display the entire cursor font using the command:

% **xfd –fn cursor**

Symbol definitions from <*X11/cursorfont.h*> are shown below; the actual cursor shapes they represent are pictured afterward.

Symbol	Value	Symbol	Value
XC_X_cursor	0	XC_lr_angle	78
XC_arrow	2	XC_man	80
XC_based_arrow_down	4	XC_middlebutton	82
XC_based_arrow_up	6	XC_mouse	84
XC_boat	8	XC_pencil	86
XC_bogosity	10	XC_pirate	88
XC_bottom_left_corner	12	XC_plus	90
XC_bottom_right_corner	14	XC_question_arrow	92
XC_bottom_side	16	XC_right_ptr	94
XC_bottom_tee	18	XC_right_side	96
XC_box_spiral	20	XC_right_tee	98
XC_center_ptr	22	XC_rightbutton	100
XC_circle	24	XC_rtl_logo	102
XC_clock	26	XC_sailboat	104
XC_coffee_mug	28	XC_sb_down_arrow	106
XC_cross	30	XC_sb_h_double_arrow	108
XC_cross_reverse	32	XC_sb_left_arrow	110
XC_crosshair	34	XC_sb_right_arrow	112
XC_diamond_cross	36	XC_sb_up_arrow	114
XC_dot	38	XC_sb_v_double_arrow	116
XC_dotbox	40	XC_shuttle	118
XC_double_arrow	42	XC_sizing	120
XC_draft_large	44	XC_spider	122
XC_draft_small	46	XC_spraycan	124
XC_draped_box	48	XC_star	126
XC_exchange	50	XC_target	128
XC_fleur	52	XC_tcross	130
XC_gobbler	54	XC_top_left_arrow	132
XC_gumby	56	XC_top_left_corner	134
XC_hand1	58	XC_top_right_corner	136
XC_hand2	60	XC_top_side	138
XC_heart	62	XC_top_tee	140
XC_icon	64	XC_trek	142
XC_iron_cross	66	XC_ul_angle	144
XC_left_ptr	68	XC_umbrella	146
XC_left_side	70	XC_ur_angle	148

The X Window System in a Nutshell

Symbol	Value	Symbol	Value
XC_left_tee	72	XC_watch	150
XC_left_button	74	XC_xterm	152
XC_ll_angle	76	XC_num_glyphs	154

Bitmaps

The standard bitmaps reside in the directory */usr/include/X11/bitmaps*. (See *bitmap* in Section 7.) Bitmaps can be used for setting window background pixmaps and possibly for application icon pixmaps. You can use these bitmaps to set the background pattern of a window in any application that allows it. For example, if you wanted to change the root window background pixmap, you could do so using *xsetroot* as follows:

```
% xsetroot –bitmap /usr/include/X11/bitmaps/wide_weave
```

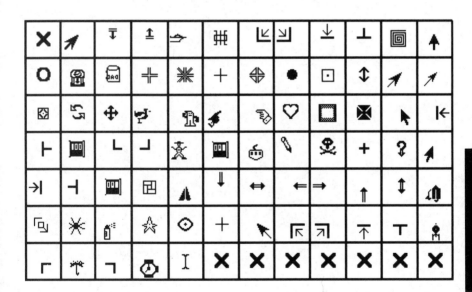

Sixty-three bitmaps are available in the R4 standard distribution, and the following 20 bitmaps have been added in R5:

Down	Right	black6	menu6
Excl	RotateLeft	box6	rdblarrow
FlipHoriz	RotateRight	grid16	
FlipVert	Stipple	grid2	
Fold	Term	grid4	
Left	Up	grid8	

All 83 bitmaps are pictured on the following pages.

1x1	2x2	Dashes	Down	Excl
FlipHoriz	FlipVert	Fold	Left	Right
RotateLeft	RotateRight	Stipple	Term	Up
black	black6	box6	boxes	calculator
cntr_ptr	cntr_ptrmsk	cross_weave	dimple1	dimple3
dot	dropbar7	dropbar8	flagdown	flagup
flipped_gray	gray	gray1	gray3	grid16
grid2	grid4	grid8	hlines2	hlines3
icon	keyboard16	ldblarrow	left_ptr	left_ptrmsk
letters	light_gray	mailempty	mailemptymsk	mailfull

mailfullmsk	menu10	menu12	menu16	menu6
menu8	noletters	opendot	opendotMask	plaid
rdblarrow	right_ptr	right_ptrmsk	root_weave	scales
sipb	star	starMask	stipple	target
terminal	tie_fighter	vlines2	vlines3	weird_size
wide_weave	wingdogs	xfd_icon	xlogo11	xlogo16
xlogo32	xlogo64			

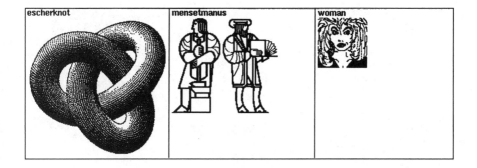

9
Translations

A translation table consists of an optional directive, which specifies how the table should be merged with any other existing translation tables, followed by a series of production rules, of the form:

[*modifier_list*]*<event>*[,*<event>*...][(*count*)][*detail*]: *action*([*args*])[*action*...]

where brackets ([ ]) indicate optional elements, an ellipsis (...) indicates repetition, and italics indicate substitution of an actual modifier, event, detail, or action name.

At a minimum, a translation must specify at least one event, specified by a predefined event name or abbreviation enclosed in angle brackets; a colon separator; and at least one action. However, a sequence of events can be specified; likewise, more than one action can be invoked as a result. The scope of event matching can be limited by one or more optional modifiers, and in the case of some events, by a "detail" field that specifies additional information about the event. (For example, for key events, the detail field specifies which key has been pressed.) Repeated occurrences of the same event (e.g., a double-click) can be specified by a count value in parentheses. A colon and optional white space separates the translation and the action.

The examples below are all valid translations:

<Enter>: doit()	*invoke doit() on an EnterWindow event*
<Btn1Down>,<Btn1Up>: doit()	*invoke doit() on a click of Button 1*
<Btn1Up>(2): doit()	*invoke doit() on a double-click of Button 1*
Button1<Btn2Down>,<Btn2Up>: doit()	*invoke doit() on a click of Button 2 while Button 1 is held down*
Shift<BtnDown>: doit()	*invoke doit() on a click of any button while the shift key is held down*
<Key>y: doit()	*invoke doit() when the y key is pressed*

A translation table is a single string, even when composed of multiple translations. If a translation table consists of more than one translation, the actual newlines are escaped with a backslash (except for the last one), and character newlines are inserted with the \n escape sequence.

The following sections provide additional detail:

- Notation
- Translation Table Syntax
- Modifier Names
- Event Types
- Examples

Notation

Syntax is specified in EBNF notation with the following conventions:

[a]   Means either nothing or "a"
{ a }   Means zero or more occurrences of "a"

All terminals are enclosed in double quotation masks (""). Informal descriptions are enclosed in angle brackets (< >).

Translation Table Syntax

The translation table file has the following syntax:

```
translationTable = [ directive ] { production }
directive        = { "#replace" | "#override" | "#augment"} "\n"
production       = lhs":"rhs" "\n"
lhs              = ( event | keyseq ) {"","(event | keyseq) }
keyseq           =""""keychar {keychar}""""
keychar          = ["^"| "$"| "\"] <ISO Latin 1 character>
event            = [modifier_list]"<"event_type">"["("count["+"]")"] {detail}
modifier_list    = ( ["!"| ":"] {modifier} ) |"None"
modifier         = ["~"] modifier_name
count            = ("1"| "2"| "3"| "4"| ...)
modifier_name    ="@ "<keysym> | <see Modifier Names table below>
event_type       = <see Event Types table below>
detail           = <event specific details>
rhs              = { name"("[params ]")"}
name             = namechar { namechar }
namechar         = {"a"-"z"| "A"-"Z"| "0"-"9"| "$"| "_"}
params           = string {","string}.
string           = quoted_string | unquoted_string
```

```
quoted_string   ="""{<Latin 1 character>}"""
unquoted_string = {<Latin 1 character except space, tab,",", newline,")">}
```

It is often convenient to include newlines in a translation table to make it more readable. In C, indicate a newline with a "\n":

```
"<Btn1Down>:     DoSomething()\n\
<Btn2Down>:      DoSomethingElse()"
```

Because a translation table is a multi-line resource, it is useful to be able to override or add individual lines to the table rather than always replace the table. XtNbaseTranslations can be used to specify a base set of translations that will be correctly overridden, augmented, or replaced by the value of the XtNtranslations resource. For maximum flexibility to the user, all X11R5 applications should specify translations in a resource file using the XtNbaseTranslations resource rather than with XtNtranslations.

Modifier Names

The modifier field is used to specify normal X keyboard and button modifier mask bits. Modifiers are legal on event types KeyPress, KeyRelease, ButtonPress, Button-Release, MotionNotify, EnterNotify, LeaveNotify, and their abbreviations; however, parsing a translation table that contains modifiers for any other events generates an error.

- If the modifier_list has no entries and is not None, it means "don't care" on all modifiers.

- If an exclamation point (!) is specified at the beginning of the modifier list, it means that the listed modifiers must be in the correct state and no other modifiers can be asserted.

- If any modifiers are specified and an exclamation point (!) is not specified, it means that the listed modifiers must be in the correct state and "don't care" about any other modifiers.

- If a modifier is preceded by a tilde (˜), it means that that modifier must not be asserted.

- If None is specified, it means no modifiers can be asserted.

- If a colon (:) is specified at the beginning of the modifier list, it directs the Intrinsics to apply any standard modifiers in the event to map the event keycode into a keysym. The default standard modifiers are Shift and Lock. The resulting keysym must exactly match the specified keysym, and the nonstandard modifiers in the event must match the modifier_list. For example, :<Key>a is distinct from :<Key>A, and :Shift<Key>A is distinct from :<Key>A.

- If a colon (:) is not specified, no standard modifiers are applied. Then, for example, "<Key>A" and "<Key>a" are equivalent.

In key sequences, a circumflex (^) is an abbreviation for the Control modifier, a dollar sign ($) is an abbreviation for Meta, and a backslash (\) can be used to quote any character, in particular a double quote ("), a circumflex (^), a dollar sign ($), and another backslash (\). Briefly:

No modifiers:	None <event> detail
Any modifiers:	<event> detail
Only these modifiers:	! mod1 mod2 <event> detail
These modifiers and any others:	mod1 mod2 <event> detail

The use of None for a modifier_list is identical to the use of an exclamation point with no modifiers.

Modifier	Abbreviation	Meaning
Ctrl	c	Control modifier bit.
Shift	s	Shift modifier bit.
Lock	l	Lock modifier bit..
Meta	m	Meta key modifier
Hyper	h	Hyper key modifier
Super	su	Super key modifier
Alt	a	Alt key modifier
Mod1		Mod1 modifier bit.
Mod2		Mod2 modifier bit.
Mod3		Mod3 modifier bit.
Mod4		Mod4 modifier bit.
Mod5		Mod5 modifier bit.
Button1		Button1 modifier bit.
Button2		Button2 modifier bit.
Button3		Button3 modifier bit.
Button4		Button4 modifier bit.
Button5		Button5 modifier bit.
ANY		Any combination.

Event Types

In translations, events can be specified either by their actual names or by their abbreviations:

Event Type	Abbrev.	Description
ButtonPress	BtnDown	Any pointer button pressed.
	Btn1Down	Pointer button 1 pressed.
	Btn2Down	Pointer button 2 pressed.
	Btn3Down	Pointer button 3 pressed.
	Btn4Down	Pointer button 4 pressed.
	Btn5Down	Pointer button 5 pressed.
ButtonRelease	BtnUp	Any pointer button released.
	Btn1Up	Pointer button 1 released.
	Btn2Up	Pointer button 2 released.
	Btn3Up	Pointer button 3 released.
	Btn4Up	Pointer button 4 released.
	Btn5Up	Pointer button 5 released.
KeyPress	Key	Key pressed.
	KeyDown	Key pressed.
	Ctrl	KeyPress with Ctrl modifier.
	Meta	KeyPress with Meta modifier.
	Shift	KeyPress with Shift modifier.
KeyRelease	KeyUp	Key released.
MotionNotify	Motion	Pointer moved.
	PtrMoved	Pointer moved.
	MouseMoved	Pointer moved.
	BtnMotion	Pointer moved with any button held down.
	Btn1Motion	Pointer moved with button 1 held down.
	Btn2Motion	Pointer moved with button 2 held down.
	Btn3Motion	Pointer moved with button 3 held down.
	Btn4Motion	Pointer moved with button 4 held down.
	Btn5Motion	Pointer moved with button 5 held down.
EnterNotify	Enter	Pointer entered window.
	EnterWindow	Pointer entered window.
LeaveNotify	Leave	Pointer left window.
	LeaveWindow	Pointer left window.
FocusIn	FocusIn	This window is now keyboard focus.
FocusOut	FocusOut	This window lost keyboard focus.
KeymapNotify	Keymap	Keyboard mappings changed.
Expose	Expose	Part of window needs redrawing.
GraphicsExpose	GrExp	Source of copy unavailable.
NoExpose	NoExp	Source of copy available.

Event Type	Abbrev.	Description
ColormapNotify	Clrmap	Window's colormap changed.
PropertyNotify	Prop	Property value changed.
VisibilityNotify	Visible	Window has been obscured.
ResizeRequest	ResReq	Redirect resize request to window manager.
CirculateNotify	Circ	Stacking order modified.
ConfigureNotify	Configure	Window resized or moved.
DestroyNotify	Destroy	Window destroyed.
GravityNotify	Grav	Window moved due to win gravity attribute.
MapNotify	Map	Window mapped.
CreateNotify	Create	Window created.
ReparentNotify	Reparent	Window reparented.
UnmapNotify	Unmap	Window unmapped.
CirculateRequest	CircRec	Redirect stacking order change to window manager.
ConfigureRequest	ConfigureReq	Redirect move or resize request to window manager.
MapRequest	MapReq	Redirect window map request to window manager.
MappingNotify	Mapping	Keyboard mapping changed.
ClientMessage	Message	Client-dependent.
SelectionClear	SelClr	Current owner is losing selection.
SelectionNotify	Select	Selection is ready for requestor.
SelectionRequest	SelReq	Request for selection to current owner.

The detail field is event-specific and normally corresponds to the detail field of the corresponding event as described by the X Protocol specification. The detail field is supported for the following event types:

Event	Event Field
KeyPress	Keysym from event detail (keycode).
KeyRelease	Keysym from event detail (keycode).
ButtonPress	Button from event detail.
ButtonRelease	Button from event detail.
MotionNotify	Event detail.
EnterNotify	Event mode (not detail).
LeaveNotify	Event mode (not detail).
FocusIn	Event mode (not detail).
FocusOut	Event mode (not detail).
PropertyNotify	Atom.
SelectionClear	Selection.
SelectionRequest	Selection.
SelectionNotify	Selection.

Event	Event Field
ClientMessage	Type.
MappingNotify	Request.

If the event type is KeyPress or KeyRelease, the detail field specifies a keysym name in standard format that is matched against the event as described above, for example, <Key>A.

For the PropertyNotify, SelectionClear, SelectionRequest, SelectionNotify, and ClientMessage events, the detail field is specified as an atom name; for example, <Message>WM_PROTOCOLS. For the MotionNotify, EnterNotify, LeaveNotify, FocusIn, FocusOut, and MappingNotify events, either the symbolic constants as defined by the X Protocol specification or the numeric values may be specified.

If no detail field is specified, then any value in the event detail is accepted as a match.

A keysym can be specified as any of the standard keysym names, a hexadecimal number prefixed with *0x* or *0X*, an octal number prefixed with *0*, or a decimal number. A keysym expressed as a single digit is interpreted as the corresponding Latin 1 keysym. For example, *0* is the keysym XK_0. Other single character keysyms are treated as literal constants from Latin 1, for example, *!* is treated as 0x21. Standard keysym names are as defined in *<X11/keysymdef.h>* with the XK_ prefix removed.

Examples

1. Always put more specific events in the table before more general ones:

   ```
   Shift <Btn1Down> : twas()\n\
   <Btn1Down> : brillig()
   ```

2. For double-click on Button 1 Up with Shift, use this specification:

   ```
   Shift<Btn1Up>(2) : and()
   ```

This is equivalent to the following line with appropriate timers set between events:

```
Shift<Btn1Down>,Shift<Btn1Up>,Shift<Btn1Down>,Shift<Btn1Up> : and()
```

3. For double-click on Button 1 Down with Shift, use this specification:

```
Shift<Btn1Down>(2) : the()
```

This is equivalent to the following line with appropriate timers set between events:

```
Shift<Btn1Down>,Shift<Btn1Up>,Shift<Btn1Down> : the()
```

4. Mouse motion is always discarded when it occurs between events in a table where no motion event is specified:

```
<Btn1Down>,<Btn1Up> : slithy()
```

This is taken, even if the pointer moves a bit between the down and up events. Similarly, any motion event specified in a translation matches any number of motion events. If the motion event causes an action procedure to be invoked, the procedure is invoked after each motion event.

5. If an event sequence consists of a sequence of events that is also a non-initial subsequence of another translation, it is not taken if it occurs in the context of the longer sequence. This occurs mostly in sequences like the following:

```
<Btn1Down>,<Btn1Up> : toves()\n\
<Btn1Up> :  did()
```

The second translation is taken only if the button release is not preceded by a button press or if there are intervening events between the press and the release. Be particularly aware of this when using the repeat notation, above, with buttons and keys because their expansion includes additional events, and when specifying motion events because they are implicitly included between any two other events. In particular, pointer motion and double-click translations cannot coexist in the same translation table.

6. For single click on Button 1 Up with Shift and Meta, use this specification:

```
Shift Meta <Btn1Down>, Shift Meta<Btn1Up>: gyre()
```

7. You can use a plus sign (+) to indicate "for any number of clicks greater than or equal to count"; for example:

```
Shift <Btn1Up>(2+) : and()
```

8. To indicate EnterNotify with any modifiers, use this specification:

    <Enter> : gimble()

9. To indicate EnterNotify with no modifiers, use this specification:

    None <Enter> : in()

10. To indicate EnterNotify with Button 1 Down and Button 2 Up and "don't care" about the other modifiers, use this specification:

    Button1 ˜Button2 <Enter> : the()

11. To indicate EnterNotify with Button1 Down and Button2 Down exclusively, use this specification:

    ! Button1 Button2 <Enter> : wabe()

You do not need to use a tilde (˜) with an exclamation point (!).

10
Errors and Warnings

This section has two main parts:

- Xlib errors

- Xt errors and warnings

Xlib Errors

Listed by return value, the Xlib errors are as follows:

1	BadRequest	11	BadAlloc
2	BadValue	12	BadColor
3	BadWindow	13	BadGC
4	BadPixmap	14	BadIDChoice
5	BadAtom	15	BadName
6	BadCursor	16	BadLength
7	BadFont	17	BadImplementation
8	BadMatch		
9	BadDrawable		
10	BadAccess		

Listed alphabetically, these errors—along with their probable cause—appear on the following pages.

BadAccess

The client attempted to grab a key/button combination that is already grabbed by another client; free a colormap entry that is not allocated by the client; store into a read-only colormap entry; modify the access control list from other than the local (or otherwise authorized) host; or select an event type that only one client can select at a time, when another client has already selected it.

BadAlloc

The server failed to allocate the requested resource.

BadAtom

A value for an Atom argument does not name a defined Atom.

BadColor

A value for a Colormap argument does not name a defined Colormap.

BadCursor

A value for a Cursor argument does not name a defined Cursor.

BadDrawable

A value for a Drawable argument does not name a defined Window or Pixmap.

BadFont

A value for a Font or GContext argument does not name a defined Font.

BadGC

A value for a GContext argument does not name a defined GContext.

BadIDChoice

The value chosen for a resource identifier either is not included in the range assigned to the client or is already in use.

BadImplementation

The server does not implement some aspect of the request. A server that generates this error for a core request is deficient. Clients should be prepared to receive such errors and either handle or discard them.

BadLength

The length of a request is shorter or longer than that required to minimally contain the arguments. This usually indicates an internal Xlib error.

BadMatch Xlib Error

An InputOnly window is used as a Drawable. Some argument (or pair of arguments) has the correct type and range but fails to "match" in some other way required by the request.

BadName Xlib Error

A font or color of the specified name does not exist.

BadPixmap Xlib Error

A value for a Pixmap argument does not name a defined Pixmap.

BadRequest Xlib Error

The major or minor opcode does not specify a valid request.

BadValue Xlib Error

Some numeric value falls outside the range of values accepted by the request. Unless a specific range is specified for an argument, the full range defined by the argument's type is accepted. Any argument defined as a set of alternatives can generate this error.

BadWindow Xlib Error

A value for a Window argument does not name a defined Window.

Xt Errors and Warnings

Here are the Xt errors and warnings, listed alphabetically by message name. This information has the form:

Message Name Category

Message Type   Default message

Note that many message names have more than one type; however, all X Toolkit errors and warnings have class XtToolkitError.

allocError Xt Error

calloc   Cannot perform calloc
malloc   Cannot perform malloc
realloc   Cannot perform realloc

ambiguousParent
Xt Warning

xtManageChildren	Not all children have same parent in XtManageChildren
xtUnmanageChildren	Not all children have same parent in XtUnmanageChildren

communicationError
Xt Error

select	Select failed

communicationError
Xt Warning

windowManager	Window Manager is confused

conversionError
Xt Warning

string	Cannot convert string "%s" to type "%s"

displayError
Xt Warning

invalidDisplay	Cannot find display structure

grabError
Xt Warning

grabDestroyCallback	XtAddGrab requires exclusive grab if spring_loaded is TRUE
xtRemoveGrab	XtRemoveGrab asked to remove a widget not on the grab list

initializationError
Xt Warning

xtInitialize	Initializing Resource Lists twice

internalError
Xt Error

shell	Shell's window manager interaction is broken

invalidArgCount
Xt Error

xtGetValues	Argument count > 0 on NULL argument list in XtGetValues
xtSetValues	Argument count > 0 on NULL argument list in XtSetValues

invalidArgCount
Xt Warning

getResources	Argument count > 0 on NULL argument list

invalidCallbackList
Xt Warning

xtAddCallbacks	Cannot find callback list in XtAddCallbacks
xtCallCallback	Cannot find callback list in XtCallCallbacks
xtOverrideCallback	Cannot find callback list in XtOverrideCallbacks
xtRemoveAllCallback	Cannot find callback list in XtRemoveAllCallbacks
xtRemoveCallbacks	Cannot find callback list in XtRemoveCallbacks

invalidChild
Xt Warning

xtManageChildren	NULL child passed to XtManageChildren
xtUnmanageChildren	NULL child passed to XtUnmanageChildren

invalidClass
Xt Error

constraintSetValue	Subclass of Constraint required in CallConstraintSetValues
xtAppCreateShell	XtAppCreateShell requires non-NULL widget class
xtCreatePopupShell	XtCreatePopupShell requires non-NULL widget class

xtCreateWidget	XtCreateWidget requires non-NULL widget class
xtPopdown	XtPopdown requires a subclass of shellWidgetClass
xtPopup	XtPopup requires a subclass of shellWidgetClass

invalidDepth   Xt Warning

| setValues | Cannot change widget depth |

invalidDimension   Xt Error

| xtCreateWindow | Widget %s has zero width and/or height |
| shellRealize | Shell widget %s has zero width and/or height |

invalidDisplay   Xt Error

| xtInitialize | Cannot open display |

invalidGeometry   Xt Warning

| xtMakeGeometryRequest | Shell subclass did not take care of geometry in XtSetValues |

invalidGeometryManager   Xt Error

| xtMakeGeometryRequest | XtMakeGeometryRequest – parent has no geometry manager |

invalidParameter   Xt Error

| removePopupFromParent | RemovePopupFromParent requires non-NULL popuplist |
| xtAddInput | Invalid condition passed to XtAddInput |

invalidParameters   Xt Error

| xtMenuPopupAction | MenuPopup wants exactly one argument |
| xtmenuPopdown | XtMenuPopdown called with num_params != 0 or 1 |

invalidParameters   Xt Warning

compileAccelerators	String to AcceleratorTable needs no extra arguments
compileTranslations	String to TranslationTable needs no extra arguments
mergeTranslations	MergeTM to TranslationTable needs no extra arguments

invalidParent   Xt Error

realize	Application shell is not a windowed widget?
xtCreatePopupShell	XtCreatePopupShell requires non-NULL parent
xtCreateWidget	XtCreateWidget requires non-NULL parent
xtMakeGeometryRequest	XtMakeGeometryRequest–NULL parent. Use SetValues instead
xtMakeGeometryRequest	XtMakeGeometryRequest – parent not composite
xtManageChildren	Attempt to manage a child when parent is not Composite
xtUnmanageChildren	Attempt to unmanage a child when parent is not Composite

invalidParent   Xt Warning

| xtCopyFromParent | CopyFromParent must have non-NULL parent |

invalidPopup   Xt Error

xtMenuPopup   Cannot find pop up in _XtMenuPopup
xtMenuPopup   Cannot find pop up in _XtMenuPopup

invalidPopup   Xt Warning

unsupportedOperation Pop-up menu creation is only supported on ButtonPress or Enter-
                      Notify events

invalidProcedure   Xt Error

inheritanceProc   Unresolved inheritance operation
realizeProc   No realize class procedure defined

invalidProcedure   Xt Warning

deleteChild   NULL delete_child procedure in XtDestroy
inputHandler   XtRemoveInput: Input handler not found
set_values_almost   set_values_almost procedure shouldn't be NULL

invalidResourceCount   Xt Warning

getResources   Resource count > 0 on NULL resource list

invalidResourceName   Xt Warning

computeArgs   Cannot find resource name %s as argument to conversion

invalidShell   Xt Warning

xtTranslateCoords   Widget has no shell ancestor

invalidSizeOverride   Xt Warning

xtDependencies   Representation size %d must match superclass's to override %s

invalidTypeOverride   Xt Warning

xtDependencies   Representation type %s must match superclass's to override %s

invalidWidget   Xt Warning

removePopupFromParent RemovePopupFromParent, widget not on parent list

invalidWindow   Xt Error

eventHandler   Event with wrong window

missingEvent   Xt Error

shell   Events are disappearing from under Shell

noAppContext   Xt Error

widgetToApplication-   Couldn't find ancestor with display information
    Context

noColormap   Xt Warning

cvtStringToPixel   Cannot allocate colormap entry for "%s"

noPerDisplay   Xt Error

closeDisplay   Couldn't find per display information
getPerDisplay   Couldn't find per display information

noSelectionProperties   Xt Error

freeSelectionProperty   Internal error: no selection property context for display

nullProc   Xt Error

insertChild   NULL insert_child procedure

registerWindowError   Xt Warning

xtRegisterWindow   Attempt to change already registered window
xtUnregisterWindow   Attempt to unregister invalid window

subclassMismatch   Xt Error

xtCheckSubclass   Widget class %s found when subclass of %s expected: %s

translation error   Xt Warning

nullTable   Cannot remove accelerators from NULL table
nullTable   Tried to remove non-existent accelerators

translationError   Xt Error

mergingTablesWithCycles   Trying to merge translation tables with cycles, and cannot resolve
                          this cycle

translationError   Xt Warning

ambigiousActions   Overriding earlier translation manager actions
mergingNullTable   Old translation table was null, cannot modify
nullTable   Cannot translate event through NULL table
unboundActions   Actions not found: %s
xtTranslateInitialize   Initializing Translation manager twice

translationParseError   Xt Warning

showLine   ... found while parsing "%s"
parseError   Translation table syntax error: %s
parseString   Missing "\"

typeConversionError   Xt Warning

noConverter   No type converter registered for "%s" to "%s" conversion

versionMismatch   Xt Warning

widget   Widget class %s version mismatch: widget %d vs. intrinsics %d

wrongParameters Xt Error

cvtIntOrPixelToXColor	Pixel-to-color conversion needs screen and colormap arguments
cvtStringToCursor	String-to-cursor conversion needs screen argument
cvtStringToFont	String-to-font conversion needs screen argument
cvtStringToFontStruct	String-to-cursor conversion needs screen argument
cvtStringToPixel	String-to-pixel conversion needs screen and colormap arguments

wrongParameters Xt Warning

cvtIntToBool	Integer-to-Bool conversion needs no extra arguments
cvtIntToBoolean	Integer-to-Boolean conversion needs no extra arguments
cvtIntToFont	Integer-to-Font conversion needs no extra arguments
cvtIntToPixel	Integer-to-Pixel conversion needs no extra arguments
cvtIntToPixmap	Integer-to-Pixmap conversion needs no extra arguments
cvtIntToShort	Integer-to-Short conversion needs no extra arguments
cvtStringToBool	String-to-Bool conversion needs no extra arguments
cvtStringToBoolean	String-to-Boolean conversion needs no extra arguments
cvtStringToDisplay	String-to-Display conversion needs no extra arguments
cvtStringToFile	String-to-File conversion needs no extra arguments
cvtStringToInt	String-to-Integer conversion needs no extra arguments
cvtStringToShort	String-to-Integer conversion needs no extra arguments
cvtStringToUnsignedChar	
	String-to-Integer conversion needs no extra arguments
cvtXColorToPixel	Color-to-Pixel conversion needs no extra arguments

Index

communicationError, Xt Error,
   384
   Xt Warning, 384
ConfigureNotify, 172
ConfigureRequest, 173
ConnectionNumber, 12
constants (defined), Above, 173
   AllHints, 163
   AllocAll, 40
   AllocNone, 40
   AllowExposures, 63, 107
   AllValues, 82
   Always, 157
   AnyButton, 67, 118
   AnyModifier, 68
   ArcChord, 147
   ArcPieSlice, 147
   AsyncBoth, 24
   AsyncKeyboard, 24
   AsyncPointer, 24
   AutoRepeatModeDefault, 151
   AutoRepeatModeOff, 151
   AutoRepeatModeOn, 151
   Below, 162, 173, 270
   BitmapFileInvalid, 88
   BitmapNoMemory, 88
   BitmapOpenFailed, 88
   BitmapSuccess, 88
   BottomIf, 162, 173, 270
   Button1, 67, 118, 170
   Button1Mask, 86, 170
   Button1MotionMask, 157, 167,
      251
   Button2, 67, 118, 170
   Button2Mask, 86, 170
   Button2MotionMask, 157, 167,
      251
   Button3, 67, 118, 170
   Button3Mask, 86, 170
   Button3MotionMask, 157, 167,
      251
   Button4, 67, 118, 170
   Button4Mask, 86, 170
   Button4MotionMask, 157, 167,
      251
   Button5, 67, 118, 170
   Button5Mask, 86, 170

   Button5MotionMask, 157, 167,
      251
   ButtonMotionMask, 157, 167,
      251
   ButtonPress, 141, 255
   ButtonPressMask, 156, 167,
      251
   ButtonRelease, 141, 255
   ButtonReleaseMask, 156, 167,
      251
   CapButt, 146
   CapNotLast, 146
   CapProjecting, 146
   CapRound, 146
   CenterGravity, 157
   CirculateNotify, 141, 255
   CirculateRequest, 141, 255
   ClientMessage, 141, 255
   ClipByChildren, 109, 148
   ColormapChangeMask, 157,
      167, 251
   ColormapInstalled, 172
   ColormapNotify, 141, 255
   ColormapUninstalled, 172
   ConfigureNotify, 141, 255
   ConfigureRequest, 141, 255
   ControlMapIndex, 70, 153
   ControlMask, 68, 86, 118, 170,
      252
   CoordModeOrigin, 49
   CoordModePrevious, 49
   CopyFromParent, 43
   CreateNotify, 141, 255
   CurrentTime, 133
   CWBackingPixel, 156
   CWBackingPlanes, 156
   CWBackingStore, 156
   CWBackPixel, 156
   CWBackPixmap, 156
   CWBitGravity, 156
   CWBorderPixel, 156
   CWBorderPixmap, 156
   CWBorderWidth, 162, 269
   CWColormap, 156
   CWCursor, 156
   CWDontPropagate, 156
   CWEventMask, 156
   CWHeight, 162, 269

Index

Index

Index

About the Editors

Ellie Cutler has been an indexer and production editor with O'Reilly & Associates since 1990. Prior to landing at ORA, she worked as a technical writer, newspaper copyeditor, and tractor-trailer driver. A professional musician, Ellie received her Bachelor of Music degree from Utah State University in 1974.

Daniel Gilly has been with O'Reilly & Associates since 1986. He's been involved with several books in the X Window series, wrote the reference section of Volume Six, *Motif Programming Manual*, and revised the Nutshell Handbook, *Learning vi*, for its 5th edition. Daniel has written a musical comedy, a radio thriller, and a one-act play. All have been performed at Boston-area colleges. He graduated from MIT in 1985 with a B.S. in Mechanical Engineering.

Tim O'Reilly is founder and president of O'Reilly & Associates, publisher of the X Window System series and the popular Nutshell Handbooks on UNIX. Tim has had a hand in writing or editing many of the books published by O'Reilly & Associates.

Tim's long-term vision for the company is to create a vehicle where creative people can support themselves by exploring interesting ideas. Technical book publishing is just the first step. Tim graduated cum laude from Harvard in 1975 with a B.A. in Classics.

X books from O'Reilly

When it comes to X, think of these books as the ultimate owner's manuals. Because of its power and flexibility, X is also extremely complex. We help you sort through that complexity with books that show you, step-by-step, how to use, program, and administer the X Window System.

The X Window System

X Protocol Reference Manual

Edited by Adrian Nye, 3rd Edition February 1992
516 pages, ISBN 1-56592-008-2

Describes the X Network Protocol which underlies all software for Version 11 of the X Window System. Includes protocol clarifications of X11 Release 5, as well as the most recent version of the ICCCM and the Logical Font Conventions Manual. For use with any release of X.

Xlib Programming Manual

By Adrian Nye, 3rd Edition July 1992
824 pages, ISBN 1-56592-002-3

Newly updated to cover X11 Release 5. Complete programming guide to the X library (Xlib), the lowest level of programming interface to X. New features include introductions to internationalization, device-independent color, font service, and scalable fonts.

Xlib Reference Manual

By Adrian Nye, 3rd Edition June 1992
1138 pages, ISBN 1-56592-006-6

Complete reference guide to the X library (Xlib), the lowest level of programming interface to X. Updated to cover X11 Release 4 and Release 5.

X Window System User's Guide

By Valerie Quercia & Tim O'Reilly
4th Edition May 1993
836 pages, ISBN 1-56592-014-7

Orients the new user to window system concepts and provides detailed tutorials for many client programs, including the *xterm* terminal emulator and window managers. Later chapters explain how to customize the X environment. This popular manual is available in two editions, one for users of the MIT software, one for users of Motif. Revised for X11 Release 5.

X Window System User's Guide

 By Valerie Quercia & Tim O'Reilly
2nd Edition January 1993
956 pages, ISBN 1-56592-015-5

Orients the new user to window system concepts and provides detailed tutorials for many client programs, including the *xterm* terminal emulator and the *twm*, *uwm*, and *mwm* window managers. Later chapters explain how to customize the X environment. Revised for Motif 1.2 and X11 Release 5.

X Toolkit Intrinsics Programming Manual

 By Adrian Nye & Tim O'Reilly
3rd Edition April 1993 (Standard Edition)
567 pages, ISBN 1-56592-003-1

A complete guide to programming with Xt Intrinsics, the library of C language routines that facilitate the design of user interfaces with reusable components called widgets. Available in two editions. The Standard Edition uses Athena widgets in examples; the Motif Edition uses Motif widgets (*see below*).

X Toolkit Intrinsics Programming Manual

 By Adrian Nye & Tim O'Reilly
2nd Edition August 1992 (Motif Edition)
674 pages, ISBN 1-56592-013-9

The Motif Edition of Volume 4 uses the Motif 1.2 widgets set in examples, and has been updated for X11 Release 5 (*see above description*).

X Toolkit Intrinsics Reference Manual

 Edited by David Flanagan, 3rd Edition April 1992
916 pages, ISBN 1-56592-007-4

Complete programmer's reference for the X Toolkit, providing pages for each of the Xt functions, as well as the widget classes defined by Xt and the Athena widgets. This 3rd Edition has been re-edited, reorganized, and expanded for X11 Release 5.

Motif Programming Manual

 By Dan Heller & Paula Ferguson
2nd Edition December 1993 (est.)
900 pages (est.), ISBN 1-56592-016-3

The *Motif Programming Manual* is a source for complete, accurate, and insightful guidance on Motif application programming. There is no other book that covers the ground as thoroughly or as well as this one. Covers Motif Release 1.2. *(Advanced orders accepted beginning November 1993.)*

Motif Reference Manual

 By Paula Ferguson & David Brennan
1st Edition June 1993
920 pages, ISBN 1-56592-038-4

A complete programmer's reference for the Motif toolkit. This book provides reference pages for the Motif functions and macros, the Motif and Xt widget classes, the *mrm* functions, the Motif clients, and the UIL file format, data types, and functions. The reference material has been expanded from the appendices of the 1st Edition of Volume 6 and covers Motif 1.2. This manual is a companion to Volume 6A, *Motif Programming Manual*.

XView Programming Manual

 By Dan Heller, 3rd Edition September 1991
739 pages, ISBN 0-937175-87-0

The *XView Programming Manual* describes both the concepts and the technical approaches behind XView, the poor-man's object-oriented toolkit for building OPEN LOOK applications for X. XView supports Internationalization, drag and drop, a mouse-less (keyboard-only) input model and instant migration into a standard sun desktop. Perfect for the beginner breaking into X programming.

XView Reference Manual

 Edited by Thomas Van Raalte
1st Edition September 1991
291 pages, ISBN 0-937175-88-9

The XView toolkit provides extensive attribute-value pair combinations, convenience routines, and object class hierarchies that are too voluminous to memorize without the aid of this comprehensive reference guide. A must-have companion for the *XView Programming Manual (see above)*.

X Window System Administrator's Guide

 By Linda Mui & Eric Pearce
1st Edition October 1992, 372 pages
Without CD-ROM, ISBN 0-937175-83-8
With CD-ROM, ISBN 1-56592-052-X

This book is the first and only book devoted to the issues of system administration for X and X-based networks, written not just for UNIX system administrators but for anyone faced with the job of administering X (including those running X on stand-alone workstations). The *X Window System Administrator's Guide* is available either alone or packaged with the XCD. The CD provides X source code and binaries to complement the book's instructions for installing the software. It contains over 600 megabytes of X11 source code and binaries stored in ISO9660 and RockRidge formats. This will allow several types of UNIX workstations to mount the CD-ROM as a filesystem, browse through the source code, and install pre-built software.

The X Window System in a Nutshell
Edited by Ellie Cutler, Daniel Gilly & Tim O'Reilly
2nd Edition April 1992
424 pages, ISBN 1-56592-017-1

Indispensable companion to the X Window System Series. Experienced X programmers can use this single-volume desktop companion for most common questions, keeping the full series of manuals for detailed reference. This book has been newly updated to cover R5 but is still useful for R4.

X Graphics

PEXlib Programming Manual
By Tom Gaskins, 1st Edition December 1992
1154 pages, ISBN 1-56592-028-7

The *PEXlib Programming Manual* is the definitive programmer's guide to PEXlib, covering both PEX versions 5.0 and 5.1. Containing over 200 illustrations and 19 color plates, it combines a thorough and gentle tutorial approach with valuable reference features. Along the way, it presents the reader with numerous programming examples, as well as a library of helpful utility routines—all of which are available online. You do not need prior graphics programming experience to read this manual.

PEXlib Reference Manual
By O'Reilly & Associates, 1st Edition December 1992
577 pages, ISBN 1-56592-029-5

The *PEXlib Reference Manual* is the definitive programmer's reference resource for PEXlib, and contains complete and succinct reference pages for all the callable routines in PEXlib version 5.1. The content of the *PEXlib Reference Manual* stands, with relatively few changes, as it was created by the MIT X Consortium.

PHIGS Programming Manual
By Tom Gaskins, 1st Edition February 1992
968 pages, ISBN 0-937175-85-4

A complete and authoritative guide to PHIGS and PHIGS PLUS programming. Whether you are starting out in 3D graphics programming or are a seasoned veteran looking for an authoritative work on a fast-rising 3D graphics standard, this book will serve your purposes well.

PHIGS Reference Manual
Edited by Linda Kosko, 1st Edition October 1992
1116 pages, ISBN 0-937175-91-9

The *PHIGS Reference Manual* is the definitive and exhaustive reference documentation for the PHIGS/PEX Sample Implementation ("PEX-SI"). It contains all the reference pages from the X Consortium release, but in upgraded form. It also contains additional reference materials. Together with the *PHIGS Programming Manual*, this book is the most complete and accessible documentation currently available for both the PEX-SI and the PHIGS and PHIGS PLUS standards.

The X Resource Journal

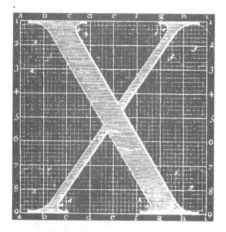

The X Resource *is a quarterly working journal for X programmers that provides practical, timely information about the programming, administration, and use of the X Window System.* The X Resource *is the official publisher of the X Consortium Technical Conference Proceedings. One year subscription (4 issues), $65. One year subscription plus the proposed Consortium standard supplements, $90.*

The X Resource: Issue 4

Edited by Adrian Nye
276 pages
ISBN 0-937175-99-4

The X Resource includes in-depth articles and documentation not available elsewhere. Articles for Issue 4 include: "The MIT X Software Distribution After Release 5"; "RPC Programming in X Applications"; "The *xgen* Application Generator"; "The Hdial Widget"; and "The Cmap Widget".

The X Resource: Issue 5

Edited by Adrian Nye
272 pages
ISBN 1-56592-020-1

The articles for Issue 5, taken from the proceedings of the 7th Annual X Technical Conference, include: "Multi-threaded Xlib"; "Supporting Mobile, Pen-based Computing with X"; and "Making the X Window System Accessible to People with Disabilities".

The X Resource: Issue 6

Edited by Adrian Nye
234 pages
ISBN 1-56592-021-X

The articles for Issue 6 include: "Writing Motif Widgets: A Pragmatic Approach"; "Interprocess Communication in Xt Programs"; and "Resolving Xt Resource Collisions".

The X Resource: Issue 7   *NEW*

Edited by Adrian Nye
150 pages
ISBN 1-56592-022-8

The articles for Issue 7 include: "A Tale of Two Toolkits: Xt vs. Inter-Views"; "Managing X in a Large Distributed Environment"; "Buddy, Can You Spare and PRPC"; and "X Application Debugging".

O'Reilly Online Services

How to Get Information about O'Reilly & Associates

The online O'Reilly Information Resource is a Gopher server that provides you with information on our books, how to download code examples, and how to order from us. There is also a UNIX bibliography you can use to get information on current books by subject area.

Connecting to the O'Reilly Information Resource

Gopher is an interactive tool that organizes the resources found on the Internet as a sequence of menus. If you don't know how Gopher works, see the chapter "Tunneling through the Internet: Gopher" in *The Whole Internet User's Guide and Catalog* by Ed Krol.

An easy way to use Gopher is to download a Gopher client, either the tty Gopher that uses curses or the Xgopher.

Once you have a local Gopher client, you can launch Gopher with:

```
gopher gopher.ora.com
```

To use the Xgopher client, enter:

```
xgopher -xrm "xgopher.rootServer:
gopher.ora.com"
```

If you have no client, log in on our machine via telnet and run Gopher from there, with:

```
telnet gopher.ora.com
login: gopher  (no password)
```

Another option is to use a World Wide Web browser, and enter the http address:

```
gopher://gopher.ora.com
```

Once the connection is made, you should see a root menu similar to this:

```
Internet Gopher Information Client v1.12
   Root gopher server: gopher.ora.com

->1. News Flash! -- New Products and
     Projects of ORA/.
   2. About O'Reilly & Associates.
   3. Book Descriptions and Information/
   4. Complete Listing of Book Titles.
   5. FTP Archive and E-Mail Information/
   6. Ordering Information/
   7. UNIX Bibliography/

Press ? for Help, q to Quit, u to go up a
menu                          Page: 1/1
```

From the root menu you can begin exploring the information that we have available. If you don't know much about O'Reilly & Associates, choose **About O'Reilly & Associates** from the menu. You'll see an article by Tim O'Reilly that gives an overview of who we are—and a little background on the books we publish.

Getting Information About Our Books

The Gopher server makes available online the same information that we provide in our print catalog, often in more detail.

Choose **Complete Listing of Book Titles** from the root menu to view a list of all our titles. This is a useful summary to have when you want to place an order.

To find out more about a particular book, choose **Book Descriptions and Information;** you will see the screen below:

```
Internet Gopher Information Client v1.12
   Book Descriptions and Information

->1. New Books and Editions/
   2. Computer Security/
   3. Distributed Computing Environment
      (DCE)/
   4. Non-Technical Books/
   5. System Administration/
   6. UNIX & C Programming/
   7. Using UNIX/
   8. X Resource/
   9. X Window System/
   10. CD-Rom Book Companions/
   11. Errata and Updates/
   12. Keyword Search on all Book
       Descriptions <?>
   13. Keyword Search on all Tables of
       Content <?>
```

All of our new books are listed in a single category. The rest of our books are grouped by subject. Select a subject to see a list of book titles in that category. When you select a specific book, you'll find a full description and table of contents.

For example, if you wanted to look at what books we had on administration, you would choose selection 5, **System Administration**, resulting in the following screen:

```
          System Administration

   1. DNS and BIND/
   2. Essential System Administration/
   3. Managing NFS and NIS/
   4. Managing UUCP and Usenet/
   5. sendmail/
   6. System Performance Tuning/
   7. TCP/IP Network Administration/
```

If you then choose Essential System Administration, you will be given the choice of looking at either the book description or the table of contents.

```
      Essential System Administration

->1.Book Description and Information.
   2.Book Table of Contents.
```

Selecting either of these options will display the contents of a file. Gopher then provides instructions for you to navigate elsewhere or quit the program.

Searching For the Book You Want

Gopher also allows you to locate book descriptions or tables of contents by using a word search. (We have compiled a full-text index WAIS.)

If you choose Book Descriptions and Information from the root menu, the last two selections on that menu allow you to do keyword searches.

Choose Keyword Search on all Book Descriptions and you will be prompted with:

Index word(s) to search for:

Once you enter a keyword, the server returns a list of the book descriptions that match the keyword. For example, if you enter the keyword DCE, you will see:

```
Keyword Search on all Book Descriptions:
                    DCE

-> 1.Understanding DCE.
   2.Guide to Writing DCE Applications.
   3.Distributed Applications Across DCE
     and Windows NT.
   4.DCE Administration Guide.
   5.Power Programming with RPC.
   6.Guide to OSF/1.
```

Choose one of these selections to view the book description.

Using the keyword search option can be a faster and less tedious way to locate a book than moving through a lot of menus.

You can also use a WAIS client to access the full-text index or book descriptions. The name of the database is

O'Reilly_Book_Descriptions.src

and you can find it in the WAIS directory of servers.

Note: We are always adding functions and listings to the O'Reilly Information Resource. By the time you read this article, the actual screens may very well have changed.

E-mail Accounts

E-mail ordering promises to be quick and easy, even faster than using our 800 number. Because we don't want you to send credit card information over a non-secure network, we ask that you set up an account with us in advance. To do so, either call us at 1-800-998-9938 or use the application provided in Ordering Information on the Gopher root menu. You will then be provided with a confidential account number.

Your account number allows us to retrieve your billing information when you place an order by e-mail, so you only need to send us your account number and what you want to order.

For your security, we use the credit card information and shipping address that we have on file. We also verify that the name of the person sending us the e-mail order matches the name on the account. If any of this information needs to change, we ask that you call our Customer Service department.

Ordering by E-mail:

Once you have an account with us, you can send us your orders by e-mail. Remember that you can use our online catalog to find out more about the books you want. Here's what we need when you send us an order:

1. Address your e-mail to: order@ora.com
2. Include in your message:
   - The title of each book you want to order (including ISBN number, if you know it)
   - The quantity of each book
   - Method of delivery: Fed Ex Economy, Fed Ex Overnight...
   - Your name and account number
   - Anything special you'd like to tell us about the order

When we receive your e-mail message, our Customer Service representative will verify your order before we ship it, and give you a total cost. If you would like to change your order after confirmation, or if there are ever any problems, please use the phone and give us a call—e-mail has its limitations.

This program is an experiment for us. We appreciate getting your feedback so we can continue improving our service.